The Trinity

The Trinity

An Interdisciplinary Symposium on the Trinity

Edited by

STEPHEN T. DAVIS
DANIEL KENDALL, SJ
GERALD O'COLLINS, SJ

OXFORD
UNIVERSITY PRESS

OXFORD
UNIVERSITY PRESS

Great Clarendon Street, Oxford OX2 6DP

Oxford University Press is a department of the University of Oxford.
It furthers the University's objective of excellence in research, scholarship,
and education by publishing worldwide in

Oxford New York

Athens Auckland Bangkok Bogotá Buenos Aires Calcutta
Cape Town Chennai Dar es Salaam Delhi Florence Hong Kong Istanbul
Karachi Kuala Lumpur Madrid Melbourne Mexico City Mumbai
Nairobi Paris São Paulo Singapore Taipei Tokyo Toronto Warsaw

with associated companies in Berlin Ibadan

Oxford is a registered trade mark of Oxford University Press
in the UK and in certain other countries

Published in the United States
by Oxford University Press Inc., New York

British Library Cataloguing in Publication Data

Data available

Library of Congress Cataloging in Publication Data
The Trinity : an interdisciplinary symposium on the Trinity / edited
by Stephen T. Davis, Daniel Kendall, Gerald O'Collins.
p. cm.
Includes bibliographical references and index.
1. Trinity Congresses.   I. Davis, Stephen T.,   1940–
II. Kendall, Daniel.   III. O'Collins, Gerald.
BT111.2.T758   1999
231'.044—dc21   99-24523

ISBN 0-19-826993-5

1 3 5 7 9 10 8 6 4 2

Typeset by Regent Typesetting, London
Printed in Great Britain
on acid-free paper by
Biddles Ltd., Guildford and King's Lynn

Preface

This book was born out of the success of a similar joint project. After the Resurrection Summit, which also met at Dunwoodie (7-10 April 1996) and a year later produced *The Resurrection* (Oxford: Oxford University Press, 1997), we decided to meet and have dialogue with scholars of a variety of disciplines on the belief at the heart of Christianity: the Holy Trinity. Hence we brought together sixteen other specialists, many of whom have already published works on God and the specific Christian belief in the tripersonal God. In planning the various papers that are published in this book, we wanted to include contributions from biblical studies, foundational (or fundamental) theology, systematic theology, moral theology, spiritual theology, patristics, the philosophy of religion, homiletics, liturgy, and the study of religious art. We managed to secure papers—sometimes more than one paper—in all these fields, and in one way or another all these fields are represented in this book.

To promote advance discussion and establish stronger connecting threads between the different contributions, we encouraged those presenting papers to circulate them in advance to all the members of the symposium. In almost every case drafts had been sent out (and in some cases also made available by e-mail) for feedback before we met at Dunwoodie (12-15 April 1998) for the Trinity Summit itself.

Our procedure and the scope of our book distinguish it from a very few other works on trinitarian belief produced in collaboration during the 1990s. The contributions to *Trinity in Process: A Rational Theology of God*, edited by Joseph A. Bracken and Marjorie Suchocki (New York: Continuum, 1997), come from one particular school, exponents of process theology. *The Trinity in a Pluralistic Age: Theological Essays on Culture and Religion*, edited by Kevin Vanhoozer (Grand Rapids, Mich.: Eerdmans, 1997), resulted from a conference held four years earlier in Edinburgh. Almost all the papers were written by specialists in systematic or dogmatic theology; no chapters came from women, Catholics, or Jews. Probably the most valuable of the recent jointly written volumes on the Trinity is Christoph Schwöbel (ed.), *Trinitarian Theology Today* (Edinburgh: T. & T. Clark, 1995). Its chapters are revised versions of papers presented five years earlier, at a 1990 conference held in London. Much attention is paid to issues in systematic theology, along with some investigations into questions of patristics and religious art. But no chapters come from biblical scholars, professional philosophers, or experts in homiletics. Once again we cannot help noticing that the contributors do not include any women, Roman Catholic, or Jewish scholars. In recalling these earlier collaborative publications on the Trinity, we are encouraged to think that both the variety of disciplines represented, the 'ecumenical' (in a broader sense) character of the participants, and the procedures adopted (which facilitated a rapid publication of the results) set our volume somewhat apart from earlier joint works on the subject of the Trinity.

Along with closely related doctrines concerned with the incarnation, life, death, and resurrection of Jesus, the doctrine of the Trinity is most central for Christian believers. This doctrine recognizably identifies their faith. Yet even (or especially?) the most learned know it to be the divine mystery *par excellence*, the paradoxical doctrine that over the centuries has provoked much controversy and even sad divisions among Christians. Various forms of modern rationalism have often found the idea of the trinitarian mystery intolerable and hence broken the paradox by holding 'one God' and rejecting 'three divine persons'. Some writers, while not jettisoning trinitarian faith, take refuge in an esoteric scholarship that allows them to avoid facing the mystery of the doctrine itself. We hope that this volume will not sin that way, but like our earlier collection *The Resurrection* will remain accessible and illuminating to its intended audience of well-educated but not overspecialized readers.

After the introductory survey (O'Collins) this collection moves from first-century, biblical questions (Evans, Fee, and Segal), through the classical contribution to trinitarian thought of the Cappadocians and Augustine of Hippo (Lienhard, Coakley, and Barnes), on to theological and philosophical debates (Alston,

Leftow, Davis, Tracy, and van Beeck). It ends with some 'practical' applications of trinitarian belief to art and preaching (Brown and Shuster). The volume proposes approaching multi-faceted trinitarian faith by reflecting on biblical, historical, systematic (both theological and philosophical), and practical data and questions.

In Chapter 1, Gerald O'Collins picks out and comments on twelve issues in current literature about the Trinity: the widespread desire to 'rehabilitate' the centrality of trinitarian faith; the biblical witness that should make christology properly trinitarian; pneumatology as central to Pauline theology; the tripersonal God according to the Cappadocians and other patristic writers; debates on the procession of the Holy Spirit; current proposals for renaming the Trinity; the place of the Trinity in interreligious dialogue; trinitarian faith as the alternative to Western atheism and agnosticism; the identity of the economic and immanent Trinity; the irreducibly special elements in trinitarian actions; the viability of personal language for the Trinity; an integral approach (through study, worship, and practice) to the trinitarian mystery. The chapter also recognizes further issues that call for attention: for instance, the distinct personal identity of the Holy Spirit, the significance for Christian faith of Jewish understanding of God, and the relevance of trinitarian faith for moral thinking and behaviour.

In Chapter 2, Craig Evans argues that early Christian expressions of the deity of Jesus originated in the teaching and activity of Jesus himself, and not simply in later contact with the cult of the emperor. He contends that Jesus' self-identification as 'the son of man' of Daniel 7, where this figure approaches the divine throne and directly from God receives kingdom and authority, takes his messianism to a new level. It is this ingredient, which evidently represents an innovation, that launches a messianic trajectory that will find its way to the more formalized expressions of trinitarian theology.

In Chapter 3, Gordon Fee proposes that Paul, always a rigorous monotheist, became a latent (economic) trinitarian as the result of his *experience* of the risen and exalted Christ and the gift of the Holy Spirit as the eschatological renewal of the promised Presence of God. In turn, the chapter examines: (1) Paul's primary trinitarian/soteriological passages, which are invariably expressed in triadic form when reflecting on the experience of salvation, and always presuppose 'equal with but distinct from'; (2) the Christ narrative in Philippians 2: 6–11, where Paul understood Christ as pre-existent, equal with God, and invested with The Name ('The Lord' by way of the LXX's use of *kyrios* to translate YHWH); this made Paul a binitarian at the least. What made him a trinitarian was his experience—and understanding—of the Spirit: as both personal and distinct from the Father and Son; as the way the risen Christ was present in the life of the believer and believing community (the Holy Spirit of God is also the Spirit of Christ Jesus); and thus as the eschatological renewal of God's Presence. The chapter concludes with some implications for the present.

In Chapter 4, Alan Segal outlines the history of binitarianism and the criticism it met within Hellenistic Jewish culture. Segal begins by identifying 'those who say there are two powers in heaven', a rabbinic heresy probably referring to Christians. He shows that Philo did not hesitate to call the logos a 'second God' because he felt it was more important to protect the immutability than the unity of God. The arguments, in turn, became the basis for Justin's christology and from there entered Christian discussions of the nature of the Trinity. At the same time, rabbinic opposition to all such notions, whether philosophical or Christian or both, intensified.

In Chapter 5, Joseph Lienhard points out how the 'Cappadocian solution' to the fourth-century trinitarian controversy, summarized in the phrase 'one ousia, three hypostaseis—(one essence and three persons)', is often presented as widely employed, and greeted with relief and enthusiasm. But the phrase, as such, is rare in the writings of the Cappadocian Fathers, and may not be the best short expression of their teaching on the Trinity. The distinction in meaning between *ousia* and *hypostasis* (both of which mean 'something that subsists') was worked out only in the late fourth century, and was—to some writers—less than convincing. Another tradition, called '*miahypostatic* theology', was more widely and forcefully represented than is usually assumed. Its most visible proponent was Marcellus of Ancyra, but it is found to some extent in Athanasius, in many other Egyptian bishops, and in much of the West. In the course of the fourth century the *miahypostatic* tradition, which first appears as a late form of monarchianism, gave up all of its distinctive contours except one: it would not accept the phrase 'three *hypostaseis*' as orthodox. The paper suggests, at the end, that perhaps some elements of this *miahypostatic* theology are worth retrieving.

In Chapter 6, Sarah Coakley outlines the recent debate that analytic philosophers of religion have conducted in defence of the so-called 'social' doctrine of the Trinity. Since appeal is characteristically made by them to Gregory of Nyssa, and especially to his *Ad Ablabium*, she focuses on Gregory, and expounds what he says in the *Ad Ablabium* in the light of his other—somewhat fragmented—expositions of the threefold unity of the Godhead. Coakley holds it crucial for an expanding of the discussion to allow for the trinitarian insights that Gregory affords when *not* explicitly discussing the (supposedly) technical meanings of *hypostasis* or *prosopon*, but describing more loosely the soul's engagement with the Trinity at the 'economic' level of operation (as, for instance, in his *Commentary on the Song of Songs*). The notion of *hypostasis* ('person') that emerges from this analysis is far less tidy than the contemporary analytic discussions have supposed; and further, a covert smuggling of 'modern' notions of the 'individual' can be detected in some authors who purport to defend Gregory, resulting in a misleading account of Gregory's perception of intra-divine relations. Finally, Coakley considers the implications of Gregory's profound apophaticism for the assessment of the *status* of his trinitarian language on the literal/analogical/metaphorical spectrum, as well as for the issues of gender which interestingly intrude into Gregory's vision of incorporation into the divine life.

In Chapter 7, Michel René Barnes shows how Augustine's trinitarian theology is best understood as a progressive appropriation of 'Nicene' trinitarian theology, developed in polemical engagement with those who deny that Nicene faith. Barnes believes that Nicene trinitarian theology fundamentally equals the understanding that the three (persons) act together, and so are one in nature. Augustine's trinitarian theology has been misunderstood because—and to the degree that—it has been read within a presumed neoplatonic context.

In Chapter 8, William Alston defends the use of substance metaphysics in formulations of the doctrine of the Trinity. The use of substance categories has been criticized by various contemporary theologians on the grounds that this leads to philosophically and theologically inadequate views of God as absolutely simple, impassible, inert, atemporal, unrelated to his creatures, and the like. By an examination of Aristotle, the fountainhead of substance meta-physics, Alston shows that features like the above are by no means necessarily connected with substance metaphysics. This is clear just from the fact that the category of substance was developed to deal with finite creatures, primarily organisms, that are far from absolutely simple, inert, atemporal, and so forth. Hence even if the contemporary theologians in question are justified in objecting to these characterizations of God, that gives them no basis for object-ing to substantialist construals of the Trinity in general.

In Chapter 9, Brian Leftow compares the 'Latin' approach to the Trinity (which takes there being one God as basic and unproblem-atic, and tries to explain how one God can be three divine persons) to the 'Social' position (which begins with three divine persons and shows how they can be one God). He examines three broad ways which Social Trinitarians use to show their versions of the Trinity to be a version of monotheism. In the end, however, he judges that none presents a doctrine of God which is both orthodox and monotheist.

In Chapter 10, Stephen Davis criticizes John Hick's recent argu-ments against orthodox views of the incarnation and the Trinity. He outlines and answers Hick's specific objections to such views, as well as his positive christological and trinitarian proposals. The conclusion is reached that Hick has failed in overturning classical views of incarnation and Trinity, that his own theology of incarn-ation is flawed, and that his account of the Trinity reveals deep fault lines in his overall theological programme.

In Chapter 11, David Tracy begins by summarizing the diffi-culties caused for trinitarian theology by three fatal modern 'separations': between feeling and thought, between theory and practice, and between form and content. He concentrates on the third 'separation'. After recalling the general Western tradition that reality is manifested in and through harmonious form, Tracy discusses the three main realistic forms for the emergence of trinitarian understanding: the history-like narratives of the gospels, the liturgical trinitarian formulae, and the doctrinal forms of the early councils. He ends by defending speculative form for trini-tarian theology as found in Western theology in general, and in the trinitarian speculations of Eckhart and Ruusbroec in particular.

In Chapter 12, after he commends theology's recent shift towards hermeneutics, Frans Jozef van Beeck analyses *participative knowledge* as it occurs, respectively, at the levels of *cosmology* (largely optional), *anthropology* (*morally* necessary), and *theology* (the heart of all knowing). His conclusion: the One God 'in whom we are alive and move and have our being' is the God whom we are *naturally* equipped to know by (mostly apophatic) *participation in the Word*, Jesus Christ, 'in whom all things were made'; *actual participation* occurs 'in the Holy Spirit', i.e. by *supernatural grace*. All this belies recent claims that the tradition has (wrongly) separated *theologia* from soteriology. Finally, van Beeck offers five proposals: (1) trinitarian theology must draw on faith and worship, not on existing theologies; (2) to enable this, a careful hermeneutics of the trinitarian tradition is called for; (3) the claim that modernity's understanding of God is 'classical theism' deserves suspicion; (4) we must study the trinitarian tradition's rootedness in the Hebrew and Jewish Scriptures; (5) we should be clear about the fact that Christian doxology and soteriology have been replaced by rational Christianity's interest in human religiosity and by efforts at defining salvation in purely human terms.

In Chapter 13, David Brown identifies three main types of approach to artistic representations of the Trinity: triadic, societal, and incarnational forms. In each case he stresses the need to judge art in relation to the wider contemporary context. Triadic repetition is seen to have deep roots in paganism and in neoplatonist assumptions at the time of the Renaissance, as well as being characteristic of today's art. Its function as an image of intensifying power is noted. Societal representations are distinguished from any automatic endorsement of a social analogy for trinitarian doctrine, and this is so in the case of Murillo's *Two Trinities*. Summary dismissal of incarnational types is shown to be often based on misunderstandings of what it is that the relevant artists were trying to achieve. Masaccio, for instance, deliberately placed the Father outside our spatial frame. In general, Brown appeals for art to be judged by its own distinctive criteria.

In Chapter 14, Marguerite Shuster explores the intuitively likely thesis that the doctrine of the Trinity has gotten short shrift in the preaching of the church, by analysing the sermons in the thirteen-volume *20 Centuries of Great Preaching* and in forty-three volumes of the journal *Pulpit Digest*. Few sermons (only twenty) explicitly on the Trinity appear. Furthermore, these sermons show marked doctrinal imprecision and largely fail to deal carefully with the biblical texts on which they are formally based. Shuster suggests that especially in an era of widespread ignorance of Christian fundamentals, preachers need to attend much more than most do to doctrinal preaching. For such preaching to be responsible, seminaries and churches must demand more precise basic knowledge of Christian theology from clergy and ministerial candidates. As the summaries offered above indicate, this volume contains a report of fourteen presentations from the Trinity Summit. In fact, each of the presentations was followed by a response that initiated the discussion of the particular paper. To avoid making this volume too long, we did not include the responses.

Inevitably, one or two reviewers will query our choice of symposiasts, and even propose the names of those we should have asked to attend. Doubtless we could have brought together a different team. To anticipate possible misunderstandings, however, let us mention that we invited some other scholars who, for a variety of good reasons, could not come to contribute and participate. Five further scholars (Michael J. Buckley, Jürgen Moltmann, Alvin Plantinga, Janet Martin Soskice, and Anthony Ugolnik) accepted our invitation but eventually had to drop out. Catherine LaCugna also agreed to come, but her premature death sadly took her away from our company in this world.

We are most grateful to the McCarthy Family foundation and, specifically, to Eugene and Maureen McCarthy, for their generous and prayerful support of our Trinity Summit. Our special thanks go to Monsignor Francis J. McAree, Rector of St Joseph's Seminary, Dunwoodie (Yonkers, NY) for his gracious hospitality and help. We wish to thank warmly the Catholic Archbishop of New York, Cardinal John O'Connor, for his support and encouragement. Fr. Gerard R. Rafferty, and other members of the Dunwoodie 'family' provided us with extraordinarily efficient assistance. Claudia Devaux and Louis Sniderman from Hewlett-Packard graciously devoted much time and effort to setting up a web site for the participants to communicate with each other before the Trinity Summit began. We also want to thank Kenneth Woodward and other journalists and representatives of the media for their vivid interest and sincere support. Lastly, we are particularly grateful to Hilary O'Shea of Oxford University Press and to all the scholars who participated in and contributed to this meeting on the Holy Trinity.

As world history moves ever closer to the third millennium, we offer the results of this interdisciplinary and international symposium to all interested readers. We dedicate our book with much affection to Eugene and Maureen McCarthy. May this volume offer some help towards understanding the faith in the tripersonal God that sets Christianity apart and remains the heart of its life and worship. We end by adapting and making our own the prayer with which St Augustine of Hippo long ago closed his glorious work on the Trinity: 'O Lord, the One God, God the Trinity, whatever we have said in these chapters that comes from you, may they acknowledge who are yours. But for whatever comes merely from ourselves, may you and they who are yours forgive us.'

STEPHEN T. DAVIS, DANIEL KENDALL, SJ, and GERALD O'COLLINS, SJ

16 June 1998

Contents

SYSTEMATIC ISSUES

List of Plates

Abbreviations

20 Centuries	Clyde E. Font, Jr, and William M. Pinson, Jr, *20 Centuries of Great Preaching*, 13 vols. (Waco, Tex.: Word, 1971)
ABRL	Anchor Bible Reference Library
ACW	Ancient Christian Writers
AGJU	Arbeiten zur Geschichte des Antiken Judentums und des Urchristentums
APAMS	American Philological Association Monograph Series
AUSS	*Andrews University Seminary Studies*
Bib	*Biblica*
CBQ	*Catholic Biblical Quarterly*
CChr, Cont. Mediaev.	Corpus Christianorum, Continuatio Mediaevalis
CCL	Corpus Christianorum Latinorum
CETEDOC	Centre de traitement électronique des documents, Catholic University of Louvain Research Institute Library of Christian Latin Texts
CH	*Church History*
CSEL	Corpus Scriptorum Ecclesiasticorum Latinorum
CTA	*Corpus des tablettes en cunéiforms alphabétiques découvertes à Ras Shamra-Ugarit de 1929 à 1939*, Mission de Ras Shamra, x (Paris: P. Geuthner, 1963)
DPL	*Dictionary of Paul and His Letters*, ed. Gerald F. Hawthorne and Ralph P. Martin (Downers Grove, Ill.: InterVarsity Press, 1993)
DS	H. Denzinger and A. Schönmetzer, *Enchiridion Symbolorum*, 35th edn (Barcelona: Herder, 1973)
EDNT	Horst Balz and Gerhard Schneider (eds.), *Exegetical Dictionary of the New Testament*, 3 vols. (Grand

Rapids, Mich.: Eerdmans, 1990–3)

EETS	Early English Text Society
ET	English Translation
ETL	*Ephemerides theologicae lovanienses*
ExpTim	*Expository Times*
GCS	Die griechischen christlichen Schriftsteller der ersten Jahrhunderte
GE	F. J. van Beeck, *God Encountered* (San Francisco/ Collegeville: Harper & Row/Glazier, 1989–)
GIBM	Greek Inscriptions in the British Museum
GNO	Werner Jaeger *et al.* (eds.), *Gregorii Nysseni Opera*, 10 vols. (Leiden: Brill, 1960–90)
HNT	Handbuch zum Neuen Testament
ICC	International Critical Commentary
IG	Inscriptiones Graecae
IGR	Inscriptiones Graecae ad Res Romanas Pertinentes
Int	*Interpretation*
JBL	*Journal of Biblical Literature*
JJS	*Journal of Jewish Studies*
JSJ	*Journal for the Study of Judaism in the Persian, Hellenistic, and Roman Period*
JSNTSup	Journal for the Study of the New Testament— Supplement Series
JSOT	*Journal for the Study of the Old Testament*
JSPSup	Journal for the Study of Pseudepigrapha Supplement Series
JTS	*Journal of Theological Studies*
LCL	Loeb Classical Library
LXX	Septuagint
MGI	John Hick, *Metaphor of God Incarnate* (Louisville, Ky.: Westminster/John Knox Press, 1993)
NIDNTT	Colin Brown (ed.), *New International Dictionary of New Testament Theology*, 3 vols. (Exeter: Paternoster, 1975–8)
NIGTC	New International Greek Testament Commentary
NIV	New International Version (of the Bible)
NPNF	Nicene and Post-Nicene Fathers
NRSV	New Revised Standard Version
NT	New Testament
NTS	*New Testament Studies*

OGIS	*Orientis Graeci Inscriptiones Selectae, Supplementum Sylloge Inscriptionum Graecarum*, ed. Wilhelm Dittenberger (Hildesheim/New York: G. Olms, 1986)
OT	Old Testament
PD	*Pulpit Digest*
PG	Patrologia Graeca (J.-P. Migne)
PL	Patrologia Latina (J.-P. Migne)
QD	Quaestiones Disputatae
RB	*Revue Biblique*
RC	Roman Catholic Sermons
RHE	*Revue d'histoire ecclesiastique*
RILP	Roehampton Institute London Papers
RSV	Revised Standard Version
RUSCH	Rutgers University Studies in Classical Humanities
SBLDS	Society of Biblical Literature Dissertation Series
SC	Sources Chrétiennes
SIG	Al. N. Oikonomides (ed.), *Sylloge Inscriptionum Graecarum et Latinarum Macedoniae* (Chicago: Ares, 1980)
ST	*Summa Theologiae*
TrinJ	*Trinity Journal*
TS	*Theological Studies*
WBC	Word Biblical Commentary
ZNTW	*Zeitschrift für die neutestamentliche Wissenschaft*

Participants in the Trinity Summit
(Easter 1998, New York)

WILLIAM P. ALSTON   Born in Shreveport, Louisiana, he earned his Bachelor's degree from Centenary College of Louisiana and his Ph.D. from the University of Chicago in 1951. Currently he is Professor of Philosophy at Syracuse University. Recent books by him include: *A Realist Conception of Truth* (1996), *The Reliability of Sense Perception* (1993), and *Perceiving God: The Epistemology of Religious Experience* (1991), *Epistemic Justification* (1989), and *Divine Nature and Human Language* (1989), all published by Cornell University Press (Ithaca, NY).

MICHEL RENÉ BARNES   Born in Decatur, Alabama, he received his Bachelor's degree from the Santa Fé campus of St John's College in 1973. He received his M.Div. (1977), Th.M. (1989), and Ph.D. (1992) from the Faculty of Theology, University of St Michael's College, Toronto, Canada. Currently he is assistant professor for patristics at Marquette University, Milwaukee. He has recently published articles in *Augustinian Studies*, *Journal of Theological Studies*, *Studia Patristica*, *Theological Studies*, and *Vigiliae Christianae*. He is the author of *The Power of God: Dunamis in Gregory of Nyssa's Trinitarian Theology* (Washington, DC: Catholic University of America Press, 1999), the co-editor of the anthology *Arianism After Arius: Essays on the Development of the Fourth Century Trinitarian Conflicts* (Edinburgh: T. and T. Clark, 1993), and is presently writing a monograph entitled *Augustine's Trinitarian Theology in its Polemical Context*.

DAVID W. BROWN   Born in Galashiels, Scotland, he obtained an MA (in Classics) at Edinburgh and a second MA (in Philosophy and Theology) at Oxford, and his Ph.D. (in Moral Philosophy) from

Cambridge. Formerly a Fellow of Oriel College, Oxford, he is currently Van Mildert Professor of Divinity in the University of Durham. Publications by him include: *The Word to Set You Free* (London: SPCK, 1995), (with David Fuller) *Signs of Grace: Sacraments in Poetry and Prose* (London: Cassell, 1995), and *The Divine Trinity* (London/La Salle, Ill.: Duckworth/Open Court, 1985). Two volumes on *Tradition and Imagination* are nearing completion.

SARAH COAKLEY   Born in London, she obtained her undergraduate degree (1973) as well as her doctoral degree (1982) from the University of Cambridge. Currently she is Edward Mallinckrodt, Jr, Professor of Divinity, Harvard University. Writings by her include: (ed.) *Religion and the Body* (Cambridge: Cambridge University Press, 1997), *God, Sexuality and the Self: An Essay 'On the Trinity'* (Cambridge: Cambridge University Press, forthcoming), (coedited) *The Making and Remaking of Christian Doctrine: Essays in Honour of Maurice Wiles* (Oxford: Clarendon Press, 1993), and *Christ Without Absolutes: A Study of the Christology of Ernst Troeltsch* (Oxford: Oxford University Press, 1988).

STEPHEN T. DAVIS   Born in Lincoln, Nebraska, he obtained his Bachelor's degree from Whitworth College in 1962, his M.Div. from Princeton Theological Seminary, and his Ph.D. from the Claremont Graduate University in Philosophy in 1970. Currently he is Professor of Philosophy of Religion at Claremont McKenna College. Books by him include: *God, Reason, and Theistic Proofs* (Edinburgh: Edinburgh University Press, 1997), *Risen Indeed: Making Sense of the Resurrection* (Grand Rapids, Mich.: Eerdmans, 1993), *Death and Afterlife* (New York: St Martin's Press, 1989), and *Encountering Jesus* (Atlanta: John Knox Press, 1988).

CRAIG A. EVANS   Born in Ontario, California, he obtained his Bachelor's degree from Claremont McKenna College in 1974, his M.Div. from Western Baptist Seminary, and his MA and Ph.D. from Claremont Graduate University in Religious Studies in 1983. Currently he is Professor and Director of Graduate Studies in Biblical Studies at Trinity Western University, British Columbia. His books include: *Jesus and His Contemporaries: Comparative Studies* (Leiden: Brill, 1995), *Word and Glory: On the Exegetical and Theological Background of John's Prologue* (Sheffield: Sheffield

Academic Press, 1993), *Luke and Scripture: Essays on the Function of Authoritative Tradition in Luke-Acts* (Minneapolis: Fortress, 1993), *Noncanonical Writings and New Testament Interpretation* (Peabody, Mass.: Hendrickson, 1992), and *Luke* (Peabody, Mass.: Hendrickson, 1990).

GORDON D. FEE   Born in Ashland, Oregon, he received his BA and MA from Seattle Pacific University (1956, 1958) and his Ph.D. from the University of Southern California in 1966. He currently teaches New Testament studies at Regent College, Vancouver, BC, where he also serves as Dean of Faculty. Books by him include: *Commentary on the First Epistle to the Corinthians* (Grand Rapids, Mich.: Eerdmans, 1987), *God's Empowering Presence* (Peabody, Mass.: Hendrickson, 1994), *Paul's Letter to the Philippians* (Grand Rapids, Mich.: Eerdmans, 1995), and *Paul, the Spirit and the People of God* (Peabody, Mass.: Hendrickson, 1996).

DANIEL KENDALL   Born in Miami, Arizona, he obtained his Bachelor's degree from Gonzaga University in 1962, his STM from Santa Clara University in 1971, and his STD from the Gregorian University in Rome in 1975. Currently he teaches theology at the University of San Francisco. Publications by him include: (with Gerald O'Collins) *Focus on Jesus* (Leominster: Gracewing, 1996), (with Stephen Davis and Gerald O'Collins) *Resurrection* (Oxford: Oxford University Press, 1997), and (with Gerald O'Collins) *The Bible for Theology* (Mahwah, NJ: Paulist, 1997).

BRIAN LEFTOW   Born in Brooklyn, NY, he obtained his BA from Grove City College in 1977, his MA from Yale in 1978, his M.Phil. from Yale in 1981, and his Ph.D. from Yale in 1984. Currently he is associate professor of philosophy at Fordham University. He has published *Time and Eternity* (Ithaca, NY: Cornell, 1991) and *Divine Ideas* (Ithaca, NY: Cornell, forthcoming), as well as recent articles in the *Journal of the Evangelical Theological Society* and the *Thomist*.

JOSEPH T. LIENHARD   Born in the Bronx, he received the BA and MA from Fordham University, the Ph.L., BD, and STM from Woodstock College, and the Dr.Theol.Habil. from the University of Freiburg im Breisgau (Germany). He is Professor of Theology at Fordham University. His most recent books are: *Augustine:*

Presbyter Factus Sum, of which he was the co-editor (New York: Peter Lang, 1993); *The Bible, the Church, and Authority: The Canon of the Christian Bible in History and Theology* (Collegeville, Minn.: Liturgical Press, 1995); his translation: *Origen: Homilies on Luke; Fragments on Luke* (Washington, DC: Catholic University of America Press, 1996); and *Contra Marcellum: Marcellus of Ancyra and Fourth-Century Theology* (Washington, DC: Catholic University of America Press, 1999).

ANSELM KYONGSUK MIN   Born in Seoul, he obtained his Bachelor's degree from St Louis University in 1966, his MA and Ph.L. from St Louis University in 1967, his Ph.D. in philosophy from Fordham University in 1974, and his Ph.D. in theology from Vanderbilt University in 1989. Currently he is Professor of Religion at Claremont Graduate University. His publications include: *Korean Catholicism in the 1970's* (Maryknoll, NY: Orbis, 1975) and *Dialectic of Salvation: Issues in Theology of Liberation* (Albany, NY: SUNY Press, 1989).

CAREY C. NEWMAN   Born in Florida, he has earned degrees from the University of South Florida (BA, 1980), Southwestern Baptist Seminary, the University of Aberdeen, and Baylor University (Ph.D., 1989). He is currently editor for Academic books of Westminster John Knox Press in Louisville, Kentucky. Recent publications include: *Jesus and the Victory of God: An Assessment with Responses* (Downers Grove, Ill.: InterVarsity Press, forthcoming), 'Resurrection as Glory: Divine Presence and Christian Origins' (in *Resurrection* (Oxford: Oxford University Press, 1997)), and *Paul's Glory-Christology* (Leiden: E. J. Brill, 1992).

GERALD G. O'COLLINS   Born in Melbourne, Victoria, he obtained his undergraduate degree from Melbourne University in 1957 and his Ph.D. from Cambridge University in 1968. Since 1974 he has taught theology at the Gregorian University in Rome. Publications by him include: *Retrieving Fundamental Theology* (Mahwah, NJ: Paulist Press, 1993), *Christology* (Oxford: Oxford University Press, 1995), (with Daniel Kendall) *The Bible for Theology* (Mahwah, NJ: Paulist Press, 1997), and (with others) *The Resurrection* (Oxford: Oxford University Press, 1997).

ALAN G. PADGETT Born in Washington, DC, he earned his BA from Southern California College (1977), M.Div. from Drew University (1981), and D.Phil. from Oxford University (1990). Currently he is Professor of Theology and Philosophy of Science at Azusa Pacific University (California). Books by him include: *God, Eternity and the Nature of Time* (London: Macmillan, 1992) and (ed.) *Reason and the Christian Religion: Essays in Honour of Richard Swinburne* (Oxford: Oxford University Press, 1994), and (with Steve Wilkens) *Christianity and Western Thought*, ii (Downers Grove, Ill.: InterVarsity Press, 1998).

ALAN F. SEGAL Born in Worcester, Massachusetts, he earned his Bachelor's degree at Amherst College in 1967 and his Ph.D. at Yale University in 1975. Currently he is Professor of Religion at Barnard College, Columbia University. Publications by him include: *The Messiah: Developments in Earliest Judaism and Christianity* (Minneapolis: Fortress, 1992), *Paul the Convert: The Apostleship and Apostasy of Saul the Pharisee* (New Haven: Yale University Press, 1990), and *Rebecca's Children* (Cambridge, Mass.: Harvard University Press, 1988).

MARGUERITE SHUSTER Born in Santa Paula, California, she obtained her Bachelor's degree at Stanford in 1968, M.Div. from Fuller Theological Seminary in 1975, and her Ph.D. from the Fuller Graduate School of Psychology in 1977. She served as a Presbyterian pastor for nearly twelve years. Currently she teaches Preaching at Fuller Theological Seminary. Her writings include: (co-edited) *Perspectives on Christology: Essays in Honor of Paul K. Jewett* (Grand Rapids, Mich.: Zondervan, 1991), doctrinal sermons in *God, Creation, and Revelation* (Grand Rapids, Mich.: Eerdmans, 1991), *Power, Pathology, Paradox: The Dynamics of Evil and Good* (Grand Rapids, Mich.: Zondervan, 1987), and editor of *Who We Are: Our Dignity as Human* (Grand Rapids, Mich.: Eerdmans, 1996).

ELEONORE STUMP Born in Germany, she obtained her Bachelor's degree from Grinnell College in 1969, her Master's degrees from Harvard University in 1971 and Cornell University in 1973, and her Ph.D. from Cornell University in 1975. Currently she is the Robert J. Henle, SJ, Professor of Philosophy at St. Louis University. Her writings include: *Reasoned Faith* (Ithaca, NY: Cornell

University Press, 1993), *Aquinas*, in the series *Cambridge Companions to Philosophy* (Cambridge: Cambridge University Press, 1993), and 'The Principle of Alternative Possibilities: Widerker's Argument against Frankfurt-Style Counterexamples', in C. H. Manekin and M. W. Kellner (eds.), *Freedom and Moral Responsibility: General and Jewish Perspectives* (Bethesda: University Press of Maryland, 1997).

DAVID TRACY Born in Yonkers, New York, he obtained his Licentiate in Theology at the Gregorian University in 1964, and his STD (also at the Gregorian) in 1969. Currently he is Professor of Theology at the University of Chicago Divinity School. His writings include: *Blessed Rage for Order* (New York: Seabury Press, 1975 (rev. and published by Chicago: University of Chicago Press, 1996)), *On Naming the Present* (London: SCM Press, 1994), *Religion and Practical Reason* (Albany, NY: SUNY Press, 1994), and *Plurality and Ambiguity* (Chicago: University of Chicago Press, 1994).

FRANS JOZEF VAN BEECK Born in Helmond, The Netherlands. Licentiates in philosophy (Berchmanianum, Nijmegen, 1954) and theology (Canisianum, Maastricht, 1964), Ph.D. in English and Italian (University of Amsterdam, 1961), John Cardinal Cody Professor of Theology at Loyola University Chicago (1985–97). Currently (1997–8) Margaret and Chester Paluch Professor of Theology at Mundelein Seminary, Illinois. Publications include: *Christ Proclaimed: Christology as Rhetoric* (New York: Paulist Press, 1979); *Catholic Identity after Vatican II: Three Types of Faith in the One Church* (Chicago: Loyola University Press, 1985); *Loving the Torah More than God?: Towards a Catholic Appreciation of Judaism* (Chicago: Loyola University Press, 1989); *God Encountered: A Contemporary Catholic Systematic Theology*, i. *Understanding the Christian Faith*, ii. *The Revelation of the Glory*: Introduction and part 1. *Fundamental Theology*, part 2. *One God, Creator of All That Is*, part 3. *Phonated and Fall* (published by Harper and Row in San Francisco and Liturgical Press in Collegeville, Minn., 1989–95).

Note: Daniel Kendall, Anselm Min, Carey Newman, Alan Padgett, and Eleonore Stump were all active and valuable participants in the Trinity Summit, but this volume does not include contributions from them.

Select Bibliography

BROWN, D., *The Divine Trinity* (London/La Salle, Ill.: Duckworth/Open Court, 1985).

CONGAR, Y., *I Believe in the Holy Spirit*, 3 vols. (London: Geoffrey Chapman, 1983).

DEL COLLE, R., *Christ and the Holy Spirit* (New York: Oxford University Press, 1994).

FEE, G. D., *God's Empowering Presence: The Holy Spirit in the Letters of Paul* (Carlisle: Paternoster, 1995).

GRESHAKE, G., *Der dreieine Gott. Eine trinitarische Theologie* (Freiburg im Breisgau: Herder, 1997).

GUNTON, C. E., *The Promise of Trinitarian Theology* (Edinburgh: T. & T. Clark, 1993).

HANSON, R. P. C., *The Search for the Christian Doctrine of God* (Edinburgh: T. & T. Clark, 1988).

HILL, E., *The Mystery of the Trinity* (London: Geoffrey Chapman, 1985).

HILL, W. J., *The Three-Personed God* (Washington, DC: Catholic University of America Press, 1982).

JENSON, R. W., *The Triune Identity: God according to the Gospel* (Philadelphia: Fortress, 1982).

JOHNSON, E. A., *She Who Is: The Mystery of God in Feminist Theological Discourse* (New York: Crossroad, 1993).

JÜNGEL, E., *The Doctrine of the Trinity: God's Being is in Becoming* (Edinburgh: Scottish Academic Press, 1966).

KASPER, W., *The God of Jesus Christ* (New York: Crossroad, 1989).

KELLY, A., *The Trinity of Love* (Wilmington, Del.: Michael Glazier, 1989).

LACUGNA, C. M., *God for Us: The Trinity and Christian Life* (San Francisco: HarperSan Francisco, 1991).

MARSH, T. A., *The Triune God* (Dublin: Columba, 1994).

MOLTMANN, J., *The Trinity and the Kingdom: The Doctrine of God* (London: SCM Press, 1981).

O'COLLINS, G., *Christology: A Biblical, Historical, and Systematic Study of Jesus* (Oxford: Oxford University Press, 1995).

O'DONNELL, J., *The Mystery of the Triune God* (Mahwah, NJ: Paulist Press, 1988).

PANNENBERG, W., *Systematic Theology*, i. (Grand Rapids, Mich.: Eerdmans, 1991).

PETERS, T. F., *God as Trinity: Relationality and Temporality in the Divine Life* (Louisville: Westminster/John Knox, 1993).

RAHNER, K., *The Trinity* (New York: Crossroad, 1997).

SCHWÖBEL, C. (ed.), *Trinitarian Theology Today: Essays on Divine Being and Act* (Edinburgh: T. & T. Clark, 1995).

STUDER, B., *Trinity and Incarnation: The Faith of the Early Church* (Edinburgh: T. & T. Clark, 1995).

SWINBURNE, R., *The Christian Concept of God* (Oxford: Oxford University Press, 1994).

THOMPSON, J., *Modern Trinitarian Perspectives* (New York: Oxford University Press, 1994).

TORRANCE, A. J., *Persons in Communion: Trinitarian Description and Human Participation* (Edinburgh: T. & T. Clark, 1996).

TORRANCE, T. F., *The Christian Doctrine of God: One Being, Three Persons* (Edinburgh: T. & T. Clark, 1996).

WELKER, M., *God the Spirit* (Minneapolis: Fortress, 1994).

ZIZIOULAS, J., *Being and Communion: Studies in Personhood and the Church* (London: Darton, Longman & Todd, 1985).

1

The Holy Trinity: The State of the Questions

GERALD O'COLLINS, SJ

After many years of relative neglect, the central doctrine of the Trinity has attracted much theological attention as the second Christian millennium draws to an end. The select bibliography (see pp. xxvii–xxviii) offers only a representative selection from much recent literature on the Blessed Trinity. For my survey I want to pick out and comment on twelve significant issues that have emerged or have been revived for current discussion.[1]

(1) Even a summary reading of current publications will reveal a widespread desire to 'rehabilitate' belief in the Trinity as the deep truth at the very heart of Christian life.[2] The way trinitarian faith seemed to have been rationally reduced to little more than a logical puzzle for the experts encouraged the situation in which Immanuel Kant (1724–1804) could state in *Conflict of the Faculties*: 'The doctrine of the Trinity, taken literally, has *no practical relevance at all*, even if we think we understand it; and it is even more clearly irrelevant if we realize that it transcends all our concepts.

---

[1] Further questions are not lacking: for instance, the maternal role of the Holy Spirit (Mother Spirit as the soul of Mother Church); the role of the Holy Spirit for the future consummation of the world; and the distinct personal identity of the Spirit. As regards the third issue, it has been too easy to play down the personhood of the Spirit and turn the Spirit into an 'aspect' of the Father and the Son, a 'mere' enigmatic and impersonal power or personification for divine action in the world— a view that Gordon Fee's chapter shows to be incompatible with St Paul's teaching. Two central questions, which in fact fail to appear in much current literature, are (*a*) the relevance of trinitarian faith for moral thinking and behaviour, and (*b*) the significance for Christian trinitarian faith of the Jewish understanding of God. I think here of the Hebrew Scriptures' personification of the powerful, life-giving 'Spirit of the Lord', and of the rabbinic fear that the Father/Son faith of Christians amounted to 'two powers in heaven', an issue that also involved gnostic and philosophical strands of thought as Alan Segal shows in his chapter.

[2] Finding the trinitarian mystery irretrievable and even intolerable, some opt for 'one God' and jettison 'three persons'. Stephen Davis's contribution to this collection examines a contemporary example of this reaction.

Whether we are to worship three or ten persons in the Deity makes no difference.'[3] A few years later F. D. E. Schleiermacher (1768–1834) queried the practical importance of trinitarian faith in *The Christian Faith*: 'Our faith in Christ and our living fellowship with him would be the same even if we had no knowledge of any such transcendent fact [as the Trinity] and even if the fact itself were different.'[4] Karl Rahner's observation about the irrelevance of trinitarian faith in the lives of most believers has been frequently quoted but it merits repetition: 'Despite their orthodox confession of the Trinity, Christians are, in their practical life, almost mere "monotheists".'[5] Bernard Lonergan used to comment wrily on the theology of the Trinity by changing the final 'no proof' in a traditional concise formulation of the doctrine of the Western Church: 'The Trinity is a matter of five notions or properties, four relations, three persons, two processions, one substance or nature, and no understanding.' At the end (in my twelfth point) I will return to this first issue and suggest some appropriate procedures for theologians and Christian philosophers of religion who are concerned about the apparent marginalization of the trinitarian faith or what Walter Kasper has called 'its present existential obscurity'.[6]

Here let me insert just one observation: those who have been emphasizing the practical irrelevance of trinitarian faith may be exaggerating. Admittedly in many churches the faithful hear sermons on the Trinity only once a year: on Trinity Sunday itself. Marguerite Shuster's chapter suggests that, even then, they may be hearing poor sermons on this utterly central belief. Nevertheless, the Nicene-Constantinopolitan Creed that churches across the world use at the Eucharist constantly reminds Christians of their trinitarian faith and does so by recalling salvation history. The

---

[3] In I. Kant, *Religion and Rational Theology*, trans. A. W. Wood and G. di Giovanni, The Cambridge Edition of the Works of Immanuel Kant (Cambridge: Cambridge University Press, 1996), 264.

[4] Trans. H. R. Mackintosh and J. S. Stewart (Edinburgh: T. & T. Clark, 1928), 741; trans. corrected.

[5] *The Trinity*, trans. J. Donceel and intr. C. M. LaCugna (New York: Crossroad, 1997), 10. A few years later Rahner published his *Foundations of Christian Faith: An Introduction to the Idea of Christianity*, trans. W. V. Dych (New York: Seabury, 1978; German original 1976). Curiously this 500-page long work has hardly anything to say about the Trinity. As Marguerite Shuster points out in her chapter, Rahner also did not include any sermon for Trinity Sunday in his published sermons for the church year.

[6] *The God of Jesus Christ*, trans. M. J. O'Connell (New York: Crossroad, 1989), ix.

celebration of baptism, along with the now more frequent renewal of baptismal vows, also recalls to the attention of believers the trinitarian faith at the heart of their lives. The Eucharist opens 'in the name of the Father, and of the Son, and of the Holy Spirit', and closes (as do normal Christian blessings) with a blessing in the name of the Trinity. The content of the eucharistic prayers, both in the East and in the West, is repeatedly trinitarian. The 'short' doxology, 'Glory be to the Father and to the Son and to the Holy Spirit', and the 'long' doxology, 'Glory to God in the Highest', address the tripersonal God. Collects in the divine office and in other liturgical ceremonies, above all in the Eucharist, end by invoking the Trinity. In short, where many preachers fail to be trinitarian in their focus, liturgical texts clearly maintain that the Trinity is *the* message of salvation. Talk of the Eucharist brings us naturally to the issue of christology and its trinitarian dimension.

(2) In the 'bad old days' one could write a christological study and largely leave out the Trinity,[7] and—vice versa—one could write a trinitarian study that made little or no reference to Jesus of Nazareth. Among other defects, such non-trinitarian christologies normally ignored the eschatological character of Christian faith: that final return of all people and things to the Father through the mission of the Son and the Spirit. Nowadays the widespread appreciation of the trinitarian face of the whole story of Jesus—from his virginal conception and baptism right through to the resurrection, the outpouring of the Holy Spirit, and his coming in glory at the end—functions against such a failure to ground christology in trinitarian doctrine. But more needs to be done, if christology is to be resolutely trinitarian. Incidentally, I want to avoid here any false dichotomy between what is 'trinitarian' and 'christological'— something Michel Barnes rightly warns against in his chapter on St Augustine.

Yet not enough has been done. Take the Synoptic Gospels' witness to the public ministry of Jesus and its heart, the proclamation of the present and coming kingdom. His filial relationship to 'Abba'

---

[7] In *The Christ of Faith: The Christology of the Church*, trans. J. Crick (London: Burns & Oates, 1957), Karl Adam, for example, pays little attention to the Trinity, apart from a few incidental remarks (233–5). The widely used manual by J. A. De Aldama, S. Gonzalez, and J. Solano, *De Verbo Incarnato*, in vol. iii of *Sacrae Theologiae Summa*, 3rd edn. (Madrid: BAC, 1956), 9–329, had practically nothing to say about the Trinity apart from a speculative section on the possibility of incarnation for any of the three persons (60–7).

has been widely discussed and treated in both biblical and theo-logical works; Craig Evans's contribution to this collection argues that Jesus' self-designation as 'Son of man' prepared the way for his being recognized as divine. But little attention has been paid to the Holy Spirit's place in the narratives of Jesus' ministry for the kingdom. Rudolf Schnackenburg's classic *God's Rule and Kingdom*[8] rarely referred to the Spirit; one can appreciate why J. D. G. Dunn needed to emphasize how the Spirit 'is the key to understanding much of the kingdom proclamation in the Synoptics'.[9] Yet, as Earl Muller remarks, in the years since Dunn's protest 'the situation has not noticeably altered'. Muller cites the failure to treat the Spirit in Dennis Duling's *Anchor Bible Dictionary* article, 'Kingdom of God, Kingdom of Heaven',[10] while also drawing attention to a few authors who have taken Dunn's observation to heart.

In *The Trinity and the Kingdom of God: The Doctrine of God*[11] and other writings, Jürgen Moltmann (b. 1926) has developed a 'social' interpretation of the Trinity; he appreciates that not only the preaching of the kingdom but also the death and resurrection of Jesus are profoundly trinitarian. It is important that we approach the death of Jesus as primarily an inner-trinitarian drama or 'the inner history of the Trinity'. Theologians and other believers need to look at Good Friday, Holy Saturday, and Easter Sunday for what they reveal of the tripersonal God before reflecting on what these holy days say about human beings and their history. Yet many fear that Moltmann's insistence on the crucifixion and resurrection as an inner-trinitarian event (with a rupture in the divine life and the Father 'ceasing' to be Father) may be confusing the intra-divine life with the story of human salvation to the point of 'imprisoning' God in the world's becoming. It is one thing to uphold a strong link

---

[8] Trans. J. Murray (New York: Herder and Herder, 1968).

[9] 'Spirit and Kingdom', *Expository Times*, 32 (1970–1), 36–40, at 36.

[10] D. N. Freedman *et al.* (eds.), iv (New York: Doubleday, 1992), 49–69. In 'The Trinity and the Kingdom', *Studia Missionalia*, 46 (1997), 91–117, at 91–2, Muller refers to this and a number of other recent studies on the kingdom that pay little or no attention to the Holy Spirit. To his list one could add J. P. Meier, *A Marginal Jew*, ii (New York: Doubleday, 1994), 237–506; in many ways this is the best cur-rent account of Jesus' proclamation of the kingdom; yet it offers little on the Spirit. In fact the whole volume of well over a thousand pages (on the mentor, message, and miracles of Jesus) does not even have an entry on 'Holy Spirit' or 'Spirit' in its subject index. Meier's particular kind of historical orientation entails a partial neglect of theology in general and of pneumatology in particular.

[11] Trans. M. Kohl (London: SCM Press, 1981).

between the theology of the cross and the doctrine of the Trinity, and emphasize that it was the Son of God who was crucified and was raised by the Father through the power of the Holy Spirit. But it is another thing to expound the crucifixion as not only affecting but even shaping the inner life of the tripersonal God.[12] If one pushes matters to an extreme and argues that the paschal mystery 'constitutes' or 'creates' the Trinity, as if God somehow needed such an historical process in order to become trinitarian, then— paradoxically—the divine persons cannot share in that mystery inasmuch as they are not present 'prior' to the event.

In various guises this question has come up since the early centuries of Christianity. The leader of the Patripassian Monarchians, Praxeas (fl. AD *c.*200), pushed the divine unity to the point of teaching that, under the name of Jesus Christ, the Father became incarnate and suffered on the cross. While rejecting this doctrine in his *Adversus Praxean* (2. 1; 29. 1–7), Tertullian (d. AD *c.*225) recognized in Christ one acting subject, and this allowed him to write of 'the crucified God' (*Adversus Marcionem*, 2. 27) and declare: 'the Son of God died' (*Adversus Praxean*, 29. 1). By the late second century, in his homily 'On the Pasch', St Melito of Sardis had already spoken of Christ's crucifixion in a way that both named him as divine Creator and predicated of him a shameful human death: 'He who hung up the earth is himself hung up; he who fixed the heavens is himself fixed [on the cross]; he who fastened everything is fastened on the wood; the Master is reviled; God has been killed' (96). Melito resembled St Justin Martyr (d. AD *c.*165) and later writers in attributing to Christ special divine actions in the Old Testament, but he differed from them by also attributing to him various sufferings: 'He was present in many so as to endure many things. In Abel he was slain; in Isaac bound; in Jacob a stranger; in Joseph sold; in Moses exposed; in David persecuted; in the prophets dishonoured' (69).

The widespread conviction that God was/is simply beyond all suffering, time, and change undoubtedly made many Christian thinkers reluctant to interpret biblical witness to God's deep involvement in history in ways that challenged a classical view of

---

[12] See J. McDade, 'The Trinity and the Paschal Mystery', *Heythrop Journal*, 29 (1988), 175–91. One could say that the crucifixion 'affected' (not shaped) the inner life of the tripersonal God inasmuch as the Son, through assuming our human condition, underwent death on the cross. In that sense one can also say that the Father (as the Father of the Son) suffered in the Son.

divine impassibility. Nevertheless, Origen could comment on passages from Deuteronomy and Ezekiel as follows:

> The Father himself, God of the Universe, he who is full of long-suffering,
> compassion, and mercy, does he not suffer in some way? Or do you not
> know that in his concern for human affairs he suffers human passion? For
> the Lord your God has taken upon himself your fortunes as he who
> carries his child (Deut. 1: 31). God, then, takes upon himself our misfor-
> tunes as the Son of God takes on our sufferings. The Father himself is not
> impassible. (*In Ezekielem*, 6. 6)[13]

Despite this last sentence, a sense of the godhead's impassibility
had made Origen qualify his language: the Father 'in some way'
suffers human passion and fortunes, whereas the incarnation
allowed Origen to state straightforwardly that 'the Son of God takes
on our sufferings'. Most of the Church Fathers who examined the
issue differed from Melito (in not speaking of the pre-incarnate
Son's sufferings) and from Origen (in not even guardedly attributing suffering to the Father); they were content to tackle the mystery of the incarnate Son suffering and dying on the cross or, as
the sixth-century patriarch, St Anastasius of Antioch put it, the
'reasons why the Word of God, otherwise impassible, came to his
passion' (*Addresses*, 4. 1–2).

In *The Crucified God*[14] and subsequent publications, however one
evaluates the particular shape of his arguments, Moltmann has
rightly urged the need to think through in a trinitarian way the
centre of christology: Jesus' crucifixion and resurrection.[15] As has
often been remarked, there is more than a passing resemblance
here to the reflections of Hans Urs von Balthasar (1905–88) on the
mystery of Calvary as an inner-trinitarian drama. Yet there is a
significant difference inasmuch as von Balthasar's interpretation is
rooted in his theology of the Trinity's 'prior', eternal life: the

---

[13] See the helpful discussion of the divine 'weakness' and 'com-passion' which
this sixth homily from Origen prompted in F. J. van Beeck, *God Encountered: A
Contemporary Catholic Systematic Theology*, vol. ii/2 (Collegeville, Minn.: Liturgical
Press, 1994), 150–68.

[14] Trans. R. A. Wilson and J. Bowden (London: SCM Press, 1974). Unfortunately,
a certain ambiguity affects this book, inasmuch as it switches from speaking of the
suffering and death *of* God to speaking of suffering and death *in* God.

[15] At the same time, one should refrain from unilaterally stressing or even abso-
lutizing the abandonment theme from Mark 15: 34 (followed by Matt. 27: 46).
Christology should also hear the somewhat different trinitarian witness to the death
(and resurrection) of Jesus coming from Luke and John.

eternal generation of the Son already expresses the 'kenosis' of the Father's heart.[16]

Christology, when studying Jesus 'in himself', has often failed to do so in a trinitarian way, or at least has failed to acknowledge the trinitarian face of the *entire* history of Jesus. It has frequently forgotten, for example, how from the virginal conception and baptism the Holy Spirit was at work sanctifying his humanity. Soteriology, in examining Christ's saving work 'for us', has often suffered from a similar failure, ignoring, for instance, how through the Holy Spirit Christ became the powerful Saviour for the whole world and its history.[17] From the time of St Anselm's extraordinarily influential work *Cur deus homo* (completed in 1098), versions of redemption have often proved non-trinitarian in character.[18] A neglect of the Holy Spirit clearly bears some responsibility for soteriologies and christologies remaining partly or even substantially non-trinitarian. A non-pneumatological approach to christology and soteriology can hardly pay anything like proper attention to the Trinity. It will become 'binitarian' and even unitarian, to the extent that it forgets the Holy Spirit and the Spirit's 'economic' mission which parallels the Son's 'sending' in Pauline and Johannine thought (e.g. Gal. 4: 4–6; John 14: 26; 20: 21). This leads to my third observation on the current scene.

(3) Contemporary trinitarian theology frequently starts from the earliest Christian reflections on the doctrine, to be found in the

---

[16] See P. Martinelli's doctoral dissertation, *Il Mistero della morte in Hans Urs von Balthasar. Il mistero pasquale come rivelazione dell'amore Trinitario di Dio* (Rome: Gregorian University, 1996). Von Balthasar's views on what it is to be a man or a woman affected his trinitarian theology (as provocatively pointed out by G. Loughlin in 'Sexing the Trinity', *New Blackfriars*, 79 (1998), 18–25) and set him apart from Moltmann.

[17] At times a one-sided concentration on Christ's 'being in himself' has led to a neglect of his redemptive 'work for us'. Such a one-sided, non-soteriological christology normally remains non-pneumatological (and non-trinitarian). It passes over the Spirit's action in consecrating Christ for his saving mission (e.g. Acts 10: 37–8); it is the Spirit who makes Jesus the last/eschatological Adam, the life-giving 'man from heaven' (1 Cor. 15: 45–9).

[18] The following representative works have little to say about God the Father and even less about the Holy Spirit: J. Rivière; *Le Dogme de la Rédemption: Étude théologique* (Paris: Lecoffre, 1914); G. Aulén, *Christus Victor: An Historical Survey of the Three Main Types of the Idea of the Atonement* (London: SPCK, 1931); F. W. Dillistone, *The Christian Understanding of Atonement* (London: SCM Press, 1984); J. McIntyre, *The Shape of Soteriology: Studies in the Doctrine of the Death of Christ* (Edinburgh: T. & T. Clark, 1992). A healthier trinitarian interest sets apart P. Fiddes, *Past Event and Present Salvation* (London: Darton, Longman & Todd, 1989) and C. E. Gunton, *The Actuality of Atonement* (Edinburgh: T. & T. Clark, 1988).

letters of St Paul. His redefining of Jewish monotheism put 'the Lord Jesus Christ' alongside 'God our Father' as the joint source of salvation or 'grace and peace' in terms of Paul's customary greeting to his correspondents. 'God our Father' is also named as the 'Father of our Lord Jesus Christ' (e.g. 2 Cor. 1: 2-3; see Rom. 15: 6). It can be easy to interpret the apostle's thought in a binitarian rather than a trinitarian fashion and leave in lower case most of the Pauline references to (*to*) *pneuma*. The merit of Gordon Fee's *God's Empowering Presence: The Holy Spirit in the Letters of Paul*[19] is to present carefully the case for reading 'Spirit' in a more personal way and recognizing the centrality of pneumatology in the apostle's understanding of Christian faith. It is too early to evaluate the long-term impact of Fee's work. But it may well help to interpret early Christian doctrine as being much more pneumatological and hence trinitarian in character. Without being anachronistic and reading later documents back into Paul's letters, Fee alerts his readers to the presence of numerous triadic formulations that in some cases the apostle may have drawn from even earlier (Christian) traditions. Paul's pneumatology went hand in hand with his 'trinitarian' thinking. What happened later, when Paul and the other New Testament witnesses had passed off the scene?

(4) From the time of Justin Martyr in the second century, post-New Testament writers wrestled with the central Christian mystery of the tripersonal God. How could they grasp, even marginally, the differentiated unity of God or the divine unity in distinction? Recent years have brought numerous studies of traditional teaching and thinking about the Trinity.[20]

In the fourth century, the Cappadocians developed their language of the three co-equal and co-eternal *hypostaseis* or persons sharing the one divine *ousia* or essence.[21] At the heart of God, they

[19] (Carlisle: Paternoster Press, 1994).

[20] See, for instance, M. R. Barnes, 'Augustine in Contemporary Trinitarian Theology', *TS*, 56 (1995), 237-50; R. P. C. Hanson, *The Search for the Christian Doctrine of God* (Edinburgh: T. & T. Clark, 1988); C. M. LaCugna, *God for Us: The Trinity and Christian Life* (San Francisco: HarperSan Francisco, 1991); E. Muller, 'The Science of Theology: A Review of Catherine LaCugna's *God for Us*', *Gregorianum*, 75 (1994), 311-41; M. Schniertshauer, *Consummatio Caritatis: Eine Untersuchung zu Richard von St. Victors De Trinitate* (Mainz: Matthias-Grünewald-Verlag, 1996); R. Williams, *Arius: Heresy and Tradition* (London: Darton, Longman & Todd, 1987).

[21] In his contribution to this book, Joseph Lienhard draws attention to the risk of

saw an interpersonal communion or *koinōnia*, with communion as the function of all three divine persons and not simply of the Holy Spirit. For this interpersonal model of the Trinity, God's inner being is relational, with each of the three persons totally related and transparent to the other two. Such a theology 'saves' the divine threeness but might seem to sacrifice the unity and lapse into tritheism—a danger not lost on the Cappadocians. In his treatise *Ad Ablabium*, to which Sarah Coakley's chapter will attend, St Gregory of Nyssa (d. AD *c.*395) took pains to argue 'that there are not three gods', or—as we would say today—'not three separate divine subjects'. Enjoying a unity infinitely closer than that between three human persons, the Trinity is not to be 'reduced' to the social analogy of a loving family or, still less, that of a committee—as Brian Leftow will argue later in this book. The subjectivity of the Father, Son, and Holy Spirit is always an infinitely radical intersubjectivity. To account for the distinctions within the Trinity so uniquely united, Gregory of Nyssa and others underlined the fact that one of the persons (the Father) relates to the other two as ultimate source and 'cause'. This 'mon-archy' of the Father could be seen, however, to favour a 'descending' view of the Trinity and even an unacceptable subordination of Son and Holy Spirit to the Father, the unoriginated fountainhead of divinity. But, properly understood, the 'mon-archy' of the Father does not mean superiority, let alone exclusive superiority.[22]

After Athanasius and the Cappadocians developed their trinitarian thinking to some extent in polemical opposition to denials of the divinity of the Son and of the Spirit, St Augustine of Hippo (AD 354–430), wrote his *De Trinitate* slowly and arguably in a somewhat less polemical way. He took seventeen years to complete the work, which—one must add—is neither his last nor his only work on the Trinity. The interpersonal relationship of paternity and filiation stand behind Augustine's model of love developed in book 8 of *De Trinitate*. The Father is the 'Lover', the Son the 'Beloved', and the Holy Spirit the mutual 'Love' that passes between Father

inaccuracy in characterizing the Cappadocian settlement as 'one *ousia* and three *hypostaseis*'.

[22] A recent study by Gabino Uríbarri Bilbao, *Monarquía y Trinidad. El concepto teológico 'monarchia' en la controversia 'monarquiana'* (Madrid: Universidad Comillas, 1996), admirably takes the edge off this suspicion of subordination, by showing the compatibility of 'monarchy' and trinitarian doctrine at least in the setting of third-century theology.

and Son (and 'proceeds' from both!). Eastern Christians have
criticized this analogy (which medieval theologians such as Richard
of St Victor were to develop in the West) for depersonalizing the
Holy Spirit, or at least for not allowing the identity of a distinct
person to come through clearly. After all in the I–Thou relationship, the love that two persons bestow on each other is not a third
person, or at least does not emerge as an activity that defines a
person distinct from the 'I' and the 'Thou'. In the *De Trinitate*
Augustine himself went on to exploit the human soul and its
faculties as the best mirror of the Trinity available. He was justified
in doing so by the way the Scriptures hint that the generation of
the Son (e.g. Matt. 11: 25–7) and the procession of the Spirit (e.g.
Rom. 5: 5) are somehow mirrored in or paralleled by the two basic
activities of the human spirit: knowing and loving. In the scheme
of 'mens/notitia/amor' Augustine found in the mind, the mind's
knowledge of itself, and the mind's love of itself an image of the
Trinity. He introduced further refinements in this trinitarian model
with the scheme of the human 'memoria/intelligentia/voluntas'
(*De Trinitate*, 9. 8; 10. 10, 14–16; 11. 11, 17–19). This psychological analogy[23] attends to the way the interior word (*verbum
mentale*) arises through a creative act that can be compared with
generation: the eternal Word or Son of God is distinct from and yet
identical with the generating Father. Similarly the divine act of love
gives rise to its eternal, immanent fruit (*impressio amati in amato*),
the Holy Spirit. Augustine's psychological analogy pre-emptively
avoids any risk of tritheism, but might be seen to encourage a
monopersonal, modalist view of God. Does the intra-personal
analogy 'save' the divine unity but 'lose' the threeness of God? One
should repeat here that Augustine's reflections on the Holy Trinity
are by no means confined to *De Trinitate*, an impression that could
be given by a widely used textbook, Henry Bettenson's *The Later
Christian Fathers*.[24] All the extracts from Augustine provided by
Bettenson (pp. 230–6) are taken from *De Trinitate*. This is to slip

---

[23] Michel Barnes rightly points out that this psychological analogy for the Trinity
is also found in such Greek authors as Eusebius of Caesarea and Gregory of Nyssa:
'Augustine in Contemporary Trinitarian Theology', 238–9. In 'Rhetorical and
Theological Issues in the Structuring of Augustine's *De Trinitate*', *Studia Patristica*,
xvii, ed. E. A. Livingstone (Leuven: Peeters Press, 1993), 356–63, at 359–60, Earl
C. Muller argues that the love analogy of book 8 is only the first step towards the
one psychological analogy Augustine wanted to develop.

[24] (Oxford: Oxford University Press, 1970); the paperback edition of 1972 had
reached its ninth impression by 1989.

over what one finds in other works by Augustine; in *The City of God* he remarks, for instance, that 'God is everything that he has except for the relations through which each person is referred to the other' (11.10.1). This remark not only anticipates St Thomas Aquinas' trinitarian theology of God as subsistent relations but also parallels a passage in *De Trinitate* (5. 5–6), which discusses inner-trinitarian relations and which Bettenson does not quote.

One should also add that in book 15 of *De Trinitate* Augustine highlighted again the love analogy to interpret the Trinity. The Holy Spirit is the Gift of mutual love between Father and Son—a theme already developed much earlier in *De Trinitate* (5. 11–12). Centuries later Richard of St Victor (d. 1173) held that mutual love, to be perfect, must be love shared with a third person. In God we find not just an I–Thou relationship of reciprocal love but also the Holy Spirit as the 'Co-beloved' (*Condilectus*). There is 'movement' from self-love (the Father) to mutual love (the Father and Son) to shared love (the Father, Son, and Holy Spirit). This view of God as absolute communion of love takes a little further Augustine's trinitarian theology of love.

(5) Reflection on the origins of the Son and the Holy Spirit in the inner life of the Trinity led the Western church to add unilaterally to the Nicene-Constantinopolitan Creed: the Spirit proceeds from the Father '*and the Son*'—the 'Filioque' addition that has helped to hold apart Eastern and Western Christianity. It is worth remarking that the original form of the Nicene-Constantinopolitan Creed (from 381) did not state that the Spirit proceeds from the Father *alone*. In confessing that the Spirit proceeds from *the Father*, it refers to One who has that name precisely because of the generation of the Son. In effect, the Creed confesses that the Spirit proceeds 'from the Father of the Son'.

In any case the addition of the 'Filioque' to the Creed found its place in Western liturgy, art, and literature. At the end of his *Paradiso* Dante Alighieri (1265–1321) envisioned God as utterly active, with 'spinning' or 'circling' symbolizing the completely actualized divine perfection; in the divine 'spinnings' the Holy Spirit proceeds from or is breathed by both Father and Son: 'in the profound and clear ground of the lofty light there appeared to me three spinnings (circlings) of three colours and of the same extent. The One seemed reflected by the Other as rainbow by rainbow, and the Third seemed fire breathed forth *equally from* the One and the

Other' (Canto 33. 115–20; italics mine). Let us recall briefly the background to the trinitarian theology espoused by Dante.

In his *Adversus Praxean*, along the lines of his image of the spring/river/canal, Tertullian wrote of the Spirit being 'from the Father through the Son' (4). More than a century later, where St Hilary of Poitiers (d. AD 367) repeated 'from the Father through the Son', Marius Victorinus (fourth century) drew on such New Testament passages as Jesus' words in John 16: 14 ('he [the Spirit of truth] will glorify me, because he will take what is mine and declare it to you') to reach the conclusion that the Son, together with the Father, 'produced' the Holy Spirit.[25] Augustine wrote of the Father endowing the Son with the 'capacity' to produce the Spirit; hence it is in a primordial or 'original' sense (*principaliter*) that the Spirit proceeds from the Father (*de Padre principaliter*). To deny this 'double procession', from the Father and from the Son 'as if from one principle' (*tanquam ab uno principio*), would violate the divine unity (*De Trinitate*, 5. 14). The Spirit proceeds from the Father through the Son, the Son being considered the 'agent' of the Father in this procession by equally 'producing' the divine Spirit. (The Son's being equal in the 'production' of the Spirit was/is important when facing Arian challenges to the Son's truly having equal divinity.) What the Son does here happens 'through the gift of the Father' and not independently, just as his divinity is derived from the Father. Being and acting in such a 'derivative' way does not exclude being equal in divinity and in the 'production' of the Spirit. Eastern theologians, however, normally reject this idea of the Son forming with the Father a single co-principle for the 'procession' of the Spirit. Such a double origin for the Spirit contradicts the divine unity. Distinguishing between the (economic) mission and the (immanent) procession of the Spirit, Eastern theologians appeal to John 15: 26: 'When the Advocate comes, whom I *will send* to you *from the Father*, the Spirit of truth *who proceeds from the Father*, he will testify on my behalf.' Only the Father is the ultimate source and fountainhead of divinity, from whom the Son and the Spirit derive—the former by generation and the latter by procession.

Here one can undoubtedly indulge over-clear, unsubtle polarities, whether it be about the procession of the Holy Spirit in par-

[25] Marius Victorinus, *Traités théologiques sur la Trinité*, SC 68 and 69 (Paris: Cerf, 1961).

ticular or about the whole doctrine of the Trinity in general—as if all the problems and differences were to go back, for instance, to the Greeks beginning with the reality of the divine persons and the Latins with the unity of the divine nature.[26] But one should respect the fear Eastern Christians have of neglecting or subordinating the Spirit. They remain strongly trinitarian in their faith because they experience the life and living witness of the Spirit in the Church. To neglect or downplay this experience will be to neglect or downplay trinitarian faith. Their problems with the Western understanding of the procession of the Holy Spirit are tied into concerns about the subordination of the Spirit to the Son (in the life of Christians) and of pneumatology to christology (in the work of theologians). In the christocentric theology of the West, which at times is hard to distinguish from christomonism,[27] the Spirit becomes the Spirit of Christ rather than the Spirit of (God) the Father.

The doctrine of the Trinity has helped to divide Eastern from Western Christianity. Nowadays within the West itself a further divisive issue has arisen: the naming of the three persons. Are 'Father, Son, and Holy Spirit' proper names for God, names that should not be replaced but retained with the assurance of St Basil of Caesarea: 'We are bound to be baptized in the terms we have received and to profess faith in the terms in which we are baptized, and as we have professed faith in, so to give glory to the Father, Son, and Holy Spirit' (*Epistle*, 125. 3)?

(6) Current proposals for renaming the godhead include: 'Source, Word, and Spirit'; 'Creator, Redeemer, and Sanctifier'; 'Creator, Liberator, and Comforter'; 'Creator, Redeemer, and Sustainer'; 'God, Christ, and Spirit'; 'the Creator, the Christ, and the Spirit'; 'Parent, Child, and Paraclete'; 'Mother, Daughter, and Spirit'; 'Mother, Lover, and Friend'; 'Spirit-Sophia, Jesus-Sophia, and Mother-Sophia'; and 'Father, Child, and Mother'. With terms for sovereignty now played down in many cultures, such names for God as 'Lord', 'King', and 'Ruler' seem threatened. Pressure for inclusive God-language would rule out the first two names. What

---

[26] Brian Leftow's contrast between Latin Trinitarianism (for which he takes the example of Thomas Aquinas) and Social Trinitarianism (for which he takes examples from twentieth-century authors) is not intended to be a typology for the patristic period.

[27] See Y. Congar, *I Believe in the Holy Spirit*, i (London: Geoffrey Chapman, 1983), 157, 159-60.

future should the more personal, more intimate, but gender-specific name of 'Father' enjoy? Has the language of divine fatherhood, by fostering a male-related image of God, legitimated male domination, underpinned the power structure of patriarchal Christianity, supported idolatrous androcentrism, helped to produce a false fixing of roles between the sexes, and proved a major (if not the major) cause of women being oppressed in the Western world (and beyond)? Did biblical traditions by naming God as 'Father' presuppose an anti-woman social orientation that should not be followed further, since calling God by that name inevitably encourages sexist disvalues and chauvinist attitudes?

Jesus compared God's saving activity to a woman searching for lost money (Luke 15: 8–10) or baking bread (Luke 13: 20–1 = Matt. 13: 33). By applying to God images associated with women of his time, and by many other details in his preaching of the kingdom, Jesus never approached depicting God in terms that would have been associated exclusively with male activities. John's Gospel pictures 'the hour' of Christ's own death and resurrection as birth pangs (John 16: 21; 17: 1) and the piercing of his body on the cross not only in terms of Christ giving rise to the Church like Adam giving rise to Eve but also as a mother nurturing her offspring (John 7: 37–9; 19: 34), as patristic authors like St John Chrysostom (*Catecheses*, 3. 19; *In Matthaeum*, 82. 5) and later writers appreciated. Reclaiming biblical (and traditional) language for God also entails recognizing that the Holy Spirit can crucially be linked with giving birth (John 3: 6; Rom. 8: 18–27). Thus attention to the full scope of the New Testament and the tradition will show that the experience of God that led to the formulated doctrine of the Holy Trinity was by no means solely associated with male activities.

Sheer abundance characterizes identification of God as 'Father' in the New Testament: 254 clear references and 4 other possible cases. Jesus' own experience and example gave rise to this development. As Raymond Brown (1928–98) puts it well, 'one is justified in claiming that Jesus' striking use of *Abba* did express his intimate experience of God as his own father and that this usage did make a lasting impression on his disciples.'[28] Far from being One whose supreme quality is power and only concern is to dominate, the compassionate 'Father' of whom Jesus spoke, knows our needs

[28] R. E. Brown, *The Death of the Messiah*, i (New York: Doubleday, 1994), 174.

before we ask, cares for all, and forgives all, even the wickedly unjust and sinful. Jesus' Father-image subverted any oppressive, patriarchal notions of God as primarily or even exclusively an authoritarian figure. Jesus also revealed the ultimate divine reality as the Father to whom he stood in a unique relationship as the Son; acting with filial consciousness he manifested the Father. Then Jesus' resurrection (with the outpouring of the Holy Spirit) made him the eldest Son of the Father's new, eschatological family (Rom. 8: 29), a family now empowered to share intimately in Jesus' relationship to the Father in the Spirit. Matthew's Gospel ends with the command to baptize 'in the name of the Father, and of the Son, and of the Holy Spirit' (Matt. 28: 19), a point of arrival for the New Testament that becomes a point of departure for the rites of initiation creeds which will take their structure around the confession of faith in the Father, the Son, and the Holy Spirit. The voices of the New Testament and the Christian tradition harmonize in presenting 'Father, Son, and Holy Spirit' as the primary (not exclusive) way of speaking about the tripersonal God. In particular, the early centuries of Christianity show how faith in Jesus as Son of God coincided with faith in God as Father. Thus, St Hilary of Poitiers called 'the very centre of a saving faith' the belief 'not merely in God, but in God as Father, and not merely in Christ, but in Christ as the Son of God' (*De Trinitate*, 1. 17).[29] One should recognize here continuity with first-century Christian usage, while rightly admitting that the fourth-century trinitarian debates used 'Father' language in a context and with connotations which were at least somewhat different from those at the time of Jesus.

'God the Father' functions validly when we align ourselves with the meanings communicated in that metaphor by the biblical witnesses (above all, by Jesus himself) and refuse to literalize it. It is these meanings that convey true information about God. 'Father' names personally the God revealed in Israel's history and known relationally as the 'Abba' of Jesus' life, death, and resurrection (together with the outpouring of the Spirit). The image and language of 'Abba' emerged from Jesus' specific experience of God. Once we agree that language and experience, while distinguishable, belong inseparably to each other, we will misrepresent Jesus' experience if we insist on replacing his central language for God.

[29] See P. Widdicombe, *The Fatherhood of God from Origen to Athanasius* (Oxford: Clarendon, 1994).

Fidelity to Jesus calls on believers to name God primarily (though
not exclusively) as 'Father', which entails acknowledging Jesus
himself (though once again not exclusively) as 'the Son of God'. By
not arguing for an *exclusive* use of male names, I recognize that we
do and should also use such gender-neutral names as 'Creator' for
the first person of the Trinity and such a female name as 'Wisdom'
for the second person. The question at issue is rather the *primary*
way of naming the Trinity.

Suppressing the traditional naming of the Trinity would mean
loss rather than gain. Such alternate proposals for the first person
as 'Source' and 'Parent' sound remote, even impersonal, and
nowhere near as directly relational as 'Father'. Unquestionably
these alternatives contain or imply personal and relational elements, and are not intended to subvert Christian belief in a personal God. But when we try using (exclusively?) 'Source', 'Parent',
and so forth as forms of address to God, we will perceive the
superiority of 'Father'. Some of the alternative triads (e.g. 'Creator,
Christ, and Spirit') have a strong Arian flavour about them, as if
only the first person of the Trinity were properly divine, possessed
the power of creation, and had in fact created Christ and the Spirit.
One might argue here that Hilary of Poitiers said something similar when he wrote of faith 'in the Creator, the Only-Begotten, and
the Gift'. Yet he used such language immediately after recalling
Jesus' mandate to baptize 'in the name of the Father, and of the
Son, and of the Holy Spirit' (*De Trinitate*, 2. 1. 33). The context for
Hilary's alternate triad removed any sense of Arian ambiguity.

Although it may claim some kind of New Testament pedigree
(perhaps in Acts 3: 13, 26; 4: 27, 30), 'Child' (as in 'Parent,
Child, and Paraclete' and 'Father, Child, and Mother') slights the
second person of the Trinity, as if the Son were not yet properly
mature. Renaming the first person of the Trinity in different ways
could well mean saying something different and changing beliefs.
A certain crypto-modalism comes through some of the alternate
proposals I listed above: 'Creator, Liberator, and Comforter', for
instance, can readily suggest a monopersonal God who behaves
towards us in creative, liberating, and comforting ways, but whose
inner life is not differentiated into three divine persons. Another
triad, 'Creator, Redeemer, and Sanctifier', can claim considerable
background in the Christian tradition. But if used by itself, it fails
to distinguish Christianity from other religions in the way that

naming 'Father, Son, and Holy Spirit' does. After all, other religions can and do profess faith in deities who create (or in some lesser way make), redeem, and sanctify human beings. The names of 'Father, Son, and Holy Spirit' tie Christian faith firmly into the revealing and saving history that culminated in the events of the first Good Friday and Easter Sunday. This, of course, does not mean that this formal, trinitarian language is the only way of speaking about and speaking to God. In these days we may need more than ever 'illogically conjunctive' language to prevent our 'Father' language from collapsing into crass literalism.[30]

All in all, I would argue that a persuasive case can be made for maintaining 'Father, Son, and Holy Spirit' as the normative, irreplaceable (but not, I repeat, exclusive) way of naming the Christian God. What St Basil of Caesarea (d. AD 379) says about 'the Holy Spirit' being the 'chief and distinguishing name' for the third person of the Trinity (*De Spiritu Sancto*, 9. 22) applies also to the traditional names of 'Father' and 'Son'. These names fix historical references, convey insights, and maintain the core of Christian identity. Alongside the name of 'Jesus', nothing else so expresses our continuity with the faith of first Christians and their successors down through the ages. It seems to me no accident that the familiar and frequent practice of 'the sign of the cross' draws together both items: the cross of Jesus and the invocation of the Trinity.

In *The Bible for Theology*[31] Daniel Kendall and I have argued more fully for the traditional naming of the tripersonal God; even then much more remains to be said. We entered into dialogue with a number of current authors. But we need to go back not only to medieval theology (examining, for example, the trinitarian language of Richard of St Victor about the Lover, the Beloved, and Co-beloved) but also to the earlier twentieth century. How should one evaluate the proposals of Karl Barth (1886–1968) about the one God who subsists in three divine 'modes of being' (the

---

[30] On this issue and the meaning of 'illogically conjunctive' language, see S. Coakley, *God, Sexuality and the Self: An Essay on the Trinity* (Cambridge: Cambridge University Press, forthcoming); and her discussion of Gregory of Nyssa in her chapter in this volume.

[31] (Mahwah, NJ: Paulist Press, 1997). That book, while discussing more fully calling God 'Father' in trinitarian contexts, should also have examined the bad effects (theological, psychological, and social) of patriarchal language in the church and beyond and investigated strategies for countering those effects.

Revealer, the Revelation, and the Revealedness) and the reflections
of Karl Rahner (1904–84) on three divine 'manners of subsistence'? Certainly the concerns of Johann Gottlieb Fichte (1762–
1814) about the finite nature of our talk of personhood should be
heard. Nevertheless, if we do not use personal language to describe
God, will we finish up saying less rather than more about God? Let
me now move from the naming of the tripersonal God to the
Trinity in interreligious dialogue.

(7) The Logos christology of Justin Martyr, Origen, Athanasius
of Alexandria, and other early Christian writers explored the way
in which the whole human race shares in the powerful presence of
the Word. At least in part they developed such a Logos christology
in dialogue with Jews and other non-Christians. Such theologizing
about 'the seeds of the Word' could encourage a kind of christomonism, which left out of the picture the work of the Holy Spirit
and hence could prove non-trinitarian.[32] Such a prominent figure
in interreligious dialogue as Jacques Dupuis, along with others, has
insisted on the universal workings of the Spirit. It is through the
Holy Spirit that God and the divine self-witness (Acts 14: 17) are
felt in human hearts; every personal encounter of God with human
beings within the Christian church *and* beyond occurs in and
through the Spirit. Such a 'spiritual' (and trinitarian) approach to
interreligious dialogue calls for more attention to some witnesses
from the first centuries of Christianity. St Leo the Great (d. AD 461),
for instance, wrote: 'When the Holy Spirit filled the Lord's disciples
on the day of Pentecost, this was not the first exercise of his role
but an extension of his bounty, because the patriarchs, prophets,
priests, and *all the holy persons of the previous ages* were nourished
by the same sanctifying Spirit . . ., although the measure of the
gifts was not the same' (*Sermo*, 76. 3; italics mine). Presumably
Leo's reference to 'all the holy persons of the previous ages' aimed
at recognizing the role of the Holy Spirit in the lives of Job, the
Queen of Sheba, Ruth, and other such non-Jews praised in the
biblical tradition. An appreciation for the universal presence of the
Spirit has led Dupuis[33] and others to recognize the trinitarian self-

---

[32] Whenever it did or does this, Logos christology forgets its origins in the Fourth
Gospel, which moves at once from the Logos (John 1: 1–14) to John the Baptist's
witness to the Holy Spirit who has descended and remained upon Jesus (John 1:
32–4).

[33] See J. Dupuis, *Toward a Christian Theology of Religious Pluralism* (Maryknoll, NY:
Orbis, 1997).

manifestation expressed, for instance, by Hindu *advaita* mysticism. The worldwide operative presence of the tripersonal God, while partly hidden, encourages such writers in their contribution to interreligious dialogue and the detection of triadic modes of religious thought. David Brown's chapter in this book draws attention to the triadic visual images with which pre-Christian Celts represented the divinity, images that helped shape subsequent representations of the Trinity in art.

(8) Where Dupuis and his colleagues engage primarily in dialogue with religious believers, Walter Kasper,[34] Michael J. Buckley,[35] and others have explored the relationship between trinitarian faith (or rather the failure on the part of Christians to maintain its integrity)[36] and the rise of modern atheism, agnosticism, and secularism in the Western world. Kasper has argued that the trinitarian confession is the only true answer to contemporary disbelief, widespread sense of meaninglessness, and the endangered human condition. Faith in the Trinity becomes then something of the greatest pastoral importance: the one effective remedy for all those threats to the human condition (and those 'fatal separations' explored by David Tracy's chapter) that cast a sombre shadow over the end of the second Christian millennium. The only viable policy is that of aligning oneself with the trinitarian narrative which not only interprets and reads off the world and its history but also uniquely fosters human freedom and dignity.[37] The next issue takes us back from dialogue with modern secularism to intra-Christian reflection.

(9) A ninth issue emerges from Catherine LaCugna's *God for Us:*

---

[34] *The God of Jesus Christ* (New York: Crossroad, 1984).

[35] *At the Origins of Modern Atheism* (New Haven: Yale University Press, 1987).

[36] In Roman Catholic theology up till the Second Vatican Council (1962–5) apologetical interests frequently downplayed the content of divine self-revelation. It needed to recapture a sense of the personal, salvific nature of the tripersonal God's self-disclosure through the missions of the Son and the Holy Spirit. See G. Heinz, *Divinam Christianae Religionis Originem Probare: Untersuchung zur Entstehung des fundamentaltheologischen Offenbarungstraktates der katholischen Schultheologie* (Mainz: Grünewald Verlag, 1984); F.-J. Niemann, *Jesus als Glaubensgrund in der Fundamentaltheologie der Neuzeit: Zur Genealogie eines Traktats* (Innsbruck: Tyrolia Verlag, 1983).

[37] To some extent the seventh issue placed trinitarian theology in the context of Asia, the natural habitat for interreligious dialogue. Our eighth issue took us to Europe and North America, the place where the challenge of post-Enlightenment disbelief has been acutely felt. A further context could be Latin America and other vast areas of the world where widespread suffering and oppression call for a trinitarian theology in the key of liberation.

The Trinity and Christian Life. She questioned the move from the 'economic' Trinity, or God revealed and actively present in the history of revelation and salvation, to the 'immanent' Trinity, or God's inner life and relatedness. *Pace* John 1: 1–2, the biblical witness does not explicitly offer some doctrine of the 'immanent' Trinity. In what way(s) then does God's historical communication to human beings reflect and reveal the eternal communion between Father, Son, and Holy Spirit? What does the 'extra-trinitarian' communication *pro nobis* tell us about the 'intra-trinitarian' life or the tripersonal God *in se*? Do the missions of the Son and the Holy Spirit in history manifest the generation of the Son and the 'proceeding' of the Spirit?

The classic dictum of Karl Rahner, that the economic Trinity *is* the immanent Trinity and vice versa, calls for some caution. Certainly there is no 'other' Trinity; the adjectives, 'economic' and 'immanent', name *one and the same* Trinity, albeit in two differing ways. Yet how far does the correspondence between the economic and the immanent Trinity go and what shape does it take? Language from St John (e.g. John 7: 39; 15: 26; 19: 30, 34; 20: 22) and St Luke (e.g. Acts 2: 33) about Jesus' giving, breathing, and sending the Spirit have led to the conclusion that the Spirit proceeds *also* from the Son both in the economy of salvation and in the immanent life of the Trinity. Nevertheless, the Synoptic Gospels' account of Jesus' baptism could suggest a different model. From the descent of the Spirit upon Jesus at the Jordan, we might derive the conclusion that, in the internal life of God, the Son is *also* generated in/by the Spirit. The virginal conception reported by Matthew and Luke might suggest the same conclusion: the Son comes from the Father *and the Spirit* (or from the Father and through the Spirit). The Father–Son relationship, revealed in Jesus' earthly life right from its very beginning, has been made possible by the Holy Spirit. Reflecting on the historical sacrifice of Jesus, some theologians like Sergius Bulgakov (1871–1944) and Vladimir Lossky (1903–58) could persuade us to interpret it as the histori-cal counterpart to something within the life of God, the eternal 'sacrificial' gift of the Son to the Father in the Spirit. In the eternal, divine life of God, the Son, not merely gives himself to the Father but gives himself up or 'dispossesses' himself in sacrifice to the Father. Or should we understand the crucifixion to indicate something different: that the Father is the Sacrificer, the Son is the

Sacrificed, and the Holy Spirit is the Sacrifice? What conclusions does some coherence between the economic and immanent Trinity suggest? Furthermore, caution is obviously in place if/when we subsequently reflect, in the opposite direction, on the coherence between the immanent and the economic Trinity. The tripersonal God, while revealed in human history, transcends infinitely the limited boundaries of that history. The Trinity's activity has repeatedly invited such cautious reflection.

(10) The issue of tripersonal activity was raised long ago by St Basil of Caesarea (d. AD 379), when he wrote in *De Spiritu Sancto* that every act of God is 'initiated by the Father, effected by the Son, and perfected by the Spirit' (16. 38). In his treatise written to Ablabius (*Quod Non Sint Tres Dei*) Gregory of Nyssa said something similar: 'We are not told that the Father does anything by himself in which the Son does not cooperate; or that the Son has any isolated activity apart from the Holy Spirit. . . . Every activity originates from the Father, proceeds through the Son, and is brought to perfection in the Holy Spirit.'[38] Michel Barnes's chapter shows how Augustine struggled with this theme of perfect unity in the Trinity's actions, and Brian Leftow's chapter illustrates how topical debates over trinitarian operations *ad extra* have remained. Granted that the divine actions *ad extra* are common, does this mean that they are undifferentiated and indistinguishable? If not, on what grounds may we distinguish them and appreciate their threefold particularity that is implied by the diversity of the verbs used by Gregory ('originates', 'proceeds', and 'is brought to perfection')? How viable is the distinction made by St Thomas Aquinas (d. 1274) between 'action *ad extra*' and the 'term' of such an action? He pointed to the example of the incarnation: all three divine persons were jointly involved in bringing it about, but the 'term' or visible point of arrival, the Incarnate Son of God with his mission, is irreducibly special to the Word.[39] Only the Son assumes a human existence and actualizes—or rather is—the

---

[38] *Gregorii Nysseni Opera Dogmatica Minora*, iii/1, ed. W. Jaeger (Leiden: Brill, 1958), 47. 21–48. 2. In *adversus Macedonianos* Gregory of Nyssa expresses the same union in divine operations: every activity which comes from God and reaches creatures 'originates from the Father, proceeds through the Son and is perfected in the Holy Spirit' (13).

[39] *ST* 3a. 3. 1–4. On the 'term' of the incarnation, see E. Muller, 'The Dynamic of Augustine's *De Trinitate*: A Response to a Recent Characterization', *Augustinian Studies*, 26 (1995), 65–91, at 76–82.

personal being of Jesus. Let us not forget the specificity of the Spirit's functional mission and ontological presence—a divine self-communication that is strictly related to the Son's mission but does not take the form of a hypostatic union.[40] Apropos of creation, Aquinas also argued for a kind of 'order', in that 'the divine persons, according to the nature of their processions, have a causality respecting the creation of things'. The 'processions of the persons are the type of the production of creatures' (*ST* 1a. 45. 6). Where Aquinas attended here to the creative causality of the divine persons, Moltmann's trinitarian theology of the cross has reflected rather on the three divine persons 'experiencing' suffering and death on Calvary but doing so differently. Here the pictorial counterpart to Moltmann's theology, the 'throne of grace', also represents the three divine persons as sharing in the crucifixion but doing so differently.

(11) This discussion of *tripersonal* activity brings us to a further issue that has already surfaced above (e.g. when facing proposals about renaming the Trinity): the concept of person (discussed in this collection by Sarah Coakley's paper). Even when we take pains to stress the other-relatedness of being personal, how does our finite language of personhood fare when applied to God?[41] One did not have to wait for Fichte to become aware of the challenge. Augustine wrote in *De Trinitate*:

> For, in truth, since the Father is not the Son, and the Son is not the Father, and the Holy Spirit, who is also called the Gift of God, is neither the Father nor the Son, then certainly there are three. Therefore, it was said in plural number: 'I and my Father are One' (John 10: 30). But when it is asked 'Three what?', then the great poverty from which our language suffers becomes apparent. But the formula 'three persons' has been coined, not in order to give a complete explanation by means of it, but in order that we might not be obliged to remain silent (5. 10).

Augustine might also have appealed here to prayer: personal language for God makes our prayer and relationship to God possible. How could one adore and glorify Rahner's 'three distinct manners

---

[40] On the irreducibly special activity of the Spirit, see O'Collins and Kendall, *The Bible for Theology*, 93–100, 163–69; and the Doctrine Commission of the General Synod of the Church of England, *We Believe in the Holy Spirit* (London: Church House Publishing, 1991).

[41] See C. Schwöbel and C. E. Gunton (eds.), *Persons: Divine and Human* (Edinburgh: T. & T. Clark, 1991).

of subsisting'[42] or Barth's 'the Revealer, the Revelation, and the Revealedness' (= three modes of being)?[43] Moreover, personal language is the highest and best language we have; whatever we say, the God revealed in Jesus Christ, cannot be less than personal. Finally, to speak of 'the persons' of the Holy Trinity should not be taken to mean that they are persons in exactly the same way. Being the Love or Gift of God who is 'breathed' by the Father through the Son, the Holy Spirit, for instance, may be seen to be not only just as personal as the (begetting) Father and the (begotten) Son but also distinctively personal.[44] In short, even if the post-Descartes world frequently understands person as such to be the centre of spiritual activity and can fall into the error of taking the three persons in God as three distinctly conscious and autonomous subjects, it seems best to retain the term. There are no clearly superior substitutes.

(12) The twelfth and last issue I wish to address is that of method and approach. When engaged with the Trinity, theology more than anywhere else should be an exercise of 'faith seeking understanding', with 'understanding' entailing intellectual expression but also coming from and issuing into a worship and practice which are profoundly trinitarian.[45] In theology and beyond, the questions we ask and the criteria (and methods) we use are inevitably shaped by the place we 'inhabit'. We cannot take a 'view from nowhere' and raise questions about the Trinity from some allegedly 'neutral' ground. A living trinitarian faith is, I hold, the only appropriate starting-point; trinitarian theology is essentially participative, as Frans Jozef van Beeck persuasively argues in his contribution to this volume. Believers experience the tripersonal God when they gather for worship in communion and witness/ work together in the fruitful practice of a life worthy of their trinitarian faith. Such community adherence is a necessary precondition for trinitarian theology, a theology that seeks understanding

---

[42] Rahner, *Trinity*, 103–15. At the same time, while pointing out how, when applied to the Trinity, 'person' in the plural can easily imply tritheism, Rahner declares: 'there is no really better word, which can be understood by all and would give rise for fewer misunderstandings' (see 56–7).

[43] See K. Barth, *Church Dogmatics*, i/1, 2nd edn. (Edinburgh: T. & T. Clark, 1975), 295–347.

[44] On the language of 'three persons', see Kasper, *The God of Jesus Christ*, 285–90.

[45] David Brown's contribution to this book vividly recalls the function of visual images of the Trinity for prayer and life.

in the service of God, the church, and society (including the academic community).

Here the three persons of the Trinity set, so to speak, the standard. Within the tripersonal God, utter self-giving and complete self-possession coincide. Within God unity (or communion) and distinction are in direct, not inverse, proportion: the unique unity (and communion) between the divine persons goes hand in hand with the unique distinction. Likewise, the closer one draws to the community of believers and, in and through them to the tripersonal God, the more 'self-possessed' and 'distinct' one will be in the whole of life and, in particular, in reflecting on the mystery of the Trinity. The lives of such trinitarian mystics as St Bonaventure (*c.*1217–74), St Catherine of Siena (1347–80), St Ignatius Loyola (1491–1556), St John of the Cross (1542–91), Blessed Marie of the Incarnation (1599–1672), and Blessed Elizabeth of the Trinity (1880–1906) showed strikingly how this self-possession grew in direct proportion to their self-giving union with the tripersonal God and human beings.[46]

This chapter has picked out for comment twelve points that shape current trinitarian theology: first, the introductory issue of the widespread desire to 'rehabilitate' the centrality of trinitarian faith. We then came to issues 2, 3, 4, and 5, which arise from the Scriptures and subsequent Christian history: New Testament questions for a properly trinitarian christology and soteriology; pneumatology as central to St Paul's theology; the differentiated unity of the tripersonal God according to the Cappadocians, St Augustine, and others; divisions that focus on the procession of the Holy Spirit. After that we took up issues 6, 7, and 8 which concern contemporary Christian life both 'within' and in dialogue with 'others': proposals for renaming the Trinity; the place of the Holy Spirit and the Trinity in interreligious dialogue with Jews, Muslims, Hindus, and others; trinitarian faith as the alternative to atheism and agnosticism. Then followed issues 9, 10, and 11, which belong to current theological discussions: the identity of the economic and immanent Trinity; the irreducibly special elements in trinitarian actions; the viability of personal language for the Trinity. We ended up with a proposal for an integral method (issue 12): a

---

[46] See C. A. Bernard, 'L'esperienza spirituale della Trinità', in E. Ancilli and M. Paparozzi (eds.), *La Mistica: Fenomenologia e riflessione teologica*, ii (Rome: Città Nuova, 1984), 295–321.

threefold approach (through study, worship, and practice) to the trinitarian mystery. The essential place of worship and practice alongside intellectual reflection could be as good a place to close this rapid survey of human responses to that divine mystery at the heart of Christian faith: the existence with us and for us of the tripersonal God.[47]

[47] For some insightful and helpful criticism on earlier drafts of this chapter, I wish to thank Frans Jozef van Beeck, Sarah Coakley, Stephen Davis, Luis Ladaria, Fred Lawrence, George Lawless, Anselm Min, Earl Muller, Alan Padgett, David Tracy, and the group which met at the Alphonsianum in Rome (Jan. 1998).

Biblical Witness

2

Jesus' Self-Designation 'The Son of Man' and the Recognition of His Divinity

CRAIG A. EVANS

Apart from the divine identity of Jesus as the Son there could not be a Trinity—at least not in the traditional Christian sense. The concept of Trinity expresses the idea that the three Persons that make it up are fully divine, fully God: God the Father, God the Son, and God the Holy Spirit. Theologians, philosophers, and apologists have debated and will continue to debate whether or not Jesus was divine and in what manner he related and/or relates to God. The historical exegete is left to explore the question whether or not our sources indicate that Jesus and/or his contemporaries understood him as in any sense divine. It is this latter point that the present paper explores.

For the last century or so biblical critics have frequently asserted or assumed that the ascription of divine status to Jesus was to be traced to early Christianity's contact with the Greco-Roman influences outside the Jewish Palestinian environment in which the movement had its beginning. The overlap between Greco-Roman language and New Testament language is extensive and meaningful. The former describes kings and emperors as 'gods', 'sons of god', 'saviours', 'lords', 'benefactors', and even 'creators'. A sampling of inscriptions will make this clear. From the Greek world, a third-century BCE inscription from Halicarnassus honours Πτολεμαίου τοῦ σωτῆρος καὶ θεοῦ ('Ptolemy, saviour and god'). The famous Rosetta Stone bears the inscription of a later Ptolemy (196 BCE), who is described as Βασιλεὺς Πτολεμαῖος αἰωνόβιος . . . ὑπάρχων θεὸς ἐκ θεοῦ καὶ θεᾶς ('King Ptolemy, the everliving . . . being a god [born] of a god and a goddess'). An inscription found over a door of a Temple of Isis on the island of Philae refers to Ptolemy XIII (62 BCE): τοῦ κυρίου βασιλ[έ]ος θεοῦ ('of the lord king god'). Another inscription comes from Alexandria and refers to Ptolemy XIV and Cleopatra (52 BCE): τοῖς κυρίοις θεοῖς μεγίστοις ('to the lords, the greatest gods').

Roman popular culture and politics adopted much of Greek ideology and put it to work to advance the cult of the emperor. The development of this cult parallels the emergence of the Julian dynasty. In its earliest stages we see it in an inscription from Ephesus, which describes Julius Caesar (48 BCE–44 BCE) as τὸν ἀπὸ Ἄρεως καὶ Ἀφροδείτης θεὸν ἐπιφανῆ καὶ κοινὸν τοῦ ἀνθρωπίνου βίου σωτῆρα ('the manifest god from Mars and Aphrodite, and universal saviour of human life').[1] The language of Titus 2: 13 is immediately called to mind: ἐπιφάνειαν τῆς δόξης τοῦ μεγάλου θεοῦ καὶ σωτῆρος ἡμῶν Ἰησοῦ Χριστοῦ ('the manifestation of the glory of our great God and Saviour Jesus Christ'). The people of Carthaea honoured Caesar as saviour and god: Καίσαρα . . . γεγονότα δὲ σωτῆρα καὶ εὐεργέτην καὶ τῆς ἡμετέρας πόλεως ('[The Carthaean people honour] Caesar . . . who has become saviour and benefactor of our city'). And again: ὁ δῆμος ὁ Καρθαιέων τὸν θεὸν καὶ αὐτοκράτορα καὶ σωτῆρα τῆς οἰκουμένης Γάιον Ἰούλιον Καίσαρα Γαίου Καίσαρος υἱὸν ἀνέθηκεν ('The Carthaean people honour the god and emperor and saviour of the inhabited world Gaius Julius Caesar son of Gaius Caesar').[2] The people of Mytilene hailed Caesar as god (θεός), benefactor (εὐεργέτης), and founder or creator (κτίστης).[3]

The dynasty's greatest ruler was Caesar's nephew Octavius, who assumed the name Caesar Augustus (30 BCE–14 CE). Queen Dunamis of Phanagoria honoured Augustus as Αὐτοκράτορα Καίσαρα θεοῦ υἱὸν θεὸν Σεραστὸν πάσης γῆς καὶ θαλάσσης ἐπόπτην ('The Emperor, Caesar, son of god, the god Augustus, the overseer of every land and sea').[4] An inscription from Halicarnassus reads: Δία δὲ πατρῷον καὶ σωτῆρα τοῦ κοινοῦ τῶν ἀνθρώπων γένους ('Hereditary god and saviour of the universal race of humanity').[5] The famous calendrical inscription from Priene refers to the birth of Augustus as ἡ γενέθλιος τοῦ θεοῦ ('the birthday of the god') and the 'beginning of the good news [εὐαγγέλια] for the world', and later refers to Augustus as τοῦ θηοτάτου Καίσαρος ('the most divine Caesar').[6] The parallel with Mark's opening verse is obvious: 'The beginning of the good news of Jesus Christ, the son of God' (Mark

---

[1] SIG 760.
[2] IG 12.5, 556–7.
[3] IG 12.2, 165b.
[4] IGR 1.901; cf. IGR 4.309, 315.
[5] GIBM 994.
[6] OGIS 458.

1: 1). Libations were offered up ὑπὲρ τοῦ θεοῦ καὶ Αὐτοκράτορος ('in behalf of the god and Emperor'). An inscription found at Tarsus reads: Αὐτοκράτορα Καίσαρα θεοῦ υἱὸν Σεβαστὸν ὁ δῆμος ὁ Ταρσέων ('The people of Tarsus [honour] Emperor Caesar Augustus son of god').[7]

With the celebrated accomplishments of Julius Caesar and Caesar Augustus the pattern was established, and the successors of these emperors imitated their great patriarchs, but not with equal success. Whereas both Julius Caesar and Caesar Augustus were officially deified posthumously, the honour was denied to all of their Julian successors: the eccentric and lecherous Tiberius (14-37 CE), the murderous and insane Caligula (37-41 CE), the stuttering and cowardly Claudius (41-54 CE)—although in his case the honour was bestowed but later rescinded—and the treacherous and maniacal Nero (54-68 CE), the last of the Julians.

That Christianity felt compelled to proclaim Jesus, Messiah of Israel and Lord of the Church, in language that rivalled the language applied to the Roman emperor is understandable. But the important question was whether the assertion of Jesus' divine status is itself to be explained in these terms. Did this tendency arise simply as a result of competition with the Roman cult of the emperor, or did it arise from things that Jesus said and did?

In what follows it will be argued that the trinitarian trajectory has its roots in Jesus' self-predication, claims, deeds, and predictions. The most important of these elements was his definition of messiahship in terms of the 'son of man' of Daniel 7. This identification heightened the significance of the honorific language found in Psalms 2 and 110, whereby Israel's anointed king was thought of as God's son seated at God's right hand. To be sure, these concepts made important contributions to Jesus' messianism,

---

[7] For fuller texts and discussion of these and many other related inscriptions and papyri, see P. Bureth, *Les Titulatures impériales dans les papyrus, les ostraca et les inscriptions d'Égypte (30 a.C–284 p.C)* (Brussels: Fondation Égyptologique Reine Élisabeth, 1964), 23–41; A. Deissmann, *Light from the Ancient East* (London: Hodder & Stoughton; New York: Harper & Row, 1927), 338–78; W. Foerster, *Herr ist Jesus: Herkunft und Bedeutung des urchristlichen Kyrios-Bekenntnisses* (Gütersloh: Bertelsmann, 1924), 99–118; P. Kneissl, *Die Siegestitulatur der römischen Kaiser: Untersuchungen zu den Siegerbeinamen der ersten und zweiten Jahrhunderts* Hypomnemata 23 (Göttingen: Vandenhoeck & Ruprecht, 1969), 27–57; D. Magie, *De Romanorum iuris publici sacrique vocabulis* (Leipzig: Teubner, 1905), 62–9; L. R. Taylor, *The Divinity of the Roman Emperor*, APAMS 1 (New York: Arno, 1931; repr. Chico: Scholars Press, 1975), 267–83.

but the appeal to Daniel 7, where the 'son of man' approaches the divine throne and directly from God receives kingdom and authority, takes this messianism to a new level.[8] It is this ingredient, which evidently represents an innovation, that launches a messianic trajectory that will find its way to the more formalized expressions of Trinitarian theology.

The points that follow will begin with Jesus' employment of imagery and self-predication from Daniel 7. Not all of the subsequent points flow from this principal argument, but it will be shown that in various ways it conditions our understanding of them. These points are five in number:

(1) Jesus' self-identification as the 'son of man' of Daniel 7 suggests a very special relationship to God.

(2) Jesus' self-identification as God's wisdom supports this suggestion.

(3) Jesus' claims to divine sonship seem to go beyond the merely honorific title that is part of messianology.

(4) Jesus' Passover request that the disciples eat meals in his memory implies that Jesus associated himself very closely with God, for Jews ate sacrificial meals in God's presence and, at Passover, in memory of God's deliverance of Israel.

(5) Jesus' claim that he would sit at God's right hand, 'coming with the clouds of heaven', implies that he would sit upon God's chariot throne, a seat reserved for the deity.

Let us now consider each of these points in turn.

I ONE 'LIKE A SON OF MAN'

One of the oddest features about the teaching of Jesus is his frequent reference to himself as 'the son of man' ($\acute{o}$ $\upsilon\acute{i}\grave{o}\varsigma$ $\tau o\hat{v}$ $\acute{a}\nu\theta\rho\acute{\omega}\pi o\upsilon$).[9] Because this epithet, which in Aramaic (בר אנש) simply

---

[8] I say 'new level' because most if not all actual attempts to act out messianic programs in Jesus' approximate time (i.e. from the death of Herod the Great to Bar Kokhba) seem primarily to have been efforts to restore an independent Jewish monarchy. Jesus' understanding of his mission seems to have been significantly different in this regard.

[9] The epithet is found in the four Gospels approximately 80 times. Outside of the Gospels, it occurs but four times (Acts 7: 56; Heb. 2: 6; Rev. 1: 13; 14: 14). Linguistically, the difference between the Greek epithet attributed to Jesus and the

means the 'human' or 'mortal', played virtually no role in the
development of christology (as attested, for example, in the letters
of Paul), it may rightly be inferred that this manner of speaking
derives from Jesus, not from the early Church. Why would the
early Church attribute such an epithet to Jesus, which in
the Greco-Roman world holds little meaning and which for
Christianity's earliest theologians made no significant contribution
to christology? The best answer is that this curious epithet originated with Jesus.

Although many scholars are willing to concede that Jesus
probably did refer to himself as 'the son of man', some doubt the
authenticity of those sayings that speak of his suffering (the so-
called Passion predictions), while others doubt the authenticity of
those that speak of the enthronement and coming of the son of
man.[10] The latter are of importance for the present concerns, for
the allusion to the figure of Daniel 7 is more obvious.[11] These
sayings will receive our attention. The material that is of especial
interest to us is that which describes the authority and dominion
granted to the 'son of man'. The pertinent material reads:

I beheld till thrones were set up, and One that was ancient of days sat
down. His clothing was white as snow, and the hair of his head like pure
wool; his throne was fiery flames, and its wheels burning fire. A fiery
stream issued and came forth from before him: thousands of thousands
ministered to him, and ten thousand times ten thousand stood before him.
The judgment was set, and the books were opened. . . . I saw in the night-
visions, and, behold, there came with the clouds of heaven one like a son
of man, and he came to the Ancient of Days, and they brought him near
before him. And there was given to him dominion, and glory, and a kingdom, that all the peoples, nations, and languages should serve him: his
dominion is an everlasting dominion, which shall not pass away, and his
kingdom that which shall not be destroyed. (vv. 9-10, 13-14)

Daniel's vision describes the setting up of thrones, one of which

---

Aramaic and Hebrew equivalents is that the Greek is always definite (i.e. 'the son
of [the] man'), while the Semitic forms usually are not.

[10] For assessments of these and related issues, see B. Lindars, *Jesus Son of Man:
A Fresh Examination of the Son of Man Sayings in the Gospels in the Light of Recent
Research* (London: SPCK; Grand Rapids, Mich.: Eerdmans, 1983); D. R. A. Hare, *The
Son of Man Tradition* (Minneapolis: Fortress, 1990).

[11] In my opinion, Jesus' Passion predictions also allude to Daniel 7. When Jesus
says the 'son of man' will 'suffer' and 'be killed', we have allusion to the struggle
described in Dan. 7: 21, 25.

is the chariot throne on which the 'One that was ancient of days' (i.e. God) sat. It is not called a chariot, but the reference to its wheels as burning fire makes that a reasonable assumption (cf. Ezek. 1: 4; 10: 6; 2 Kgs. 2: 11–12). Daniel's vision presupposes Ezekiel's much more elaborate description of God's chariot throne. The vision goes on to describe the appearance of 'one like a son of man', that is, a human-like being. Exactly who this human is, or whether it really is a human (it is said to be *like* a son of man), is much debated. In any case, this being stands in contrast to the violent, war-like beasts (which represent various Pagan kingdoms) described in chapter 7 and elsewhere in Daniel. The human-like being approaches God and is given 'dominion, and glory, and a kingdom'. In Greek 'dominion' is rendered 'authority' (ἐξουσία). The result is that 'all the peoples, nations, and languages should serve him' and his kingdom 'shall not be destroyed'.

The feature that is particularly interesting, and would prove to be controversial among some rabbinic interpreters, is that more than one throne is set up (note the plural 'thrones' in v. 9) and that the human-like being is brought before God. What is the meaning of the plural 'thrones' the rabbis asked? 'One is for Him; the other is for David.'[12] So opined Rabbi Aqiba. But this interpretation scandalized Rabbi Yose, who replied: 'Aqiba, how long will you profane the Divine Presence?' It was unthinkable that a mere mortal could sit next to God. But Aqiba's interpretation enjoys the support of Psalm 122: 5, which speaks of the tribes going up to Jerusalem, where 'sit thrones for judgment, thrones for the house of Israel'.[13] The association of the plural thrones of Psalm 122 with the plural thrones of Daniel 7 is based on the frequently invoked rabbinic interpretive principle of *gezera šawa*, whereby scriptural passages containing common terminology may interpret one another. Aqiba evidently thought it possible that a mortal could sit next to God, or perhaps he thought that the Messiah (i.e. 'David' in the rabbinic context) was more than a mere mortal.

That this human-like being could be brought before God is especially surprising when it is remembered that not even the great lawgiver Moses was permitted to see God's face (as in Exod. 33–4). He is told, 'No man shall see me and live' (Exod. 33: 20). Yet, the

---

[12] See b. Sanh. 38b; b. Hag. 14a.

[13] See the longer, more involved interpretation preserved in Midr. Tan. B on Lev. 19: 1–2 (*Qedošin* §1).

'son of man' in Daniel 7 is ushered right into the very presence of God himself, seated on his throne. Indeed, according to Aqiba, David (or the Messiah, and probably the son of man of Daniel 7) will take his seat next to God on his own throne.

The ancient background from which the imagery of the son of man and the Ancient of Days derives is probably Canaanite[14] and seems to parallel the relationship of Baal to 'El.[15] The former is well known in Ugaritic texts as the 'rider of the clouds', while the latter is called 'father of years' and is often depicted as aged. As such this description seems to parallel Daniel's 'Ancient of Days'. Like the 'son of man' in Daniel 7, Baal is promised an 'everlasting kingdom' and 'dominion for ever and ever'.[16] Although 'El confers kingship on Baal, the latter remains subordinate to the former.

John Collins rightly argues that Daniel is not directly dependent on Ugaritic sources (which date to the fourteenth century BCE), but on subsequent traditions, whether Pagan or Jewish, that made use of them. According to Collins: 'What is important is the pattern of relationships: the opposition between the sea and the rider of the clouds, the presence of two godlike figures, and the fact that one who comes with the clouds receives everlasting dominion. These are the relationships that determine the structure of the vision in Daniel 7. No other material now extant provides as good an explanation of the configuration of imagery in Daniel's dream.'[17] This background helps to clarify Daniel's visionary scene. It also suggests that all of the characters in this celestial drama, the Ancient of Days, the one that is like a son of man, and the holy ones are heavenly beings, not mortals.

Interpreters of Daniel 7 in late antiquity almost always understood the 'son of man' figure as referring to an individual, often

---

[14] So J. A. Emerton, 'The Origin of the Son of Man Imagery', *JTS* 9 (1958), 225–42; L. Rost, 'Zur Deutung des Menschensohnes in Daniel 7', in G. Delling (ed.), *Gott und die Götter: Festgabe für Erich Fascher zum 60. Geburtstag* (Berlin: Evangelischer Verlag, 1958), 41–3; see now more recently P. G. Mosca, 'Ugarit and Daniel 7: A Missing Link', *Bib* 67 (1986), 496–517, who emphasizes the royal setting of the traditions.

[15] *CTA* 2.1.21.

[16] *CTA* 2.4.10.

[17] J. J. Collins, *Daniel*, Hermeneia (Minneapolis: Fortress, 1993), 291; see also the comments on pp. 293–4. J. D. G. Dunn (*Christology in the Making: A New Testament Inquiry into the Origins of the Doctrine of the Incarnation* (London: SCM, 1980), 72) is correct to observe that there is no firm evidence that the 'Son of man' was understood in a messianic sense prior to the time of Jesus.

to the Messiah (as in the Gospels, 1 Enoch, and 4 Ezra).[18] Many modern interpreters, however, think the one 'like a son of man' is none other than the archangel Michael, the prince or guardian of Israel, who receives from God the kingdom in Israel's behalf, and that the 'holy ones' who struggle against the evil forces also are angels.[19] It is not necessary to choose between these interpretations. It is significant to note that this celestial figure, closely associated with God and with the angels of heaven, was also understood as a messianic figure in some circles in late antiquity. That this messianic figure might actually have been understood as a supernatural figure, such as an angel, would only add to his heavenly status. That Jesus chose to define himself and, by implication, his messiahship in this way is very significant.

The vision of the 'son of man', or 'human', in Daniel 7 lies behind the following sayings of Jesus:

1. But that you may know that the son of man has authority on earth to forgive sins (Mark 2: 10)

2. so that the son of man is lord even of the sabbath (Mark 2: 28)

3. For whoever shall be ashamed of me and of my words in this adulterous and sinful generation, the son of man also shall be ashamed of him, when he comes in the glory of his Father with the holy angels (Mark 8: 38)

4. For the son of man also came not to be ministered to, but to minister, and to give his life as a ransom for many (Mark 10: 45)

5. And then shall they see the son of man coming in clouds with great power and glory (Mark 13: 26)

6. I am; and you shall see the son of man sitting at the right hand of Power, and coming with the clouds of heaven (Mark 14: 62)

7. The son of man shall send forth his angels, and they shall gather out of his kingdom all things that cause stumbling, and those who do iniquity (Matt. 13: 41)

8. Truly I say to you, that you who have followed me, in the regeneration when the son of man shall sit on the throne of his glory, you also shall sit upon twelve thrones, judging the twelve tribes of Israel (Matt 19: 28 = Luke 22: 28–30; cf. Mark 10: 35–45)

9. For as the lightning comes forth from the east, and is seen even to the west; so shall be the coming of the son of man (Matt 24: 27)

10. and then shall appear the sign of the son of man in heaven: and

---

[18] See the discussion by A. Y. Collins in the excursus, '"One Like a Human Being"', in J. J. Collins, *Daniel*, 305–8.

[19] Ibid. 310.

then shall all the tribes of the earth mourn, and they shall see the son of man coming on the clouds of heaven with power and great glory (Matt. 24: 30)

11. And as were the days of Noah, so shall be the coming of the son of man (Matt. 24: 37)

12. and they knew not until the flood came, and took them all away; so shall be the coming of the son of man (Matt. 24: 39)

13. Therefore be also ready; for in an hour that you think not the son of man comes (Matt. 24: 44)

14. But when the son of man shall come in his glory, and all the angels with him, then shall he sit on the throne of his glory (Matt. 25: 31)

15. And I say to you, Every one who shall confess me before people, the son of man shall also confess him before the angels of God (Luke 12: 8; cf. Matt. 10: 32)

16. But watch at every season, making supplication, that you may prevail to escape all these things that shall come to pass, and to stand before the son of man (Luke 21: 36)[20]

In the first saying, Jesus' claim to have 'authority on earth' alludes to the heavenly scene of Daniel 7. That is, the implication is that the son of man not only has authority in heaven, where that authority was received, but he has it on earth, where he currently ministers. The authority is also understood to extend to the forgiveness of sins. Jesus' critics had reacted to Jesus' pronouncement of forgiveness with the question: 'Why does this man speak thus? It is blasphemy! Who can forgive sins but God alone?' (Mark 2: 7). Some think that Jesus' pronouncement of forgiveness constitutes infringement on priestly prerogatives, but then we should have expected the question to be 'Who can forgive sins but priests alone?' In essence Jesus has claimed an authority that bypasses the function of the priests whereby acting in God's place, or perhaps as God's vice regent, he extends forgiveness in an immediate and unmediated manner.

A similar authority is seen in the pronouncement made in the second saying listed above. As the son of man, Jesus 'is lord even of the sabbath' (Mark 2: 28). Given the high view of the sabbath, the day sanctified by God himself (cf. Gen. 2: 2–3), any claim to be 'lord of the sabbath' implies a remarkable degree of authority. Apart from God himself, who could possess such authority? Only

---

[20] Limitations of space prohibit discussion of the authenticity and meaning (in Jesus and later in the respective evangelists) of each and every saying. Such discussion will be taken up in future studies.

the son of man of Daniel 7, who received authority directly from God, could possess such authority.

In the third and fifth sayings Jesus speaks of the son of man coming 'in the glory of his Father with the holy angels' (Mark 8: 38; cf. 13: 26). In the Greek version of Daniel 7: 14 the son of man receives 'all glory', while later in Daniel's vision we hear of the 'holy ones', who are probably to be understood as angels. Indeed, in the seventh saying Jesus speaks of 'his angels' (Matt. 13: 41; cf. the fourteenth saying, Matt. 25: 31). The references to glory and to angels are consistent with the vision of Daniel 7. Even the reference to 'his angels', which implies a measure of authority over the angels, fits the picture in Daniel 7.

In the sixth saying Jesus affirms that he is indeed 'the Messiah, son of the Blessed' (cf. Mark 14: 61) and that the High Priest and his colleagues will 'see the son of man sitting at the right hand of Power, and coming with the clouds of heaven' (Mark 14: 62). The implication of judgement is found in the tenth saying, where 'all the tribes of the earth mourn', the eleventh and twelfth sayings, which make comparison with Noah's flood, the thirteenth and sixteenth sayings, which enjoin preparedness so that one may 'stand before the son of man' and, presumably, escape condemnation. The fifteenth saying makes the remarkable claim, again consistent with the heavenly scene of judgement in Daniel 7, that the son of man will 'confess before the angels of God' every person who confesses him 'before people'.

The ninth saying depicts the suddenness and drama of the appearance of the son of man, 'as the lightning comes forth from the east, and is seen even to the west'. This description is consistent with the heavenly scene of Daniel 7. The tenth saying is similar, referring to a 'sign of the son of man in heaven'. The thirteenth saying underscores the element of suddenness: 'in an hour that you think not the son of man comes'.

Finally, some of these sayings speak of enthronement. The eighth saying promises that the 'son of man shall sit on the throne of his glory' and his disciples also will 'sit upon twelve thrones, judging the twelve tribes of Israel'. What is described here is in effect a new government, a celestial government establishment on earth by which all twelve tribes of Israel will be faithfully governed, perhaps even protected.[21] The fourteenth saying also speaks of the son of

[21] What is probably meant is that the tribes will be 'judged' in the Old Testament

man sitting 'on the throne of his glory'. This is consistent with the plural 'thrones' of Daniel 7: 9 and the later interpretation seen in 1 Enoch[22] and the even later interpretation in rabbinic literature.[23]

Taken together, these sayings (and there are others that were not cited) constitute a remarkable portrait of a figure who has received heavenly authority and acts in many ways as a heavenly being. This may very well explain Jesus' questioning of the scribal tendency to call the Messiah 'the son of David' (Mark 12: 35–7). Jesus counters this interpretation by noting that David calls the Messiah 'lord', thus implying that the Messiah is no mere son of David (which according to conventions of Jewish culture could imply that the Messiah is subordinate to his great ancestor) but is something greater. Yes, the Messiah would be greater than David if he is the one 'like a human' of Daniel 7, the being who receives authority and kingdom from God and possesses prerogatives usually thought to be God's. This is consistent with Jesus' claim to be 'greater than Solomon' (Matt. 12: 42)—David's (mere) son—and even stronger than Satan the strong man (Mark 3: 27).[24] How can

sense as in the Book of Judges. The tribes will not be condemned (as some patristic interpreters for polemical purposes chose to understand the passage).

[22] The 'son of man' is virtually deified in 1 Enoch 37–71 (or the Similitudes of Enoch), where we are told that the 'son of man' had the countenance of 'holy angels' (46: 2), that was given the name 'Before-Time' and was so named in God's presence (48: 2), and that he was concealed in God's presence prior to the creation of the world (48: 6; 62: 7). He is also called the 'Chosen One' (48: 6), 'Elect One' (49: 2; 51: 4; 52: 6; 53: 6; 55: 4; 61: 8; 62: 1), and 'Messiah' (48: 10; 52: 4). We are told that the day is coming when 'all the kings, the governors, the high officials, and those who rule the earth shall fall down before him on their faces, and worship and raise their hopes in that Son of Man; they shall beg and plead for mercy at his feet' (62: 9). In 1 Enoch the epithet 'son of man' has become titular (and so has been capitalized).

[23] The 'bar naphle' pun in b. Sanh. 96b–97a links Dan. 7: 13 to Amos 9: 11 (the promise to raise up the fallen tent of David). In Greek *nephele* means 'cloud', so *bar nephele* means 'son of the cloud'; while in Aramaic/Hebrew *bar naphle* means 'son of the fallen'. Dan. 7: 13 is understood in a messianic sense elsewhere in rabbinic literature (cf. b. Sanh. 98a; Num. Rab. 13.14 [on Num. 7: 13]; Midr. Ps. 21. 5 [on Ps. 21: 7]; 93. 1 [on Ps. 93: 1]; Frag. Tg. Ex. 12: 42).

[24] The possibility that Judaism of late antiquity could regard as divine a being other than God is seen in the presentation of Melchizedek in one of the Scrolls from Qumran (11QMelch). In this document Isa. 61: 2 is paraphrased to read: 'the year of Melchizedek's favour'. Here the name Melchizedek is substituted for the 'Lord'. Verses from the Psalms are applied to this mysterious figure: 'A godlike being has taken his place in the council of God; in the midst of the divine beings he holds judgment' (Ps. 82: 1). Scripture also says about him, 'Over it take your seat in the highest heaven; A divine being will judge the peoples' (Ps. 7: 7–8). It is interesting that Melchizedek, like the son of man of Daniel and of Jesus' sayings, takes a seat

Jesus be stronger than Satan, a heavenly being against whom the archangels have struggled with difficulty (Dan. 10: 13; 12: 1)? Jesus can be stronger only if he is the one 'like a son of man' who was presented to God and from him received authority and the kingdom.

Jesus' identification of himself as the being of Daniel 7 not only confirms his messianic self-understanding, but defines the nature of his messianism. It suggests that he saw himself as more than a popular messiah whose mission was to throw off the Roman yoke and restore the kingdom of Israel, as in the days of David and Solomon. The frequent appeal to the figure of Daniel 7 to define himself, his mission, his struggle, his death, and subsequent vindication strongly implies that Jesus understood himself in terms that transcend those of a mere mortal. In the points that follow we shall explore further indications that support this implication. These additional points will be treated more briefly.

II JESUS AS GOD'S WISDOM

The very style of Jesus' teaching and ministry may have prompted his earliest followers to view him as Wisdom incarnate.[25] Perhaps the most intriguing saying in the dominical tradition is the one in which Jesus speaks as Wisdom personified: 'Come [δεῦτε] to me [πρός με] all who labour [κοπιᾶν] and are heavy laden, and I will give you rest [ἀναπαύειν]. Take my yoke [ζυγός] upon you and learn from me, for I am meek and lowly in heart, and you will find rest [ἀνάπαυσιν] for your souls [ψυχή]. For my yoke [ζυγός] is easy and my burden is light' (Matt. 11: 28–30).[26] This language reminds us

in heaven and judges people. Still later in this document it is said that Melchizedek, a 'divine being ('el)', 'reigns' (quoting Isa. 52: 7).

Probably also relevant is the prediction in 4Q521 that 'heaven and earth will obey his Messiah'. It is hard to see how a messianic figure of such expectation would have been thought of as a mortal and nothing more. 4Q246 should also be mentioned, where there is expected one who will be called 'son of God' and 'son of the Most High'. 4Q369 also speaks of a 'first-born son', a 'prince and ruler', whom God will instruct 'in eternal light'.

[25] See B. Witherington, *Jesus the Sage: The Pilgrimage of Wisdom* (Edinburgh: T. & T. Clark, 1994), 147–208.

[26] A few scholars have regarded Matt. 11: 28–30 as authentic dominical tradition, cf. E. Klostermann, *Das Matthäusevangelium*, 4th edn., HNT 4 (Tübingen: Mohr [Siebeck], 1971), 102; A. M. Hunter, 'Crux Criticorum—Matt. 11. 25–30', NTS 8

of Wisdom's summons: 'Come to me [πρός με]' (Sir. 24: 19; cf.
Prov. 9: 5); 'Come [δεῦτε], therefore, let us enjoy the good things
. . .' (Wisd. 2: 6); 'Come [δεῦτε], O children, listen to me, I will
teach you the fear of the Lord' (LXX Ps. 33: 12 [34: 11]).
Especially interesting is Sirach 51: 23-7: 'Draw near to me [πρός
με], you who are untaught . . . Put your neck under the yoke
[ζυγός], and let your soul [ψυχή] receive instruction; it is to be
found close by. See with your eyes that I have laboured [κοπιᾶν]
little and found for myself much rest [ἀνάπαυσιν].'[27] These sayings
hint that Jesus may have understood himself as God's Wisdom (or
as Wisdom's messenger). This suspicion is confirmed when he
claims to be 'greater than Solomon' (Luke 11: 31 = Matt. 12: 42),
Israel's famous patron of Wisdom.[28] In light of these passages and
others Martin Hengel has concluded that Jesus understood himself
as the messianic teacher of wisdom, indeed as Wisdom's envoy.[29]

The significance of this wisdom element in Jesus' lifestyle and
self-reference lies in the observation that Wisdom personified was
viewed as a way of speaking of God. Spirit, Wisdom, and Word
were three important abstractions that often in late antiquity

(1962), 241-9; S. Bacchiocchi, 'Matthew 11: 28-30: Jesus' Rest and the Sabbath',
AUSS 22 (1984), 289-316; J. P. Meier, *A Marginal Jew: Rethinking the Historical
Jesus*, 2 vols., ABRL 3 and 9 (New York: Doubleday, 1992-4), ii. 335, 387 n.174.
Others have contested this view, cf. R. H. Gundry, *Matthew: A Commentary on his
Literary and Theological Art* (Grand Rapids, Mich.: Eerdmans, 1982), 219; C.
Deutsch, *Hidden Wisdom and the Easy Yoke: Wisdom, Torah and Discipleship in
Matthew 11.25-30*, JSNTSup 18 (Sheffield: JSOT Press, 1987), 51; D. C. Allison and
W. D. Davies, *The Gospel according to Saint Matthew*, 2 vols., ICC (Edinburgh: T. &
T. Clark, 1988-91), ii. 293. If the substance of Matt. 11: 28-30 does indeed go
back to Jesus, there can be little question that the tradition has been heavily edited
(cf. Allison and Davies, *Matthew*, ii. 287-91). But even if inauthentic, Matt. 11:
28-30 does reflect aspects of Jesus' manner of speaking and acting as Wisdom's
envoy.

[27] See Dunn, *Christology in the Making*, 163-4.

[28] R. Bultmann (*The History of the Synoptic Tradition*, 2nd edn. (Oxford: Basil
Blackwell, 1968), 112-13) accepts the saying as authentic. Meier (*A Marginal Jew*,
ii. 689-90) makes the point that there is no evidence that the early Church showed
a tendency to enhance or exploit a Solomon typology.

[29] M. Hengel, 'Jesus als messianischer Lehrer der Weisheit und die Anfänge der
Christologie', in J. Leclant *et al.* (eds.), *Sagesse et religion: Colloque de Strasbourg,
Octobre 1976* (Paris: Bibliothèque des Centres d'Études Supérieures Spécialisés,
1979), 147-88, esp. 163-6, 180-8. See also Witherington, *The Christology of Jesus*,
51-3, 221-8, 274-5; B. L. Mack, 'The Christ and Jewish Wisdom', in J. H.
Charlesworth (ed.), *The Messiah: Developments in Earliest Judaism and Christianity*,
The First Princeton Symposium on Judaism and Christian Origins (Minneapolis:
Fortress, 1992), 192-221, esp. 210-15.

functioned as hypostases, carrying on the divine function on earth. Among other things, this way of speaking and conceptualizing enabled the pious to affirm the transcendence of God, on the one hand, and the immanence of God, on the other. In Jewish thinking of the first century, Jesus' speaking and acting as though he were God's Wisdom would have made a significant contribution to early christology, out of which ideas of deification [= belief in Jesus' divine status, eds.] would have readily and naturally sprung. The christology of the fourth Gospel is indebted to Wisdom traditions.[30] Indeed, what is only hinted at in a few places in the Synoptics is ubiquitous and explicit in the fourth Gospel. To a certain extent Pauline christology is also indebted to Wisdom traditions. This is seen in the apostle's assertion that 'Christ (is) the power of God and the wisdom of God' (1 Cor. 1: 24; cf. 1: 30: 'Christ Jesus, whom God made our wisdom').

III JESUS' CLAIM TO DIVINE SONSHIP

Another important element in Gospel tradition is the various references to Jesus as the 'son', 'son of God', or 'son of the Most High'. The cries of the demonized (Mark 3: 11 = Luke 4: 41: 'You are the son of God!'; Mark 5: 7: 'Jesus, son of the Most High God') are in all probability rooted in authentic tradition.[31] These epithets remind us of 4Q246, where we find reference to one who will be called 'son of God' and 'son of the Most High'. This Aramaic text, dating from the first century BCE, confirms the expectation of a coming world saviour who would be thought of as 'son of God'; it also confirms that this concept was right at home in Palestine.[32] Two other

---

[30] See M. Scott, *Sophia and the Johannine Jesus*, JSNTSup 71 (Sheffield: JSOT Press, 1992). Statements such as 'He who has seen me has seen the Father' (John 14: 9) are illustrative of wisdom christology.

[31] It has to be admitted that these cries complement Markan christology; cf. R. A. Guelich, *Mark 1–8: 26*, WBC 34A (Dallas: Word, 1989), 148–9. On the possibility of the authenticity of the tradition, see R. H. Gundry, *Mark: A Commentary on his Apology for the Cross* (Grand Rapids, Mich.: Eerdmans, 1993), 158–9.

[32] See the discussion by J. J. Collins, 'The *Son of God* Text from Qumran', in M. C. De Boer (ed.), *From Jesus to John: Essays on Jesus and New Testament Christology in Honour of Marinus de Jonge*, JSNTSup 84 (Sheffield: JSOT Press, 1993), 65–82; J. D. G. Dunn, '"Son of God" as "Son of Man" in the Dead Sea Scrolls? A Response to John Collins on 4Q246', in S. E. Porter and C. A. Evans (eds.), *The Scrolls and the*

references have a reasonable claim to authenticity, though some have challenged them. Jesus asserts that no one knows the eschatological hour, 'not even the son, only the Father' (Mark 13: 32).[33] In one of the Wisdom passages Jesus affirms that 'no one knows the Father except the son' (Matt. 11: 27).[34] These references to 'son', especially in contrast to the 'Father', should be understood as a shortened form of 'son of God'. To be called 'son of God', as opposed to 'prophet of God' (cf. Ezra 5: 2; Luke 7: 16)/'prophet of Yahweh' (1 Sam. 3: 20) or 'man of God' (cf. 1 Kgs. 17: 24), carries with it the implication that one shares in the divine nature. This is the implication of the inscriptions seen above, where various kings and despots call themselves 'son of God' and 'God'. There is no reason to think that Jesus' Jewish contemporaries, who were themselves very much part of the Greco-Roman world,[35] would have thought of these expressions in terms significantly different from those held by Gentiles. This is not to say that the epithet 'son of God' necessarily implied divinity, for it could be honorific or mystical (as I think we have it in the case of certain Jewish holy men who were supposedly addressed by heaven as 'my son').[36] But such an epithet, given its usage in late antiquity, would have contributed to belief in Jesus' heavenly status.

IV 'DO THIS IN MEMORY OF ME'

The words of institution, uttered on the occasion of the Last Supper, are themselves suggestive of Jesus' heavenly status. Jesus associates his body and blood with the Passover sacrifice, implying that in his death a new covenant is established: 'And he took a cup, and when he had given thanks he gave it to them, and they

---

Scriptures: Qumran Fifty Years After, JSPSup 26; RILP 3 (Sheffield: Sheffield Academic Press, 1997), 197–209.

[33] On the authenticity of this passage, see Gundry, *Mark*, 747–8, 792–5; *idem*, *Matthew*, 492; Meier, *A Marginal Jew*, ii. 347. Gundry comments: 'That Mark does not exclude Jesus' ignorance of the exact time bears tribute to Mark's respect for the tradition' (*Mark*, 747–8).

[34] On the authenticity of this passage, see Gundry, *Matthew*, 218; A. E. Harvey, *Jesus and the Constraints of History* (London: Duckworth, 1982), 160–73.

[35] Hengel's discussion in *The 'Hellenization' of Judaea in the First Century after Christ* (London: SCM; Philadelphia: Trinity Press International, 1989) is apposite.

[36] Jewish legends relate a story about God addressing Hanina ben Dosa: 'My son Hanina' (cf. b. Ta'an. 24b; b. Ber. 17b).

all drank of it. And he said to them, "This is my blood of the covenant, which is poured out for many"' (Mark 14: 23-4).

In what sense could the blood of an ordinary sacrificial victim, even that of a pious human, effect the promise of the new covenant (cf. Jer. 31: 31; Zech. 9: 11)? The sacrifice of one whose status is of a heavenly order, however, may establish a new covenant. Indeed, the words 'my blood of the covenant' in Mark approximate the words in Zechariah 9: 11: 'the blood of my covenant'. Because it is *God* who speaks in Zechariah's prophecy, the verbal parallel is suggestive.

In what is probably an authentic fragment of the words of institution, Paul concludes this scene with these words: 'Do this, as often as you drink it, in memory of me' (1 Cor. 11: 25). The Passover request that the disciples remember Jesus is in itself interesting, for the Passover was instituted to commemorate God's salvific action in the exodus. Apparently Jesus asks his disciples to remember his action in going to the cross, presumably to effect salvation once again for his people. Remembering God's saving act and Jesus' saving act appear to be parallel.

Indeed, the idea of sharing a meal in memory of Jesus, as though Jesus were present, is in itself very interesting. It may parallel the idea that Israelites shared meals with God when they partook of the sacrifice (usually the so-called fellowship offerings). Just as an Israelite eats a special meal with God, so the disciple eats a special meal with Jesus. The parallel is intriguing and to my knowledge unique in Judaism of late antiquity.

Finally, in the Greco-Roman world drinking and pouring libations in honour of or in memory of various gods, including the Roman emperor, was a common practice. The words of institution, in all probability deriving from Jesus, and not from the post-Easter Church, may also have contributed to the early belief in the divinity of Jesus.

V SEATED AT THE RIGHT HAND

With this last point, we return to an important element that derives from Daniel 7. This element is found in the passage that describes Jesus' hearing before Caiaphas and members of the Sanhedrin (Mark 14: 55-65). Searching for an incriminating charge the High Priest asks Jesus: 'Are you the Messiah, the son of the Blessed?' (Mark 14: 61).[37] Jesus replies: 'I am; and you will see the son of man seated at the right hand of Power and coming with the clouds of heaven' (Mark 14: 62). Caiaphas accuses Jesus of 'blasphemy' (Mark 14: 63). Jesus' answer is not blasphemous simply for affirming that he is the Messiah (or Christ), nor is it necessarily blasphemous for affirming that he is the 'son of God', since sonship was probably understood by many to be a concomitant of messiahship (as seen in Ps. 2: 2, 7; 2 Sam. 7: 14). Jesus' blasphemy lay in his combination of Psalm 110: 1 ('sit at my right hand'[38]) and Daniel 7: 13 ('son of man coming with the clouds of heaven'), implying that he will take his seat in heaven next to God.

The juxtaposition of these Scriptures suggests to me that Jesus interpreted Daniel 7: 9 much as Aqiba is said to have done almost one century later. That is, the Messiah was to sit on a throne next to God, or at God's right hand (as Psalm 110 requires).[39] As Hengel has shown, sitting at God's right hand may actually have implied that Jesus was asserting that he would sit at God's right hand *in God's throne* (cf. 1 Chr. 29: 23: 'Solomon sat on the throne of the Lord as king'). Such an idea is not only part of primitive royal traditions in the Old Testament but can even be found in the New Testament in reference to the resurrected Christ: 'I will grant him who conquers to sit with me on my throne, as I myself conquered and sat down with my Father on his throne' (Rev. 3: 21). When we remember that the throne of Daniel 7: 9 had burning wheels, we should think that Jesus has claimed that he will sit with God on the Chariot Throne and will, as in the vivid imagery of Daniel 7, come with God in judgement.[40] This tradition, which I do not

[37] 'The Blessed' is a circumlocution for 'God' (cf. m. Ber. 7: 3) and is probably an abbreviated form of the longer phrase, 'the Holy One blessed be He', which is ubiquitous in rabbinic literature.

[38] Gundry (*Mark*, 915–18) could be right in his suggestion that Jesus' own words were 'seated at the right hand of Yahweh' and that in the 'public' version of Jesus' offence, the circumlocution 'Power' was introduced (as prescribed in m. Sanh. 6: 4; 7: 5).

[39] See C. A. Evans, *Jesus and His Contemporaries: Comparative Studies*, AGJU 25 (Leiden: Brill, 1995), 204–10.

[40] Recognition that it is the chariot throne that is in view makes unnecessary D. A. Juel's suggestion (*Messiah and Temple: The Trial of Jesus in the Gospel of Mark*, SBLDS 31 (Missoula, Mont.: Scholars, 1977), 95) that Mark 14: 62 is a clumsy and inauthentic combination of contradictory materials. He finds contradiction in the aspects of *sitting* and *coming*. But Juel does not adequately assess the underlying

think early Christians understood well nor exploited, is authentic and not a piece of Christian confession or scriptural interpretation.[41]

VI CONCLUDING COMMENTS

The recognition of Jesus' divine status was a long process, culminating in the creeds affirming the Trinity and the full humanity and full deity of Jesus. Although it cannot be shown that all of the elements of Chalcedonian christology are plainly taught in Scripture, the belief in the deity of Jesus appears to be rooted in his teaching and activities and not simply in post-Easter ideas. This is probable, not only for the reasons argued above, but also because the affirmation of Jesus as Israel's Messiah required no confession of his divinity. That the awaited Messiah might possess divine attributes was a possibility, given what is said of him in 1 Enoch and his identification with the son of man figure in Daniel, but it was not a requirement. Popular expectation seems to have looked more for a Davidic-like figure who would drive the Romans from Israel and restore the kingdom along the lines of the classical period.[42]

Had Jesus not claimed to be Israel's awaited Messiah, it is not likely that his disciples would have later said that he had. Easter alone would have provided no motivation to infuse the content of Jesus' teaching with messianism. If Jesus had been no more than a righteous prophet or beloved rabbi, a teacher of national reform or of personal salvation, then why not proclaim his resurrection to be vindication of his prophecy or teaching? Why introduce messianism, a new agenda, and a foreign body of teaching? If Jesus allowed his disciples to think of him as Israel's Messiah, but possessing no qualities of divinity or special relationship to God whereby divinity might reasonably be inferred, then why would the disciples introduce this element, when conventional messianism did not require it and strict, Jewish monotheism would not encourage it?

Danielic imagery. Being seated on the divine Chariot Throne and coming with the clouds of heaven are complementary elements.

[41] For further discussion, see Evans, *Jesus and His Contemporaries*, 210–11, 431–3.

[42] See Ibid. 53–81.

These questions are raised at the end of this essay to show that the burden of proof rests on the sceptic who wishes to maintain that the tradition of the Gospels and subsequent Christian interpretation of this tradition should be discounted. The sceptic not only must refute the points argued above, but must also answer the questions in the previous paragraph. In my judgement, the Gospels' presentation of Jesus' teaching and conduct as ultimately messianic and in places connoting divinity is compelling. The most plausible explanation of the Gospels as we have them and of the earliest Church's proclamation is that Jesus claimed to be Daniel's heavenly son of man figure through whom God would defeat his enemies and bring about the everlasting kingdom. From this claim and from related teachings and actions the early Church rightly inferred Jesus' divinity, which in view of other theological and philosophical considerations led to the formulation of the doctrine of the Triunity of the Godhead. [The doctrine of the Trinity could never have arisen, unless Christians had accepted the divinity of Jesus and, as the next chapter argues, the personal and divine identity of the Holy Spirit. eds.]

3

Paul and the Trinity: The Experience of Christ and the Spirit for Paul's Understanding of God

GORDON D. FEE

It has been rightly said that 'the New Testament contains no doctrine of the Trinity'.[1] Fully developed doctrine, no, but experienced reality, yes. At issue for the study of the Trinity in Paul (and the rest of the New Testament) is not doctrinal exposition of the One and the Three. Rather it is the explication of his—and his churches'—experience[2] of Christ and the Spirit as the experience of the only and living God, expressed in a variety of descriptive and theological affirmations that attribute deity to both.

The reluctance on the part of New Testament scholarship to use trinitarian language when referring to these affirmations is understandable;[3] but that reluctance is often expressed in ways that

I wish here to extend my thanks to my Regent College colleagues, who vigorously interacted with an earlier version of this paper at a recent faculty retreat. That discussion helped me to sharpen up my concerns at several points, so much so that I rather thoroughly reconfigured the whole.

[1] Donald H. Juel, 'The Trinity and the New Testament', *Theology Today*, 54 (1997) 313.

[2] Although some may object to, or be anxious about, the language of 'experience' (it raises spectres of Schleiermacher or contemporary patterns of 'truth based on feeling'), it has Pauline precedent (Gal. 3: 4) and seems to be the best English word to express the experienced nature of the reception of the Spirit that Paul appeals to on several occasions (e.g., 1 Thess. 1: 5–6; 1 Cor. 2: 4–5; Gal. 3: 2–5; Rom. 15: 18–19); and in any case, it is not 'inner feeling' or religious experience per se that I refer to, but always to an experienced encounter with the living God (Father, Son, and Spirit) of a kind that the Scriptures are full of.

[3] This reluctance is writ large throughout the academy in a variety of ways. It can be seen most recently in reviews of two of my recent books. In his review of *God's Empowering Presence* James Dunn takes issue with what he calls 'Fee's rather glib assumption that Paul's theology can be properly described as trinitarian. It is

cause one to wonder what the real issue is. Is it the word Trinity itself, because it implies speculative ontological questions of a later time? Or does it have to do with what the Pauline affirmations are actually saying about Christ and the Spirit? Here is where the pigeon comes home to roost, for the denial of trinitarian language seems very often to preface denials about the *deity* of Christ and/or the Spirit as well, not to mention denials of the *personal nature* of the Spirit.

Thus, the primary issues in Paul's 'economic trinitarianism' are christological and pneumatological. About Christ it is ultimately a question of Incarnation and pre-existence; about the Spirit it is a question of his being 'person', plus his relationship to both God the Father and Jesus Christ the Son expressed in later theology in terms of 'equal to' but 'distinct from'.

The pneumatological issue has been further exacerbated by the practical binitarianism of so many orthodox Christians. On the one hand, in light of the full biblical data—from Matthew's 'God with us' to John's worship 'of the One who sits on the throne and of the Lamb', not to mention John's Gospel and Paul's letters along the way—and despite offshoot groups like the Ebionites, one can scarcely imagine the Christian faith not having expressed itself finally in terms of God as Binity. That is, the biblical texts were (correctly) understood by the orthodox majority as overwhelmingly supporting Christ's full deity, but in the context of rigorous monotheism. Once that was resolved, then at issue, besides the

not that he fails to attempt to justify the use of the term. . . . It is rather that to make use of a later technical term, without addressing or clarifying the issues involved in that term . . . is to erect an orthodox flag without an adequate flagpole' (*Theology*, 1996, 152). Likewise David Kaylor's review of *Paul's Letter to the Philippians* remonstrates: 'Those who resist the tendency to let theological assumptions determine exegetical outcomes will find difficulties precisely at this point. Is there really "an intentional Trinitarian substructure" here (see pp. 179, 302), or is Fee reading later theological constructs into Paul?' (*Int*, July 1997, 303)—as though his view of Paul were without theological assumptions! In both cases the objection is to the use of this word, since neither scholar would deny that Paul's understanding of salvation included God's loving initiative, Christ's effectual work on the cross, and the Spirit's making it an experienced reality. What language, one wonders, should we use for such a view of God? Is not a 'rose by any other name . . .'? Paul's understanding of salvation was triadic, and the triad was divine. So why not Trinity, especially since the Father and Son are personal, as is the Spirit, or so it is argued here? I am not here contending for the language as such, but for a way to express Paul's insistence on the Oneness of God, while at the same time using the language of deity for Christ and the Spirit.

christological question per se,[4] was what to do with the Spirit—how to express a trinitarian faith that included the Spirit fully in the Godhead, and not as a kind of divine stepchild.

It seems to me that historically most orthodox Christians have gone the latter route (treated the Spirit as a divine stepchild);[5] the primary reason for which is probably related to the later church's understanding of the ongoing role of the Spirit in the life of the church.[6] But abetting such a view is the very real problem of human beings' relating to the concept of 'spirit'. Father and Son are easily recognizable metaphors for God and potentially easy to relate to. But for many the Spirit is, in the words of a former student, 'a gray oblong blur'; and relating to the Spirit is especially difficult since all of our images are *im*personal. How does one relate to water, wind, oil, fire, or dove in the same way one does to a father or son?[7]

The purpose of this paper is to examine the Pauline christological and pneumatological data once again, with a view towards seeing Paul as a latent trinitarian. My thesis is that the key to Paul's new and expanded ways of talking about God as Saviour—while at the same time rigorously maintaining his monotheism—is to be found in the *experience of the Spirit*, as the one who enables believers to confess the risen Christ as exalted Lord, and as the way God and Christ are personally present in the believer and the believing community.

[4] That is, how Son of God and son of man co-exist as one being, fully God and fully man—another reality supported by the biblical data but never addressed as such.

[5] See esp. the discussion by Elizabeth Johnson, *She Who Is* (New York: Crossroad, 1992), 128–31, who says, picking up the language of many whom she has just quoted, 'Faceless, shadowy, anonymous, half-known, homeless, watered down, the poor relation, Cinderella, marginalized by being modeled on women—such is our heritage of language about the Spirit' (131). She goes on to cite Kilian McDonnell, 'Anyone writing on pneumatology . . . is hardly burdened by the past.'

[6] For what is involved here, see the helpful overview by George S. Hendry, *The Holy Spirit in Christian Theology*, 2nd edn. (London: SCM, 1965), 53–71; cf. Johnson, *She Who Is*, who notes that in her own Roman Catholic tradition Mary has assumed the biblical role of the Spirit, citing among several examples Pope Leo XIII: 'Every grace granted to human beings has three degrees in order; for by God it is communicated to Christ, from Christ it passes to the Virgin, and from the Virgin it descends to us' (p. 129).

[7] Cf. a story from Dorothy Sayers (as related by Madeleine L'Engle, *A Circle of Quiet* (San Francisco: Harper, 1972), 50) about 'the Japanese gentleman who, in discussing the mysterious concept of the Trinity in Christianity, said, "Honorable Father, very good. Honorable Son, very good. Honorable Bird I do not understand at all"'.

To make this point I propose first to examine Paul's triadic statements themselves as to their latent trinitarianism, since these statements are invariably both soteriological and experiential. Then, in the light of these statements I propose to examine (*a*) the issue of pre-existence and (*b*) the implications of calling Christ *kyrios*. Finally, with regard to the Spirit, I wish to explore (*a*) the issue of 'personhood', (*b*) what it means for the Spirit of God also to be the Spirit of Christ, and (*c*) the implications of the experience of the Spirit as the experience of the renewed Presence of God, understood also as the presence of the risen Christ.

At the end I raise some theological implications from these data, as to both the essentially experienced nature of the Spirit as our way of knowing God in a truly relational way, and the need for our theology to keep in step with the Pauline way of talking about the Trinity by way of narrative, which was maintained especially by the early creeds.

I THE TRIADIC EXPERIENCE OF GOD AS SAVIOUR[8]

At the heart of Paul's theology is his gospel, and his gospel is essentially about *salvation*—God's saving a people for his name through the redeeming work of Christ and the appropriating work of the Spirit. Paul's encounter with God in salvation, as Father, Son, and Holy Spirit,[9] alone accounts for the expansion and transformation of his theological language of God and of God's saving work. In light of this reality and the great number of texts that support it—with trinitarian language—these passages rightly serve as the starting point for any study of the Trinity in Paul.

The evidence here is found in two sets of texts: several explicitly triadic texts (2 Cor. 13: 14; 1 Cor. 12: 4–6; Eph. 4: 4–6) and the many passages where Paul succinctly encapsulates 'salvation in Christ' in triadic terms, sometimes in semi-creedal fashion, but always in non-reflective, presuppositional ways.

---

[8] Much of what is said in this section has appeared earlier in very much the same form in *Paul, the Spirit, and the People of God* (Peabody, Mass.: Hendrickson, 1996), 39–46.

[9] Although I will fall into traditional usage (Father/Son/Spirit) from time to time, I consciously try most often to stay with Paul's most frequent usage (God/Christ/Spirit)—although Paul himself contributes to the traditional language in such passages as Gal. 4: 6 ('God sent forth the Spirit of His Son into our hearts, crying *Abba*, i.e., Father').

1. The remarkable grace-benediction of 2 Corinthians 13: 14 offers us all kinds of theological keys to Paul's understanding of salvation, and of God himself.[10] The fact that the benediction is composed and intended for the occasion,[11] rather than as a broadly applicable formula, only increases its importance in hearing Paul. Thus what he says here in prayer appears in a *thoroughly pre-suppositional* way—not as something Paul argues for, but as the *assumed, experienced reality* of Christian life.

First, it summarizes the core elements of Paul's unique passion: the gospel, with its focus on salvation in Christ, equally available by faith to Gentile and Jew alike. That the *love of God* is the foundation of Paul's view of salvation is stated with passion and clarity in passages such as Romans 5: 1–11, 8: 31–9, and Ephesians 1: 3–14. The *grace of our Lord Jesus Christ* is what gave concrete expression to that love; through Christ's suffering and death on behalf of his loved ones, God accomplished salvation for them at one moment in human history.

The *participation in the Holy Spirit* continually actualizes that love and grace in the life of the believer and the believing community. The *koinonia* ('fellowship/participation in') *of the Holy Spirit* is how the living God not only brings people into an intimate and abiding relationship with himself, as the God of all grace, but also causes them to participate in all the benefits of that grace and salvation— that is, by indwelling them in the present with his own presence, and guaranteeing their final eschatological glory.

Second, this text also serves as our entrée into Paul's understanding of God himself, which had been so radically affected for him by the twin realities of the death and resurrection of Christ and the gift of the Spirit. Granted, Paul does not here *assert* the deity of Christ and the Spirit. What he does is to *equate the activity of the three divine Persons* (to use the language of a later time) in *concert and in one prayer*, with the clause about God the Father standing in second place (!). This suggests that Paul was in fact trinitarian in any meaningful sense of that term—that the believer knows and experiences the one God as Father, Son, and Spirit, and that when

---

[10] For a more thorough analysis of this text, see *God's Empowering Presence* (Peabody, Mass.: Hendrickson, 1994), 362–5.

[11] That it is both ad hoc and Pauline is clearly demonstrated by the twofold reality that it functions precisely as do all of his other grace-benedictions, which all *begin* exactly this way, with 'the grace of our Lord Jesus Christ', and that this beginning point thus determines the unusual order of Christ, God, the Spirit.

dealing with Christ and the Spirit one is dealing with God every bit as much as when one is dealing with the Father.

Thus this benediction, while making a fundamental distinction between God, Christ, and Spirit, also expresses in shorthand form what is found everywhere throughout his letters, namely, that 'salvation in Christ' is the cooperative work of God, Christ, and the Spirit.[12]

The same trinitarian implications also appear in 1 Corinthians 12: 4-6 and Ephesians 4: 4-6. In the former passage Paul is urging the Corinthians to broaden their perspective and to recognize the rich diversity of the Spirit's manifestations in their midst (over against their apparently singular interest in speaking in tongues). He begins in vv. 4-6 by noting that diversity reflects the nature of God and is therefore the true evidence of the work of the one God in their midst. Thus, the Trinity is presuppositional to the entire argument, and these opening foundational words are the more telling precisely because they are so unstudied, so freely and unselfconsciously expressed. Just as there is only One God, from whom and for whom are all things, and One Lord, through whom are all things (1 Cor. 8: 6), so there is only One Spirit (1 Cor. 12: 9), through whose agency the One God manifests himself in a whole variety of ways in the believing community.

In Ephesians 4: 4-6 one finds the same combination as in 2 Corinthians 13: 14—a creedal formulation expressed in terms of the distinguishable activities of the triune God. The basis for Christian unity is the one God. The *one body* is the work of the *one Spirit* (cf. 1 Cor. 12: 13), by whom also we live our present eschatological existence in *one hope*, since the Spirit is the 'down payment on our inheritance' (Eph. 1: 13-14). All of this has been made possible for us by our *one Lord*, in whom all have *one faith* and to which faith all have given witness through their *one baptism*. The source of all these realities is the *one God* himself, 'who is over all and through all and in all'. Again, because at issue is the work of the Spirit ('the unity the Spirit creates', v. 3), the order

---

[12] It should also be pointed out that affirmations like this also shut down all possibilities that Paul ever identified the risen Christ with the Spirit. For a critique of this mistaken bypath taken by several recent NT scholars, see my 'Christology and Pneumatology in Romans 8: 9-11—and Elsewhere: Some Reflections on Paul as a Trinitarian', in I. H. Marshall *Festschrift*, J. B. Green and M. Turner (eds.), *Jesus of Nazareth Lord and Christ: Essays on the Historical Jesus and New Testament Christology* (Grand Rapids, Mich.: Eerdmans, 1994), 312-31.

is the same as in 1 Corinthians 12: 4–6—Spirit, Lord, God—which works from present, experienced reality to the foundational reality of the one God.

If the last phrase in this passage re-emphasizes the unity of the one God, who is ultimately responsible for all things—past, present, and future—and subsumes the work of the Spirit and the Son under that of God, the entire passage at the same time puts into creedal form the affirmation that God is *experienced* as a triune reality. Precisely on the basis of such experience and language the later church maintained its biblical integrity by expressing all of this in explicitly trinitarian language. And Paul's formulations, which include the work of both Christ the Spirit, form a part of that basis.

2. That the work of the Trinity in salvation is foundational to Paul's understanding of the gospel is further evidenced by the large number of texts in which salvation is formulated in less explicit, but clearly triadic terms, which are full of trinitarian implications. This is especially true of larger passages such as Romans 5: 1–8; 2 Corinthians 3: 1–4: 6; Galatians 4: 4–6; Ephesians 1: 3–14; or Titus 3: 4–7.

Let us take Galatians 4: 4–6 as an example. This passage serves to sum up the argument that began in 3: 1. In showing the folly of the Galatian believers' readiness to come under the provisions of the Jewish law, Paul has appealed first of all to their common, and obviously lavish, experience of the Spirit (vv. 3–5) and then second to the work of Christ especially as bringing the time of Torah to an end. At the end of this argument, and in a context that emphasizes the temporal role of the Law, Paul concludes that 'in the fulness of time God sent forth his Son', whose task was to redeem those who were under bondage to Law and do so by giving them adoption as God's own children.[13] The experiential evidence of this work of Christ in the believers' lives comes about because God also 'sent forth the Spirit of his Son into our hearts', who cries out from within us the *Abba*-cry of the Son to the Father, thus indicating that we, too, are 'sons' of the Father. It is a passage like this that caused H. B. Swete to remark so perceptively, 'Without the mission

---

[13] While 'children' is certainly the correct sense of the Greek, it has the misfortune of losing Paul's play on the word *υἱός*, where Christ as 'Son' brings about adoption as 'sons' evidenced by the Spirit of the Son being sent into our hearts to cry the *Abba*-prayer of the Son to the Father.

of the Spirit the mission of the Son would have been fruitless; without the mission of the Son the Spirit could not have been sent'.[14]

Such texts reveal an unmistakably trinitarian experience of God
on the part of the Apostle. God sends the Son who redeems; God
sends *the Spirit of his Son* into *our hearts*, so that we may realize
God's 'so great salvation'—and the experienced evidence of all this
is the Spirit of the Son prompting us to use the language of the Son
in our own relationship with God.

But besides these grand and thus well-known moments in Paul,
this 'trinitarian' understanding of salvation is also true of many
other texts in which salvation is portrayed in the same triadic way
as is encapsulated in 2 Corinthians 13: 14. (Among these passages,
listed in my view of their chronological order, see especially the
semi-creedal soteriological passages, such as 1 Thess. 1: 4–6; 2
Thess. 2: 13–14; 1 Cor. 6: 11; 2 Cor. 1: 21–2; Rom. 8: 3–4; and
8: 15–17. But see also many other such texts, soteriological or
otherwise: 1 Cor. 1: 4–7; 2: 4–5; 2: 12; 6: 19–20; 2 Cor. 3:
16–18; Gal. 3: 1–5; Rom. 8: 9–11; 15: 16; 15: 18–19; 15: 30;
Col. 3: 16; Eph. 1: 3, 17–20; 2: 17–18; 2: 19–22; 3: 16–19; 5:
18–19; Phil. 1: 19–20; 3: 3.)

All of these in some form or another reflect the threefold activity
of Father, Christ, and Spirit in effecting salvation. Take, for
example, 2 Thessalonians 2: 13, where God's people are 'beloved
by the Lord (through his death)', because God elected them for
salvation through the sanctifying work of the Spirit; or 1 Cor. 6:
11, where God is the implied subject of the 'divine passives' (you
were washed, justified, sanctified), accomplished in the name of
Christ and by the Spirit. And so with each of these texts; only those
with eyes deliberately closed could fail to see how thoroughgoing
this three-dimensional understanding of God as Saviour is in Paul.

One of the more remarkable features of these passages is the
frequency and consistency with which the Spirit is mentioned in
purely soteriological texts. Equally remarkable is the paucity of
such texts (e.g. 1 Thess. 1: 9–10; 5: 9–10), where the Spirit is not
mentioned. What makes this so noteworthy is that most often
when Paul refers to God's saving work as it was effected in history,
he (understandably) focuses altogether on the work of Christ; but
when that work is effectively applied to the life of the individual,

---

[14] *The Holy Spirit in the New Testament* (London: Macmillan, 1910) 206.

that is, when he refers to the experienced reality of salvation, the narrative almost always includes the agency of the Spirit.

The point of all of this, of course, is that salvation in Christ is not simply a theological truth, predicated on God's prior action and the historical work of Christ. Salvation is an experienced reality, made so by the person of the Spirit coming into our lives. One simply cannot be a Christian in any Pauline sense without the effective work of God as Father, Son, and Holy Spirit.

But these statements serve only as the beginning point in our investigation of Paul as a 'trinitarian'. Equally important is a careful look at what he says about *who Christ and the Spirit are*, whether what is implied theologically in the benediction in 2 Corinthians 13: 14 noted above can be found elsewhere. We begin with christology.

II CHRIST: PRE-EXISTENT AND EXALTED LORD

All trinitarian conversation must begin with the Incarnation; here the reality of God as Trinity stands or falls in terms of divine self-disclosure.[15] And the presupposition of the Incarnation is our Saviour's pre-existence. Thus, those scholars who wish to contest whether Paul understood Christ in terms of deity have especially contested pre-existence as a Pauline category. The five texts[16] that have traditionally been so understood are thus given alternative interpretations, so as to cast doubt on whether Paul should be understood in a Johannine way.

My concern here is not to offer a full rebuttal of these views, but simply to note the exegetical weaknesses of the alternative exegesis[17]—vis-à-vis, the strengths of the traditional understanding—of

---

[15] On this matter, see esp. Catherine Mowry LaCugna, *God for Us: The Trinity and Christian Life* (San Francisco: HarperSanFrancisco, 1993), 209-41.

[16] Rom. 8: 3; 2 Cor. 8: 9; Gal. 4: 4; Phil. 2: 6; Col. 1: 16-17, to which one should probably add such texts as 1 Cor. 8: 6.

[17] See, *inter alia*, Norman K. Bakken, 'The New Humanity: Christ and the Modern Age. A Study Centering in the Christ-Hymn: Philippians 2: 6-11', *Int* 22 (1968), 71-82; J. D. G. Dunn, *Christology in the Making* (London: SCM, 1980), 114-21; John Harvey, 'A New Look at the Christ Hymn in Philippians 2. 11', *ExpTim* 76 (1964-5), 337-9; George Howard, 'Phil 2: 6-11 and the Human Christ', *CBQ* 40 (1978), 368-87; Jerome Murphy-O'Connor, 'Christological Anthropology in Phil. II, 6-11', *RB* 83 (1976), 25-50; Charles H. Talbert, 'The Problem of Pre-existence in Philippians 2: 6-11', *JBL* 86 (1967), 141-53.

the most significant of these texts, Philippians 2: 6-11, which I have had recent occasion to examine in some detail.[18]

The alternative understanding begins with two important pre-suppositions: that Paul is citing a prior text, with whose particulars he may not necessarily be in full agreement; and that vv. 6-8 are a reflection of Paul's Adam-Christ christology, in which Paul sees Christ here merely in his humanity, who was (as Adam) in God's 'image', but vis-à-vis Adam did not try to seize God-likeness.

Whether the passage had prior existence or not is a debatable point, but the suggestion that the text may not reflect Paul's own christology should be forever laid to rest. The obvious fact is that, now embedded as it is in a thoroughly Pauline sentence which *the Apostle dictated as his own*, one may assume that what Paul 'cites' as a model to be emulated he thoroughly agrees with.

On the second point, several observations: (1) Whether there is an Adam-Christ analogy at work here is a highly debated point. If so, it is purely 'conceptual' not linguistic.[19] On the other hand, if so, it must also be urged that Paul's perspective in the opening sentence (vv. 6-7c) has little to do with Christ in his humanity; that is, if the analogy is intended, it has nothing to do with the two Adams' being in God's image *in their humanity*, and everything to do with how each Adam *handled* being in that 'image'. To press the analogy to suggest 'mere humanity without pre-existence' is to stretch Paul's own grammar and language nearly beyond recognition.[20] (2) The metaphor inherent in the main verb of the first

---

[18] For a fuller exposition of what is given in outline form here, see *Paul's Letter to the Philippians* (Grand Rapids, Mich.: Eerdmans, 1995), 191–229.

[19] The one tie that is often suggested, that there is a semantic overlap between Paul's μορφή and the LXX's εἰκών, is both an assertion that has not been demonstrated and a thoroughly illegitimate use of linguistic data. That the two words are fully interchangeable and would have automatically been understood so by the readers is scholarly mythology based on untenable semantics. This is to imply that because in certain instances they share a degree of semantic overlap, therefore an author could—or would—use either one or the other at will. Since Paul is quite ready to speak of Christ as 'in the image (εἰκών) of God', and since that is the word used in Genesis, how is it possible, one wonders, that Paul was *intending* this analogy and then wrote μορφή?

For an objection to the need for a linguistic tie in order for the Philippians to have perceived a conceptual tie, see J. D. G. Dunn, *The Theology of Paul the Apostle* (Grand Rapids, Mich.: Eerdmans, 1997), 274–5. While his point, that one does not necessarily need linguistic ties for there to be an allusion, is conceded, the question still remains as to how in this instance the Philippians would have had a clue without such a tie.

[20] In fact one of the major weaknesses of the view is methodological, in that it

sentence, ἐκένωσεν ('he emptied himself'), seems strikingly inappropriate to refer to one who is already (and merely) human. Paul's point is that it was while 'being in God's nature' and thus 'equal with God'[21] that Christ disdained acting out of 'selfish ambition or vain conceit' (v. 3), but rather showed God-likeness precisely in his 'pouring himself out by taking on the form of a slave'. (3) The one described in the opening participle (v. 6) as 'being in the form of God' and thus 'equal with God' is described at the end of the sentence as being 'made/born in human likeness'; which is then picked up as the first item in the second sentence in terms of his being 'found in human appearance'. This, too, is an especially strange thing to say of one who was merely human from the start. (4) This view ultimately divests the narrative of its essential power, which rests in the pointed contrast between the opening participle ('being in the form of God') and the final coda ('death of the cross').[22] (5) Finally the structure itself supports the traditional view, in which the participle that begins the second clause ('and being found in appearance as a human being') stands in clear contrast to that which begins the first clause ('who being in the "form" of God'), so that the first sentence narrates how Christ acted as God and the second how he acted in his humanity.

Paul's nicely balanced sentences are in fact written precisely to counter the two negative attitudes expressed in v. 3 ('selfish ambi-

requires a considerable accumulation of merely possible, but highly improbable, meanings, *all of which are necessary to make it work.* Conclusions based on such a procedure are always suspect. For refutations, see Paul D. Feinberg, 'The Kenosis and Christology: An Exegetical-Theological Analysis of Phil 2: 6–11', *TrinJ* 1 (1980), 21–46; L. D. Hurst, 'Re-enter the Pre-existent Christ in Philippians 2: 5–11?', *NTS* 32 (1986), 449–57; Peter O'Brien, *Commentary on Philippians*, NIGTC (Grand Rapids, Mich., 1991), 263–8; C. A. Wanamaker, 'Philippians 2. 6–11: Son of God or Adamic Christology?', *NTS* 33 (1987), 179–93; T. Y.-C. Wong, 'The Problem of Pre-existence in Philippians 2, 6–11', *ETL* 62 (1986), 167–82. For a helpful overview and sane conclusions on this matter, see L. W. Hurtado, *DPL* 743–6.

[21] Too many NT scholars have passed over the plain sense of Paul's grammar in these opening clauses, where the anaphoric τό before εἶναι ἴσα θεῷ points back to Christ's 'being in μορφή θεοῦ'; thus the clause grammatically reads: 'being in the form of God, he did not consider (the) to be equal with God to be ἁρπαγμόν'. See further, my *Philippians*, 207–8.

[22] Indeed, in order to make this view work, one must resort to the dreadful redundancy of making *both* participles that refer to Christ's humanity begin the final sentence ('Coming to be in the likeness of human beings and being found in appearance as a human being, he humbled himself . . .'). For a refutation, see my *Philippians*, 214 n. 3.

tion' and 'vain glory'), so that Christ as God 'emptied himself by taking the form of a slave' and as man 'humbled himself by becoming obedient to the point of death on the cross'. All of this makes perfectly good sense in terms of Paul's understanding of Christ as pre-existent and 'equal with God', but very little sense *in this context* as emphasizing his role in contrast to Adam which assumes a view of Christ that begins from below.

When we turn to vv. 9–11, we come to the other point I wish to make regarding Paul's presuppositional christology, namely the appellation of κύριος given him at his exaltation by God the Father. As long as the heavy hand of Wilhelm Bousset, with his rich learning but *religionsgeschichtlich* presuppositions, was laid upon our discipline,[23] many NT scholars found it convenient to back away from the christological implications of the earliest Christian confession that 'Jesus is Lord'. But it is clear from a large variety of data that the early believers came by this title through the Septuagint, not from pagan or imperial influences; and Paul serves as both our earliest and most definitive witness to this.

In the first place the very subtlety of many of the Pauline usages must catch our attention. Without hesitation Paul takes a series of κύριος phrases and sentences from the OT which refer to Yahweh and applies them to Christ: e.g., 'the day of the Lord' is for him 'the day of our Lord Jesus Christ' (1 Cor. 1: 8 *et al.*), and the 'Spirit of the Lord' is now also 'the Spirit of Christ' (see esp. Rom. 8: 9). In contrast to the 'gods many and lords many' of the pagan cults, 'for us [believers in Christ]', Paul says, 'there is one God, the Father, from whom are all things and we for him, and one Lord, Jesus Christ, *through whom are all things* and we through him.' Thus, the one God of Israel, Yahweh, who is designated *kyrios* in the LXX, is now, on the basis of Jesus' own use of *Abba* that he passed on to his followers (Gal. 4: 6; Rom. 8: 15), designated 'Father', while the appellation *kyrios* comes to be used almost exclusively of Christ.[24]

---

[23] See *Kyrios Christos* (first German edn., 1913); translated by J. E. Steely from the fifth German edition with a foreword by Rudolf Bultmann (Nashville: Abingdon, 1970). For an assessment and critique, see L. W. Hurtado, 'New Testament Christology: A Critique of Bousset's Influence', *TS* 40 (1979), 306–17.

[24] Among scores of such passages, see the interesting usage in Rom. 14: 1–12, where 'the Lord' before whom one does or does not eat is Christ, who assumed the role of Lord of both the living and the dead through his own death and resurrection.

But none of these is perhaps as telling as is the way Paul uses Isaiah 45: 23 in Philippians 2: 10-11. First, 'at the name of Jesus', who in his exaltation has been given The Name (i.e. κύριος/the Lord), 'every knee shall bow'. The whole created order shall give him obeisance. The 'bowing of the knee' is a common idiom for doing homage, sometimes in prayer, but always in recognition of the authority of the god or person to whom one is offering such obeisance.[25] The significance of Paul's using the language of Isaiah in this way lies with his substituting 'at the name of Jesus' for the 'to me' of Isaiah 45: 23, which refers to Yahweh, the God of Israel. In this stirring oracle (Isa. 45: 18-24a), Yahweh is declared to be God alone, over all that he has created and thus over all other gods and nations. And he is Israel's saviour, whom they can fully trust. In vv. 22-24a Yahweh, while offering salvation to all but receiving obeisance in any case, declares that '*to me* every knee shall bow'. Paul now asserts that through Christ's resurrection and at his ascension God has transferred this right of obeisance to the Son; he is the Lord to whom every knee shall eventually bow.

Also in keeping with the Isaianic oracle, but now interrupting the language of the citation itself, Paul declares the full scope of the homage that Christ will one day receive: every knee 'of those in the heavens and of those on earth and of those under the earth' shall bow to the authority inherent in his name. In keeping with the oracle, especially that 'the Lord' is the creator of the heavens and the earth (45: 18), Paul is purposely throwing the net of Christ's sovereignty over the whole of created beings.[26]

Second, not only shall every creature bend the knee and offer the worship that is due Christ's name, but 'every tongue' shall express that homage in the language of the confessing—but currently suffering—church: Jesus Christ is Lord. In its Pauline occurrences this confession always takes the form, 'the Lord is Jesus', to which he here adds 'Christ'. For Paul this confession is the line of demarcation between believer and non-believer (Rom. 10: 9). In Romans

[25] See e.g. Ps. 95: 6; Mark 15: 19; Luke 5: 8; 22: 41; Acts 7: 60; 9: 40; Eph. 3: 14; cf. the discussions in *NIDNTT*, ii. 859-60 (Schönweiss), and *EDNT*, i. 257-58 (Nützel).

[26] Those 'of heaven' refer to all heavenly beings, angels and demons (so most interpreters); those of earth refer to all those who are living on earth at his Parousia, including those who are currently causing suffering in Philippi; and those 'under the earth' probably refer to 'the dead', who also shall be raised to acknowledge his lordship over all.

10: 9, this confession is linked with conviction about the resurrection of Jesus; that same combination is undoubtedly in view here.

Such a passage thus affirms the deity of Christ in unmistakable terms: equal with God, he became incarnate; in his humanity he became obedient to the point of death on the cross, all the while never ceasing to be God; raised and exalted, he is given The Name, so that the Lord is none other than Jesus Christ, at whose name every created being shall eventually do obeisance. Such language seems to force upon us at least a binitarian view of God on the part of Paul.

But for all the well-known christocentricity of Paul's theology, he was not in fact a binitarian, but a thoroughgoing trinitarian in his experience of God and his articulation of that experience. Crucial to all of this is the reality that for Paul the confession of Jesus as Lord is possible solely through the experience of the Spirit (1 Cor. 12: 3). Thus, Paul's 'high christology' does not begin with doctrinal reflection but with experienced conviction. Those who have received the Spirit of God have been enabled to see the crucifixion in new, divine light. Those who walk 'according to the Spirit' can no longer look on Christ from their old 'according to the flesh' point of view (2 Cor. 5: 15–16). They now know him to be the exalted Lord, ever present at the Father's right hand making intercession for them (Rom. 8: 34).

It is in this light that we now turn to Paul's understanding of the Spirit, since his thoroughly trinitarian experience of God was ultimately determined by his and his churches' experience of the Spirit—as the fulfilment of God's promise, including especially the promise of the renewal of the divine Presence with God's people.

III THE SPIRIT: THE PERSONAL PRESENCE OF GOD AND CHRIST

Since the difficulty most people face when dealing with the Holy Spirit is with 'personal-ness', that is the rightful place for this discussion to begin. Unfortunately, this very understandable difficulty has been abetted by the reticence of NT scholarship on this matter, which has taken two forms. On the one hand, it is argued that Paul is largely dependent on the OT for his understanding of the Spirit, and that there the Spirit appears most often as not much more than some kind of extension or emanation of God, or of power coming from God. And since in the OT—and in Paul—the primary function of the Spirit of God is some form of agency, there is nothing inherent in Paul's understanding that would require us to think of the Spirit in personal terms.

On the other hand, some have argued that Paul's understanding of the Spirit is best viewed in terms of identification with the risen Christ, that is, that the risen, exalted Christ and the Spirit are essentially the same reality. If by this one means that the Spirit is how the risen Christ is continually present with his people, there are no objections to be raised. After all, this is exactly how we understand God the Father to be with us as well. But the language in the literature suggests far more than that, moving very close to full identification, so that 'distinct from' is almost totally lost in the rhetoric of identification.

Since I have addressed this latter issue at some length in an earlier paper,[27] here I wish only to revisit some Pauline texts that seem to demand (*a*) that Paul understood the Spirit in very personal terms, and not simply as an extension of God, personifying his power as it were, (*b*) that he understood the Spirit as the 'Spirit of Christ' as well as the 'Spirit of God (the Father)', and clearly as 'distinct from' Christ, and (*c*) that one key to Paul's enlarged understanding of the one God in trinitarian terms lies with his understanding the Spirit to be the renewed Presence of God and thus also the presence of the risen Christ.

1. While it is true that Paul does not speak directly to the question of the Spirit's *personal nature*, nonetheless, two passages in particular make it clear that he understood the Spirit in personal terms, intimately associated with God, yet distinct from him.

(*a*) In 1 Corinthians 2: 10–12 Paul uses the analogy of human interior consciousness (only one's 'spirit' knows one's mind) to insist that the Spirit alone knows the mind of God. At issue in this passage is the Corinthians' radical misunderstanding of the Spirit, which in turn has led to a radical revaluation of the cross (actually devaluation). Having argued vigorously for the centrality of the cross (1: 18 to 2: 5), Paul now sets out to demonstrate that the Spirit—whom the Corinthian believers have indeed received as the source of their supernatural giftings (chs. 12–14; cf. 1: 5–7)— must first of all be understood as the one who has revealed God's

[27] See n. 12 above.

heretofore hidden mystery: that the 'foolishness and weakness' of the crucifixion is in fact the ultimate expression of God's wisdom and power.

Paul's concern with the analogy in vv. 10–11, therefore, is not ontological (that God is like us in his being, in that he has a 'spirit'), but epistemological (how we can know the mystery of the cross that has lain hidden in the 'depths of God'). His point is that only through self-revelation one can penetrate into another's consciousness. Indeed, the analogy breaks down precisely at the point of ontology; but with regard to ours, not God's. Whatever else is clear in Paul's pneumatology, the present *locus* of God's Spirit is not interior to God as a way of expressing self-consciousness, but 'external' to God, in the sense that the Spirit presently dwells in and among God's people.[28] Thus, Paul's concern in using the analogy has to do with revelation, pure and simple. The Spirit whom they have come to understand in a triumphalistic way is rather to be understood as the source both of their getting it right with regard to the cross (as God's wisdom) and also of their living life in the present in a cruciform way, as their maligned apostle does (which is quite the point of 1 Cor. 4).

Nonetheless, by use of this analogy Paul does in fact draw the closest kind of relationship between God and the Spirit. The Spirit alone 'searches all things', even 'the depths of God'; and because of this unique relationship with God, the Spirit alone knows and reveals God's otherwise hidden wisdom (1 Cor. 2: 7). What is significant for our present purposes is that such language assumes personhood in a most straightforward way. The Spirit 'searches, knows, reveals, and teaches' the 'mind of God', so that having received the Spirit ourselves, 'we have the mind of Christ', Paul concludes (2: 16).

Some mystery is involved here, of course, because finally we are dealing with divine mysteries. But there can be little question that Paul sees the Spirit as distinct from God; yet at the same time

---

[28] The passages here are numerous, most of them reflecting Paul's use of the language of the LXX from Ezek. 36: 26 (πνεῦμα καινὸν δώσω ἐν ὑμῖν; 'I will give a new Spirit in you', followed by the analogy of a heart of 'flesh' replacing the heart of stone) and 37: 14 (καὶ δώσω τὸ πνεῦμά μου εἰς ὑμᾶς καὶ ζήσεσθε; 'and I will give my Spirit into you and you shall live'). Among many texts in Paul, see 1 Thess. 4: 8 (for the precise language of Ezekiel); Rom. 8: 11 and 1 Cor. 3: 16 (for the concept of 'indwelling'); Gal. 4: 6 (for the location as 'in our hearts'); and 1 Cor. 6:19 (for the abbreviated 'in you').

the Spirit is both the interior expression of the unseen God's personality and the visible manifestation of God's activity in the world. The Spirit is truly God in action; yet he is neither simply an outworking of God's personality nor all there is to say about God.

(*b*) Even more significantly, in Romans 8: 26-7 this same reality is expressed in reverse; now it is God who *knows the mind* of the Spirit. This passage comes at the end of a sudden and extraordinary influx of σύν-compounds that express our relationship with the Spirit and Christ (and includes the now-subjected creation as joining with us in 'sighing' in our present 'already/not yet' eschatological existence). In v.16 Paul has stated that the Spirit 'bears witness together [συμμαρτυρεῖ] with our spirits that we are God's children'; now, following the brief, but theologically significant, interlude describing our present existence in weakness (vv. 18-25), he concludes with this final word about our present life as life in the Spirit: 'Likewise (just as the Spirit bears witness with our spirits), the Spirit also joins together with us to aid us (συναντιλαμβάνεται) in our weakness, by interceding from within us with inarticulate groanings.' Paul's ultimate concern here is to show the absolute sufficiency and adequacy of such praying in the Spirit, the effectiveness of whose intercession lies precisely in the fact that God, who searches *our* hearts, likewise 'knows the mind of the Spirit', that he is interceding for us κατὰ θεόν (according to God!).

Thus, not only does the Spirit himself (αὐτὸ τὸ πνεῦμα) intercede on behalf of the saints (a very personal activity, it must be pointed out), but the saints can have complete confidence in such prayer, even if they do not understand the words, because *God knows the mind of the Spirit, that the Spirit intercedes according to God.* One can scarcely miss the significance of such a sentence for Paul's understanding of the Spirit, as both personal (the Spirit intercedes; God knows the Spirit's mind) and 'distinct from' God the Father.

2. It is of further importance with regard to this latter text to note that some few sentences later (v. 34) Paul mentions the present intercessory activity of Christ in our behalf. Whereas the Spirit intercedes from 'within us' (see 8: 9, 15), Christ in his exaltation intercedes for us 'at the right hand of God'. This collocation of intercessory texts, one by the Spirit (from within the human breast) and the other by Christ (at the right hand of the Father)

should put to rest any idea that Paul identified the risen Christ with the gift of the Spirit.

On the other hand, and here is the crucial matter, on three occasions, when at issue is the risen Christ's presence with him, Paul freely and readily denominates the Spirit of God to be 'the Spirit of Christ (Jesus)' (Rom. 8: 9; Gal. 4: 6; Phil. 1: 19). Although such usage admittedly says something more christological than pneumatological, what it does say of the Spirit is especially significant, since herein most likely lies an important key to Paul's trinitarian understanding of God. As he insists elsewhere, there is only one Spirit (1 Cor. 12: 4, 9; Eph. 4:4); but as his usage in various contexts makes plain, the one Spirit is the Spirit of both the Father and the Son.

Crucial here is that the reception of the Spirit is thus the way Paul experiences—and therefore relates to—both the Father and Christ. It would be hard to minimize the significance of this reality for our understanding of Paul's latent trinitarianism. To some Gentile believers who are sorely tempted to relate to God by means of (impersonal) Torah observance, Paul asserts that the Son of God who loved me and gave himself for me (past tense) also 'lives in me' (present tense), so that I am dead with reference to Torah and alive to God (Gal. 2: 19–20). And it is equally clear from Romans 8: 9–10 that 'Christ lives in me' is Pauline shorthand for 'the risen Christ lives in me by his Spirit [i.e. by the Spirit of God who is also the Spirit of Christ]'.

Thus, just as Paul knows God to be personally present with him through his experience of the Spirit, so also when Paul speaks of Christ as living in me/you/your hearts (as he does on five occasions[29]) this is realized by the Spirit as well. This, surely, is of no small consequence for our coming to terms with Paul's own enlarged understanding of God as Saviour.

What this says in terms of our understanding the Spirit is equally important, of course, since this combination of realities (that the Spirit of God is equally the Spirit of Christ) means that just as Christ put a human face on God, as it were, so also has he put a human face on the Spirit. No longer can one think of the Spirit as some 'it', some emanation from God; the Spirit of God is also to be henceforth known as the Spirit of Christ. He is thus

---

[29] Rom. 8: 10; 2 Cor. 13: 5; Gal. 2: 20; Eph. 3: 17; Col. 1: 23.

the very personal presence of Christ with and within us during our present between-the-times existence.

3. That leads us at last to a final set of texts, which make clear what we have been noting right along—that Paul views the Spirit as the eschatological renewal of God's presence with his people. While this motif stems in part from the language of 'indwelling' found in the new covenant promises of Jeremiah and Ezekiel, it emerges especially in Paul's use of temple imagery, part of the significance of which is that the metaphor functions both for the corporate, gathered community as well as for the individual believer.

The theme of God's presence with his people is one of the keys to the structure of the book of Exodus. When Israel comes at last to the holy mount, the place of God's 'dwelling', it is also a place where they are forbidden to go on the threat of death. Only Moses is allowed into God's presence. But God plans to 'move' from the mount and dwell among his people by means of a 'tabernacle'. So after the giving of the Book of the Covenant (chs. 20–4), Moses receives the precise instructions for constructing the tabernacle (chs. 25–31). But this is followed by the debacle in the desert (ch. 32), followed by God's announcing that 'my presence will *not* go with you'; an angel will go instead (ch. 33). Moses recognizes the inadequacy of this solution and intercedes: 'If your Presence does not go with us, do not send us up from here. How will anyone know that you are pleased with me and with your people unless you go with us? What else will distinguish me and your people from all the other people on the face of the earth?' (33: 15–16 NIV). God's Presence with Israel is what distinguishes them, not the Law or other 'identity markers'. This in turn is followed by the further revelation of God's character (34: 4–7) and the actual construction of the tabernacle, all of which concludes with the descent of God's *glory* (his Presence) which 'filled the tabernacle' (40: 35). With that, they set out for the place which 'the Lord your God will choose as a dwelling for his name' (Deut. 12: 11 and *passim*). At a later point in time the motif of the divine presence, as outlined here, was specifically equated with 'the Holy Spirit of the Lord' (Isa. 63: 9–14; cf. Ps. 106: 33), which language and theme Paul himself deliberately echoes in Ephesians 4: 30.[30]

---

[30] This is often noted in the commentaries, but then rather summarily dismissed. Paul's Greek reads καὶ μὴ λυπεῖτε τὸ πνεῦμα τὸ ἅγιον τοῦ θεοῦ; the LXX of Isa. 63:

The deuteronomic promise is finally fulfilled in the construction of Solomon's temple, where the same 'glory' as in Exodus 40 descended and 'filled his temple' (1 Kgs. 8: 11). But Israel's failure caused them to forfeit God's presence. This is the tragedy. The temple in Jerusalem, the place where God has chosen to dwell, is finally destroyed; and the people are not only carried away captive, but both the captives and those who remained were no longer a people distinguished by the presence of the living God in their midst—although it is promised again in Ezekiel's grand vision (40-8). The second temple itself evinces mixed feelings among the people. In light of Solomon's temple and the promised future temple of Ezekiel, Haggai complains, 'Who of you is left who saw this house in its former *glory*? How does it look to you now? Does it not seem to you like nothing?' (2: 3). In many circles, therefore, the hope of a grand, rebuilt temple with the renewal of God's presence—his glory—still awaited the people of God.

It is this complex of ideas and images that Paul picks up in 1 Corinthians 3: 16-17 and elsewhere (cf. 6: 19; 2 Cor. 6: 16; Eph. 2: 21-22), as his introductory, 'do you not know that, . . .' followed by 'you are *the* temple of God [in Corinth]', strongly suggests. And what makes them God's temple in Corinth, his alternative to all the pagan deities to which they were formerly enslaved (1 Cor. 12: 2), is the Spirit. The church, corporately and individually (1 Cor. 6: 19), is now the place of God's own personal presence, by the Spirit. This is what marks God's new people off from 'all the other people on the face of the earth'. Hence Paul's consternation with the Corinthians' present behaviour which has the effect of banishing the Spirit, the living presence of God that makes them his temple, the place of God's present dwelling.

Thus, this imagery, which understands God's presence with Israel in terms of the Spirit, is what is exploited by Paul. Their corporate experience of the Spirit's gifting, rather than being

---

10 reads παρώξυναν τὸ πνεῦμα τὸ ἅγιον αὐτοῦ. That Paul is here 'citing' the LXX best explains both the unusual 'fullness' to the name ('the Spirit, the Holy, of God') and the word order. The two linguistic differences between Paul and LXX Isaiah are easily explained. Paul substitutes τοῦ θεοῦ for αὐτοῦ because in Paul's sentence the pronoun would otherwise have no antecedent (but in making the substitution he keeps the word order of the LXX). He substitutes λυπεῖτε for a form of παρωξύνω most likely because the latter means 'irritate' or 'vex', and Paul understands the Piel of עצב to mean 'grieve' (correctly so; this is the only instance in the LXX where עצב is rendered with παρωξύνω).

turned into demonic self-focused spirituality, must be for their corporate building up. All things the Spirit does among them is for their common good and for the edification of the body. And this, precisely because the evident manifestations of the Spirit among them are evidence of God's own presence among them.

All together these series of texts indicate in the strongest kind of way that Paul understood the Spirit in personal terms. It is in light of what seems reasonably clear in these texts that then causes one to see the same reality in all of the other texts where the Spirit's agency is personal—in the same way as Christ's is[31]—and where the Spirit is the subject of verbs that presuppose personhood.[32]

Not only so, but these texts also give certain evidence that for Paul this new eschatological experience of God's presence is also the experience of the presence of the risen Christ 'living in me'. The net result is that the experience of the Spirit finally provides the key to Paul's trinitarianism. The Spirit whom God 'sent into our hearts' is thus 'distinct from' God himself, just as is the Son whom God sent to redeem. At the same time the Spirit is the Spirit of Christ and is thus 'distinct from' Christ, who now lives in us by means of 'the Spirit of Christ'.

To be sure, Paul's experience and understanding of the Spirit as God's personal presence inevitably leads us into some deep waters. At issue *for us* is with *how* God exists in his essential being as triune. How can God be known as Father, Son, and Spirit, one being, yet each 'person' distinct from the other? And we tend to think that a person is not a true trinitarian unless they have a working formulation in response to this question.

To put the question this way, however, is to get ahead of Paul, not to mention to define trinitarianism by later standards. What makes this an issue for us at all is the fact that Paul, the strictest of monotheists, who never doubted that 'the Lord thy God is one', wrote letters to his churches that are full of presuppositions and

---

[31] For this discussion, see esp. my *Paul, the Spirit, and the People of God*, 26–7.

[32] Besides the texts noted above, the Spirit also *teaches* the content of the gospel to believers (1 Cor. 2: 13), *dwells* among or within believers (1 Cor. 3: 16; Rom. 8: 11; 2 Tim. 1: 14), *accomplishes* all things (1 Cor. 12: 11), *gives life* to those who believe (2 Cor. 3: 6), *cries out* from within our hearts (Gal. 4: 6), *leads* us in the ways of God (Gal. 5: 18; Rom. 8: 14), *bears witness* with our own spirits (Rom. 8: 16), *has desires* that are in opposition to the flesh (Gal. 5: 17), *works* all things *together* for our ultimate good (Rom. 8: 28), *strengthens* believers (Eph. 3: 16). Furthermore, the fruit of the Spirit's indwelling are the personal attributes of God (Gal. 5: 22–3).

assertions which reveal that he *experienced* God, and then *expressed* that experience, in a fundamentally trinitarian way. Thus Paul affirms, asserts, and presupposes the Trinity in every kind of way, but especially soteriologically—the very heart of Pauline theology. And those affirmations—that the one God known and experienced as Father, Son, and Holy Spirit, each distinct from the other, is yet only one God—are precisely the reason the later church took up the question of 'how'.

IV CONCLUSIONS AND IMPLICATIONS

In sum: Paul's various triadic expressions of God's saving activity, as the combined activity of Father, Christ, and Spirit, stem not only from his prior understanding of God as Saviour and his encounter with the risen Christ on the Damascus Road, but especially from his experience of the Spirit, who made that work effectual in his and others' lives. Furthermore, the risen Christ is now the exalted 'Lord', the OT language for God, about whom Paul spoke as the pre-existent Son of God and to whom he attributed every imaginable activity which Paul's Judaism reserved for God alone. That the issue is Trinity, however, and not Binity, comes directly out of the church's personal experience with God through the Spirit, who is at once the renewed Presence of God and the way the risen Christ lives in him/them. The question is, Did Paul in fact have a trinitarian faith, even if he did not use the language of a later time to describe God? Our analysis of the Pauline data suggests that indeed he did.[33]

One may grant that Paul's trinitarian assumptions and descriptions, which form the basis of the later formulas, never move towards calling the Spirit 'God' and never wrestle with the philosophical and theological implications of those assumptions and descriptions. But neither is there evidence that he lacked clarity as to the distinctions between, and the specific roles of, the three divine 'persons' who accomplished so great salvation for us all.

I would thus urge my colleagues in the NT academy, that in our

---

[33] On this whole question, and especially on Paul as a Trinitarian, see further the section entitled 'What about the Trinity?' by David Ford, in Frances Young and David Ford, *Meaning and Truth in 2 Corinthians* (Grand Rapids, Mich.: Eerdmans, 1987), 255–60.

desire to be good historians we not dismiss too easily the fact that the 'historical Paul' had plenty of theological muscle. If his concern is less with 'God in his being' and more with 'God our Saviour', there is plenty of good reason to see Paul as presuppositionally an ontological trinitarian as well. The fact that the Spirit alone knows the mind of God, 'the deep things of God', as Paul puts it, and that God knows the mind of the Spirit indicates not only functional trinitarianism, but something moving very close to 'ontological' trinitarianism. So also with the clear evidence of the Spirit's 'unity' with Christ—in receiving a fresh supply of the Spirit, it is the Spirit of Jesus Christ whom Paul receives (Phil. 1: 19)—yet the clear distinction between Christ and the Spirit remains.

We may wish for more, but then on what theological point might we not always be wishing for more. Such is the way of ad hoc documents whose concern is primarily, as in the Judaism to which Paul is heir, with the way God's people live in the world, so that even when he addresses their thinking it is to change the way they are living. May our own trinitarian discussions never lose sight of this end as well.

Which leads me to note that perhaps even more important than how Paul contributes to later ontological articulation, is what he may contribute to our own experience of and relationship with God. Fundamental to Paul's Judaism is that God's people are expected to 'know God', which of course has little to do with doctrinal articulation and everything to do with knowing God relationally, in terms of his character and nature. Paul carries this fundamental understanding with him, but insists on putting it into perspective: our knowing is preceded by God's 'knowing us' (Gal. 4: 9; cf. 1 Cor. 13: 12).

As a follower of Christ, Paul rephrases 'knowing' in terms of 'knowing Christ', for the surpassing value of which he has 'suffered the loss of all things' (Phil. 3: 8). '*Being found* in him', he goes on, has as its final goal 'to know him, both the power of his resurrection and participation in his sufferings, so as to be made like him in his death' (v. 10). It is clear from any number of passages that for Paul 'knowing God' comes by way of 'knowing Christ' (cf. 2 Cor. 4: 6); and 'knowing Christ' comes by way of 'the Spirit's wisdom and revelation' (Eph. 1: 17). At the heart of all of this is Paul's conviction that Christian life means to 'live by, walk in, be led by' the Spirit. Living the life of the Spirit means for the Spirit to bear his fruit in our individual and corporate lives; and that fruit is nothing other than God's character, as lived out by Christ, being reproduced in his people.

Hence to be a trinitarian of the Pauline kind means to be a person of the Spirit; for it is through the Spirit's indwelling that we know God and Christ relationally, and through the same Spirit's indwelling that we are being transformed into God's own likeness 'from glory to glory' (2 Cor. 3: 18).

Finally, whatever else we learn from Paul's kind of trinitarianism, we need to recognize that if Rahner is right, that the economic and immanent Trinity are one, then our trinitarianism is terribly defective if we spend our labours on the ontological questions in such a way as to lose the essential narrative about God and salvation that raised those questions in the first place. The instincts of the earlier creeds were right on at this point, by insisting that we confess our faith in God by way of this narrative (God as Creator, Christ as Redeemer); where their instincts failed was in excluding the Holy Spirit from the narrative as such—although one could argue that 'the holy catholic church' is the Spirit's role in the narrative.

In any case, rather than simply use Paul as the quarry for later theological reflection, something might be said for keeping Paul's form of trinitarian expression as part of the final equation.[34]

---

[34] Which, it should be noted, is also part of Catherine LaCugna's agenda in *God for Us* (see esp. ch. 7).

4

'Two Powers in Heaven' and Early Christian Trinitarian Thinking

ALAN F. SEGAL

I LORD AND GOD

Along with 'O Lord, Come', 'Christ is Lord' may be the most primitive of all Christian proclamations. It is already clearly in use in the writing of Paul:

For what we preach is not ourselves, but Jesus Christ as Lord, with ourselves as your servants for Jesus' sake.

For it is the God who said, 'Let light shine out of darkness,' who has shone in our hearts to give the light of the knowledge of the glory of God in the face of Christ. (2 Cor. 4: 5-6)

Paul identifies the Christ with Lord and, as the next verse shows, then clearly identifies that figure with the God who created in Genesis 1. That identification is an important step in early Christian thought for in that simple identification is the kernel of all trinitarian thinking to follow. For Paul this identification is achieved through the Glory of the Lord, a well-known technical term for the human apparition of God which followed the Israelites through the desert and was manifest to Moses at Sinai (Exod. 23-34) and again with the exiles in Babylonian captivity (Ezek. 1: 26). In Paul, this identification was without doubt made on the basis of his visions and apocalypses, as he tells us. But it was based on the Easter events experienced by the apostles and by converted followers like Paul himself.

Paul both had his own visions and listened to the primitive church traditions which he learned after his conversion. Since Jesus died as a martyr, expectations of his resurrection would have been normal in sectarian Judaism. But the idea of a crucified messiah was unique. In such a situation, the Christians only did what other believing Jews did in similar circumstances: they turned to biblical prophecy for elucidation. No messianic text suggested itself as appropriate to the situation. But Psalm 110: 1 was exactly apposite: 'The Lord says to my Lord: "Sit at my right hand, until I make your enemies your footstool".' This description of enthronement of a Davidic descendant was now understood as a heavenly enthronement after death and resurrection. Yet nothing in the text makes the death or resurrection part of the narrative inevitable. It must have come from the historical experience of the early Christian community, after they experienced these events. Thereafter, Psalm 110: 1 could be combined easily with Daniel 7: 9–13, the description of the enthronement of another human figure on the throne, the 'son of man'—literally, the human figure.

The Gospels, for their part, usually identify Jesus with the famous 'son of man' prophecy in Daniel 7: 13. Jesus apparently used the term *son of man* while alive, though deciding what he meant by the phrase remains problematic. After his crucifixion and the Easter experience of the church, the son of man phrases Jesus used were put in the context of the statement in Daniel 7: 13 about the enthronement of the son of man, and Jesus' disciples believed that his victory of death was followed by his ascension and enthronement in heaven as the divine figure who was to bring God's coming justice. Through the imagery of the 'son of man', the man Jesus was associated with the figure on the throne in Daniel 7: 13 while the traditions of Jesus' messianic function were associated with traditions about the son of man, taking on a uniquely Christian interpretation.

An exegesis of this novelty and importance should have left traces and reactions among the various Jewish groups contemporary with Christianity. We have some hints of Jewish reaction in the New Testament. But it is hard to find much reaction to the notion of the Trinity until the fourth century. However, the reaction to the identification of the Lord as a figure different from God seems to be more immediate.

II 'Two Powers in Heaven'

If the following evidence is any indication, it was the difference between the father and son that most disturbed the rabbis who heard the Christian confession. Those heretics whom the rabbis called 'two powers in heaven' (שׁתי רשׁויות בשׁמים) present a promising start for uncovering the vexed relationship between Judaism, and developing trinitarian Christianity. Although some kind of dualistic doctrine seems inherent in the rabbinic designation, several scholars have seen a relationship between 'two powers' and Christianity.[1] Furthermore, most of the rabbinic texts define 'two powers in heaven' as a binitarian heresy, raising the possibility that the rabbis are reacting to some of the early Christian proclamations about the divinity of the Christ. However, the texts were written over a long period of time, probably referring to a variety of different phenomena, so only an outline of the complete problem can be presented here.[2]

III The Mekhiltas

The best way to begin is to turn to some characteristic occurrences of the designation and try to outline the history of the heresy. The most significant passage may be found in several places in

---

[1] The study of rabbinic heretics (the *minim*) has had several distinguished forebears. See e.g. M. Joël, *Blicke in die Religionsgeschichte zu Angang des zweitens christlichen Jahrhunderts*, ii (Breslau: Schottlaender, 1880), 71 ff.; I. Elbogen, *Der jüdische Gottesdienst in seiner geschichtlichen Entwicklung* (Hildesheim: Georg Olms, 1962), 36; M. Simon, *Verus Israel: Étude sur les relations entre Chrétiens et Juifs dans l'Émpire romain* (Paris: Éditions É. de Boccard, 1964), 217 ff.; R. T. Herford, *Christianity in Talmud and Midrash* (New York: Ktav Publishing House, 1975), 362 ff.; S. M. Wagner, 'Religious Non-conformity in Ancient Jewish Life', Diss. (Yeshiva University, 1964); A. Marmorstein, *Religionsgeschichtliche Studien* I (Schotschau: Selbstverlag des Verfassers, 1901), 66–81; A. Buechler, 'The Minim of Sepphoris and Tiberius in the Second and Third Centuries', *Studies in Jewish History* (Oxford: Oxford University Press, 1956). See also the works of S. Lieberman (*Hellenism in Jewish Palestine: Studies in the Literary Transmission of Beliefs and Manners of Palestine in the I Century B.C.E.-IV Century C.E.* (New York: Jewish Theological Seminary of America, 1962)) and E. E. Urbach (*The Sages: Their Concepts and Beliefs*, in Hebrew (Jerusalem: Magnes Press, 1969); English trans. by Israel Abrahams (Cambridge, Mass.: Harvard University Press, 1979)).

[2] For further detail, see my book *Two Powers in Heaven: Early Rabbinic Reports about Christianity and Gnosticism* (Leiden: E. J. Brill, 1977). This paper condenses several arguments from the book and has been used with permission.

Midrashic literature and is alluded to in many more. The tradition occurs often in different versions in the *Mekhiltot*. A simple form of the tradition occurs in the Mekhilta of Rabbi Simeon bar Yohai (hereafter cited as MRSBY). In the Mekhilta of Rabbi Ishmael (hereafter cited as MRI) the passage occurs in two places (Bahodesh 5 and Shirta 4) in virtually identical form. In Bahodesh alone, a closely related tradition, adduced in the name of R. Nathan, was added because of its obvious relevance. Finally, the tradition was known and discussed in Pesikta Rabbati (hereafter cited as PR), but there it has undergone considerable development.[3]

MRSBY	MRI
Bashalah 15, p. 81	
Another interpretation:	
YHWH is a man of war, YHWH is His name.	*I am YHWH your God*
	Why is this said?
Because, when the Holy one Blessed be	Because
He was revealed at the sea,	when he was revealed at the sea
He appeared to them as a young man making war.	He appeared to them as a young man making war. As it is said *YHWH is a man of war*
YHWH is His name.	

---

[3] Another comment: *Face after face* R. Levi said: 'God faced them in many guises. To one He appeared standing, and to one seated; [see Gen. 28: 13 and Isa. 6: 1] to one as a young man, and to one as an old man. How so? At the time the Holy One, Blessed be He, appeared on the Red Sea to wage war for His children and to requite the Egyptians, he faced them as a young man, since war is waged best by a young man, as it is said:

The Lord is a man of war, the Lord is His name [Exod. 15: 3]. And when the Holy One, Blessed be He, appeared on Mount Sinai to give the Torah to Israel, He faced them as an old man, for Torah is at its best when it comes from the mouth of an old man. What is the proof? The verse: *With aged men is wisdom and understanding in length of days* [Job 12: 12]; and therefore Daniel said: I beheld till thrones were placed, and one that was Ancient of days did sit [Dan. 7: 9]'. In regard to God's guises R. Hiyya bar Abba said: 'If a whoreson should say to you, "They are two gods," quote God as saying in reply: I am the One of the Sea and I am the One of Sinai.' (Another comment) R. Levi taught that at Sinai the Holy One, blessed be He, appeared to them with many faces, with a threatening face, with a severe face, with an angry face, with a joyous face, with a laughing face, with a friendly face. How so? . . . In regard to God's many faces, R. Hiyya bar Abba taught: 'Should a whoreson say to you, "They are two gods," reply to him, Scripture does not say "The Gods have spoken . . . face after face" but *The Lord has spoken with you face after face.*' (see PR I piska 21 100b; William G. Braude, *Pesikta Rabbati*, i (New Haven: Yale Univeristy Press (1968), 421–2).

He appeared to them at Sinai like an old man, full of mercy.

He appeared at Sinai like an old man, full of mercy:
and it was said: *and they saw the God of Israel* [Exod. 24: 10]. And of the time after they had been redeemed what does it say? *And the like of the very heaven for clearness* [Exod. 24: 10]
Again, it says,
I beheld 'till thrones were set down [Dan. 7: 9]. And it also says *A fiery stream issued and came forth from Him.* Scripture would not give an opportunity to the nations of the world to say
'There are two powers in heaven,' but declares:

And of the time after they had been redeemed what does it say? *And the like of the very heaven for clearness* [Exod. 24: 10]

I beheld 'till thrones were set down [Dan. 7: 9]

So as not to give an opportunity to say 'There are two powers in heaven.'
Rather
YHWH is a man of war [Exod. 15: 3]

Another interpretation:
YHWH is a man of War.
YHWH fought in Egypt.
YHWH fought at the Sea.
And He is at the Jordan,
He is at the Arnon streams.
And He is in this world
And He is in the world to come.
He is in the past
And He is in the future

I was in Egypt.
I was at the Sea

I was in the past
I will be in the future
I am in the world
I will be in the world to me.

And it is said: *Behold now, that I, even I, am He* [etc.] [Deut. 32: 39]

As it is said: *Behold now, that I, even I, am He,* [etc.] [Deut. 32: 39]
Even unto old age I am the same [Isa. 46: 4]

Thus says YHWH the king of Israel, [etc.]
I am YHWH, the first and the last [Isa. 44: 6]

Thus says YHWH the king of Israel and his redeemer, the Lord of Hosts I am the first and the last [Isa. 44: 6]
And it says: *Who has wrought and done it? He that called the generations from the Beginning. I the Lord am the first and to the end, I am He* [Isa. 41: 4]

In MRSBY the subject is introduced as an exegetical comment on the two statements made about YHWH in Exodus 15: 3. The exegesis notes the repetition of the name YHWH in Exodus 15: 3 and explains its significance. 'YHWH is a man of war' is to be interpreted as a literal description, referring to God's manifestation as a young warrior when he destroyed the Egyptians at the Red Sea. 'YHWH is His name' is necessary because at Sinai, he will reveal himself as an old man, showing mercy. Hence, it is important for the Israelites to realize that the same God is speaking in both places, though the manifestations look different.[4]

The text in MRI is even more complex and is obviously the result of a long history of redaction. First, the issue is no longer merely the repetition of the divine name YHWH, because the biblical verse differs slightly. In this case, the dangerous doctrine is the idea that there are two different manifestations of God—one, a just, young man, appearing at the sea; the other, a merciful, old man, appearing at Sinai.[5] Neither MRI nor MRSBY can itself be the most ancient tradition. However, both are variations of it. The most ancient layer, which will later appear to be Tannaitic, must be carefully uncovered in comparing them and then comparing the rabbinic evidence with the Christian material, which can be accurately dated to the first century.

The common tradition must have been an exegesis of the meaning of the divine names, and probably also centred around the Sinai theophany. Daniel 7: 9–10 is a common proof text against the heresy. However, it is also likely to be the locus of a heretical argument, since the passage describes two different figures in heaven in Daniel's night vision. Of course, the rabbis objected to

---

[4] See J. Lauterbach, 'Some Clarifications of the Mekhilta' (in Hebrew), *Sefer Klausner: A Collection of Science and Belle-lettres gathered for Professor Klausner on his Sixtieth Birthday Celebration*, ed. N. H. Torchyner, A. Tcherikover, A. A. Kubeck, B. Shortman. (Tel Aviv: Hotsaat, 1937), 181–8, esp. 184–8. See also Judah Goldin, *The Song at the Sea* (New Haven: Yale University Press, 1971), 126 ff.

[5] Space does not allow a complete discussion of the passage. But it should be noted that the rabbinic doctrine of the two *middoth* or 'measures' of God is implicit in this discussion in MRI. This aspect was missing in the version occurring in MRSBY. MRI has developed a special tradition about the discussion of God's attributes of justice and mercy, though the actual technical terms do not appear. The theme of God's justice and mercy is very important for dating the whole rabbinic tradition. We shall see that Philo and the *midrash* both record similar traditions about God's justice and mercy. For more detail on this aspect of the passage, see N. A. Dahl and Alan F. Segal, 'Philo and the Rabbis on the Names of God', *JSJ* 9 (1978), 1 ff.

such an idea, saying that the repetition of divine names and the change in divine appearances were planned by God. From the rabbinic perspective, repetition of the divine name did not identify 'two powers'; rather it emphasized that the Israelites would have to recognize God in different forms throughout their history. In attempting to identify the heresy we should look for a doctrine which did associate 'two powers' with the different names of God.

Other interesting details emerge from this passage. It is clear that the heretical doctrine in this particular case involves believing in two corresponding or cooperating deities. This means that the heretics who provoked this response from the rabbis are not dualists. Nor can they have been Marcionite Christians or extreme gnostics. Rather we have to look among the sects contemporary with the early rabbis for theologies with two complementary figures in heaven to find candidates for the heresy. This would include several of the apocalyptic systems where a central figure, like Michael, Melchizedek, or even a 'son of man' were important partners of God in bringing redemption. No doubt, many varieties of Christians were also included, for Christianity was exceptionally interested in the interpretation of Daniel 7: 9-10 and Christianity is foremost among those sects declaring a second divine hypostasis to share in the coming kingdom.

Though Christianity's theology is trinitarian, it may not have appeared so in its original context. For one thing, Christian mention of the 'Holy Spirit' would neither have been considered unique nor heretical by the rabbis. For another thing, Christianity of the period was much more concerned with the relationship between the Father and the Son. The concept of the 'Holy Spirit' was not a source for the same kind of speculation.[6]

The rabbinic response to the heresy is clear. The rabbis appeal to scripture to show that God is unitary. Deuteronomy 6, Isaiah 44-7, and Exodus 20 are used by the rabbis to show that God is unique. These verses are probably being employed against heretical interpretations of Daniel 7: 9-10; they are certainly being used against the idea that the names of God denote different divinities. This pattern of scriptures is characteristic both of the heresy and the defence against it. It will be especially important for recon-

---

[6] See Jaroslav Pelikan, *The Christian Tradition: A History of the Development of Doctrine*, i. *The Emergence of the Catholic Tradition* (100-600) (Chicago: University of Chicago Press, 1971), 172-225.

structing the history of the heresy and for understanding the radicalization of gnosticism.

However, the other aspects of the heresy are more mysterious. Determining the identity of the groups of heresy in question remains a serious question. MRI describes those professing belief in the doctrine as 'gentiles'. PR calls a person with such beliefs either a 'whoreson' or a 'son of heresy' depending upon the translation. So there can be no definite identification of the heresy from the terminology in the rabbinic writings. There is some evidence connecting this argument with a rabbinic polemic against Christianity. Elsewhere, PR 22 comments on 'My God, my God, why hast thou forsaken me?' which in Aramaic is supposed to have been Jesus' last words (Matt. 27: 46). The rabbis say that the first 'my God' refers to the sea while the second 'my God' refers to Sinai. Since no other heretical group found this verse relevant for their doctrine, one may suppose that Christianity was identified as a 'two powers heresy'; but the rabbinic charge of 'two powers' may not have been originally or exclusively used against it. The many descriptions of the heresy in the different versions of the tradition suggest that the charge was used against several groups of heretics in different times and places. This logical conclusion can be demonstrated more soundly later, as more evidence is revealed.

In these passages, one becomes aware of the development of a single tradition in many different ways and probably over considerable periods of time. Traditions with so many layers present immense dating problems. Approximations alone can be made for the date of each layer. Although these texts occur in the 'Tannaitic' Midrashim, recent scholarship has shown that the traditional attributions should not be accepted without question.[7] The traditions may go back as far as the first century but the texts are not equally ancient. Even so, parts of the early layers of the tradition may be isolated.[8]

[7] For more information about the new attempt to date rabbinical traditions, see e.g. Jacob Neusner, 'The Rabbinic Traditions about the Pharisees before 70 A.D.: The Problem of Oral Transmission', *JJS* 22 (1971), 1–18. Also see some of his longer works, such as, *From Politics to Piety: The Emergence of Pharisaic Judaism* (Englewood Cliffs, NJ: Prentice-Hall, 1973); *The Rabbinic Traditions about the Pharisees before 70* (Leiden: Brill, 1971); *Eliezer ben Hyrcanus: The Man and the Legend* (Leiden: Brill, 1973).

[8] The criticism of S. Cohen (*AJS Review*, 10: 1 (Spring 1985), 114–17) that the exegesis of Exod. 15: 3 is entirely theoretical and bears no relationship to actual heretics has been shown mistaken by J. Fossum in *The Name of God and the Angel of*

IV PHILO

With external evidence like Christianity, it is possible to push the origin of this tradition back much further than the rabbinic tradition would itself allow. Philo, too, attests to the pervasiveness and antiquity of the problem of God's appearances as well as his different aspects. His doctrine of the λόγος commands our attention first because Philo explicitly calls the λόγος a second God (δεύτερος) in several places:

Yet there can be no cowering fear for the man who relies on the hope of the divine comradeship, to whom are addressed the words 'I am the God who appeared to thee in place of God.' (Gen. 31: 31). Surely a right noble cause of vaunting it is, for a soul that God deigns to show himself to and converse with it. And do not fail to mark the language used, but carefully inquire whether there are two Gods; for we read 'I am the God that appeared to thee,' not 'in my place' but 'in the place of God,' as though it were another's. What then are we to say? He that is truly God is one, but those that are improperly so-called are more than one. Accordingly, the holy word in the present instance has indicated Him who truly is God by means of the articles, saying, 'I am the God,' while it omits the article when mentioning him who is improperly so called, saying 'who appeared to thee in the place' not 'of the God' but simply 'of God.' (Som. 1.227-9, trans. Colson)

Why does (Scripture) say, as if (speaking) of another God, 'In the image of God He made man' and not 'in His own image?' Most excellently and veraciously this oracle was given by God. For nothing mortal can be made in the likeness of the Most High One and father of the universe but (only) in that of the second God, who is His λόγος. For it was right that the rational part of the human soul should be formed as an impression of the divine λόγος, since the pre-*logos* God is superior to every rational nature. But He who is above the λόγος exists in the best and in a special form— what thing that comes into being can rightly bear His likeness? Moreover, Scripture wishes to show that God most justly avenges the virtuous and

the Lord (Tübingen: Mohr, 1985), 228 ff. There we see that the Samaritan *Malef* 3: 5 contains real traditions of mediation attached to Exod. 15: 3: 'The Glory too seemed to be saying: "O congregation, keep yourself from me, for is there not before me a mighty deed? I slew, I oppressed, I destroyed, I made alive; and, with you, I did all this when I was at the sea and showed you every wonder and made you cross with great marvels by the mighty power of God"'. There is no guarantee that this is an old tradition, but it is certainly an actual heretical one. The Samaritans, of course, did not canonize the book of Daniel, which was so important to the Christian interpretation.

decent men because they have certain kinship with His λόγος, of which the human mind is a likeness and image.[9]

He believes that 'second God' is an appropriate and fitting title but criticizes those who cannot distinguish between the original god and the angelic copy:

Here it gives the title of 'God' to His chief Word, not from any superstitious nicety in applying names, but with one aim before him, to use words to express facts. Thus, in another place, when he had inquired whether He that is has any proper name, he came to know full well that He has no proper name [the reference is to Exod. 6: 3] and that whatever name anyone may use for Him he will use by license of language; for it is not the nature of Him that is to be spoken of, but simply to be. Testimony to this is afforded also by the divine response made to Moses' question whether He has a name, even 'I am He that is' (Exod. 3: 14). It is given in order that, since there are not in God things which man can comprehend, man may recognize His substance. To the souls indeed which are incorporeal and are occupied in His worship it is likely that He should reveal himself, conversing with them as friend with friends; but to souls which are still in a body, giving Himself the likeness of angels, not altering His own nature, for He is unchangeable, but conveying to those which receive the impression of His presence a semblance in a different form, such that they take the image to be not a copy but that original form itself. (Som. 1.230-5 Loeb, 5. 419-21, trans. Colson and Whitaker).

Here, the issue for Philo is the meaning of scriptural anthropomorphisms. This is a theme which runs throughout Philo's discussion of the 'second god'.[10] At the same time, Philo stresses that there is no God besides God the Most High and uses Deuteronomy 4: 39, as the rabbis do, to deny that any other figure can be considered a God:

But let Melchizedek instead of water offer wine, and give to souls strong drink, that they may be seized by a divine intoxication, more sober than sobriety itself. For he is a priest, even Reason, having as his portion Him that is, and all his thoughts of God are high and vast and sublime: for he is the priest of the Most High (Gen. xiv. 18), not that there is any other not Most High—for God being One 'is in heaven above and on earth beneath and there is none beside Him' (Deut. 4: 39)—but to conceive of

---

[9] QG 2.62 (*Philo*, in ten volumes and two supplementary volumes, trans. F. H. Colson, G. H. Whitaker, and R. Marcus (Cambridge, Mass.: Harvard University Press, 1971)).

[10] See also Mig. 86-93 where Philo speaks of extreme allegorizers. The issue in that place, however, is loyalty to the commandments.

God not in low earthbound ways but in lofty terms, such as transcend all other greatness and all else that is free from matter, calls up in us a picture of the Most High. (Leg. 3.81)

In this particular case, Philo denies that any other being can be God's agent, for there is only one God. It is interesting that Philo picks the allegory of Melchizedek as λόγος to discuss this issue, since elsewhere he allows that the λόγος can be considered as a 'second god' and divine mediator. It appears as though Philo is opposed to some concepts of mediation, even while he maintains the agency of the λόγος.[11]

Philo also knows that the names of God connote his aspects of mercy and justice, just as the rabbis do. But Philo identifies the divine names, κύριος and θεός (= YHWH and Elohim), with the aspects of God in exactly the opposite ways that the rabbis do. Generally Philo equates YHWH with the attribute of strict justice and Elohim with the attribute of mercy, the exact opposite of the standard rabbinic doctrine. Philo's system is, however, the same configuration of terms that underlies the MRI passage.[12]

That Philo knows the issue of a 'second god' and the themes of justice and mercy suggests a possible origin well before the birth of Jesus. But Philo's writings suggest more than a continuous issue. He employs very similar scripture, indicating the existence of a widespread scriptural tradition, since the rabbis, a century later, know nothing of him directly and are not indebted to him for their exegesis. In fact, Philo elsewhere credits some of his exegetical information to traditions that he has learned from the elders (Vit. Mos. beginning). This provides a second unambiguous first-century location for this dispute, which is present but not datable in Midrash. Again, extra-rabbinic evidence helps establish the antiquity of certain issues within early rabbinic Judaism, the reverse of the more standard methodological procedure. Preliminary indications are, therefore, that many parts of the Jewish

[11] Melchizedek was a heavenly figure of note in Qumran. See Fred. L. Horton, Jr., *The Melchizedek Tradition: A Critical Examination of the Sources to the Fifth Century A.D. and in the Epistle to the Hebrews* (Cambridge: Cambridge University Press, 1976). See M. Friedlaender, *Der vorchristliche juedische Gnosticismus* (Goettingen: Vandenhoeck und Ruprecht, 1898), 30–33. See also Birger Pearson, 'Friedlaender Revisited: Alexandrian Judaism and Gnosticism', *Studia Philonica*, 2 (1973), 26 for a discussion of this important text.

[12] See Cher. 9, 27–8, Fug. 18, 95, 100; also H. A. Wolfson, *Philo*, i (Cambridge: Cambridge University Press, 1962), 223.

community in various places and periods used the traditions which the rabbis claim is an heretical conception of the deity. This is certainly in line with our previous discovery that Christianity must have been accused of believing in 'two powers in heaven'. Christianity was vitally concerned with the concept of the λόγος, though, unlike Philo, Christians associated a definite personality with the mediating figure. Furthermore, the Jews in the Gospel of John are represented as opposing Jesus because he claims to be equal with God (John 5: 18–21; 8: 58–9; 10: 33). Λόγος theology also interested many Church Fathers, as we shall see.

V   The Opposition to Rabbinic Judaism

Though the rabbis did not enter into detail about their Christian opponents, they certainly seized upon a principal point of the *kerygma* of the primitive church; Jesus had ascended to the Father and received the title 'Lord', one of the titles reserved for God in rabbinic tradition. Many documents in the New Testament witness that this ascension took place as part of Jesus' exaltation, though Paul, in Philippians, probably states it most succinctly: 'Therefore God has highly exalted him and bestowed upon him the name which is above every name, that at the name of Jesus every knee should bow in heaven and on earth and that every tongue confess that Jesus Christ is Lord to the glory of God the Father' (Phil. 2: 9–11).

It seems unlikely, however, that the rabbis invented the argument to counter Christianity. The notion of a split in the Godhead existed in Philo and there is little specifically anti-Christian material in the rabbinic exegesis. Rather the rabbis and Philo appear to reflect the same exegetical issue which has taken on primal importance in the development of Jewish Hellenistic thought, although they witness to the issue at a different stage of development and in a different social context. But the issue at the core seems to be the same: the names of God are not to be understood as separate hypostases of God. This argument was then put to use by the rabbis to counter Christian claims about the meaning of Jesus' divine name.

Justin, the gentile Christian, is the one Church Father whose relationship to the 'two powers controversy' has been noted previously by several scholars.[13] Justin Martyr was born at the beginning of the second century in Shechem, then called Flavia Neapolis, in Samaria. He called himself a Samaritan, which meant only that he was descended from people living in that part of the country and not part of that religious sect (Dial. 120), because he stated that he was uncircumcised (Dial. 29). Nevertheless, the details of Justin's life and his familiarity with a variety of exotic Jewish doctrines add evidence for the relationship we have already suspected between the Samaritans and early gentile Christianity. Justin's *Dialogue with Trypho* also evinces real polemical use of almost all the scriptural exegesis which the rabbis thought dangerous.

The setting for the *Dialogue* was Ephesus where Justin had migrated in his Christian mission. The date for the *Dialogue* must have corresponded closely with the Bar Kokhba Revolt, for Justin mentions it often (e.g. Dial. 108; Apol. 1.31) and Trypho is described as a Jewish fugitive who escaped from the turmoil.

Justin's use of Midrashic traditions has sometimes been taken as evidence that the *Dialogue* is fictional, serving as a purely literary framework for presenting Justin's views. Yet it certainly reflects one side of the debate between Judaism and Christianity in the early and mid-second century, whether the immediate incident be wholly fact, embellished incident, or pure fiction.

By means of Genesis 19: 24, Justin proceeds to show that a second divine figure, Christ, is responsible for carrying out divine commands on earth:

'The previously quoted Scriptural passages will make this evident to you,' I replied. 'Here are the words: "The sun was risen upon the earth, and Lot entered into Segor. And the Lord rained upon Sodom brimstone and fire from the Lord out of Heaven. And He destroyed these cities and all the country round about."' Then the fourth of the companions who remained with Trypho spoke up: 'It must therefore be admitted that one of the two angels who went down to Sodom, and whom Moses in the Scriptures calls Lord, is different from Him who is also God, and appeared to Abraham.' 'Not only because of that quotation,' I said, 'must we certainly admit that,

---

[13] Several scholars have pointed out Justin's relationship to the Haggadah. See A. H. Goldfahn, *Justinus Martyr und die Agada* (Breslau: Glutsch, n.d.). M. Friedlaender, *Patristische und talmudische Studien* (Vienna: Alfred Helder, 1878). Buechler has further emphasized the relevance of Justin for the 'two powers controversy' around Sepphoris and Tiberius, see *Minim*. Also L. Ginzberg, *Die Haggada bei den Kirchenvaetern. Erster Theil. Die Haggada in den pseudohieronymischen* '*Questiones*' (Amsterdam: s.n., 1899).

besides the creator of the universe, another was called Lord by the Holy Spirit. For this was attested to not only by Moses, but also by David, when he said: "The Lord said to my Lord: Sit Thou at My right hand, until I make Thy enemies Thy footstool," and in other words: "Thy throne, O God is forever and ever; the scepter of Thy kingdom is a scepter of uprightness. Thou hast loved justice, and hated iniquity; therefore God, Thy God hath anointed Thee with the oil of gladness above Thy fellows (Ps. 45: 7–8)."' (Dial. 56)

It is a Jew, not Justin, who admits that another divine being, 'The Lord', was present at the destruction of Sodom and Gomorah, and that this divine being was different from God. Genesis 19: 24 is actually mentioned by the rabbis as the source of heresy (b. Sanh. 38b), where the defence against heresy is attributed to the Tanna R. Ishmael b. Yosi (CE 170–200). From our previous discussion, there is no reason to doubt that such heterodox Jews existed as early as Philo. Justin only endeavoured to prove that this second divinity is the Christ. It is significant that the angelic figure is accepted by the Jew, only his messianic status is questioned. This is another piece of evidence that Christianity was the first to connect the messiah and the principal angel. In this place Judaism relies primarily on the various descriptions of vindication and enthronement found in the Psalm texts.

Like Philo, Justin calls the λόγος another God (ἕτερος θεός), distinct in number, if not in essence (ch. 56; see also 127). The sharply drawn personality of this manifestation, together with the doctrine of the incarnation, is the element which most distinguishes Justin's concept of λόγος from Philo's. But, as Goodenough has persuasively argued, both Justin and Philo should be understood to express variants of the same Hellenistic Jewish traditions.[14] Like Philo, Justin believes the λόγος is an angel in that it is a power (δύναμις) radiating from God. Like the angels it has freedom of choice, but unlike the angels, Justin's λόγος has self-direction (ch. 88). Therefore, although Justin implies that the λόγος is the same as an angel, he prefers to emphasize its distinctiveness in ways that never occurred to Philo.

As further evidence that these traditions had a background in Hellenistic Judaism before they were put to Christian use,

---

[14] E. R. Goodenough, *The Theology of Justin Martyr: An Investigation into the Conceptions of the Earliest Christian Literature and its Hellenistic and Judaistic Influences* (Jena: Verlag Frommannsche Buchlandlung, 1923), 147 ff.

Goodenough shows that most of the titles applied to the λόγος by Justin are the same as those used by Philo and other Hellenistic Jewish writers: θεός, κύριος, ἄγγελος, δύναμις, ἀνατολή, λίθα, πέτρα, ἀρχή, ἡμέρα, φῶς, σοφία, ἀνήρ, ἄνθρωπος, Ἰσραήλ, Ἰακώβ, etc.[15]

As Justin says:

'So my friends,' I said, 'I shall show from Scripture that the God has begotten of Himself a certain rational power as a beginning before all other creatures. The Holy Spirit indicates this power by various titles, sometimes the Glory of the Lord, at other times, Son or Wisdom or Angel or God or Lord or Word. He even called himself the commander-in-chief when he appeared in human guise to Josue, the son of Nun.' (Dial. 61, 244)

One of the most significant titles is 'the Glory of the Lord', which links the figure with the λόγος of the fourth gospel and also the human figure on the throne which Ezekiel saw. To substantiate the claim of the λόγος's primacy in the divine economy, Justin points to the grammatical plural referring to God in Genesis 1: 26 and Genesis 3: 22 (Dial. 62). After this he adduces passages to support the incarnation from the virgin birth to the ascension (Dial. 63–5). Of course, the argument is not well received by his Jewish opponents, even those who admit the existence of the second power, so Justin goes over the same scripture from a variety of different perspectives. At one point he goes into a rather fanciful exegesis to show that the name of God, which the angel in Exodus 23: 21 carried, is 'Jesus', a motif which cannot be original to the name of God tradition:

Now from the book of Exodus we know that Moses cryptically indicated that the name of God himself (which He says was not revealed to Abraham or to Jacob) was also Jesus. For it is written: 'And the Lord said to Moses, say to this people: Behold, I send my angel before thy face, to keep thee in thy journey, and bring thee into the place that I have prepared for thee. Take notice of him, and obey his voice; do not disobey him, for he will not pardon thee, because My name is in him.' Consider well who it was that led your fathers into the promised land, namely he who was at first named Auses (Osee), but later renamed Jesus (Josue). If you keep this in mind, you will also realize that the name of him who said to Moses, 'My name is in him,' was Jesus. Indeed he was also called Israel, and he similarly bestowed this name upon Jacob. (Dial. 75)[16]

---

[15] Ibid. 168–72.
[16] Probably another form of the traditions evinced in the Prayer of Jacob lies behind this argument.

While it is clear that Justin is using 'two powers' traditions to describe Jesus as λόγος and Christ, the traditions could have hardly originated with the identification of Jesus as the angel in Exodus. The attempt to see Jesus (Joshua) as the angel's name is secondary. Rather, Justin is taking over a previous exegetical, possibly mystical tradition, applying the name of his particular saviour, and defending his belief against the other candidates for the office of angelic mediator. The tradition itself, without the Christian colouring, can be seen as early as Philo. Some of this tradition can be seen in Ignatius' *Letter to the Antiochenes*, 2. Here Ignatius makes use of the same biblical traditions and especially Genesis 19: 24 to demonstrate that both Lord and God are divine. He does not use the *logos* doctrine, however.

But this is not the only way in which two powers language in Hellenistic Judaism is used in Christian discourse as well. One of the earlier arguments between 'orthodoxy' and 'heresy' is also profoundly influenced by 'two powers' language growing out of an exacerbated polemical context. Polemic was present in earliest Christian life. The Gospel of Thomas, which is often parallel to the synoptic tradition, says:

Jesus said, 'Whoever blasphemes against the Father will be forgiven, and whoever blasphemes against the son will be forgiven, but whoever blasphemes against the holy spirit will not be forgiven, either on earth or in heaven.'

'Truly, I say to you, all sins will be forgiven the sons of men, and whatever blasphemies they utter; but whoever blasphemes against the Holy Spirit never has forgiveness, but is guilty of an eternal sin.' (Mark 3: 28–9)

'Therefore I tell you, every sin and blasphemy will be forgiven men, but the blasphemy against the Spirit will not be forgiven. And whoever says a word against the Son of man will be forgiven; but whoever speaks against the Holy Spirit will not be forgiven, either in this age or in the age to come.' (Matt. 12: 31–2)

'And every one who speaks a word against the Son of man will be forgiven; but he who blasphemes against the Holy Spirit will not be forgiven.' (Luke 12: 10)

This passage has clearly developed in a polemical context. In its original setting, probably in Mark, it cautions against criticizing the workings of the Holy Spirit. In its Lucan and Matthean version it begins to be taken up into debate on the nature of Christ's divinity.

It identifies Jesus with the Son of Man securely. By the time of the version in the Gospel of Thomas, we have a mature trinitarian statement which is now considered to be sacrosanct. The Gospel of Thomas, therefore, has undergone considerable development with regard to this particular saying.

Several traditions corresponding to the rabbinic ones are found in another second-century Church Father, Theophilus of Antioch.[17] His relationship with Midrashic traditions has been noticed before, but no conclusions have previously been drawn about his relationship to the 'two powers' controversy. He too uses Christ as equivalent to *logos*, on the basis of John 1, but he uses several interesting scriptural quotations to prove his point (*Ad Autolycum*, 1: 3; 2: 22; also Gen. 1: 26 is used in 2: 18). He witnesses to the traditions we saw in Philo in which the *logos* is described as God's 'place': 'Since the *logos* is God and derived his nature from God, whenever the Father of the Universe wills to do so, He sends him into some place where he is present and is heard and seen' (*Ad Autolycum*, 2: 22).

Further, after claiming that another title for the *logos* is 'light', Theophilus could posit the idea that the *logos* helped God in the process of creation: 'The unique spirit occupied the place of light and was situated between the water and the heaven so that, so to speak, the darkness might not communicate with the heaven which was nearer to God, before God said: "let there be light"' (*Ad Autolycum*, 2: 13).

Theophilus also opposes the idea that two different gods were involved in creation—one creating man, therefore masculine in nature; the other creating woman, therefore feminine in nature:

You shall be like gods—so that no one could suppose that one god made man and another made woman, He made the two together. Moreover, He formed only man from the earth so that thus the mystery of the divine unity might be demonstrated. At the same time, God made woman by taking her from his side, so that man's love for her might be greater. (*Ad Autolycum*, 2: 28)

Irenaeus gives evidence for some of the same exegetical traditions which Justin and Theophilus evinced (see e.g. Iren. 3.6.1; 3.24.3). He uses Genesis 19: 24 quite significantly. But Irenaeus brings the scriptural passages to bear primarily against gnosticism.

---

[17] J. Barbel, *Christos Angelos* (Bonn: P. Hanstein, 1941), 61 ff.

Marmorstein noticed the relationship between Irenaeus' and the rabbis' exegesis.[18] It was, however, his opinion that the Church Fathers and the rabbis were absolutely independent and could only be explained by assuming that both were original responses to gnosticism. That is not the probable conclusion because when Irenaeus explicitly mentions some of the scriptural passages which the gnostics used, they do not correlate highly with the scriptures we are tracing. For instance, Marcosians used Genesis 1, Exodus 33: 20, Isaiah 1: 3, Hosea 4: 1, Psalm 13: 3, and Daniel 12: 9. According to Irenaeus most of these passages are useful for show-ing that Israel is ignorant of its real, high God. Therefore, the rabbinic polemic had other, earlier targets in mind.

However, when Irenaeus defends orthodoxy against the Marcionite gnostics, he himself uses 'two powers' traditions. Jesus comes from the Father, being foretold by the prophets in the following verses: Genesis 19: 24; Psalms 45: 7, 50: 1, 82: 1, 110: 1. By quoting from these passages he tries to show that the OT made mention of both the Christ (as Lord) and the Father (as God)—though, at the same time, uniquely one true God. We are familiar with the use of Psalm 110 by the NT and Genesis 19: 24 by the rabbis and Justin. The latter proved that the Son had received power to judge the Sodomites. Two of the new Psalms references—namely, Psalms 45: 7 and 82: 1—are similar to Psalm 110 in that they describe an enthronement scene, which is taken to be the enthronement of the Son in heaven. Psalm 50: 1 is more significant because it occurs as dangerous scripture in a late passage in Amoraic Midrash along with Joshua 22: 22 and 24: 19 (j. Ber. 12d–13a). There is no specific evidence to demonstrate that the other passages were used as early as Psalm 50: 1—El, Elohim, YHWH—so it is equally likely to have been used as a proof of the Trinity, though not by Irenaeus. Irenaeus uses the passage merely to prove that the Son is one with the Father. He does this because the Greek translation of the psalm used a genitive plural to translate one name of God: *Theos, Theōn kyrios* making a total of two figures. Thus, Irenaeus shows us that the enthronement and theophany passages in the OT were very important to the Christian community and, in fact, heavily used by Church Fathers to fight against the new idea that the God of the OT was not the God

---

[18] *Religionsgeschichtliche Studien*, i. 61 ff.

of salvation—a doctrine such as we find in Marcionism and gnosticism.

The heresy of 'two powers' is often related to the Church's debate about the nature of the Trinity in ways that have not yet been adequately treated. Tertullian (c.160–220) and Hippolytus (d. 235) both devoted their energies to defeating gnosticism and Marcionism (see e.g. Hippolytus, *Refutat. Omn. Haer.* 7: 17). Tertullian, for instance, accuses Marcion of believing in 'two gods' (c. *Marcion*, 1.2.1, 1.2.16). However, they are also concerned to define the orthodox nature of Christianity. In doing so, they were, more than once, charged with believing in 'two gods' by Christians of modalist and monarchianist persuasion.[19] As early as Justin's time, there were Christians who objected to the idea that the *logos* was numerically different from the High God. The first theologian of this type, of whom we have significant record, is Noetus of Smyrna. Hippolytus tells us that Noetus believed so strongly in the unity of God that he had to maintain that the Father suffered and underwent death along with the Son (patripassianism: *contra Noetum* and also *Ref.* 9; see also Epiphanius, 57.1.8). For scriptural support, he and his supporters relied on some familiar rabbinic proof texts (Exod. 3: 6, 20: 3; Isa. 44: 6; 45: 14f. and others from the NT) implying the unity of God. And, of course, from here the charge was carried down through the anti-heresiological literature. For example, Cyril rails against Marcion and Cerdo as 'two God' heretics (*Procatechesis* 6, 'of heresies' 12–13).

Tertullian also debates with the adherents of this 'modalistic' heresy. In doing so, he makes binitarian use of all of the scriptures which we have associated with the heresy of 'two powers'. Furthermore, he is at pains to show that *two Gods* are presupposed by the Bible, one who spoke at creation, the second who created (*Adv. Praxean*, 13). The second God is called 'the Christ' in various places demonstrated by using Isaiah 45: 7, Amos 4: 13, and other scriptural passages deemed dangerous by the rabbis. But he goes on to correct the implication of dualism, saying that it is not fit to derive from these scriptures a notion of two separate beings, only 'two Gods' in number: 'God forbid that there are only two gods in number'. Apparently, some modalists were accusing Tertullian of believing in 'ditheism' whereas he admits to the term 'binitarian'.

---

[19] See J. N. D. Kelly, *Early Christian Doctrines* (New York: Harper, 1958), 83–132.

By this time, it is clear that no rabbinic Jews would have granted an ounce of difference between the two conceptualizations.

The modalists also used the vocabulary of 'two gods' to express their positions. Novatian puts in the mouth of these heretics the criticism that orthodoxy believes: 'If the Father is one and the Son another, and if the Father is God and Christ God, then there is not one God, but two Gods' (*de Trin.* 30). Hippolytus also accuses Callistus of the same crime, even though the latter was presumably aware of the dangers of patripassianism. Most interesting of all, Hippolytus records one of the charges made against him by Callistus as ditheism (*ditheous*). It seems likely that the Church continued to use the stronger term 'two gods' whenever it needed a strong polemical statement against its heretics but admitted to binitarianism until such time as the doctrine of the Trinity was firmly entrenched in the third and fourth centuries. This would suggest that the synagogue must have ceased to be actively involved in polemic when it prudently changed to the designation 'two powers' at the end of the Tannaitic and beginning of the Amoraic period.

Origen (*c.*183–250), however, was heir to the Philonic tradition and is clearly influenced by middle Platonism as well, so he has no compunction about continuing the old vocabulary. He felt that the Son of God, as *logos*, could be called a *deuteros theos* (*Contra Celsum*, 5: 39, 6: 61, 7: 57; *de Oratione*, 15: 1; *Com. Ev. Joh.*, 2: 2, 10: 37). In his *Dialogue with Heraclides*, the issue between the two men is centred on the Eucharist. Apparently, both agreed that Christianity could be said to believe in 'two gods', although only in a special way: 'We are not afraid to speak, in one sense of two gods, in other sense of one God' (*Dial. Heracl.* 2. 3, Oulton. edn. 1. 124–5).

His reservations against describing Christianity as believing in 'two gods' are understandable. Jews, Christian modalists, and even pagans could accuse him of violating monotheism. In fact, he is forced to defend himself from such a charge levelled by Celsus, who says that Christians believe that two lords rule the world (*Contra Celsum*, 8: 12). By now, many different groups of people were using the same arguments in a variety of contrasting ways. Of course, wherever the charge of 'two gods' was brought, the familiar scriptural passages of Deuteronomy and Isaiah as well as 'The father and I are one' (John 10: 3), Origen can bring the passages in to defend the monotheism of Christianity, even while maintaining 'two Gods' elsewhere (see *Contra Celsum*, 2: 24).

The third and fourth centuries bring a much fuller and more interesting development of Christological discussion, and the term 'power' is central to the whole controversy, as Michel René Barnes has shown:

Indeed, I imagine that power theology had such play in the fourth century controversies precisely because of the traditional presence of power theology. The first understanding asserts that there is only one 'power of God', and identifies that divine power with the Son of the Word. In the fourth century this is the belief of Nicenes like Athanasius and Marcellus as well as some who were not Nicenes but were self-consciously anti-'Arian'. The second understanding asserts that there is only one 'power of God', the Father's own, and that the Son or the Word is identified as the 'power of God' only as a second 'imaged' power, a power produced by the first power. In the fourth century this is the belief of Arians, non- and anti-nicenes such as Asterius, Eusebius of Caesarea, Eunomius, and Palladius of Ratiaria as well as the Dedication creeds. The third understanding asserts that there is only one 'power of God', that this single power is the principle of unity in the divine, and that it is possessed commonly among the three. This is the belief of pro-Nicenes like Hilary, Ambrose, Gregory of Nyssa, and Augustine. I construct this account in the full confidence that power—δύναμις, virtus/potestas—was, for the early church, a foundational term in trinitarian theology, foundational in the way that σοφία and λόγος are understood to have been.[20]

This development may be seen as an interpretation of 1 Corinthians 1: 24 and its context: 'but to those who are the called, both Jews and Greeks, Christ the power of God and the wisdom of God' (αὐτοῖς δὲ τοῖς κλητοῖς, Ἰουδαίοις τε καὶ Ἕλλησιν, Χριστὸν θεοῦ δύναμιν καὶ θεοῦ σοφίαν). There is no question that it is also part of the philosophical vocabulary of Late Antiquity; so the verse serves as the occasion to discuss a much wider philosophical dilemma. The details of this discussion are best left to Professor Barnes, who has studied them in more detail than anyone else. But one of the discussions is particularly interesting because it also uses the vocabulary of 'two powers'—the argument between Athanasius

---

[20] Michel René Barnes, 'The Power of God: Dynamis and Gregory of Nyssa's Antieunomian Conflict', Ph.D. diss. (Toronto School of Theology of the University of Toronto: CUA at University of Toronto, exp. 1998); 'One Nature, One Power: Consensus Doctrine in Pro-Nicene Polemic', *Studia Patristica*, 29 (1997), 205–23, at 205–6.

and Origen. Origen is willing to use the terminology of 'two powers' to describe God's own eternal and proper power, the second being the derived power in the son, which has its own existence. Eusebius of Caesarea also follows this path in calling for two essences, two things, or two powers.

The alternative, that of Athanasius and the Nicene fathers, is to identify the second person as *the power of God* making the Son or Word or Wisdom of God the same as the power of God's existence. Since power is regularly regarded as part of the essence of the object according to the Hippocratic and Platonic physics assumed in this analysis, the issue of the relationship between the two persons of the Trinity is neatly resolved as an identity in essence. Power is a normal and regular aspect of the essence of substance in the same way that heat is a normal and regular part of fire.[21] As Athanasius says it: 'God has a Son, the Word, the Wisdom, the Power, that is, His image and radiance from which it at once follows that [the Son] is always; that He is from the Father; that He is like; that He is the eternal offspring of [the Father's] essence.'[22]

From this evolves Gregory's trinitarian doctrine. According to Barnes, in virtually every place where Gregory describes the unity of the Trinity, he refers to the relationship between fire and heat as an analogy for that unity.[23] Thus, from the point of view of the rabbis, all Christians seem to be 'two powers' sectarians; but from the point of view of orthodoxy, only those who incline in the direction of Origen and Eusebius are.

Among the Greek philosophers, just as among the theosophists who produced the hermetic literature, the concept of 'second god' appears to have achieved some limited use, partially based on Plato's idea of the demiurge in the Timaeus and partially based on the application of the idea to the λόγος by Philo. Numenius of Apamea, for instance, though his work survives only in fragments, is known to have been influenced by Jewish scriptures.[24] Origen, in the *Contra Celsum* (4. 52), remarks that Numenius was familiar

---

[21] See ibid. 209.

[22] See Athanasius *Discourse*, 2.18.34; NPNF 4: 368, as quoted in ibid. 214.

[21] Ibid. 219.

[24] For the history of scholarship on Numenius, see the new edition of the *Fragments*, edited by Edouard des Places (Paris: Belles Lettres, 1973). The numbering of the fragments will be according to des Places's system, not according to the numbering of Leemans.

with the scriptures of the Hebrews, which he endeavoured to synthesize with Greek philosophy by means of allegory. Numenius calls the first divinity 'The Good' or 'Reason' or 'Thought' (Fr. 16-17), even 'the Standing God' (Fr. 15).[25] But because Numenius also distinguishes radically between God and matter, he finds it necessary to assume a 'second god' who mediates the chasm while participating both in divinity and matter. With this cosmology, Numenius has appeared to many scholars as a gnostic.[26] However, he can hardly be a radical gnostic, for the soul, while divine in origin, is distributed in sentient beings through the rational agency of the second god (Fr. 13).[27] Thus, Numenius' second god is not the evil demiurge of the radical gnostics. However, when seen together with the *Hermetic Literature*[28] and possibly even the *Chaldaean Oracles*, Numenius' writing suggests that there was an occasional interest in Jewish thought among the pagan mystics and incipient neoplatonists of the second century.[29] Perhaps some philosophers like Numenius, as successors to Philo, together with gentile Christians were included among the 'nations of the world' identified by the rabbis as believing in 'two powers in heaven'. This philosophical usage of the term 'second god' in the successors of Philo may be the basis of the use of the term in rabbinic literature and the christological controversies of the second and third centuries.

[25] Notice the affinities with Philo's discussion of God, based on the LXX phrase, 'place where God stands' (Exod. 24: 10). In fact, since the study of K. S. Guthrie, *Numenius of Apamea: The Father of Neo-Platonism* (London: G. Bell, 1917), some relationship between Philo and Numenius has been generally assumed.

[26] See e.g. the study of Beutler in *Pauly-Wissowa*, Supplement 7 (1950).

[27] In this fragment Numenius uses the metaphor of a planter of a vineyard for God, as is common in Philo and Jewish tradition in general.

[28] *Deuteros theos* appears CH 8:5(16).

[29] For a more detailed study of this question, see A.-J. Festugière, *La Révélation d'Hermés Trismégiste* (Paris: J. Gabalda, 1950-3), esp. vols. iii and iv.

Patristic Witness

5

Ousia and *Hypostasis*: The Cappadocian Settlement and the Theology of 'One *Hypostasis*'

JOSEPH T. LIENHARD, SJ

I THE CAPPADOCIAN SETTLEMENT

If anyone with even a basic knowledge of the history of doctrine were asked what the 'Cappadocian settlement' was, he would undoubtedly say, 'one *ousia*, three *hypostaseis*', μία οὐσία, τρεῖς ὑποστάσεις. G. L. Prestige wrote, for example: 'The Cappadocian Settlement finally fixed the statement of Trinitarian orthodoxy in the formula of one *ousia* and three *hypostaseis*.'[1] In other words: as the orthodox response to the Arian heresy, the three Cappadocian Fathers taught that God is one *ousia* in three *hypostaseis*, thus both preserving Christian monotheism and accounting fully for the biblical confession of Father, Son, and Holy Spirit.

The Cappadocian settlement is often presented as one that was widely and readily employed, and accepted with relief and enthusiasm. But the exact formula is, in fact, more a piece of modern academic shorthand than a quotation from the writings of the Cappadocians. In the short form just quoted, the formula is rarely found in their writings. It is perhaps more common in an Alexandrian milieu, in the *De trinitate* attributed to Didymus the Blind,[2] although the authenticity of that work is much disputed. Textbooks can also be misleading. Johannes Quasten wrote that 'this formula . . . appears for the first time in the *Discourse against Arius and Sabellius*'.[3] Frances Young wrote, with even more con-

---

[1] G. L. Prestige, *God in Patristic Thought*, 2nd edn. (London: SPCK, 1952), 233.
[2] PG 39, cols. 269–992.
[3] Johannes Quasten, *Patrology*, iii (Westminster: Newman, 1960), 93. The

viction, that the *Adversus Arium et Sabellium* 'is the earliest work in
which the formula "one *ousia* and three *hypostases*" appears; was
Didymus the architect of this brilliant solution to the contentions
of the East?'[4] But the 'formula', as such, does not appear in this
work. One of the few instances of the formula in the writings of the
Cappadocians is found in Gregory of Nazianzus's *Oration on the
Great Athanasius*, in which Gregory wrote: 'We, in an orthodox
sense, say one *ousia* and three *hypostaseis*, for the one denotes the
nature of the Godhead, the other the properties of the three'.[5]

One also reads, sometimes, that the Council of Constantinople of
AD 381 canonized the formula.[6] But it is not found in the creed of
that council. The two terms *ousia* and *hypostasis* do occur together
in the letter addressed by the Synod of Constantinople of AD 382
to the Western bishops, in a passage that is more typical of
Cappadocian thought. The authors do not use *ousia* and *hypostasis*
exclusively, but three terms for what is one in God (divinity, power,
and essence), and two for what is three (subsistences and persons):
'[The 318 Fathers of Nicaea] teach us to believe in the name of the
Father, and of the Son, and of the Holy Spirit: clearly, to believe in
one divinity and power and essence [οὐσία] of the Father, Son, and
Holy Spirit; in their dignity of equal honour and in their coëternal
reign, in three most perfect subsistences [ὑποστάσεις] or three
perfect persons [πρόσωπα].'[7]

Adversus Arium et Sabellium is printed in PG 45, cols. 1281-1301, and in GNO iii/1,
71-85.

[4] Frances Young, *From Nicaea to Chalcedon* (Philadelphia: Fortress, 1983), 85.

[5] *Τῆς γὰρ μιᾶς οὐσίας, καὶ τῶν τριῶν ὑποστάσεων λεγομένων μὲν ὑφ' ἡμῶν
εὐσεβῶς—τὸ μὲν γὰρ τὴν φύσιν δηλοῖ τῆς θεότητος, τὸ δὲ τὰς τῶν τριῶν ἰδιότητας,*
(Gregory of Nazianzus, Oration 21 *On the Great Athanasius*, 35 (SC 270, 184-6;
trans. C. G. Browne and J. E. Swallow, NPNF 2nd series, vii. 279, altered)).

[6] Basil Studer e.g. writes: 'A complete picture of the extent to which the formula
mia ousia—treis hypostaseis proved significant for the history of dogma cannot be
gained without also taking into consideration the council of Constantinople (381),
which officially recognized this formula' (Basil Studer, *Trinity and Incarnation: The
Faith of the Early Church*, trans. Matthias Westerhoff (Collegeville, Minn.: Liturgical,
1993), 144). But Studer then cites the synodical letter of the Synod of
Constantinople of AD 382, quoted just below.

[7] *Πιστεύειν εἰς τὸ ὄνομα τοῦ πατρὸς καὶ τοῦ υἱοῦ καὶ τοῦ ἁγίου πνεύματος, δηλαδὴ
θεότητος καὶ δυνάμεως καὶ οὐσίας μιᾶς τοῦ πατρὸς καὶ τοῦ υἱοῦ καὶ τοῦ ἁγίου πνεύματος
πιστευομένης, ὁμοτίμου τε ἀξίας καὶ συναϊδίου τῆς βασιλείας, ἐν τρισὶ τελειοτάταις
ὑποστάσεσιν, ἤγουν τρισὶ τελείοις προσώποις* (quoted from *Decrees of the Ecumenical
Councils*, ed. Norman P. Tanner (London: Sheed & Ward, and Washington:
Georgetown University Press, 1990), i. 28). The letter is preserved by Theodoret,
Historia ecclesiastica 5, 9 (GCS Theodoret, 289-94).

More typically, the Cappadocians used a range of three or four terms to speak of what is one in God, and what is three. Gregory of Nyssa can serve as a good example. In his *Oratio catechetica magna* he speaks of a 'distinction of *hypostaseis* in the unity of the nature'.[8] In a passage in his *Refutatio confessionis Eunomii* he does employ both *ousia* and *hypostasis*.[9] In his work *To Ablabius* Gregory writes of confessing three *hypostases*, and recognizing no distinction of nature in them, but one divinity of the Father and the Son and the Holy Spirit.[10] In the same work he writes of the doctrine of the *hypostases*, of which the nature is one,[11] and of saying 'the three *hypostases*' and one God.[12]

Nor was the acceptance of such a formula—specifically, of the phrase 'three *hypostaseis*'—so ready. To give, at this point, only one example: in a tone that verges on hysteria (in itself not unusual for him), Jerome, c.376, wrote to Pope Damasus about the phrase 'three *hypostases*' that he had just heard: 'Accordingly, now—O woe!—after the Nicene creed, after the Alexandrine decree (with the West equally in accord), I, a Roman, am importuned by the Campenses, that offspring of Arians, to accept a newfangled term, "three *hypostaseis*." What apostles, pray tell me, authorized it? What new Paul, teacher of the Gentiles, has promulgated this doctrine?'[13]

---

[8] Διάκρισις ὑποστάσεων ἐν τῇ ἑνότητι τῆς φύσεως (*Oratio catechetica magna* I, I (GNO iii/4, 8)).

[9] 'In regard to essence (οὐσία) he is one (ἕν); . . . but in regard to the attributes indicative of the persons (ὑποστάσεις), our belief in Him is distinguished into belief in the Father, Son, and Holy Spirit' (*Refutatio confessionis Eunomii* 6 (GNO ii, 314-15); trans. NPNF, 2nd series, v. 102 (altered)).

[10] *Ad Ablabium* (GNO iii/1, 38).

[11] Ibid. (GNO iii/1, 40-1).

[12] Ibid. (GNO iii/1, 46).

[13] Jerome, Ep. 15, 3 (trans. Charles Christopher Mierow, *The Letters of St. Jerome* 1, ACW 33 (New York: Newman, 1963), 71 (altered)). The identity of the 'Campenses' is uncertain; but they are probably representatives of the homoeousian party. Jerome wrote this letter after he had heard the teaching of Apollinaris of Laodicea but before he heard Gregory of Nazianzus and Didymus the Blind, who accepted 'three *hypostaseis*'. The passage continues: 'We ask what three *hypostaseis* may be supposed to signify. "Three subsistent persons," they say. We reply that this is what we believe. The meaning is not enough for them; they demand the word itself, because some bane lies hid in its syllables. We exclaim: "Whosoever does not confess three *hypostases* as three *enhypostata*, that is, in the sense of three subsistent persons, let him be anathema!" And because we have not uttered the specific terms we are adjudged heretics. "Furthermore, whosoever interprets *hypostasis* as *ousia* and does not say that there is one *hypostasis* in three persons, he is a stranger to Christ." By reason of this confession you and I are alike marked with the brand of

In contrast, the Easterners found the Westerners obtuse and their language deficient.[14]

In what follows, my goal is quite limited. I would like, first of all, briefly to trace the history of the formula. This part, admittedly, is more concerned with words than ideas. It looks precisely to the gradual growth of a distinction in meaning between *ousia* and *hypostasis*, and to their gradually increasing use as technical terms in reflection on the one God whose name is Father, Son, and Holy Spirit. I will then describe another current, the current that resisted the confession of three *hypostaseis*, and suggest that it was much stronger, and much more widespread, than is normally assumed. This part is concerned with an idea, the impact of which was loaded into a single word. There existed in the fourth century a theological tradition that gradually blended with the larger tradition on all points but one: it resolutely refused to use the phrase 'three *hypostaseis*' of God. As an addendum to this section, Basil of Caesarea is viewed as one of the more petulant and impatient opponents of this tradition. Finally, I would like to suggest some possible conclusions. I do not venture into contemporary systematic questions, although some of the points raised here are the result of conversations with Fr. Piet Schoonenberg, SJ, who has read some of my work and encouraged me to look for its implications.

I do not offer a uniform translation of *ousia* and *hypostasis*. Such a refusal arises not only from cowardice, but also from the recognition of a fact: fourth-century authors themselves were wary of

union' (ibid. 71–2). This last phrase, which translates 'inurimur cauterio unionis', may suggest an accusation of unitarianism. W. H. Fremantle (NPNF, 2nd series, vi. 19) translates the phrase 'branded with the stigma of Sabellianism', which is probably a good interpretation.

[14] Basil wrote (Ep. 214, 4): 'As to the point that person and substance are not the same thing, even the brethren of the West themselves, as I believe, subscribe to this, in as much as they were aware of the poverty of their own language and gave the word for substance in the Greek tongue, in order that, if there should be any distinction of meaning, it might be preserved in the well-defined and unconfused differentiation of the terms' (trans. Roy J. Deferrari, *St. Basil: The Letters*, LCL, iii. 233–5). Gregory of Nazianzus was sharper, writing of the use of *ousia* and *hypostasis*: 'The Italians mean the same, but, owing to the scantiness of their vocabulary, and its poverty of terms, they are unable to distinguish between Essence and Hypostases, and therefore introduce the term Persons, to avoid being understood to assert three Essences. The result, were it not piteous, would be laughable' (*Oration* 21, 35 (trans. Browne and Swallow, NPNF, 2nd series, vii. 279)).

explaining the meaning of the two words, and generally resorted to comparisons rather than definitions. As will be shown below, the words were perceived, first and foremost, as synonyms. Hence they will be left in transcription.

Basil Studer offers a precaution,[15] and I gratefully repeat it here. Dogmatic formulas such as 'one *ousia* in three *hypostaseis*' have limited value. They have little place in the Church's preaching, and occur mostly in apologetic or polemical writings, or in works addressed to intellectuals. Creeds, for example, contain a confession of the one God who is Father, Son, and Holy Spirit, but generally do not include the word 'Trinity', or dwell on abstract terms like *ousia* or *hypostasis*. The Church prays to almighty God through Jesus Christ his Son in the Holy Spirit. The formula 'one *ousia* in three *hypostaseis*' was crafted on the workbench of theologians; and even for them, it is more of a convenient abbreviation than the last word that might be uttered.

II History of the Formula

In standard Greek, and in Christian theological usage for much of the fourth century, the words *ousia* and *hypostasis* were synonyms. The history of the formula is the history of the growth of a distinction in meaning between them, and the fact that the Cappadocians had to struggle to explain the distinction shows that it was anything but obvious.

Fourth-century Greek had three words for something that subsists: οὐσία, ὑπόστασις, and (in one of its senses) ὕπαρξις; to these three nouns there corresponded three verbs that mean 'to subsist': εἶναι, ὑφίστασθαι, and ὑπάχειν.

In Christian usage, the words were also synonyms, at least until the later fourth century. The Council of Nicaea, in its anti-Arian anathemas, used the words *ousia* and *hypostasis* as parallel (but not, therefore, necessarily as synonyms).[16] The Western Council of Sardica wrote of 'one *hypostasis* (which the heretics themselves call

---

[15] Studer, *Trinity and Incarnation*, 141–2.

[16] Τοὺς δὲ λέγοντας· . . . ὅτι . . . ἐξ ἑτέρας ὑποστάσεως ἢ οὐσίας . . . ἀναθεματίζει ἡ καθολικὴ ἐκκλησία (August Hahn, *Bibliothek der Symbole und Glaubensregeln der Alten Kirche*, 3rd edn. (repr. Hildesheim: Georg Olms, 1962), §142, pp. 161–2). The phrase rejects the assertion that the source of the Son's being was other than the Father.

ousia)'.[17] Fifty years later Jerome, who had learned Greek in the East, could write, 'The entire school of secular literature recognizes *hypostasis* as no different than *ousia*.'[18] Epiphanius of Salamis also wrote that they are synonyms.[19]

As the writings of Athanasius show, for more than thirty years after Nicaea, the attention of theologians and controversialists was not centred on the word *homoousion*, or on any other technical term. It was the Synod of Sirmium in AD 357 that drew attention to such terms, precisely by prohibiting their use: 'But inasmuch as some or many were troubled about substance (*substantia*), which in Greek is called *usia*, that is, to make it more explicit, *homousion* or the term *homoeusion*, there ought to be no mention of these at all and no one should preach them.'[20] The Homoeousian Synod of Ancyra in AD 359, shocked into action by the Blasphemy of Sirmium, still used the two terms as synonyms.[21]

The beginning of a change is attested by Marius Victorinus (who stands quite outside the tradition); he reported, *c.*360, that some Greeks were speaking of 'three *hypostaseis* out of one *ousia*'.[22]

The Synod of Alexandria, which took place in AD 362, was a decisive moment. At this synod, held after he returned from his third exile, Athanasius tried to reconcile the opposing parties in Antioch. The church there was divided over loyalty to two, then three, bishops. The party that was loyal to Eustathius (who had been deposed by the Arians just after the Council of Nicaea) was led by Paulinus. The situation was exacerbated when Lucifer of Calaris hastily ordained Paulinus a bishop in 361. Another, larger group was loyal to Meletius, whose theological identity remains disputed. The Arians gave their loyalty to Euzoius.[23] As long as the

---

[17] Μίαν εἶναι ὑπόστασιν, ἣν αὐτοὶ αἱρετικοὶ οὐσίαν προσαγορεύουσι (Hahn, *Bibliothek*, §157, p. 188).

[18] *Ep.* 15, 4 (trans. Mierow, ACW 33, 72).

[19] *Panarion* 69. 72. 1 (GCS Epiphanius iii. 220).

[20] Quoted from J. N. D. Kelly, *Early Christian Creeds*, 3rd edn. (London: Longman, 1972), 285–6. The spelling of Greek terms is kept from the Latin original. Hilary (*De synodis* 11) preserves the Latin original (repr. in Hahn, *Bibliothek*, §161, p. 200). Athanasius has a Greek translation in *De synodis* 28. Hilary (*De synodis* 10) named this document the 'Blasphemy of Sirmium'.

[21] See Epiphanius, *Panarion* 73. 12. 3 (GCS Epiphanius iii. 285).

[22] Marius Victorinus, *Adversus Arium* 2, 4; 3, 4 (CSEL 83, 178 and 198).

[23] See Kelley McCarthy Spoerl, 'The Schism at Antioch since Cavallera', in Michel R. Barnes and Daniel H. Williams (eds.), *Arianism after Arius: Essays on the Development of the Fourth Century Trinitarian Conflicts* (Edinburgh: T & T Clark, 1993), 101–26.

church in this patriarchal see remained divided, doctrinal consensus could never be achieved. In the justly famous *Tome to the Antiochenes*, sent by Athanasius and other Egyptian bishops to Antioch, the Meletians were granted the validity of the expression 'three *hypostaseis*', while the Eustathians were accepted as confessing 'one *hypostasis*'.[24] After his death, Athanasius was praised by Gregory of Nazianzus for his diplomatic skill at this synod: 'He conferred in his gentle and sympathetic way with both parties, and after he had carefully weighed the meaning of their expressions, and found that they had the same sense, and were in nowise different in doctrine, by permitting each party to use its own terms, he bound them together in unity of action.'[25] But the importance of this concession lay only in Athanasius' tolerance of the two formulas; the *Tome* did not relate the two expressions to each other or distinguish them in meaning. Athanasius himself continued the old usage and, a decade later, still wrote of *ousia* and *hypostasis* as synonyms.[26]

Basil of Caesarea was the first to attempt to distinguish explicitly between *ousia* and *hypostasis*. Eunomius of Cyzicus had identified unbegottenness (ἀγεννησία) with God's essence (οὐσία), and concluded that the Son, as begotten, could not be God. Basil contended that unbegottenness was proper to the Father, not common to all three.[27] In epistle 125, the confession of faith dictated for Eustathius of Sebaste in AD 373, Basil insisted that the terms *ousia* and *hypostasis* were distinct in meaning, without defining them. Sabellians, he wrote, take *hypostasis* and *ousia* to be the same thing, with an appeal to the anathemas of the Creed of Nicaea.[28] In another letter[29] Basil dealt with a neo-Arian charge against himself, that he said that the Son is 'one in being with the Father in his *hypostasis*' (ὁμοούσιος κατὰ τὴν ὑπόστασιν). He replies that to speak of the one *hypostasis* of Father, Son, and Holy Spirit, while teaching the distinction of *prosôpa*, leaves one open to a charge of Sabellianism. He repeats his point, made in epistle 125, that

---

[24] *Tome to the Antiochenes* 5 (PG 26, cols. 801A and C).
[25] Gregory of Nazianzus, Oration 21 *On the Great Athanasius*, 35 (trans. Browne and Swallow, NPNF, 2nd series, vii. 279).
[26] *Epistula ad Afros* 4 (PG 26, col. 1036B).
[27] Basil, *Contra Eunomium* 2, 28 (PG 29, col. 637).
[28] Basil, Ep. 125, 1 (ed. Yves Courtonne, *Saint Basile: Lettres* (Paris: Les Belles Lettres, 1957–66), ii. 31).
[29] Ep. 214, 3 (ed. Courtonne, ii. 204).

hypostasis and *ousia* are not the same thing, but now adds an explanation: *ousia* is related to *hypostasis* as the common (τὸ κοινόν) to the proper (τὸ ἴδιον);[30] the Son is *homoousion* with the Father, but the Father, Son, and Holy Spirit must each be confessed in his own *hypostasis*.[31] In another letter (epistle 236 to Amphilochius) Basil repeats the distinction again, but this time adds a defence of using *hypostasis* and not *prosôpon*, a remark probably directed at the Marcellians: 'And those who say that οὐσία and ὑπόστασις are the same are forced to confess different "persons" (πρόσωπα) only, and in hesitating to speak of three "subsistents" (ὑποστάσεις) they fail to avoid the evil of Sabellius.'[32]

Gregory of Nazianzus seldom paired one *ousia* with three *hypostaseis*. The word he preferred for what is one in God was *physis*. Anthony Meredith writes that it is to Gregory 'that we owe the formula of one nature and three hypostases'.[33] Gregory had other concise formulas for what is one in God, just as he employs several terms for what is three. He writes, for example: 'If our hymn has been worthy of its theme, it is the grace of the Trinity, of the Godhead one in three';[34] or: 'The aim is to safeguard the distinctness of the three persons (*hypostaseis*) within the single nature and quality (*physis, axia*) of the Godhead.'[35] He writes that Sabellius contracts 'the Three into One, instead of defining the One in Three Personalities' (μίαν φύσιν ἐν τρίσιν ἰδιότησιν); and: 'But they [Gregory's flock] worship the Father and the Son and the Holy

[30] Basil (Ep. 214, 4 (ed. Courtonne, ii. 205)) also names the distinguishing characteristics of the three *hypostaseis*: 'So even here the concept of existence or substance [οὐσία] is generic, like goodness, divinity, or any other abstract concept; but the person is perceived in the special character of fatherhood, or sonship, or of holy power' (trans. Roy J. Deferrari, *St. Basil: The Letters*, LCL, iii. 235). Gregory of Nazianzus defined the *idia* more neatly as unbegottenness, generation, and procession: ἀγεννσία, γέννησις, and ἔκπεμψις or πόρευσις (Oration 25, 16 (SC 284, 198)); cf. 26, 19 (SC 284, 270–2); 29, 2 (SC 250, 178–80); 31, 29 (SC 250, 310–12)).
[31] Ep. 214, 4 (ed. Courtonne, ii. 204–6).
[32] Ep. 236, 6 (ed. Courtonne, ii. 54; trans. Deferrari, LCL, iii. 403, altered). Deferrari's printed translation reads: 'And those who say that substance and persons are the same are forced to confess different Persons only, and in hesitating to speak of three Persons they fail to avoid the evil of Sabellius.' He translates both *hypostasis* and *prosôpon* as 'person', and does not distinguish plural from singular.
[33] Anthony Meredith, *The Cappadocians* (Crestwood, NY: St Vladimir's, 1995), 44, citing *Oration* 31, 9 (see below).
[34] *Oration* 28, 31 (trans. and ed. Frederick W. Norris, ed., *Faith Gives Fullness to Reasoning: The Five Theological Orations of Gregory Nazianzen* (Leiden: Brill, 1991), 244).
[35] *Oration* 31, 9 (ibid. 283).

Spirit, One Godhead; God the Father, God the Son and (do not be angry) God the Holy Spirit, One Nature in Three Personalities, intellectual, perfect, Self-existent, numerically separate, but not separate in Godhead.'[36] Elsewhere he writes that God is one Light and three, three *idiotêtes* or *hypostaseis* or *prosôpa*, but one *ousia* and *theotês*.[37]

Gregory of Nyssa further clarified the distinction between *ousia* and *hypostasis*,[38] especially in his *Contra Eunomium* and his treatise *On the Distinction between* Ousia *and* Hypostasis (usually printed as Basil, ep. 38). In this well-known treatise, Gregory's opponents are those who consider *hypostasis* and *ousia* as synonyms. He explains *koinon* as genus, *idion* as individual, just as 'man' is generic and Peter, Andrew, and John are individuals. The word *hypostasis* clarifies 'what is said proper to the individual' (τὸ ἰδίως λεγόμενον) while *ousia* designates 'what is common and uncircumscribed' (τὸ κοινόν τε καὶ ἀπερίγραπτον).[39] Gregory also undertakes one of the few attempts made to specify the sense of *hypostasis*: 'it is the conception which, by means of the specific notes it indicates, restricts and circumscribes in a particular thing what is general and uncircumscribed'.[40]

Thus, it is clear that the 'Cappadocian settlement' was less than it is often taken to be. Slowly, and in relatively few places, Basil of Caesarea began to insist on a distinction between *ousia* and *hypostasis*; and Gregory of Nyssa generally explained the distinction with a comparison without providing definitions of the two terms.

III THE MIAHYPOSTATIC TRADITION

The Cappadocian settlement met with resistance from several quarters. Resistance came, of course, from the neo-Arians, of whom Eunomius was the best known. Eunomius identified God's essence as unbegottenness, and concluded that the begotten Son

---

[36] *Oration* 33, 16 (SC 318, 192–4; trans. Browne and Swallow, NPNF, 2nd series, vii. 334 (altered)). Cf. also *Oration* 25, 17 (SC 284, 198).

[37] *Oration* 39, 11 (SC 358, 170). Gregory here identified *prosôpon* with *hypostasis*, thus placing a stronger emphasis on the divine unity.

[38] See *Refutatio confessionis Eunomii* 205 (GNO ii. 399).

[39] *Ep.* 38, 3 (ed. Courtonne, i. 82–4).

[40] Ἡ τὸ κοινόν τε καὶ ἀπερίγραπτον ἐν τῷ τινὶ πράγματι διὰ τῶν ἐπιφαινομένων ἰδιομάτων παριστῶσα καὶ περιγράφουσα [ἔννοια] (*Ep.* 38, 3 (ed. Courtonne, i. 82–3)).

was therefore not God. Both Basil and Gregory of Nyssa wrote extensive works against Eunomius.

But resistance also came from another direction, too; and one of its most vocal proponents was Marcellus of Ancyra. In older histories of dogma, Marcellus is treated as a lone figure, the odd heretic who professed an expanding and contracting Godhead, and against whom the clause in the Creed of Constantinople, 'of his kingdom there will be no end', is directed. Such histories see him as one dismissed as a heretic in the 330s and soundly (but anonymously) criticized by Athanasius in the *Fourth Oration against the Arians*. Both Newman and Gwatkin[41] held that the *Fourth Oration* was authentic, and thus that Athanasius rejected and refuted Marcellus. Once the authenticity of the *Fourth Oration* is denied (as it now universally is), then evidence that Athanasius rejected Marcellus evanesces.[42] Not only that, but other evidence can then be reinterpreted: evidence that Athanasius remained in communion with Marcellus, and also in theological sympathy with him. And they were not alone: the Westerners, especially the Romans, remained sympathetic to the sort of theology that Athanasius and Marcellus represented. So did the party of Paulinus at Antioch, and some bishops in Greece, too. Study of documents from the fourth century shows that there existed a theological tradition that was ready to oppose the Arians' teaching, but also insisted that it was proper to call God one *hypostasis*, just as He was called one *ousia*. Elsewhere I have named this tradition 'miahypostatic theology';[43] it was more widespread, and more tenacious, than is generally assumed.

Miahypostatic theology can be described in a typical or ideal form.[44] Its point of departure is strict Christian monotheism. There is one God, who subsists; He is one *hypostasis*, one *ousia*, and (in some authors) one *prosôpon*. This one God utters a Word, or begets a Son, and sends forth his Holy Spirit. The miahypostatic tradition readily takes over these names from the rule of faith, and willingly

---

[41] J. H. Newman, *Arians of the Fourth Century* (London: Rivington, 1833); H. M. Gwatkin, *Studies of Arianism*, 2nd edn. (Cambridge: Deighton Bell, 1900).

[42] See Joseph T. Lienhard, 'Did Athanasius Reject Marcellus?', in Barnes and Williams (eds.), *Arianism after Arius*, 65–80.

[43] Joseph T. Lienhard, 'The "Arian" Controversy: Some Categories Reconsidered', *TS* 48 (1987), 415–37.

[44] This and the next two paragraphs are adapted from ibid. 425–6.

confesses faith in the Father, the Son, and the Holy Spirit. But it cannot readily explain, in speculative language, what the Word and the Spirit are. It hesitates to assign any plurality to the Godhead. In general, in speaking of God, saying 'one' is always safe, whereas saying 'two' is always dangerous. Plurality is rather located in the Incarnate.

The Incarnation is the decisive moment in the history of salvation, and marks a new stage in the history of the Logos. At the Incarnation God himself is united with a human nature, and thereby with human nature itself. Human nature is conceived as a collectivity, so that, when the Word assumed a human nature (ὁ ἄνθρωπος)—it also assumed—and thereby elevated—humanity in general (ἡ ἀνθρωπότης). Miahypostatic theology applied to the incarnate Christ, or to Christ's flesh, all the biblical texts that suggested the Son's subordination to the Father. It is the Incarnate, as man, who says, 'The Father is greater than I' (John 14: 28) or who knows neither the day nor the hour (Mark 13: 32). In principle, at least, this point gave these authors an opportunity to reflect on Christ's human soul or mind.

Salvation, in this tradition, is essentially a divine act by which the human race is elevated and deified, and takes place in the order of being: God acts, and the human race is thereby saved. Athanasius expressed this concept in his famous axiom, 'The Word of God became man so that man might become divine.'[45]

The sources of this tradition are not immediately obvious. Miahypostatic theology had little enthusiasm for Origen, guarded monotheism carefully, and feared predicating plurality of the Godhead; it seems to be a theology that developed, insulated from the influence of Origen (or, in the West, Tertullian), out of an older, monarchian tradition.

IV Marcellus of Ancyra and his Theology

Marcellus' life can be summarized briefly. He must have been born c.280/85. He is first mentioned as a participant in the Synod of Ancyra that met in AD 314; he is one of the signers of its *acta*.[46]

---

[45] *On the Incarnation of the Word*, 54.

[46] K. J. von Hefele and H. Leclercq, *Histoire des conciles*, i (Paris: Letouzey, 1907), 298-326.

He also attended the Council of Nicaea in AD 325, where, by his own testimony, he refuted certain men who were thereafter convicted of heresy.[47]

After the Council of Nicaea, the role of spokesman for the Eusebian party went to Asterius the Sophist, who composed a 'little book' (συνταγμάτιον), which defended the teaching of Eusebius of Nicomedia. In response to Asterius's defence of Eusebius of Nicomedia, Marcellus composed his fateful work, the *Contra Asterium*.[48] In 336 Marcellus, in Constantinople, presented the emperor with a copy of a little book, undoubtedly the *Contra Asterium*. Marcellus' book gave the Eastern bishops the chance they sought, to depose him. They did so at a synod in Constantinople in 336, and replaced him with Basil of Ancyra, later the leader of the Homoeousians. The threat that Marcellus posed appeared serious enough that Eusebius of Caesarea, the most learned of the Eastern bishops, among the last works that he composed, wrote two refutations of him: the *Contra Marcellum* and the *De ecclesiastica theologia*. For the rest of his life, almost forty years, Marcellus was either an exile or the leader of a small group of followers in Ancyra.

By accident or by agreement, Marcellus also became an ally of Athanasius. Perhaps they met in the summer of 335, at the Synod of Tyre. If not, they certainly were together in Rome in 340-1.

After 343, Marcellus is known only indirectly. He remained in communion with individuals and groups with whom Athanasius was in communion. When Athanasius, with the *Tome to the Antiochenes*, tried to reconcile the schismatic parties at Antioch in 362, his plan was precisely to have the Meletians be reconciled to the Eustathians, who were led by the presbyter Paulinus. Marcellus had consistently been in communion with the Eustathians, as Athanasius had, too. In 371, Marcellus' deacon Eugenius, writing for Marcellus and those loyal to him, asked Athanasius to confirm their orthodoxy, which Athanasius did. Marcellus died in 374. In 376, the remaining Marcellians confirmed their communion with a group of exiled Egyptian bishops. When Jerome wrote his *De viris*

---

[47] Marcellus, *Letter to Julius* (frag. 129; GCS Eusebius 4, 214-15).

[48] Its original title is unknown. It is generally called *Contra Asterium*, as Maurice Geerard does in the *Clavis Patrum Graecorum*. More recently Klaus Seibt (*Die Theologie des Markell von Ankyra* (Berlin: de Gruyter, 1994)) has suggested the title *Opus ad Constantinum imperatorem*.

illustribus in 393, he could still report that Marcellus had been in communion with Julius of Rome and with Athanasius.[49]

Although the *Contra Asterium* survives only in fragments, the fragments are extensive enough that a clear picture of Marcellus' own doctrine, and of the doctrines that he set out to refute, can be derived from them. In Marcellus' eyes, the principal, and most dangerous, of the Eusebians' theses was the assertion that the number 'two' (or 'three') could be predicated of the Godhead. The Eusebians had said that the two names 'Father' and 'Son' must have a referent in the Godhead itself.[50] 'Son' was their preferred title for the second person; 'Word', they said, was metaphorical.[51] The Eusebians held that there are in the Godhead two essences, hypostases, persons, powers, natures, objects, or Gods.[52] They described the unity of the Godhead with the word *symphônia*, harmony of will.[53] Further, they reasoned that, since there cannot be two coexisting first principles, the Father must be the source of the Son's being and thus—in this sense, at least—the Son came to be. Further, plurality in the Godhead necessarily implied subordination. They often used 1 Timothy 2: 5 ('For there is one God, and there is one mediator between God and men, the man Christ Jesus') to establish the distinction between God and Christ,[54] and Colossians 1: 15 ('He is the image of the unseen God') to show the Son's subordinate rank.[55] The Eusebians could speak of a 'first creation' of the Son,[56] or of his being 'begotten',[57] or even of Christ as a creature.[58] They saw no radical difference between the preincarnate Son and the incarnate Christ, and applied biblical titles such as 'Life', 'Way', 'Day', 'Resurrection', 'Door', and 'Bread' to the Preincarnate as easily as to the Incarnate.[59]

Marcellus's own teaching can also be gleaned from the extant fragments of the *Contra Asterium*. There is one God, who may also be called 'Father'. This God has a Logos, by which Marcellus always means 'word', and never 'reason'. God and his Word cannot be distinguished in *dynamis* or *hypostasis*, any more than a man

---

[49] Jerome, *De viris illustribus* 86.
[50] Marcellus, frag. 65. The fragments of Marcellus's *Contra Asterium* are printed in GCS Eusebius 4.
[51] Frag. 45; 46.
[52] Frag. 35; 40; 63; 67; 76; 80-4.
[53] Frag. 72-4.
[54] Frag. 100-2.
[55] Frag. 90; 93; 97.
[56] Frag. 5; 29.
[57] Frag. 3; 18; 28; 36; 96.
[58] Frag. 40.
[59] Frag. 43.

and his word can.[60] The Word is Son only from the time that the
Virgin conceived. All other titles of the Word apply to the
Incarnate.[61] Just as there is one *hypostasis* in God, there is one
prosôpon, too. Asterius had held that Father and Son are two
prosôpa. But if they are, then either the Spirit received its mission
from the Father, but not the Son, or the Spirit does not proceed
from the Father. But in God there is one *prosôpon*, one source of
action, and the Spirit proceeds from the Father and is commissioned and conferred by the Son.

One of the most distinctive characteristics of Marcellus' theology
is his refusal to apply the number 'two', in any sense, to the
Godhead: there are not two *ousiai*, or *hypostaseis*, or *dynameis*, or
prosôpa. Marcellus did not, on his own, use the terms *ousia* or
hypostasis of the Godhead; when he does use them, he is generally
quoting his opponents. His preferred word is *prosôpon*: there is one
prosôpon, one subject, in God. When he employs *hypostasis*, it is
usually in the dative, and means the reality behind the *prosôpon*.
Marcellus can argue that Exodus 3: 14 must be the words of
Father and Son, undivided in hypostasis; otherwise, when one says
'I am who am', he implies that the other is not.[62]

V MIAHYPOSTATIC THEOLOGY AFTER AD 336

Four documents allow us to trace the miahypostatic tradition up to
376, five years before the Council of Constantinople. They are
the letter that Marcellus wrote to Julius of Rome in 340 or 341;
the exposition of the faith from the Council of Sardica in 343; the
letter of Eugenius the Deacon to Athanasius in 371; and the letter
of the Marcellians to exiled Egyptian bishops of 376.

1. *Marcellus' Letter to Julius of Rome*

Julius of Rome convoked a synod there in 341. The Easterners had
originally suggested it, but then refused to send delegates. Among
other points, the synod examined Athanasius and Marcellus and

---

[60] Frag. 61. Marcellus accused the Eusebians of 'wanting to invent a second god
who is distinct from the Father in *hypostasis* and *dynamis*' (frag. 77).

[61] Frag. 43.

[62] Frag. 64.

acquitted them of heresy (in Marcellus' case) or of wrongdoing (in Athanasius' case). Julius then addressed a letter to the Eastern bishops, somewhat high-handed in tone; and this letter had fateful consequences. The letter regularly linked the names of Athanasius and Marcellus, and thus gave the impression that Athanasius and Marcellus formed one party. Moreover, undoubtedly following Athanasius' lead, Julius also called the Easterners 'Arians'. Athanasius had been deposed from office for disciplinary reasons; but, perhaps through his conversations with Marcellus in Rome, he effectively turned the dispute into a theological one. Thus, Julius' letter marked the moment when 'Arianism' as such was born— born as Athanasius' designation for all those bishops of the East who had voted to depose him, or who disagreed with him.

In his letter to Julius,[63] Marcellus accuses the Eusebians of teaching that the Son is 'another *hypostasis*', distinct from the Father. He writes that, if the Eusebians teach that the Son is a creature, then he is not God's own word and wisdom and power. Otherwise, God would have been without word, wisdom, and power before he created the Son. This created Son would then be 'another *hypostasis*, distinct from the Father'.

In the last section of the letter, Marcellus states his thesis: 'the Godhead of the Father and of the Son is indivisible'.[64] A separation of the Son–Word from God the Pantokrator would lead to unacceptable conclusions: either there are two Gods, or the Word is not God.

2. *The Exposition of the Faith from Sardica* (AD 343)

The clash between East and West reached its angriest moment at the Council of Sardica (Philippopolis) in 343. The Easterners, who had refused to be seated with the deposed bishops Athanasius and Marcellus, withdrew to Philippopolis and held a synod of their own. The Western Council of Sardica decreed that Athanasius, Marcellus, and other bishops deposed by the Easterners were innocent, and reinstated them in office.

This is a difficult document; even the text is doubtful in places.[65]

---

[63] Frag. 129.

[64] Ἀδιαίρετον εἶναι τὴν θεότητα τοῦ πατρὸς καὶ τοῦ υἱοῦ (frag. 129; GCS Eusebius 4, 215, 25).

[65] In this case the text in Hahn's *Bibliothek* must be disregarded. Friedrich Loofs published a critical edition in *Das Glaubensbekenntnis der Homousianer von Sardica*

Harnack is often quoted as saying that this exposition is the most unambiguous expression of Western thought on the Trinity.[66] It also represents Marcellus' thought more than Athanasius'. The level of hatred and anger in the synodical letter and the exposition of faith cannot have come from the Western bishops alone; the tone suggests an outburst of rage on the part of those who had suffered deposition and exile for ten or fifteen years at the hands of the Eusebian party.

The exposition begins with a challenge: the bishops confess that 'there is one *hypostasis*—which the heretics themselves call *ousia*— of the Father and the Son and the Holy Spirit'. The Son's *hypostasis* or subsistence, they say, is the same as the Father's; and they take this to mean that the Father never was and never could be without the Son, or the Son without the Father. In other words, the doctrine of one *hypostasis* is understood as affirming the eternal existence of the Son. The bishops then quote John 14: 10 and 10: 30, which Marcellus had quoted in his letter to Julius. They then need to defend themselves against the charge of denying any plurality in the Godhead: they do not deny the term 'begotten', but deny that the Son was begotten to serve as the agent of creation.[67] They explicitly reject grounding the divine unity in 'harmony' (συμφωνία) or 'agreement' (ὁμόνοια).[68] The whole passage reveals some of the weaknesses of an exclusive insistence on 'one *hypostasis*'.

Marcellus, in the *Contra Asterium*, had assigned all titles but

---

(Abh. Berlin: Königliche Akademie der Wissenschaften, 1909). The edition is filled with conjectures and corrections. Parmentier, in his edition of Theodoret (GCS), prints a more conservative text, but takes Loofs's work into consideration. The comments here are based on the most recent edition of Parmentier's text, but Loofs's article has been consulted regularly.

[66] *History of Dogma* 4, 3rd edn., trans. Neil Buchanan (New York: Dover, 1961), 68 n. 1.

[67] Theodoret, *Historia ecclesiastica* 2. 8. 41-2 (GCS Theodoret 114-15). The passage is difficult. Parmentier translates it thus: 'No one of us denies that he was begotten, but we deny that he was begotten for some end, wholly for those things that are called "unseen and seen," a begotten craftsman of archangels and angels and the world, and begotten for the human race, [just] because Scripture says: "Wisdom, the crafter of all, taught me" (Prov 8: 22) and "Through him all things came to be" (Jn 1: 3).'

[68] Ibid. 2. 8. 45 (GCS Theodoret 116), as Origen maintained in the classic passage in *Contra Celsum* 8. 12: 'They are two objects in subsistence, but one in agreement and harmony, and in the identity of their will' (ὄντα δύο τῇ ὑποστάσει πράγματα, ἓν δὲ τῇ ὁμονοίᾳ καὶ τῇ συμφωνίᾳ καὶ τῇ ταὐτότητι τοῦ βουλήματος).

'Logos' to the Incarnate. In the letter to Julius he gave up the attempt. Here the bishops—perhaps under Marcellus' influence— try to explain some titles without yielding their insistence upon saying μία ὑπόστασις.

3. *The Letter of the Deacon Eugenius to Athanasius* (AD 371)

The learned Benedictine editor of Athanasius' works, Bernard de Montfaucon, discovered *c.*1700 a short document that sheds new light on Marcellus' relations with Athanasius.[69] The document is a letter that the deacon Eugenius[70] and 'the clergy and others gathered in Ancyra of Galatia with our father Marcellus'[71] sent to Athanasius, and includes a confession of the Marcellians' faith.

The *Expositio* cannot be dated by any internal evidence. Guesses in the past have ranged from 347 through 362 to 373.[72] The text of the *Expositio* shows that Marcellus himself was with Eugenius and the others at Ancyra.[73] Zahn preferred a date *c.*371.[74] Tetz, probably correctly, believes that it was Basil of Caesarea's well-known opposition to the Marcellians that caused them to seek Athanasius' support, and hence agrees with Zahn on the date 371.

Positively, the Marcellians confess their adherence to Nicaea; they write that they believe 'as our fathers confessed at the Synod of Nicaea', and then cite the two key phrases from the Creed of Nicaea, 'from the being of the Father' (ἐκ τῆς οὐσίας) and 'one in being with the Father' (ὁμοούσιον τῷ πατρί).[75] The Marcellians formulate their own confession in a carefully phrased sentence that stresses, on the one hand, the real and eternal existence of Father, Son, and Holy Spirit, but, on the other hand, adheres just as clearly and determinedly to the doctrine of one divine *hypostasis*:

---

[69] Both the critical edition of the text and an excellent analysis are provided by Martin Tetz, 'Markellianer und Athanasios von Alexandrien. Die markellianische Expositio fidei ad Athanasium des Diakons Eugenios von Ankyra', ZNTW 64 (1973), 75-121. What follows depends heavily on Tetz's work.

[70] As Tetz (ibid. 78) suggests, this Eugenius may be identical with the deacon Hyginus, whose signature appears in the Marcellians' confession of AD 376 (in Epiphanius, *Panarion* 72. 11).

[71] *Expositio* 1, 1 (Tetz, 'Markellianer', 78).

[72] Tetz, 'Markellianer', 84-9.

[73] *Expositio* 1, 1.

[74] Zahn, *Marcellus von Ancyra. Ein Beitrag zur Geschichte der Theologie* (Gotha: F. A. Perthes, 1867), 90.

[75] *Expositio* 2, 1; cf. 3, 2.

'For we confess the eternal Father of the eternal Son, who exists and subsists, and the Holy Spirit eternally existing and subsisting. For we do not say that the Triad is not subsistent, but we acknowledge it in subsistence.'[76]

What the Marcellians clearly and obviously avoid is saying that there are three *hypostaseis* in the Godhead—or, for that matter, three of anything. They accept the term 'Triad', but not the numeral 'three'.

The Marcellians also accept three distinct functions for Father, Son, and Holy Spirit, expressed by three different prepositions. Both equality within the Triad and distinction are expressed in a noteworthy sentence: 'For our perfection is given and comes to be in Father and Son and Holy Spirit, and there is one faith in one God through the Son in the Holy Spirit.'[77] Moreover, they confess that the Word is also Son, Wisdom, and Power of the Father,[78] as Marcellus already had written in 340 in his letter to Julius of Rome.

Thus, the Marcellians have given up most of the peculiar aspects of Marcellus' teaching from the *Contra Asterium*, such as the expansion of the Godhead from a Monad to a Triad, and the univocal use of 'Word' for the Preincarnate. But they retain the aspect of Marcellus' teaching that was key to his thought: the insistence on one *hypostasis* in the Godhead.

4. *The Marcellians' Letter to Egyptian Bishops* (AD 376)

Upon the death of Valentinian in 375, neo-Arian forces again made their influence felt. Perhaps as a result of pressure from neo-Arians, eleven Egyptian bishops were exiled to Diocaesarea in Palestine. They addressed a letter (lost) to the clergy at Ancyra who had remained faithful to Marcellus and asked about their faith. The Ancyrans answered and Epiphanius preserved their letter.[79]

The Ancyrans attest that Athanasius had sent them a letter (also lost) of communion, undoubtedly in answer to Eugenius's *Expositio*

---

[76] Ἡμεῖς γὰρ ὁμολογοῦμεν πατέρα ἀΐδιον υἱοῦ ἀϊδίου ὄντος καὶ ὑφεστῶτος καὶ πνεῦμα ἅγιον ἀϊδίως ὂν καὶ ὑφεστός. οὐ γὰρ ἀνυπόστατον τὴν τριάδα λέγομεν, ἀλλ' ἐν ὑποστάσει αὐτὴν γινώσκομεν (ibid. 2, 4).

[77] Καὶ γὰρ ἡ τελειότης ἡμῶν ἐν πατρὶ καὶ υἱῷ καὶ ἁγίῳ πνεύματι δίδοται καὶ γίνεται, καὶ μία πίστις ἐστὶν εἰς ἕνα θεὸν δι' υἱοῦ ἐν πνεύματι ἁγίῳ (ibid. 3, 3).

[78] Ibid. 2, 2.

[79] The letter is in *Panarion* 72. 11-12 (GCS Epiphanius iii. 265-6).

fidei, and that they had shown this letter to the Egyptian bishops. The bishops asked the Ancyrans for a profession of faith, which the Ancyrans made in this letter. They explicitly professed the Nicene faith, and ended the letter with the creed of Nicaea and its anathemas, copied verbatim. They condemned those who say that the Holy Spirit is a creature, and—by name—the heresies of Arius, Sabellius, Photinus, and Paul of Samosata.

They also anathematized some teachings that had long been considered typical of Marcellus. The first was denying that the Holy Trinity is three *prosôpa,* uncircumscribed, subsistent, consubstantial, coeternal, and perfect in themselves.[80] The second was saying that the Son was an expansion, or a contraction, or an activity of the Father.[81] The third applies the first point to the Son: 'God the Word [is] God's Son, eternal, coeternal with the Father, subsistent and perfect in himself, the Son of God.'[82] The only crucial expression that the Marcellians do not confess is 'three *hypostases*'.[83]

Then, to reassure the Egyptian bishops, the Marcellians formulate three anathemas of their own. They read:

If anyone says that Father, Son and Holy Spirit are the same, let him be anathema.

If anyone ascribes a beginning or an end to God's Son and Word, or to his kingdom, let him be anathema.

If anyone says that the Son or the Holy Spirit is part of the Father, and does not confess that the Son of God was begotten of the Father's being before all thought (ἐπίνοια), let him be anathema.[84]

---

[80] 'Those who do not say that the Holy Trinity comprises persons that are uncircumscribed, *enhypostatic,* one in being, coeternal, and perfect in themselves' (τοὺς μὴ λέγοντας τὴν ἁγίαν τριάδα πρόσωπα ἀπερίγραφα καὶ ἐνυπόστατα καὶ ὁμοούσια καὶ συναΐδια καὶ αὐτοτελῆ) (*Panarion* 72. 11. 5 (GCS Epiphanius iii. 266)). In the *Contra Asterium* (frag. 76) Marcellus had insisted on one *prosôpon.*

[81] Πλατυσμός, συστολή, ἐνέργεια (*Panarion* 72. 11. 6 (iii. 266)). Marcellus had used 'expand' of the Monad, and called the Son the Father's activity.

[82] Τὸν θεὸν λόγον τὸν υἱὸν τοῦ θεοῦ, προαιώνιον καὶ συναΐδιον τῷ πατρὶ, καὶ ἐνυπόστατον καὶ αὐτοτελῆ υἱὸν καὶ θεόν (ibid.).

[83] See André de Halleux, 'Hypostase et "personne" dans la formation du dogme trinitaire (ca. 375–381)', *RHE* 79 (1984), 313–69, 625–70.

[84] *Panarion* 72. 12. 1 (iii. 266).

VI BASIL OF CAESAREA'S OPPOSITION TO THE PARTY OF 'ONE *HYPOSTASIS*'

The Marcellians' letter of 376 is best explained as a defensive move, made to protect themselves and their views from Basil of Caesarea; the clearest example of opposition—theological and political—to the miahypostatic tradition can be garnered from Basil's correspondence. Basil tried to propagate the phrase 'three *hypostaseis*'; and his correspondence shows how widespread the resistance to the phrase was.[85] Typical is the ominous sentence at the end of a letter Basil wrote in 375 to the clergy of Neocaesarea: 'Do not set aside the *hypostaseis*'.[86]

Soon after his election in 370, Basil of Caesarea set out to unify the non-Arian elements in the church, and to win three groups over to his side: the Western church, the Egyptian church under Athanasius' leadership, and some parties in Asia Minor who opposed him. All three showed sympathy for Marcellus of Ancyra, and all resisted, in one way or another, saying 'three *hypostaseis*'.

The first step had to be the resolution of the schism at Antioch in favour of Meletius. In Basil's mind, the one thing that would unite Athanasius and the Westerners with himself and the Meletians was the condemnation of Marcellus. Even in 371, Marcellus was hardly isolated or deserted. He was in communion with the Eustathians at Antioch under Paulinus, with Athanasius, and with bishops in Greece and Macedonia, and still evoked considerable loyalty from Athanasius.

Within a year, Basil wrote six letters to Athanasius. In his first letter,[87] he tells Athanasius that what is needed is agreement from the bishops of the West: specifically, the Westerners should condemn certain unnamed Easterners who are guilty of heresy (κακοδοξία), just as they condemned one or two Westerners. In a paragraph filled with flattery, Basil implores Athanasius to send envoys to the West to receive such condemnations. In his next letter,[88] Basil makes it clear to Athanasius that he wants all the parties at Antioch to be united under Meletius, the opposite of what

---

[85] See Joseph T. Lienhard, 'Basil of Caesarea, Marcellus of Ancyra, and "Sabellius"', *CH* 58 (1989), 157–67.

[86] Τὰς ὑποστάσεις μὴ ἀθετεῖτε (Ep. 207, 4 (ed. Courtonne, ii. 88)).

[87] Ep. 66.

[88] Ep. 67.

Athanasius intended in the *Tome to the Antiochenes*. In the following letter,[89] Basil finally shows his hand: he wants Athanasius to
secure a Western condemnation of Marcellus. Basil was impatient
with the Westerners, writing that they do not cease anathematiz-
ing Arius, but refuse to censure Marcellus.[90] Basil appealed to
Athanasius, not to be divided over the 'persons' (*prosôpa*), perhaps
using *prosôpon* in place of *hypostasis* because it would be more
acceptable to Athanasius. Basil, in a final letter,[91] reports in
unspecific terms a move towards unity on the part of those whose
faith is like his, and implores Athanasius for a general letter to
Eastern bishops. Athanasius left Basil's letters unanswered, and
never acted. Basil later complained that his letters to Athanasius
had accomplished nothing.[92]

In 376, as shown above, the adherents of Marcellus, in Ancyra,
wrote to the exiled Egyptian bishops and confirmed their own
mutual communion. But Basil of Caesarea, the relentless enemy of
Marcellus, was not satisfied with their confession. In 377 he sent a
letter to three of the Egyptian bishops. He first warned them about
Apollinaris of Laodicea's innovations, and then about 'the party of
Marcellus'. Basil is concerned particularly with the Marcellians who
want to rejoin communion. He warns the Egyptians that to readmit
such men to communion is a momentous step; once they are
satisfied with the Marcellians' orthodoxy, they should tell the
whole church what they had done. The Egyptians' action apparently caused grave scandal in some—unnamed—quarters.[93] The
Egyptians exiled in Diocaesarea must have written to Peter of
Alexandria, the new patriarch, complaining about Basil's meddling.
Peter presumably wrote to Basil and forwarded the exiles' complaint. Basil wrote a letter (ep. 266) to Peter, meekly apologizing for
the tone of his actions and for any misunderstanding he had
caused.[94] Nevertheless, Basil is willing to accept the Nicene confession of the Marcellians; and with this gesture, the last of
Marcellus' disciples are reconciled with the Church, and Marcellus'
teaching is relegated to the growing register of dead heresies.

---

[89] Ep. 69.
[90] Ep. 69, 2.
[91] Ep. 82.
[92] Ep. 89, 2 to Meletius.
[93] Basil, Ep. 265, 3. Ep. 266 to Peter of Alexandria, Athanasius's successor, also
deals with the reconciliation of Marcellians.
[94] See Zahn, *Marcellus*, 91–2.

VII CONCLUSIONS

1. The 'Cappadocian settlement', in the form of the precise phrase 'one *ousia*, three *hypostaseis*', is rare in the writings of the Cappadocians.

2. More commonly, several terms, usually *physis* ('nature') and *theotês* ('deity'), as well as *ousia*, designate what is one in God; and *idiotêtes* ('properties') and *prosôpa* ('persons'), along with *hypostasis*, are common designations for what is three in God.

3. Of all the terms used of God after the Council of Nicaea, *hypostasis* was the only one about which application to God in the singular or the plural was disputed. Hence this term, more than any other, became the focal point of theological controversy in the fourth century.

4. My own research has shown that the miahypostatic tradition was held by a group larger than is generally assumed, and one that resisted the phrase 'three *hypostaseis*' well up to the time of Constantinople I. By 376 the Marcellians had yielded on every point in Marcellus's theology that was objected to, except this one. 'Three *hypostaseis*' still sounded tritheistic to them.

5. One reason for this phenomenon is the persistent sense that both words, *ousia* and *hypostasis*, mean 'something that subsists'. In some modern interpretations, the phrase 'one *ousia* in three *hypostaseis*' is understood principally as a statement of negative theology: 'God is truly One, and God is truly Three'; the phrase is a call for silent adoration before a mystery.

6. G. L. Prestige, in his exacting analysis of Greek theological vocabulary,[95] found two different senses of the word *hypostasis*. One derives from the middle voice, or intransitive use, of the verb ὑφίστημι. In this sense, *hypostasis* means 'sediment' or 'deposit'; 'the hidden part of any object'; 'basis' or 'foundation'; and 'substance'. The other derives from the active voice, or transitive use, of ὑφίστημι. In this sense—the normal sense—it means 'support'; 'perdurability', and the 'objective resistance of solid fact'; and 'positive, concrete, distinct existence'.[96] In a summary statement Prestige wrote: 'Thus it may mean either that which underlies, or that which gives support'.[97] It is tempting to say that the two groups I have delineated simply misunderstood each other; one

[95] *God in Patristic Thought*, 162–78.   [96] Ibid. 174.   [97] Ibid. 163.

used *hypostasis* in the sense of 'substance', and could confess one *hypostasis* in God, whereas the other used it in the sense of 'positive, concrete, distinct existence', and confessed three *hypostaseis* in God. But it is always risky, if not foolhardy, to say that we understand the language of the Fathers better than they themselves did. These educated men surely understood their own language. And to many of them, well up to the end of the fourth century, 'three *hypostaseis*' said something that they did not want to say. And if Prestige's analysis is right, they did not want to say that there are three 'positive, concrete, distinct existences' in God.

7. In a sentence that is widely quoted, but perhaps misleading, Prestige also tried to explain the distinction between *ousia* and *hypostasis*. He wrote: 'Ousia tends to regard internal characteristics and relations, or metaphysical reality; while hypostasis regularly emphasises the externally concrete character of the substance, or empirical objectivity.'[98] His learning was impressive, and one hesitates to disagree with him. Yet the sentence suggests a sort of modalism.

8. Thus. the Cappadocian settlement was a gain—in clarity—but it was also a loss. The range of terms used to name God was narrowed. While the old thesis of Zahn and Harnack, that the Cappadocians were in fact Homoeousians and therefore practically tritheists has long since been refuted, and rightly so, still, the value of some names for the Second Person—such as Word, Image, Power, and Wisdom—diminished. The Cappadocian settlement still has something about it that can also be unsettling.

[98] Ibid. 188.

6

'Persons' in the 'Social' Doctrine of the Trinity: A Critique of Current Analytic Discussion

SARAH COAKLEY

I INTRODUCTION AND STATEMENT OF THESIS

Let me begin this essay by sketching out some intriguing features of the context in which the current trinitarian debate is taking place. In the remarkable recent outpouring of writing on the doctrine of the Trinity we may detect, I suggest, an interesting double paradox.

On the one hand, sophisticated logicians amongst the analytic philosophers of religion have devoted much energy to defending the so-called 'Social' (or 'Plurality') doctrine of the Trinity, whilst decrying the coherence of a 'Latin' (or 'Unity') model.[1] In so doing, however, they have—with only one or two important exceptions, to be examined below—paid relatively little attention to the *type* of entity that they are calling 'person' when they count 'three' of them in the Godhead. Indeed, when we probe a little with the tools of the hermeneutics of suspicion, we may detect distinct whiffs of influence from 'modern' perceptions of 'person' (or 'individual') smuggled into the debate, and read back into the patristic texts which are being claimed as authoritative.

On the other hand, and simultaneously, systematic theologians have been at work debunking precisely those 'modern' notions of individualism that they perceive to have distorted Christian anthropology since the Enlightenment and to have undermined trinitarian conceptuality altogether.[2] For them, construing 'persons' *as* 'rela-

---

[1] Brian Leftow's paper for this conference provides a useful introduction to this issue and the literature concerned.

[2] I think here of recent work by British theologians such as Colin Gunton, Alistair McFadyen, or (rather differently) Elaine Graham. Harriet A. Harris's article, 'Should

tions' (whatever this means exactly) has become a theological watchword. Unhappily, these two camps of scholarship, despite their shared commitment to the reinstatement of trinitarian theology, show little mutual regard for each other's work.

This paradox of intention and starting point recapitulates itself, in a rather curious way, in intra-feminist debates on the Trinity—a fact so far rarely commented upon; but this is why I speak of a 'double paradox'. On the one hand, we have the radical feminist spoof of trinitarianism (in Mary Daly's work) as the so-called 'Men's Association', a barely concealed symbolic endorsement, in Daly's view, of the all-male club, which on rare occasions admits a stereotypical 'feminine' principle into its magic circle as a token presence ('You're included under the Holy Spirit. He's feminine'[3]). Clearly what underlies Daly's deliberately 'absurd' accusation here is a deep—and not altogether unfounded—suspicion that modern patriarchal thinking has here found its projective trinitarian manifestation as an association of like-minded males. In contrast to Daly's dismissive rejection of trinitarianism, the patiently irenic work of Elizabeth Johnson on the Trinity attempts to reclaim its significance for feminism by concentrating on its celebration of 'mutuality' and 'relationship'.[4] So the divergence between analytic philosophers of religion and theologians on the Trinity is in some form recapitulated in the feminist camp: whilst Daly assumes a threefold 'individualism' in the doctrine (and rejects it), Johnson prefers to construe 'persons' *in terms of* 'relationships'.

It will be the central thesis of this paper that *neither* side in either of these somewhat curiously parallel disjunctions has fully grasped the complexity and subtlety of late fourth-century trinitarianism at its best. Moreover, it will be suggested by the end that the modern contestants' predetermined commitments to (divergent) perceptions of 'personhood' may lead, in the end, to insoluble difficulties. In arguing thus I shall take Gregory of Nyssa as my focus and example, a figure whose trinitarian contribution is often too easily conflated with that of the other 'Cappadocians', but whose pro-

We Say that Personhood is Relational?', *Scottish Journal of Theology*, 51 (1998), 214–34, contains an astute account and criticism of this strand of thinking.

[3] Mary Daly, *Gyn/Ecology* (Boston: Beacon Press, 1978), 38.

[4] See Elizabeth A. Johnson, *She Who Is* (New York: Crossroad, 1992); see e.g. 'The ontological priority of relation in the idea of the triune God has a powerful affinity with women's ownership of relationality as a way of being in the world' (p. 205).

foundly apophatic sensibilities make the assessment of the intended *status* of his trinitarian language a particularly subtle matter for reflection. One of the more surprising conclusions to which my argument will lead is that Gregory's approach to the Trinity is not 'social' in the sense often ascribed to that term today; it does not 'start' with three and proceed to the one. Nor does it attempt to 'nail' the meaning of divine *hypostasis* by particular reference to the analogy of three individual men: the analytic discussions here have been misled by an over-concentration on Gregory's *Ad Ablabium*, as well as by an insufficiently nuanced reading of that text. If we take a wider view of Gregory's corpus (and especially if we look at the rich range of imagery on the Trinity that he uses in contexts not restricted to the polemical or apologetic), a rather different perception of his trinitarian theology emerges, one which is in no doubt about the *unity* of the divine will in action, but which is highly diffident about probing the details of the nature of God in Godself beyond a certain, cautiously delimited point. Such diffidence may appear intrinsically unsatisfactory to the analytic school of philosophy of religion; but it raises questions about apophaticism that are, at the very least—or so I shall argue—worthy of greater analytic attention, and have implications for our understanding of the linguistic status of trinitarian claims.

If the gender interests of the feminist debates seem somewhat irrelevant to the analytic discussion as currently pursued, Gregory's example should also give pause for thought. The perplexing fluidity of gender reference which characterizes Gregory's trinitarian discussions as a whole gives the lie to attempts to sanitize the matter from any such taint; as we shall attempt to show, Gregory's approach demonstrates how unwise it is to dislocate trinitarian debates from the matrix of human transformation that is that Trinity's very point of intersection with our lives. If Gregory is right, moreover, such transformation is unthinkable without profound, even alarming, shifts in our gender perceptions, shifts which have bearing as much on our thinking about God as on our understanding of ourselves.

In what follows, I shall first take a brief look at the analytic defence of the 'social' doctrine of the Trinity with an eye to the notions of 'person' that may be in play here. Then I shall turn to an explication of some suitably representative trinitarian texts in Gregory, and thereby suggest that those from the analytic school who have sought to explicate his trinitarian intentions may have in large part missed the mark. (Current theology may be in no better shape, however, from such a 'Nyssan' perspective, if it seeks to *reduce* 'personhood' to 'relationality'.) I shall then suggest the implications of my analysis of Gregory for the *status* of his trinitarian language—how it stands on the literal/analogical/metaphorical spectrum now commonly utilized in analytic philosophy of religion, and what difference Gregory's profoundly apophatic perception of God makes to this account. Finally I shall give a brief account of the gender-complexities of Gregory's understanding of the process of incorporation into the life of the trinitarian God, and argue that such complexities are central, and not peripheral, to what needs to be considered in any coherent defence of the notion of God as Trinity. Whilst this short essay cannot attempt a full philosophical defence of the coherence of Gregory's viewpoint, it is intended as a first (albeit mainly exegetical) step towards undertaking such a task more fully.

II 'Persons' in the Current Analytic Defence of the 'Social' Doctrine of the Trinity

Let us first take a brief sampling of some of the more sophisticated analytic defences of the 'social' Trinity, so called, with an eye not only to how the 'social' view here is construed, but also to what notion of 'person' is in play, whether explicitly or implicitly. Because they represent rather different positions within this type, I take as my examples Peter van Inwagen, Richard Swinburne, and David Brown.

Peter van Inwagen's seminal essay applying the notion of 'relative identity' to the Trinity explicitly states that 'it is Tritheism that I shall risk'.[5] He gives the (not incontestable) following two reasons for such a move: first, that the Creeds steer us away from Modalism anyway, but second, that Modalism is nonetheless a 'far easier heresy than Tritheism to fall into in our time'.[6] This announcement (asserted rather than argued) becomes the basis for van Inwagen's

---

[5] Peter van Inwagen, 'And Yet They Are Not Three Gods But One God', in Thomas V. Morris (ed.), *Philosophy and the Christian Faith* (Notre Dame, Ind.: University of Notre Dame Press, 1988), 247.

[6] Ibid.

willingness to risk a tritheistic reading. But everything then depends on how the notion of divine 'person' is construed at the outset; and although van Inwagen acknowledges this, he irritatedly deflects the suggestion that the meaning of divine *hypostasis* might be significantly different from the 'everyday' meaning of 'person'. Without providing a definition of the latter, van Inwagen presses on regardless, merely citing the view of Peter Geach that the 'normal' (*sic*) use of 'person' ultimately owes much to the technical patristic debates about Trinity and Incarnation.[7] The upshot of this (theologically unsatisfactory) section on the notion of 'person' is that van Inwagen never clearly tells us what sort of entities are at stake in his calculus; and since logic—however sophisticated—can only formalize pre-logical intuitions, we are left with a fundamental hiatus in the argument. The strong suspicion that it is three individual people that he has visually in mind (in the 'normal' sense of 'person'?) recurs when he returns in closing to the question of the danger of tritheism and addresses the problem of the potential 'clash' of divine wills.[8] In sum, as van Inwagen himself acknowledges, his appeal to 'relative identity' can, at most, only explicate how ' "is the same being as" does not dominate "is the same person as" '; it leaves the *explanation* of such a possibility, and the nature of the persons involved, quite untouched.[9] But the overwhelming impression of the article is that divine 'persons' are not intended to be thought of as significantly different from human 'persons'.

If van Inwagen's approach merely *suggests* the model of a closely meshed community of divine individuals, Swinburne's unashamedly embraces it. The embarrassingly tritheistic overtones of his early discussion of the matter ('Could There be More than One God?'[10]), is, to be sure, significantly modified in the more recent *The Christian God*,[11] but merits brief reflection nonetheless. It is doubtless significant that an (otherwise appreciative) footnote on van Inwagen's essay chides him for making the matter unduly 'mysterious'.[12] Swinburne's alternative makes no bones about its *unmysterious* vision of three 'Gods' (*sic*), each characterized in

---

[7] Ibid. 248.
[8] Ibid. 270–1.
[9] Ibid. 271–2.
[10] *Faith and Philosophy*, 5 (1988), 225–41.
[11] (Oxford: Clarendon Press, 1994).
[12] *Faith and Philosophy*, 5 (1988), 240 n. 19.

Cartesian terms as bodiless and self-conscious 'individuals' ('individual centres of consciousness and will'), though of course also possessing the necessary divine features of omniscience, omnipotence, and so on. The initial worry is that these three individuals might want to 'annihilate' each other (granted their assumed total freedom); but on reflection this power cannot be used for such a purpose, for it would be 'bad' to do so, and each depends on the others.[13] In *The Christian God* this picture undergoes some considerable modification and clarification, but the fundamental image of three Cartesian 'individuals' endures, bound now by a more rigorously worked-out perception of their 'logical inseparability'.[14] Swinburne describes his position as a 'moderate form of social trinitarianism', and declares his sympathies to be more with Moltmann (and his 'three different consiousnesses') than with Barth's modalism.[15] It is noteworthy that Swinburne now cites Gregory of Nyssa's *Ad Ablabium* as his classic exemplar for the explication of innertrinitarian differentiation in terms of causal relations;[16] but his understanding of 'person' is, as we shall shortly show, very far indeed from Gregory's intentions in that text. It is much more the inspiration of Richard of St Victor's argument (in his *De Trinitate*, III) for the necessity of three persons' cooperation in non-possessive love that propels Swinburne's 'social' doctrine than the intricacies of Gregory of Nyssa's explicit rejection of tritheism.[17] But Swinburne transmutes the Victorine view of self into a 'modern', Cartesian one, which continues to haunt the picture even after the sophisticated modifications of *The Christian God*.

So far we have suggested that both van Inwagen and Swinburne import notions of 'person' into their 'social' doctrines of the Trinity that are implicitly, or explicitly, beholden to modern forms of 'individualism',[18] and that lead their understandings of the doctrine

[13] Ibid. 233.
[14] *The Christian God*, 189. Swinburne's definition of 'person' in this book (see p. 31: having a 'mental life of at least the kind of richness and complexity which humans have'), still shelters a fundamentally 'Cartesian' set of presumptions in which one is 'constituted' by having a 'soul', which is then 'connected to a human body' (p. 26).
[15] Ibid. n. 26.
[16] ibid. 184.
[17] See ibid, 190-1.
[18] At the Summit, conversation focused on what qualifies as a 'modern' view of 'individualism'. Autonomy, privacy, individual rights, and reflective self-consciousness were all suggestions made by William Alston, who was the respond-

to veer dangerously towards tritheism. The same charge can by no means be brought against David Brown, who above all such 'social' trinitarians has given the greatest amount of thought to the perils of importing anachronistic notions of 'person' into the patristic texts, and has attended to Gregory of Nyssa's work on the Trinity with especial care.[19] I wish here only to draw attention to two (to me puzzling) features of Brown's distinguished contribution to this debate. The first is, that despite previous disavowals of such a solution, Brown finally utilizes a 'modern' notion of 'person' (as 'self-conscious') in his construal of the Trinity, but shifts the locus of this self-consciousness to the Godhead as a whole, rather than to the three 'persons'.[20] Obviously this represents a considerable modification of the triplicated 'centres of consciousness' model, such as we saw in Swinburne, and it also marks a significant strengthening of Brown's own earlier position (in *The Divine Trinity*) that the 'persons' might be seen as unified merely in the way that some couples are unified in a 'successful marriage'.[21] But it raises the question why 'self-consciousness' *need* be the defining characteristic of divine 'personhood' at all, especially granted Brown's underscoring of the lack of attention to this criterion in the patristic period, and the complications Brown's 'solution' creates in splitting 'consciousness' and 'self-consciousness' apart in the Trinity.[22] Gregory of Nyssa, as we shall see, is more interested in underscoring the unity of divine *will* in the Trinity (and it remains unclear to me on Brown's analysis how many 'wills' are in play there).

The other point of exegetical contention raised by Brown's analysis is precisely the extent to which Gregory can be constrained into the category of 'social' trinitarianism *as Brown understands it*. Brown is himself admirably explicit about his under-

ent to my paper. David Brown's discussion of the modern overtones of this term is useful here: see his 'Trinitarian Personhood and Individuality', in Ronald J. Feenstra and Cornelius Plantinga (eds.), *Trinity, Incarnation, and Atonement* (Notre Dame, Ind.: University of Notre Dame Press, 1989). Brown distinguishes 'individualism' (with the overtones of autonomy) from 'individuality' and 'individuation'. I do intend the definition of 'individualism' as given here.

[19] See ibid. and also *idem, The Divine Trinity* (London: Duckworth, 1985), and *idem*, 'Trinity' in Philip L. Quinn and Charles Taliaferro (eds.), *A Companion to Philosophy of Religion* (Oxford: Blackwell, 1997), 525–31.

[20] 'Trinitarian Personhood and Individuality', 69.

[21] *The Divine Trinity*, 300.

[22] See again 'Trinitarian Personhood and Individuality', 57ff.

standing of (what he chooses to call) the 'Plurality Model' (PM); and it is clear that he sees Gregory as the prime historical instantiation of the type. For Brown, 'PM [is] the belief that what is fundamentally a trinitarian plurality is also ultimately a unity in the Godhead'; what is at stake then is whether one 'starts' with the 'threefoldness', as is the case with PM.[23] Put in experiential terms, PM implies that 'the experience of distinct Personhood antedates the realisation of a common identity'.[24] On Brown's reading, Gregory's utilization of the trinitarian analogy of individual men and the genus of humanity allows us to read him as a PM trinitarian in the sense described, and even also entitles us to find in him something close to a 'modern' concept of the person.

It is precisely these claims that I would now like to move to question. It will I trust have become clear from this section of the essay (as more fully in Brian Leftow's careful analysis[25]) that 'social' trinitarianism can come in more than one form, and—unsurprisingly, granted the intense contemporary philosophical debate on the defining characteristics of 'personhood'[26]—that the notion of 'person' in play is also capable of variation. What we have noted in each of the cases discussed, however, is the presumption that on a 'social' model one *starts* with the 'three'—whose individual identities are at least initially clearly and distinctively bounded—and that the task thereafter is to account for the unifying *community* which they share.

Is this then what Gregory of Nyssa is doing? I shall now argue that his trinitarianism subscribes to none of the features just described.

---

[23] See *The Divine Trinity*, 243.

[24] Ibid. 287.

[25] See Brian Leftow, 'Anti Social Trinitarianism' (Ch. 9 of this book), pp. 203-49.

[26] See e.g. the range of opinions expressed in Amélie Oksenberg Rorty (ed.), *The Identities of Persons* (Berkeley: University of California Press, 1976). At the Summit, William Alston noted the confusing plethora of definitions of 'personhood' currently in play, but nonetheless urged that there is a 'core concept of person' as a 'cognitive and conative subject' and that this could apply both to humans and to God. The trouble with this, as I see it, is that it begs precisely the question that Gregory is struggling with: *does* he intend 'persons' in the Godhead to have individualized wills, thoughts, and intentions, as human persons do?

III WHY GREGORY OF NYSSA IS NOT A 'SOCIAL' TRINITARIAN: SOME KEY TEXTS

What must first of all be openly admitted is that Gregory is not a wholly consistent or systematic thinker: it is not hard to find loopholes and terminological lapses in his work on the Trinity.[27] Once this is granted, however, it is possible, I suggest, to range a number of cumulative points together here to indicate how he has been misinterpreted as a 'social' trinitarian:

(1) *Gregory does not 'start' from the three apologetically.* As Joseph Lienhard shows in his excellent paper for this volume, the (somewhat messy political) context of Gregory's major apologetic writings on the Trinity does not present us with the opportunity for such a trimphant clarification of terms as the textbooks may lead us to expect.[28] The reality was not that neat: Gregory is countering both Sabellianism and Arianism at different points in his argument. But the anti-Eunomian writings, especially, are significant for their insistent stress on the divine *unity* as a counteraction to late Arianism. Persistently Gregory reminds us of the unified *will* and *power* of God; persistently he decries Eunomius' suggestion that there is a 'greater' and 'less' in the divine.[29] Apologetically, therefore, Gregory has every reason to give prime emphasis to the *unity* of the divine Nature.[30]

[27] G. Christopher Stead is noted for his work exposing precisely such inconsistencies in Gregory: see, *inter alia*, his 'Ontologie und Terminologie bei Gregor von Nyssa', in Heinrich Dörrie, Margarete Altenbuger, and Uta Schramm (eds.), *Gregor von Nyssa und die Philosophie* (Leiden: Brill, 1976), 107-27. I am greatly indebted in what follows to the meticulously careful work of Lucian Turcescu, whose unpublished paper 'Gregory of Nyssa's Understanding of Divine Persons in *Ad Graecos* (*Ex Communibus Notionibus*)', given at the North American Patristics Society, 1997, discerns an important lapse in the consistency of Gregory's uses of the terms *hypostasis* and *prosopon*. Despite these moments of inconsistency, it is my view that we can give a good account of Gregory's (generally consistent) intentions. In what follows it will be clear to the discerning reader that my interpretation differs in significant respects from that of Cornelius Plantinga in his important article, 'The Social Analogy of the Trinity', *The Thomist*, 50 (1986), 325-52. To anticipate: I interpret the import of the 'three men' 'analogy' differently from Plantinga, and this is partly because I take very seriously the *other* 'analogies' that Gregory holds up to us in *Ad Ablabium* and related texts.

[28] Joseph T. Lienhard, SJ, '*Ousia* and *Hypostasis*: The Cappadocian Settlement and the Theology of "One *Hypostasis*"' (Ch. 5 of this book), esp. pp. 99-107.

[29] See e.g. *Contra Eunomium*, I. 22; II. 3; III. 5, etc. (= NPNF, 2nd ser., v. 61, 103, 147).

[30] Thus, in *Contra Eunomiun* (NPNF, 2nd ser., v. 61 = GNO i. 101) Gregory dis-

(2) *The ordering of causality in the 'persons' gives a logical pre-eminence to the Father.* If any *logical* priority is at stake, it must surely be granted to the Father, rather than to three 'individuals'. In *this* sense Gregory 'starts' with this *one* 'person', as source and cause of the others: 'the Father [alone] is uncreate and ungenerate as well'.[31] But there is no sense of disjunction created thereby: 'there is one motion and disposition of the good will that is communicated from the Father through the Son to the Holy Spirit.'[32]

(3) *The analogy of three men united by 'manhood' is also a significant disanalogy.* Here we come to the argument (especially as rehearsed in the *Ad Ablabium*) that has caused Brown (and others) to insist on Gregory's prioritizing of the 'three', and even to suggest a 'modernizing' or individualizing notion of the 'person' in play. But it should be underscored, first, that Gregory meets the initial objection of Ablabius thus: 'The argument that *you* state is something like this . . .', viz., that we freely call Peter, James, and John three men, even though we know them to be 'one nature'; so why not, asks Ablabius, call Father, Son, and Holy Spirit three Gods, even though we know that they too have 'no difference of nature'?[33] The first point to note, therefore, is that it is Ablabius who 'starts with the three' here, not Gregory who recommends it. Gregory simply receives the gauntlet as it is thrown down. Second, Gregory goes on to assert *both* the radical unity effected by the analogy if it is taken seriously (since on the view of what Maurice Wiles has called Gregory's 'radical Platonism' the universal is *more real* than the particular[34]), *and* to question the analogy by stressing how profoundly different the divine case is from the human. For 'In the case of the Divine nature we do not [as in the case of men] learn that the Father does anything by Himself in which the Son does not work conjointly, or again that the Son has any special operation apart from the Holy Spirit.'[35] Thus we note that on both

cusses Eunomius' subordinationism and insists first and foremost on the nature of God as 'simple, uniform [and] incomposite'.

[31] *Contra Eunomium*, I. 22; NPNF, 2nd series, v. 61 = *GNO* i. 102.

[32] *Ad Ablabium*, NPNF, 2nd ser., v. 334 = *GNO* iii/1, 48–9.

[33] NPNF, 2nd ser., v. 331 = *GNO* iii/1, 38.

[34] Maurice Wiles, *The Making of Christian Doctrine* (London: Cambridge University Press, 1967), 133 ff.

[35] Gregory, *Ad Graecos*, 24–25 = *GNO* iii/1, 47. G. Christopher Stead's article, 'Why Not Three Gods?', in Hubertus R. Drobner and Christophe Klock (eds.), *Studien zu Gregor von Nyssa und der christlichen Spätantike* (Leiden: Brill, 1990), 149–63, brings out well the double logic of Gregory's analogy *and* disanalogy in the

(somewhat problematically related) gambits, the emphasis is again thrown away from the 'threeness' to the unity.

(4) *On an experiential (as opposed to logical) ordering, we might say Gregory 'starts' with the Holy Spirit, which then inexorably brings the other two 'persons' with it.* Since according to Gregory in the *Ad Ablabium* 'the same life is wrought in us by the Father, and prepared by the Son, and depends on the will of the Holy Spirit',[36] there is a sense in which the Spirit acts as the experiential point of entry into the divine flow from the 'spring' of the Father. But since the operations of the three are by definition inseparable, even this apparent experiential distinctness has an illusory quality to it: 'there is *one* motion . . .'.[37]

(5) *There is no suggestion that three 'consciousnesses' are in play; 'hypostasis' does not denote consciousness or self-consciousness.* If we may ascribe to Gregory the *Letter* 38 previously contained in Basil's corpus,[38] then there we find Gregory providing a rare definition of *hypostasis*: it is, he says, 'the conception which, by means of the specific notes it indicates, restricts and circumscribes in a particular thing what is general and uncircumscribed'.[39] We note that this 'definition' is peculiarly devoid of any overtones of 'personality', let alone of 'consciousness'. A *hypostasis* is simply a distinct enough entity to bear some 'particularizing marks'—in the case of the Trinity the distinctions of differing causal relations within the Godhead. As for the word *prosopon*, more commonly used by Gregory, but arguably less technically, *prosopon* in its human sense and evocations is nonetheless severely tempered when applied to God. As Gregory puts it in one intriguing passage in the *Ad Graecos*:

All the persons belonging to Man [i.e. Humanity] do not directly possess . . . their being from the same person, but some from this one and some from that one, so that with respect to the individuals caused there are also many and diverse causes. But with regard to the Holy Trinity, such is not the case, for there is one and the same Person, that of the Father, from

argument here, though with less respect for the success of the argument than I have.

[36] NPNF, 2nd ser., v. 334 = *GNO* iii/1, 48–9

[37] Ibid.

[38] This ascription is still debated, and may never find complete resolution. For the purposes of this essay I follow Cavallin, Hübner, and Fedwick (amongst others) in attributing this letter to Gregory.

[39] *Ep.* 38, St Basil, *The Letters*, trans. Roy J. Deferrari, LCL, 4 vols. (Cambridge, Mass.: Harvard University Press, 1950), i. 200–1.

whom the Son is begotten and the Holy Spirit proceeds. . . . For the Persons of the Divinity are not separated from one another either by time or place, not by will or by practice, not by activity or by passion, not by anything of this sort, such as is observed with regard to human beings.[40]

(6) *The talk is of 'communion' (koinōnia) between the 'persons', not of 'community'.* This distinction is significant, and crucial to the argument in *Letter* 38. Gregory is in this letter most certainly not enjoining the unification of separate 'individuals' into a 'community', as seems to be the model in the analytic discussion of 'PM'. On the contrary, he writes that 'there is apprehended among these three a certain ineffable and inconceivable communion (*koinonia*) and at the same time distinction (*diakrisis*)'—which latter, however, does not 'disintegrate the continuity of their nature'.[41]

(7) *Number cannot strictly apply to God.* Although the *hypostaseis* have relational 'distinguishing marks', it is only in a Pickwickian sense that they are 'three', according to Gregory; as H. A. Wilson comments on the argument in *Ad Ablabium*, 'if [Gregory] has been willing to carry the use of numerical terms rather further than S. Basil was prepared to do, he yet is content in the last resort to say that number is not in strictness applicable to the Divine *hypostaseis*, in that they cannot be contemplated *kat'idian perigraphen*, and therefore cannot be enumerated by way of addition.'[42] Such a perception may be deeply infuriating to contemporary analytic philosophers of religion; but it does indeed seem to be Gregory's view: we cannot 'add up' the numbers in the Trinity in the *same* way as we count heads at a gathering of humans.

(8) *Gregory's favoured analogies for the Trinity stress the indivisibility of the 'persons' and even a certain fluidity in their boundaries.* If we can thus prevent ourselves being imaginatively dominated by the analogy of the three 'men' (which in any case we now see is treated by Gregory with great caution), we can allow some other (arguably more favoured) analogies to have their force. We have already mentioned the long-established analogy of a 'spring' from which water gushes forth in a continuous stream.[43] To this

---

[40] Gregory, *Ad Graecos*, 24–5 = *GNO* iii/1, 47; trans. in Daniel F. Stramara, 'Gregory of Nyssa, *Ad Graecos* . . .', *Greek Orthodox Theological Review*, 41 (1996), 385; see commentary on p. 379.

[41] *Saint Basil: The Letters* I, trans. Roy J. Deferrari (Cambridge, Mass.: Harvard University Press, 1926), 210, 211.

[42] In the 'Prolegomena', NPNF, 2nd ser., v. 27.

[43] *Ad Ablabium*, ibid. 334.

Gregory adds, in *Letter* 38, the idea of the inseparable links in a 'chain' ('just as he who grasps one end of a chain pulls along with it the other end also to himself, so he who draws the Spirit . . . through the Spirit draws both the Son and the Father along with It'[44]). Even more interesting, in this same letter, is the extended discussion of the analogy of the rainbow. Here, the 'light from light' of the Creeds is given the more colourful, and also directionally reflexive, imagery of the 'bow': 'When the sunbeam, intercepting obliquely the compact and opaque portion of the cloudy mass, then causes its own circle to impinge in a straight line upon a particular cloud, there occurs a sort of bending of the light and its return upon itself, for the sunlight returns in the opposite direction from what is moist and shiny. . . . when the rays of all the colours are seen together, they are both distinct and yet at the same time filch from our view the points of their juncture with one another . . .'.[45] This analogy, then, has the particular and additional merits of stressing the incorporative, reflexive flow of the divine 'persons', as well as the indeterminate boundaries, at least from our human perception, of the 'persons'' distinctness. Thus it is that Gregory can conclude this discussion by underscoring that pictorial 'analogies' such as this do better justice to the matter in hand than strict dogmatic definitions; for they appropriately draw attention to how we become 'dizzy' in the making of such distinctions, just as we become dizzy if we look into the sun.[46]

It is also worth reminding ourselves that Gregory can on occasion use a 'psychological' analogy for the Trinity (our 'word' and our 'breath' being distinct features of the self[47]), a ploy of course more commonly associated with Augustine and the West, but also giving the lie to the suggestion that Gregory is uniquely fixated on the image of 'three men'.

(9) *A strongly apophatic sensibility attends any talk of the 'essence' of God.* This point is reiterated constantly even in the more philosophical and apologetic writings we have so far been covering. But if we turn now to the fascinating, and correlated, account of the

---

[44] St Basil, *The Letters*, LCL, i. 210–11.

[45] St Basil: *The Letters* I, LCL, Ibid. 213–15.

[46] Ibid. 216–17. 'We fall into a matter difficult to understand and become dizzy when we face the conflict of the different propositions'.

[47] See 'The Great Catechism', ch. II, in NPNF, 2nd ser., v. 477 = ed. J. H. Srawley, *The Catechetical Oration of Gregory of Nyssa* (Cambridge: Cambridge University Press, 1903).

effects of trinitarian incorporation in Gregory's *Commentary on the Song of Songs*, we find a wealth of discussions of the dark 'incomprehensibility' of the divine nature. It is as well to remember that the whole life-work of 'ascent' in Gregory culminates in noetic darkness, as did Moses' ascent of Mt Sinai, and we cannot afford to ignore this epistemological complication when considering Gregory's account of the Trinity. Again, it should give us pause when pronouncing on the effectiveness, or otherwise, of *particular* dominating models for the Trinity. In the *Song* it is the haunting image of the 'hand of the bridegroom', reaching out to draw us into darkness, that reminds us of the deep impossibility of circumscribing the divine 'essence' in intellectual terms: ' "My beloved has put his hand through the hole of the door". Human nature is not able to contain the infinite, unbounded divine nature.'[48]

(10) *Freer, and more instrumental, imagery for the divine 'persons' is thus also used evocatively by Gregory in his exegetical work, without any apparent concern for philosophical precision.* With this apophaticism constantly underlined, Gregory is thereby freed up to allow a plethora of other (less philosophically precise) images for the process of trinitarian 'incorporation' into the divine, and these should also be borne in mind when assessing the full texture of his trinitarianism. I draw gratefully here on a (as yet unpublished) paper by my pupil Francis Yip ('The Trinity and Christian Life in the Dogmatic and Spiritual Writings of Gregory of Nyssa'). Yip fascinatingly supplements the material usually surveyed by dogmaticians and philosophers in assessing Gregory's trinitarianism by drawing attention to a number of creative—even bizarre— trinitarian images in the *Song*: the 'arrow' of the Word which wounds the soul and the tip of the arrow that is the Spirit,[49] for instance, or the wind of the Spirit blown against the ship of the church of which Christ is the pilot.[50] Often these images mutually bombard one another in a flood of inter-corrective ideas. Such, it seems, is precisely Gregory's intention, since he wishes us not to fixate on one set of images, but to allow all of them to be permeated by the profoundly apophatic sensibility that propels us from one to the other.

---

[48] *In Cant.* 11; ET *Commentary on the Song of Songs*, trans. Casimir McCambley (Brookline, Mass.: Hellenic College Press, 1987), 208 = GNO vi. 336.

[49] *Cant.* 4; ibid. 103 = GNO vi. 127–8.

[50] *Cant.* 12; ibid. 213 = GNO vi. 341–2.

To sum up this section of the argument: what, then, have we learnt from these ten cumulative points? It has been my concern above all to divert the analytic discussion from the mesmeric hold that the 'three men' argument has appeared to have on it, and to suggest that even when Gregory uses that analogy he is deeply concerned to underscore its limitations. Nor is there any suggestion, on my reading, of a 'modern' sense of 'individual' in play (with, for instance, a focus on 'self-consiousness', or 'autonomy') even when this analogy is to the fore. Rather, what we are presented with is the idea of a unified *flow* of divine will and love, catching us up reflexively towards the light of the 'Father', and allowing to the 'persons' only the minimally distinctive features of their different internal causal relations. Such, I suggest, is very far from the tritheistic-tending accounts of the analytic material discussed in our previous section; and equally far (though this point cannot be spelled out in detail here) from the well-meaning, but arguably finally incoherent, accounts of human 'personhood *as* relation' (only?) which have become popular in recent theological writing, often on the basis of trinitarian appeals.[51] Gregory is quite clear about the *difference* between human and divine 'persons', as I trust has now been established. And he does not, whether apologetically, logically, or experientially, 'start' with 'three'. This is not a 'community' of 'individuals'; nor, incidentally, does it—on my reading—*prioritize* 'person' over 'substance' (a matter that has become polemical in the thought of John Zizioulas[52]). A final irony, in the terms of our conference, is that my account of Gregory's trinitarianism can I think rather more easily shelter under what Brian Leftow defines as 'Western' 'LT' than under his (and other analytic philosophers') account of 'Eastern' 'ST'.

What, then, is the precise linguistic status of the various components of Gregory's trinitarian terminology? To this somewhat tricky question we shall now devote an exploratory short section, before turning, finally, to the (related) complications of gender.

---

[51] Harriet A. Harris (see n. 2) points out the oddity of this kind of appeal: 'We cannot jump from recognising the relationality involved in being a person to affirming that persons are relational entities. Persons are ontologically prior to relations'.

[52] See John D. Zizioulas, *Being as Communion* (Crestwood, NY: St Vladimir's Seminary Press, 1985). The interpretation I have offered here, in which Gregory's 'radical Platonism' is stressed, gives logical priority to the divine *ousia*.

IV What Sort of Language is Trinitarian Language for Gregory of Nyssa?

This question is a doubly complicated one if we choose to apply contemporary philosophical distinctions to patristic texts that do not utilize these particular distinctions, and which are in themselves already complex and disputed. Nonetheless a brief exploration will be attempted here. In what follows I am assuming (not uncontentiously!) that neither 'metaphorical' nor 'analogical' language for God is incompatible with 'literal' claims. (I use 'literal' speech here to mean making a statement in which 'one is attributing to the subject the property with which the predicate is associated by its semantic status in the language', rather than merely meaning 'univocal with common usage', as in some discussions.[53]) If I am right, then a profound apophatic sensibility about the divine 'essence', such as Gregory exemplifies, does not necessarily lead to a 'pan-metaphoricism', nor even to the claim that metaphors are irreducible.

If we allow that 'metaphorical' language, first, involves (at least in its inception) a *surprising* conjunction of terms whose meaning is disclosed by context, there is no need to assume, as many do, that no purchase on reality is thereby attempted or achieved;[54] on the contrary, there may be realms of linguistic endeavour (many theological statements included) where such artful conjunction *best* suits the attempt to make serious metaphysical claims. Moreover, metaphors of this creative sort can, on reflection, often be seen to *encode* 'literal' meanings.[55] If I say, for instance, that 'Christ is a rock', I clearly do not mean this 'literally' (it is a metaphor); but I do mean ('literally') that Christ is reliable, unchanging, etc.

How one construes what a theological 'analogy' is, in contrast, may differ according to one's prior metaphysical and theological commitments (whether, for instance, one accepts on authority, revelation or reasoned argument that 'pure perfection' terms such

---

[53] See Richard Swinburne, *Revelation* (Oxford: Clarendon Press, 1992), ch. 1, for the 'univocal' meaning; compare William P. Alston, *Divine Nature and Human Language* (Ithaca, NY: Cornell University Press, 1989), chs. 1 and 2, esp. p. 25, for the meaning I am using. The definition of 'literal' speech provided here was suggested by William Alston at the Summit.

[54] For the contextual understanding of metaphor, see Swinburne, *Revelation*, ch. 3.   [55] See Alston, *Divine Nature*, ch. 1.

as 'love' belong supremely to God and therefore only secondarily, and by analogical extension, to humans). A good rule-of-thumb definition of an 'analogy' is that it involves 'stretch[ing] [a term] to fit new applications, . . . *without generating for the native speaker any imaginative strain*'[56] (with which we contrast the imaginative *frisson* of the newly coined metaphor). But of course we need to know in any given case *which* way we are 'stretching'; that is (to continue the example above) it matters whether we know—on one of the grounds already mentioned—that God supremely embodies love and humans embody it only derivatively, or whether the 'analogy' here is merely a settled (or 'dead') metaphor, that speaks of God as love as imaginatively 'obvious' simply because we have had several centuries to get used to a conjunctive idea that was originally coined as a metaphor. If it is the latter case, then, as Swinburne has recently argued, the lines between 'metaphorical' and 'analogical' language for God are often transitionally and diachronically blurred.[57]

If we take this much as read, what sort of language *is* trinitarian language for Gregory? The answer, I suggest, is different depending on what term or terms we are discussing, and how fluid their own 'common' meanings are. *Hypostasis,* for instance, can mean a bewildering number of things in the patristic era; but in the technical sense explicitly delimited by Gregory (that which 'restricts and circumscribes in a particular thing what is general and uncircumscribed'), I see no reason to deny its 'literal' status as applied to Father, Son, and Holy Spirit in the Godhead. *Prosopon,* however (also translated 'person' in English, but having a more obviously 'relational' or 'psychological' meaning as visage or personal presentation[58]), is utilized more commonly than *hypostasis* by Gregory, but with a more profound sense of its disjunction from its usage as applied to humans, as we have already noted above: 'For the Persons [*prosopa*] of the Divinity are not separated from one another either by time or place, not by will or by practice, not by activity or by passion, not by anything of this sort, such as is observed with regard to human beings.'[59] On these grounds it

[56] Janet Martin Soskice, *Metaphor and Religious Language* (Oxford: Clarendon Press, 1985), 64.

[57] See again Swinburne, *Revelation*, ch. 3.

[58] See the discussion in Stramara, 'Gregory of Nyssa', 379.

[59] Ibid.

would seem that the language of *prosopon* used for the divine
entities in the Trinity is best seen as analogical (and perhaps even
metaphorical in its original coinage).

The case of 'Father' language in the Trinity, however, is more
subtle and difficult again. It might be tempting to judge it metaphorical, granted the great lengths that Gregory goes to *distinguish*
human fatherhood from divine fatherhood in the late Arian
debates; but the picture is complicated by a strain of thought in
Gregory that sees the language of God as 'Father', 'Son' and 'Holy
Spirit' as authoritatively *given* in revelation. In *Contra Eunomium*
2[60] there is an interesting passage where Gregory insists: 'Once for
all, from the Lord . . . we have learned this, that is the Father and
the Son and the Holy Spirit. We say that it is a terrible and soul-
destroying thing to misinterpret these Divine utterances and to
devise in their stead assertions to subvert them,—assertions pre-
tending to correct God the Word, Who appointed that we should
maintain these statements as part of our faith.' This non-negotiable
and revelatory appeal is perhaps reminiscent of a notable passage
in Athanasius, where Athanasius avers that the *proper* meanings
of 'Father' and 'Son' (which logically imply one another) reside in
the divine prototype rather than being applied from the creaturely
realm of passion and bodies.[61] It is not entirely clear to me that
Gregory is making a parallel move here; but if he is, then human
'father' language would become an analogical derivative from the
divine, rather than divine 'Father' language being either metaphorical or analogical language on the basis of human prototypes.

In the case of the visual trinitarian images such as 'chain', 'rainbow', 'spring', or 'humanity' (as are in play in *Ep.* 38 and the *Ad
Ablabium*, and argued above to be vital to understanding Gregory's
position on the Trinity), we have what Gregory *calls* 'analogies',
but would seem to be more appropriately described as 'metaphors'
in terms of the modern distinctions we have rehearsed. Each of
these also bears with it a strong accompanying sense of the finally
inexpressible nature of the divine; as such, the metaphorical status
of the language does not detract from the realistic seriousness of

[60] NPNF, 2nd ser., v. 101–2 = *GNO* ii. 298.

[61] See Athanasius, *Contra Arianos*, I. 21; there is an illuminating discussion of
this point in Catherine Osborne, 'Literal or Metaphorical? Some Issues of Language
in the Arian Controversy', in Lionel R. Wickham and Caroline P. Bammel (eds.),
Christian Faith and Greek Philosophy (Leiden: Brill, 1993), 148–70.

the claim, but merely draws our attention to the limitations of what we can 'nail down' linguistically where God is concerned.

Such, it seems, is the unavoidable complexity of attending to the linguistic status of the various strands of Gregory's trinitarian argument.

But there is yet one further complication to add: that of the 'gender fluidity' that Gregory sees both in God-in-Godself, and in the human seeking of that (trinitarian) God. If I am right, then any account of Gregory's trinitarian theology that fails to explore his own literature of spiritual assimilation into the divine has given only an excerpted version of the whole.

V THE TRINITY AND GENDER ACCORDING TO GREGORY

I made the claim at the beginning of this paper that it is deeply unwise to divorce Gregory's more apologetic or expository works on the Trinity from his trinitarian spirituality of human transformation. Especially in his late work the *Commentary on the Song of Songs*, Gregory charts in highly imagistic and eroticized language the ascent of the soul into intimacy with the life of the Trinity. Two features are especially striking about this process, as recent work by Verna Harrison on gender in Gregory has fascinatingly demonstrated.[62]

First, the stages of ascent to God that Gregory maps out in this work and elsewhere (most notably in the *Life of Moses*), involve a progressive and final *darkening* of the mind; at the height of the ascent on the mountain, Moses, the 'type' of the Christian soul, finds his mind no longer able to absorb what God is giving him: 'When, therefore, Moses grew in knowledge, he declared that he had seen God in darkness, that is, that he had then come to know that what is divine is beyond all knowledge and comprehension . . .'.[63] When this theme of noetic darkness is discussed in the erotic language of the *Commentary on the Song of Songs*, it becomes clear that another set of faculties (the 'spiritual senses') take over

[62] See Verna E. F. Harrison, 'Gender, Generation, and Virginity in Cappadocian Theology', *JTS* 47 (1996), 38–68; and *eadem*, 'Male and Female in Cappadocian Theology', *JTS* 41 (1990), 441–71.

[63] Gregory of Nyssa, *The Life of Moses*, trans. Abraham J. Malherbe and Everett Ferguson (New York: Paulist Press, 1978), 95 = GNO vii/1, 87.

from the *nous* (intellect) in this heightened state of intimacy with the divine. What has occurred is a profound transformation of the physical senses (sight, however, is significantly omitted) into a deep receptive sensitivity. At the same time, Gregory charts a symbolic gender reversal: what has up to now been the spiritual quest of an ardent 'youth' going courting for Sophia, becomes here conversely the 'more mature character of the bride who actively seeks, yet is still more open to receive, the divine bridegroom'.[64]

The gender fluidity that Gregory charts at the *human* level of transformation finds also its metaphysical counterpart, secondly, in God. Whilst Sophia (Christ) is being actively courted by the soul, she is described as a 'manly woman'; but when the soul adopts the darkened epistemological state of active receptivity, Christ becomes the bridegroom seeking *her*. A further complication arises when we add the fully trinitarian picture of incorporation that tends to emerge in fits and starts in the *Commentary on the Song of Songs*. In the seventh Homily[65] the bridegroom's *mother* is aligned with God the Father: Gregory explains that the names 'father' and 'mother' are effectively the same in meaning, granted that we know that there is really 'neither male nor female' (see Gal. 3: 28) in God. In the fifteenth Homily[66] the Holy Spirit is perceived as a dove who is also the mother of the bride. In all these transferences and reversals, the message Gregory evidently wishes to convey is that gender stereotypes must be reversed, undermined, and transcended if the soul is to advance to supreme intimacy with the trinitarian God; and that the language of sexuality and gender, far from being an optional aside or mere rhetorical flourish in the process, is somehow necessary and intrinsic to the epistemological deepening that Gregory seeks to describe.[67]

What then are the implications of this discussion for the question of trinitarian conceptuality with which we started this essay? The answer as I see it is twofold: on the one hand, the *Commentary*

---

[64] Harrison, 'Gender, Generation, and Virginity', 61.

[65] *Commentary*, trans. McCambley, 145 = *GNO* vi. 212–14.

[66] *Commentary*, 468–9 = *GNO* vi. 468–9.

[67] It is important to note that this gender-play bespeaks shifts in human epistemological *capacity* which cannot be gained except through painstaking spiritual growth. If Gregory is right about this, then there may be different (more or less spiritually mature) ways of discussing the Trinity, depending on the spiritual growth of the discussants. This is a complication, we note, that is as yet completely ignored in analytic discussions of the matter.

material is vital further evidence that the 'three men' analogy of the *Ad Ablabium* is a highly partial one in Gregory's view for expressing the spiritual complexity and richness involved in the ascent and incorporation into the realm of the Trinity.[68] (In this sense Mary Daly's spoof is vindicated, although in a way more subtle and positive for an alternative trinitarian picture than Daly would ever acknowledge.) Second, it is clear from Gregory's *Commentary* material that a *reduction* of 'persons' to 'relationality' is not what he intends. To be sure, we are forced back to his expository doctrinal texts for a more precise account of how the *hypostaseis* actually distinguish themselves without separation (as we have sketched); but what the overlapping and bombarding images of the *Song* commentary remind us is that the 'persons' of the Trinity are always being reconfigured and reconstrued as the soul advances to more dizzying intimacy with the divine. And in this progress the engagement of the self with deep levels of erotic as well as epistemological re-evaluation are unavoidably predictable. Hence, whatever 'analogy' (in Gregory's meaning) seems most adequate to express the doctrine of the Trinity convincingly in doctrinal or philosophical terms, the less we should become permanently fixated upon it, and the more the profusion of available biblical and allegorical allusions should draw us on beyond complacency.

VI CONCLUSIONS

The material I have covered in this essay has taken us in a number of different directions. My chief goal has been to call into question a tendency to read Gregory's trinitarianism solely in terms of the 'three men' analogy, especially with the overtones of psychological self-consciousness or 'individualism'. Along the road I have gathered some other pieces out of Gregory's trinitarian armoury which are, I have argued, insufficiently attended to in the current philosophical debate. Gregory's expository and apologetic

---

[68] In an illuminating discussion at the Trinity 'Summit', Michel Barnes posited the *genesis* of the reading of Gregory I am here questioning, and attributed it to de Régnon's influence. See the illuminating section on Gregory and de Régnon's interpretation of him in Michel René Barnes, 'Augustine in Contemporary Trinitarian Theology', *TS* 56 (1995), 245-6.

works on the Trinity should at all costs be read in tandem with his 'spiritual' writings and his intriguing (if disturbing) views about gender and epistemological transformation. Without these *addenda*, I want to suggest, we do not appreciate the subtlety, spiritual depth, and striking contemporary challenge of his trinitarian alternative. The explication of these complexities thus remains a challenging future task for the analytic school of philosophy of religion.

7

Rereading Augustine's Theology of the Trinity

MICHEL RENÉ BARNES

It is impossible to do contemporary trinitarian theology and not have a judgement on Augustine; unfortunately, this is *not* the same thing as saying that it is impossible to do contemporary trinitarian theology and not have *read* Augustine.[1] Strangely, it is not just possible but quite common to have a 'reading' of Augustine without ever having read Augustine. My purpose in this essay is to offer a reading of Augustine's trinitarian theology which attempts to stand free (in the sense of not being dependent upon, or repeating as if by rote) of the account or reading of Augustine's trinitarian theology which is widely circulated in treatments of that theology by systematicians and some historians of doctrine. Briefly put, that reading identifies the root conceptual idiom of Augustine's trinitarian theology as 'neoplatonic'. The substantial influence of neoplatonism upon Augustine's trinitarian theology is said to result in (or to express itself in) an overly metaphysical portrait of God, one which diminishes the reality of the Trinity to the point of being functionally modalist, and which divorces the God-who-is-Trinity from our experience in revelation. While I think this account of Augustine's trinitarian theology is, frankly, dead wrong, it is not my purpose in this essay to engage directly in the various expressions of this account. What I hope to do is to offer a careful, informed reading of a few early writings by Augustine on the Trinity, and in so doing to draw out what I consider to be a more accurate and honest representation of Augustine's theology. Such an account is not as comprehensive as it might be, and in particular I will not approach the issue of 'neoplatonism' directly,

---

[1] There is a remark by Gerald Bonner which is quite apt here: 'More than most authors Augustine has been the object of unjustified denunciation by those who have not read him.' This remark is quoted as the very first line on the first page of John M. Rist's *Augustine* (Cambridge: Cambridge University Press, 1994).

e.g. parsing passages in *de Trinitate* for what they do or do not owe
to 'neoplatonism'. I would rather use this opportunity to offer
something more 'constructive'.[2]

Moreover, it is important not to lend too great a credibility to the
'proof'-like quality of characterizations of the monist or neoplatonic
nature of Augustine's trinitarian theology. Such characterizations
are rarely offered with the requisite apparatus to be considered
'proofs'; they are, rather, episodes in an overall narrative which
begins with the presupposition of a fundamental monism or neoplatonism. Since such characterizations are in fact not 'proofs', any
offering of refutations or counter-proofs ('facts') will not dislocate
the 'monist Augustine' narrative. What I am offering instead is a
counter-narrative, a relatively new set of categories within which
Augustine's trinitarian theology may be understood. I am in fact
offering only the first chapter, the first act, of such a counter-
narrative, but I believe that the fundamental categories of the re-
narrating can be identified and communicated by working through
two early texts by Augustine. I had originally intended to treat
Augustine's trinitarian theology in three stages or phases: early
(e.g. from *Ep.* 11 to *de Trinitate*, I–V), middle (*de Trinitate* VI–XV,
various sermons and *Tractates*, etc.), and late (*Twentieth Tractate on
John, Against the 'Arian Sermon'*, the writings against Maximinius,
and *De Fide ad Catechumenos*). Two developments changed all
that, one 'negative' development, one 'positive' development. The
'negative' development was the simple realization that there was
not space enough wholly to construct a new narrative within the
page-limitations for our essays. The 'positive' development was that
I saw that in working from only the early texts I was able to
identify the key features of Augustine's theology of the Trinity.
Doubtless there is further development in Augustine's trinitarian
theology, and new things to uncover, but what I consider to be the
fundamental concerns of that theology were substantially present
in the early writings I have been able to consider here. Just as
importantly—for my purpose of providing a new narrative or a
'rereading' of Augustine's theology of the Trinity—is the fact that,
if I could find in the early writings the presence of a trinitarian
theology which owed not to neoplatonism but to Nicene theology,
which was polemical in its structure, and with an intense focus on

---

[2] I want to thank (alphabetically) Lewis Ayres and John M. Rist for their
comments and suggestions after reading earlier drafts of this essay.

the Incarnation, then I have found all these under those conditions widely regarded to be least hospitable to my rereading.

I READING AUGUSTINE ON THE TRINITY

One burden that has fallen upon the reading of Augustine's trinitarian theology is the existence of a tradition or habit of reading the texts of that theology in a dismembered form. Augustine has been read in bits and pieces. Indeed, in bits and pieces sometimes seems to be the only way that Augustine's trinitarian theology has been read. The medievals who read him read him in that way. The moderns who read him have continued the practice. Undoubtedly all of Augustine's trinitarian writings have been physically 'read' together (i.e. by one person), yet within the discipline of theology the texts have not been 'read together' in the sense of setting the theology from each text in: (*a*) the context of all of Augustine's trinitarian writings; (*b*) the context of other late fourth-/early fifth-century Latin trinitarian writings; (*c*) the context of fourth-century Latin polemical literature; and (*d*) the context of authoritative Latin trinitarian theology from the second and third centuries. Augustine's trinitarian writings *have* been read in the context of late fourth- and early fifth-century Latin neoplatonism—or, more frequently, in the context of an idealized understanding of what neoplatonism then was. Where there has been a comparative reading of Augustine and other doctrinal authors, that comparative reading has been functionally a reading of two decontextualized and fragmented authors or texts, e.g. a dismembered Augustine and a dismembered Ambrose. It is ironic that while today there is some formal pressure towards doing readings which decontextualize, in point of fact there may have never been a 'contextualized' reading of Augustine. What is today being held up as a new hermeneutical goal is rather a restatement of what has been unconscious (and conscious) practice. Let me suggest, as an alternative, that now is the time to do something radically new and excitingly different: to read Augustine's trinitarian theology as a whole and in its context. In this essay I am certainly not going to produce all of what could be produced from a single reading of Augustine in such a new manner, but whatever I have to say about Augustine's trinitarian theology in this essay will follow from an attempt at a reading mindful of all that Augustine wrote on the Trinity,[3] and the variety of contexts in which he wrote. My intention in this essay is that my 'rereading' of Augustine's trinitarian theology will constitute a kind of re-membering of the texts of that theology.[4]

One illustrative and important example of a decontextualized, dismembered reading of Augustine's trinitarian theology may serve as an indication of how such readings have been significant in Western trinitarian theology. We can take the case of the trinitarian controversy involving Joachim of Fiore, Peter Lombard, and the Fourth Lateran Council, where, as Fiona Robb has recently noted, both Lombard and the Fourth Lateran Council emphasized the category of '*quaedam summa res*' as the fundamental category for describing the divine unity. Robb remarks that Peter's 'concept of the divine essence as a *quaedam summa res*, [was] attacked by Joachim but enshrined in the [Fourth] Lateran decree. The *quaedam summa res* represented both an abstract concept and a view of

---

[3] Presently the best study available of Augustine's doctrine of God is Basil Studer's *The Grace of Christ and the Grace of God in Augustine of Hippo: Christocentrism or Theocentrism?* (Collegeville, Minn.: Liturgical Press, 1997). Despite some limitations, the book does an excellent job of articulating Augustine's theology in its own terms, that is, following Augustine's theology out via its own logic. See also Johannes Arnold, 'Begriff und heilsökonomische Bedeutung der göttlichen Sendungen in Augustinus *De Trinitate*', *Recherches Augustiniennes*, XXV (1991), 3–69; and Studer's 'History and Faith in Augustine's *de Trinitate*', *Augustinian Studies*, 28 (1997), 7–50.

[4] Since 1995 my work on Augustine has been conducted in continuous conversation with Lewis Ayres (Trinity College, Dublin) regarding his work on parallel and overlapping themes. Our daily exchange of research and texts via e-mail means that it is difficult to acknowledge all the points at which this detailed conversation has influenced both our accounts. My own understanding of Augustine has been influenced particularly by Ayres's work on what he calls the 'anthropological' component in Augustine's trinitarian thought, especially the epistemological significance of the Second Person. See 'The Discipline of Self-knowledge in Augusine's *De trinitate* Book X', in L. Ayres (ed.), *The Passionate Intellect: Essays on the Transformation of Classical Traditions Presented to Professor Ian Kidd*, RUSCH VII (Brunswick, NJ: Transaction, 1995), 261–96; and 'Christology and Faith in Augustine's *De trinitate* XIII: Toward Relocating Books VIII–XV', *Augustinian Studies*, 29 (1998), 111–139, as well as 'Augustine on the Unity of the Triune God', in R. Dodaro and G. Lawless (eds.), *Augustine and his Critics* (London: Routledge, forthcoming). Ayres is presently writing a book entitled *Augustine's Trinitarian Theology*. I have also benefited substantially from two articles by Rowan Williams, 'Sapientia and the Trinity: Reflections on *de Trinitate*', *Collectanea Augustiniana*, ed. I. B. Bruning (Leuven: Leuven University Press, 1990), 317–32; and 'The Paradoxes of Self-Knowledge in the *De trinitate*', in *Collectanea Augustiniana*, ed. Joseph Lienhard, Earl Muller, and Roland Teske (New York: Peter Lang, 1993), 121–34.

divine unity quite at odds with Joachim's own.'[5] Robb then goes on to note that the category of *quaedam summa res* owed much to Augustine, and here she refers to Book I.5 of *On Christian Doctrine* which contains a formula by Augustine which reads, in part, '*pater et filius et spiritus sanctus eademque trinitas, una quaedam summa res . . . unus deus, et singulus quisque horum plena substantia et simul omnes una substantia*'.[6] Robb makes the point that it is Augustine's '*plena substantia*' as well as the '*quaedam summa res*' which supports Lombard's own usage of '*quaedam summa res*'.

The trinitarian debate between Joachim and Peter Lombard is frequently treated in modern trinitarian theologies as an exemplary case of an encounter between a trinitarian theology with a strong emphasis on the reality of the different Divine Persons (Joachim's) versus a trinitarian theology with a strong emphasis on the reality of the unity of the divinity (Lombard's), and it may in fact have been just that. I would not want to dispute the judgement that Lombard may have either been given doctrinal insight or found a convenient authority in Augustine's *On Christian Doctrine*. I would want to suggest, however, that Lombard's reading of Augustine's trinitarian theology cannot be given much weight in terms of his reproducing an Augustinian insight for development in his own trinitarian theology. The reason why I say this is simple: the one and only time that Augustine ever uses either the phrase '*plena substantia*' or '*summa res*' is at *On Christian Doctrine* I.5; neither phrase ever again occurs in any of Augustine's writings.[7] The uniqueness of Augustine's trinitarian usage in *On Christian Doctrine* I.5 does indeed pose questions for Augustine scholars to try to answer (such as whether the use of this usage is tied specifically to the overall question of signification in *On Christian Doctrine*). But, most importantly, whatever importance '*plena substantia*' (following Robb) or '*summa res*' (simply following Peter Lombard) had for later theologians that importance can only stand apart from Augustine's own trinitarian theology. Peter's reading of Augustine is a clear—and influential—example of the decontextualized and dismembered way Augustine's trinitarian theology has been read. Modern trinitarian theologies which accept at face value Lombard's

---

[5] 'The Fourth Lateran Council's Definition of Trinitarian Orthodoxy', *Journal of Ecclesiastical History*, 48 (1997), 22–43; here, p. 25.

[6] CCL 32, I.V.6.9–10, emphasis added

[7] I make this claim on the basis of CETEDOC searches for both phrases.

reading of Augustine—with whatever sympathy for either of the two sides in the debate—are in fact simply reproducing that dismembered reading.

Let me offer, then, a few methodological observations which I believe reflect necessary prerequisites for any credible reading of Augustine. I cannot claim that these comments are earth-shaking; indeed, I provide (and require) such prerequisites of work by my graduate students, so they can hardly be new to present readers. Nonetheless, it is the question of what a historically credible reading of Augustine's trinitarian theology might be that is at the heart of my essay here, and my methodological presuppositions are best made explicit. These criteria may also, I hope, make more clear what I intend to do in this essay.

There are, I propose, seven different criteria by which one judges a historical reading (or interpretation) of a text. A given reading is more credible as a work of scholarship in direct proportion to its degree of success in fulfilling these criteria. First, the reading must locate the text (or topic) in its original context, and use that context to 'unpack' the meaning or sense of the text. Second, the reading must identify the presence and hence, effect of tradition in the text (or topic), and use that presence to identify the meaning or sense of the text. Third, the reading must identify and place the content of the text in a larger 'external' narrative which supports the reading(s) derived from the previous steps by making such a content possible (or even, happy day, *likely*). Fourth, the reading must utilize a knowledge of scholarship on the author, text, and topic; the broader and more detailed the engagement with scholarship the more sophisticated the reading. Fifth, there must be close reading or exegesis of the text which uncovers the key steps in the author's logic or expression. Sixth, the reading must identify, and show a fluency with, those conceptual idioms that are the key building blocks of the author's logic or expression. Seventh and finally, judgements on the sense of any part (a sentence, a phrase) of the text must relate that sense to the text as a whole (and test that proposed sense against the whole text). Such a relating of the part to the whole is necessary to avoid the danger of a 'historical fundamentalism' (akin to 'biblical fundamentalism') in which sentences or phrases are interpreted apart from the text within which the words stand. Steps such as these (and there is nothing definitive about this list or the order) are, I would argue, necessary for a credible reading of *any* theological (or philosophical) text, but it is enough for now to identify with such criteria the credibility of the reading of a text which falls under the rubric of 'historical theology'.

One would imagine that there have been a variety of studies of Augustine's trinitarian theology which place that theology and the key texts (e.g., *de Trinitate, Tractates on John*) in their original context, either in terms of the late fourth-/early fifth-century context within which Augustine developed his doctrine of the Trinity, or in terms of the context of Augustine's writings on the Trinity considered as a whole. However, there is no variety of such studies; indeed, studies of this sort can hardly be found at all. The key scholarly works on Augustine's trinitarian theology—e.g. those of Schmaus or Schindler[8]—either make only the most superficial historical placing of the theology, or are wrong about the details of that setting (or both). The most detailed contextual study of Augustine's trinitarian theology does not even have that theology as its proper subject: Olivier du Roy's detailed and very influential work, *L'Intelligence de la Foi en la Trinité selon saint Augustin*[9] is about, as its title indicates, understanding and faith. Moreover, du Roy's study limits itself to works written before AD 391, and, most importantly, by design limits itself almost exclusively to philosophical background.

Likewise, scholarly treatments which identify the presence (or effect) of tradition in the texts (or topics), and which use that presence to recover the meaning or sense in the text are very few. As I noted earlier, there are no serious studies of Augustine's debt to second- and third-century Latin trinitarian theology, nor are there monographs on Augustine's relationship to Latin Nicene polemical works of the fourth century (such as those by Phoebadius of Agen, Gregory of Elvira, Hilary of Poitiers, Eusebius of Vercelli, and Ambrose of Milan).[10] There are a few comments on this relation-

---

[8] Michael Schmaus, *Die psychologische Trinitätslehre des heiligen Augustinus* (Münster: Aschendorff, 1927), and Alfred Schindler, *Wort und Analogie in Augustins Trinitätslehre* (Tübingen: Mohr, 1965).

[9] *L'Intelligence de la foi en la Trinité selon saint Augustin* (Paris: Études Augustiniennes, 1966).

[10] Although one should now see the very recent article by Christoph Markschies, 'Was ist latinischer "Neunizanismus"?', *Zeitschrift für Antikes Christentum*, 1 (1997), 73–95, which argues for a body of Latin 'neo-Nicene' theology stretching from the second half of the fourth century in continuity through to Augustine.

ship made *en passant*, and there are comments in articles and books which presume this or that relationship, but there are no serious studies.[11] Scholarship identifying the role of 'tradition' is largely limited to the study of the genre of *de Trinitate*, particularly its relationship to the 'ascent' motif in neoplatonism.[12] Obviously it is true that historical theology, especially scholarship on the development of trinitarian doctrine during the patristic period, has not been as productive or responsible as one would think it should have been. On the other hand, this lack of productivity (resulting in a lack of trustworthy insight or 'facts') has not visibly stopped anyone in the field of Systematics from saying whatever they wanted to say about Augustine's trinitarian theology.

Two of the criteria for judging the historical quality of a reading have collapsed into one another: it is often now the case that the placing of the text in a larger narrative is functionally equivalent to reproducing (sometimes unconsciously) specific scholarly judgements. For many theologians writing about Augustine's trinitarian theology, the larger 'external' narrative is simply de Régnon's grand scheme of 'western trinitarian theology *begins with* (in the sense of "presumes" and "is ultimately concerned with") divine unity (i.e., the essence) while eastern trinitarian theology *begins with* divine diversity (i.e., the persons)'. The narrative provided by de Régnon's paradigm is filled in, as it were, with du Roy's work to provide the following 'historical context': 'the emphasis in Augustine's trinitarian theology on divine unity is indebted to the influence of neoplatonism'. I have elsewhere argued the hidden character of the origins of this judgement, and I will not repeat that argument here.[13] What I will suggest now is that the judge-

---

[11] There is one well-known account of Augustine's relationship to Greek theology, Irenée Chevalier, *S. Augustin et la pensée grecque: Les Relations trinitaires* (Fribourg en Suisse: Librairie de l'Université, 1940), but it is impossible now to credit the argument of that work. There are, however, a number of treatments of Augustine's trinitarian theology written during the 1950s, in the first blush of Chevalier's publication, which take his conclusions as authoritative.

[12] As I pointed out in 'The Arians of Book V, and the Genre of *de Trinitate*', *JTS* 44 (1993), 185–95, in older scholarship the emphasis on genre has served functionally as a way of removing *de Trinitate*, and the trinitarian theology it expresses, from any historical context.

[13] I have argued that the narrative presupposed by many modern accounts of Augustine's trinitarian theology is that of Théodore de Régnon—or rather, a greatly simplified version of de Régnon's study. See my 'The Use of Augustine in Contemporary Trinitarian Theology', *TS* 56 (1995), 237–51 and 'De Régnon Reconsidered', *Augustinian Studies*, 26 (1995), 51–79.

ment of the 'neoplatonic' character of Augustine's trinitarian theology may have once had the function of placing that trinitarian theology within a historical context and within a narrative of the development of doctrine (namely, placing that trinitarian theology within the historical context of late fourth-, early fifth-century Latin neoplatonism). But if such a judgement on *the 'neo-platonic' character of Augustine's emphasis on unity* ever had the function of locating that theology within a historical context, the judgement does not, cannot, continue to do so credibly any longer. There are several reasons why reading Augustine's trinitarian theology as an event in Latin neoplatonism can no longer credibly serve to locate that theology historically, of which I shall only three name. The first reason is that the understanding of neoplatonism as a historical phenomenon which was presumed for that narrative is itself no longer viable from a scholarly point of view.[14] The second reason is that the secondary work which supposedly supports such a judgement (e.g. du Roy's) in fact does not.[15] The third reason why reading Augustine's trinitarian theology as an event in Latin neoplatonism can no longer credibly serve to locate that theology historically is the point of departure of this essay: such a location fails to reflect the doctrinal content of the texts it is supposed to explain, depending as it does upon an *a*historical, decontextualized, or dismembered reading of the texts.

This brings us to the last three criteria: an identification of and fluency with conceptual idioms that are the building blocks of the author's logic or expression; a close reading or exegesis of the text which uncovers the key steps in the author's logic or expression;

---

[14] Let me offer an obvious example: the last chapter of A. H. Armstrong's *The Architecture of the Intelligible Universe in the Philosophy of Plotinus* (1940; rpt. Amsterdam: Adolf M. Hakkert, 1967) is on Plotinus' doctrine of the λόγος. In this work Armstrong argues that Plotinus had a 'subordinationist' understanding of λόγος and he suggests that this Plotinian understanding had been absorbed into any Christian trinitarian theology influenced by Plotinus. Later, however, Armstrong recanted of this position, having recognized that the λόγος doctrine he had attributed to Plotinus was in fact Philo's. Thus, Armstrong's treatment of Plotinus in *The Cambridge History of Later Greek and Early Medieval Philosophy* (Cambridge: Cambridge University Press, 1967) makes no mention of the λόγος critique so prominent in *The Architecture of the Intelligible Universe*.

[15] It is too frequently assumed that a triadic analysis of existence is 'neoplatonic', but there is no historical reason for such an assumption. The authority for many observations on triadic usage in Augustine's trinitarian theology, namely du Roy, does not identify the triad as neoplatonic since he is well aware of the alternative sources.

and reading the parts of the text in relation to the whole. This essay will utilize these three techniques especially (or most explicitly) in order to develop an alternative account of Augustine's trinitarian theology. I will focus on three conceptual idioms (or motifs) in Augustine's trinitarian theology. First, the doctrine of inseparable activity as the fundamental expression of divine unity; second, the epistemic character of the Incarnation as the decisive revelation of divine unity, that is, of the Trinity, especially as the decisive revelation of their inseparable activity; and third, the 'hermeneutical' circle of faith by which true doctrine leads to the process of personal imaging (of the Trinity), which leads to greater doctrinal insight which leads to greater imaging of the Trinity, etc. This essay is principally a series of text-studies, but the reader should find that with these three conceptual idioms (or motifs) we find the basis for a rereading of Augustine, one which better represents Augustine's trinitarian theology by better fulfilling the seven criteria just articulated. The narrative of that rereading may be summarized: as one would expect of a late fourth-/early fifth-century Latin writing on the Trinity, Augustine's basic frame of reference for understanding the Trinity is the appropriation of Nicaea. That appropriation takes place within a polemical context, and, moreover, involves rearticulating the creed of Nicaea in terms which were not originally part of that text. In Augustine's time, the most important of such articulations is that 'the unity of the Trinity is found in its inseparable activities or operations'.

II The Theology of *Epistle* 11

The earliest written treatment of the doctrine of the Trinity by Augustine is in his *Epistle* 11,[16] a letter to Nebridius, a friend and fellow North African who shared his experiences in Italy.[17] Augustine clearly functioned as a mentor to the community of serious-minded young Christians he moved within in Italy and in

[16] I use the English translation of Sister Wilfred Parsons in the Fathers of the Church series, vol. 12 (1951).

[17] *Epistle* 11, written in AD 389, is not simply the first time Augustine uses the term 'trinitas' in his extant writings but—according to James J. O'Donnell—the only time the word is used by Augustine before his ordination in AD 391. See O'Donnell's commentary *Augustine—The Confessions*, 3 vols. (Oxford: Clarendon Press, 1992), iii. 309, which is his note on *Confessions* 12.7.7. Despite the seemingly obvious

Africa. In a series of letters which constitute the occasion for the earliest of Augustine's preserved correspondence, Nebridius asks Augustine to explain *how is it that if the Trinity do all things together in unity, then why is the Son alone said to be incarnated and not the Father and the Holy Spirit as well?* Answering this question leads Augustine first into Trinity and then—seamlessly—into christology, a fact which will deserve some attention. But first, Nebridius' question itself requires comment.

The point of departure for Nebridius' question is 'Nicene' theology as it had been developed—in both East and West—by the AD 380s. By the 380s, 'Nicene' trinitarian theology had developed substantially beyond the doctrine first articulated in the creed of Nicaea, 325. There had developed, for example, a sensitivity to the need for usage which positively identifies the separate existence of the Father, Son, and—with somewhat lesser emphasis—the Holy Spirit. Such a sensitivity is nowhere to be found in the original theology of Nicaea, 325. However, a very important development in the 'Nicene' trinitarian theology of the 380s is the way in which the unity among the Three is conceived and articulated. Obviously the usage of 'Father' and 'Son', and the continuity of nature presupposed in any 'fatherly' generation of a 'son', articulate a notion of a kind of unity within the Trinity. But the understanding that the very usage of 'Father' and 'Son' applied to God is to be understood as identifying the kind of continuity of nature presupposed in any 'fatherly' generation of a 'son' is precisely what is to be proved in the trinitarian controversies (since the opposition will argue that these titles are to be understood adoptively). It is this conclusion which anti-Arians strive for, not the demonstration of the unity.[18]

---

significance of *Ep.* 11 as an occasion to perceive Augustine's earliest trinitarian theology, the recent substantial article by Nello Cipriani, 'Le Fonti Christiane della Dottrina Trinitaria nei primi Dialoghi di S. Agostino', *Augustinianum*, 34 (1994), 253–312, contains no treatment whatsoever of the letter. See, however, Ayres's forthcoming treatment of *Ep.* 11 in his 'Augustine on the Unity of the Triune God', in R. Dodaro and G. Lawless (eds.), *Augustine and his Critics*. Presently, the most extensive study of *Ep.* 11 remains du Roy's in his *L'Intelligence de la foi en la Trinité selon saint Augustin*, 391–401.

[18] Which is not to deny the fact that in anti-Arian polemics attempts are made to 'save' Father and Son terminology from any conceptual weakness (e.g. the idea that calling God 'father' is implicitly to attribute passionate generation to Him). Moreover, arguments are made, e.g. by Basil of Ancyra and the Homoiousians, which explicitly advance the 'Father'-'Son' model as the paradigm of descriptions of the Trinity in conscious opposition to anti-Nicene theology.

I would suggest, rather, that the most fundamental conception and articulation in 'Nicene' trinitarian theology of the 380s of the unity among the Three is the understanding that *any action of any member of the Trinity is an action of the three inseparably*. This development in 'Nicene' trinitarian theology, which begins in the late 350s, becomes the most distinctive feature of pro-Nicene polemic, and—by the 380s—is identified as the substance of 'Nicene' theology.[19] Hilary of Poitiers' use of such an argument is probably the most appropriate to specify here, since his book will be read later by Augustine. In his *de Trinitate* VII. 17-18, Hilary says that 'the whole mystery of our faith' (*omne sacramentum fidei nostrae*[20]) is contained in the teaching that the Son does the same work as the Father and that 'the same things the Father does are all done likewise by the Son' (*ut omnia quae Pater facit, eadem omnia similiter facit et Filius*[21]). This truth Hilary calls 'our confession of Father and Son' (*Et ut maneret salutaris in Patre et Filio confessionis nostrae ordo*[22]).

The question which Augustine answers in *Epistle* 11 reflects Nebridius' attempt at understanding the 'Nicene' faith which he wants to hold properly. Nebridius understands that catholic trinitarian theology holds that all actions performed by the Father, Son, and Holy Spirit are performed in common. Augustine himself recognizes the source—and, if you will, the 'canonical' context—of Nebridius' question when he begins his answer by making explicit that source or context: 'According to the Catholic faith, the Trinity is proposed to our belief and believed . . . as so inseparable

---

[19] The terms 'neo-Nicene' and 'pro-Nicene' are technical, if still somewhat fluid, names for two kinds of trinitarian theology based on Nicaea. To a certain extent it is appropriate to understand these two theologies as two understandings of Nicaea, and one can also understand the difference between the two to be that of sequence: pro-Nicene is later (although pro-Nicene theology does not wholly replace neo-Nicene theology). The two terms correspond approximately to the difference between Athanasius' trinitarian theology and the trinitarian theology of, e.g. Gregory of Nyssa. Distinguishing features of the two forms of 'Nicene' theology would include: (*a*) neo-Nicene theology is not engaged in the debate over John 5: 19, while pro-Nicene is, and (*b*) neo-Nicene theology identifies the Son as the single, proper 'Power' of God, while pro-Nicene theology understands both the Father and Son to share the 'Power' of God, and thus to share the same nature. See my 'One Nature, One Power: Consensus Doctrine in Pro-Nicene Polemic', *Studia Patristica*, XXIX (1997), 205-23.

[20] CCL 62, 277

[21] Ibid. 279.

[22] Ibid. 278.

that whatever action is performed by It [the Trinity] must be thought to be performed at the same time by the Father and by the Son and by the Holy Spirit.'

One last comment on the context of Nebridius' question: it is almost the same question that Augustine will refer to at the beginning of *de Trinitate*. At *de Trinitate*, I. 8, immediately after the work's original beginning (at I. 7), and just after repeating the same summary of Catholic faith found earlier in *Epistle* 11, Augustine says: 'Yet this faith worries some people, when they hear that the Father is God and the Son is God and the Holy Spirit is God, and yet this threesome is not three gods but one God. They wonder how they are to understand this, especially when it is said that the Trinity works inseparably in everything that God works. . . .'[23] Augustine completes this observation with the remark, 'People ask us these questions to the point of weariness . . .'. When, at the beginning of the fifth century, Augustine wrote these words Nebridius had been dead for nearly ten years. It was not the persistent requests of his old friend which so wearied Augustine the bishop; it was the problem of understanding a trinitarian theology which one wanted to believe—even as that theology was, as *de Trinitate*, I. 9 makes clear, still facing criticism and competition from an alternative theology (namely, the theology of the Homoians).[24] The inherently difficult task of attempting to understand catholic or Nicene trinitarian theology is a task Augustine admits he shares, must share, with Nebridius. Augustine's reply to Nebridius begins by admitting the difficulty of the issue and the tentativeness of his answer. That tentativeness is something to which we shall return.

Augustine's answer to Nebridius starts with the thesis that any

---

[23] *The Trinity*, trans. Edmund Hill, *The Works of St Augustine* (Brooklyn, NY: New City Press, 1991), I/5, 70.
[24] The standard account of Latin Homoianism is Michel Meslin, *Les Ariens d'Occident 335–430* (Paris: Éditions du Seuil, 1967). A substantial description of Latin Homoianism can be found in the 200-page introduction by Roger Gryson for his translation, *Scolies Ariennes sur le Concile d'Aquilée*, SC 267 (Paris: Les Éditions du Cerf, 1980). A very good recent account of the growth of Western Homoianism can be found in Daniel H. Williams, *Ambrose of Milan and the End of the Nicene–Arian Conflicts* (Oxford: Clarendon Press, 1995). In *The Search for the Christian Doctrine of God* (Edinburgh: T. & T. Clark, 1988), R. P. C. Hanson has a chapter describing 'Homoianism' which purports to describe both Greek and Latin Homoian theology, but in fact the chapter contains a significant treatment only of *Latin* Homoian theology (as though there were no differences between it and Greek Homoianism).

nature may be analysed in or through three characteristics: that the nature *is* (or exists); that such a nature *is this or that* (i.e. that something was specific identity); and that it *continues to be* what it is (its identity endures). Such an analysis might suggest an analogy to the Trinity because Augustine understands that the first characteristic of a nature—that it is—'shows us the very cause of nature from which all things come', while the second characteristic of a nature—that a nature is this or that 'shows us the appearance in which all things are fashioned and in a certain sense formed'. That a characteristic should indicate 'the cause from which all things come' seems analogous to the distinctive characteristic of the Father, while 'appearance' and 'form' seem christological in character—at least retrospectively, given what Augustine says in *Epistle* 14 and develops further in his later writings.

The rest of Augustine's argument is peculiarly cast: if we could observe any existing nature or substance which failed to possess one (or two) of these characteristics, then one of the Trinity could possibly act without the other two. But we never observe any existing nature or substance to lack one of the three characteristics, so the Trinity does indeed act in unity. Augustine adds that if one understands the logical necessity that mandates each of the three characteristics of being then one can similarly understand that the Trinity must act in unity. Augustine introduces the triad not because it is a trinitarian analogy in the sense that each of the three 'characteristics' stands for one of the three persons. The point of the triadic analysis of substance or nature is to provide an example of a common operation which serves as an analogue to the understanding that Augustine is ultimately working through—namely, that the Three share common operations, and that such common operations indicate (and are caused by) their common nature.

There are many comments to make about this argument by Augustine. Whether or not the argument is quite so spectacularly 'subtle' as Augustine claims it is, the argument is not very convincing: it is, perhaps, too subtle by half. Having said that, some slightly more constructive observations can be offered. First, the argument is an argument for the unity of action among the Three and not an argument that the Three are One. The description of unity among the Three in terms of the unity of action is very much a traditional Nicene way of speaking about trinitarian unity. A second observation, which goes to the heart of Augustine's argument, is that the ontological analysis Augustine offers of *the kinds of action* that we are talking about in trinitarian theology *as unified* is similar to other pro-Nicene polemics, like that of Gregory of Nyssa, in its probable debt to a technical philosophical analysis of being. Gregory's debt is to Plotinus' notion of power;[25] Augustine, of course, has a *triadic* analysis of being—which is unlike Hilary of Poitiers and Gregory of Nyssa, but like Marius Victorinus. We cannot, however, say *where* that triadic analysis is coming from or what philosophical influence it represents. Cicero? Quintillian? Porphyry? Marius Victorinus?[26] The most important thing, which needs emphasizing, is that recourse in trinitarian doctrine to a philosophical analysis of being is typical of Nicene and pro-Nicene argument or reasoning, and such recourse is not in itself distinctive to Augustine, nor, obviously, is it an innovation.

The underlying question of the pro-Nicene doctrine that unity of nature is demonstrated in the unity of action surfaces again in *Epistle* 14, another letter written to Nebridius which continues the conversation already begun in *Epistle* 11. Nebridius remarks upon the fact that although he (Nebridius) and Augustine are separate persons they do many of the same things as the other (e.g. they both walk).[27] Nebridius then refers to the sun and the other stars:

---

[25] See my 'Eunomius of Cyzicus and Gregory of Nyssa: Two Traditions of Transcendent Causality', *Vigiliae Christianae*, 52 (1998), 59–87.

[26] Du Roy's treatment of the triadic language in *Ep.* 11 is substantial, and his identification of the different possible sources for the language remains as the authoritative account. However, while in his treatment of *Ep.* 11 du Roy is circumspect about attributing a specific source for the usage, in his lengthy 'Conclusion' he is less circumspect and it is this part of the study which supports characterizations of Augustine's trinitarian theology as constituted fundamentally by neoplatonic triads.

[27] Although this is not the place for a full treatment of this fact, it is nonetheless worth noting that Nebridius' reference to 'walking' as the activity shared by Augustine and himself indicates the Stoic provenance of the topoi employed in the discussion. Stoics regularly use walking as an exemplary example of continuity between intention (or impulse) and doing. Moreover, walking features in Stoic arguing points for the reality of individual acts over against Platonic and Aristotelian over-evaluation of the universal. In short, in these early epistles we have evidence of the influence of philosophical authorities other than neoplatonism, and, to push this point, insofar as we can recognize the continuity between what Augustine speaks of in his letter and the philosophical discussion he is drawing upon, then it seems as though Augustine is employing arguments used by Stoics to argue *against* the very sort of reification of universals Augustine is often accused of maintaining. See Seneca, *Epistle* 113. 18–24; John M. Rist, *Stoic Philosophy* (rpt. 1980; Cambridge: Cambridge University Press, 1969), 33–4; and Brad Inwood, *Ethics and Human Action in Early Stoicism* (Oxford: Clarendon Press, 1985), 52, 156.

the sun does not do the same things the other stars do. The point
of such remarks for trinitarian theology is fairly straightforward:
catholic trinitarian theology argues that whatever shares the same
nature performs the same actions, and what performs the same
actions must have the same nature; the Father and the Son perform the same actions so they must have the same nature, and
sharing the same nature they act in unity. But, Nebridius observes,
Nebridius and Augustine share the same nature (i.e. humanity)
and perform many of the same actions: is that the kind of unity
the persons of the Trinity have? Moreover, the sun and the stars,
seemingly possessed of the same nature, do not perform the same
actions (the sun heats us, stars do not, etc.). How does this affect
the logic of the argument that whatever shares the same nature
performs the same actions?

Augustine's reply is informative for what it reveals about his
logic. In the same way as he had already argued in *Epistle* 11,
Augustine begins by transposing the question. In *Epistle* 11
Augustine argues for the necessity of the unity of the triadic
characteristics of being, and the presence of all three of the
characteristics in the Trinity, by simply saying that having the
proper understanding of being we see that each occasion of being
demonstrates the presence of the three characteristics. Those three
characteristics—with their attendant unity—must therefore obtain
in the Trinity. In *Epistle* 14 Augustine begins his reply with the
same kind of transposition: if it is true that you and I—we
humans—do the same actions, then whatever else has the same
nature must also do the same actions. If we move, Augustine tells
Nebridius (and we do, both of us walking), then the sun and the
stars also move. Just as we both awaken, the sun and the stars all
shine. The reality of *common nature–common action* that we know
serves as the basis for knowing that other cases of common nature
result in common action. The provocative character for us of this
argument by Augustine is due, to a degree not to be underesti-
mated, to our not recognizing, these ignorant centuries later, the
rhetorical or logical school of discourse in which Augustine is
implicitly casting his argument for Nebridius. But the provocative
character for us of Augustine's argument is also due to discursive
moves within the text (and thus within Augustine's logic or rhetorical form) which begin to reveal themselves after a close reading. I
shall return to this remark in a moment.

If, in *Epistle* 14, Augustine argues that our experience that identical activities must follow from natures which are in fact identical provides a basis for our knowing that the sun and the stars must share common activities since they share common natures, there must be, nonetheless (Augustine asserts), a significant qualification to all such comparisons. No two physical existents, no two bodies, ever really perform the same operation since no two bodies can occupy the same space at the same time.[28] And if two bodies never really perform the same operation so much more is there an intrinsic incommensurability in comparisons between intellectual operations and the actions of bodies: the unity in a common act of contemplation exceeds comparison with the unity in a common physical act. In other words, in terms of the overall argument what Augustine really wants Nebridius to consider is what might be called the formal character of his arguments. Comparisons between physical and intellectual realities are always bound by intrinsic limitations or incommensurateness. Despite the limitations, there is, however, a certain utility to the comparisons. Articulating that utility brings us back to *Epistle* 11 and the initially provocative character of Augustine's argument noted above.

In *Epistle* 11, after Augustine has articulated his three-characteristics-of-nature argument, he turns to the topic of the Incarnation. Nebridius' original question was, after all, a question focused upon the Incarnation: if the Three act as one, then why do we attribute Incarnation only to the Son and not to the Father and Holy Spirit as well? Augustine describes the Son in terms of a distinguishing characteristic such as those already introduced. But the distinguishing characteristic is not immediately one of the original three which the reader might have suspected were trinitarian analogues (especially a twentieth-century reader primed to look for trinitarian analogues). The distinguishing characteristic of the Son is expressed in rather idiosyncratic terms by Augustine: a 'system of life' and a 'sort of art' and the understanding which forms a mind in its thoughts. Such titles suggest the unique role the Son plays—particularly in the Incarnation—in revealing the content and practice of knowledge and a way of life which are necessary in order for us to understand God the Trinity. This act of

---

[28] This observation by Augustine also echoes the Stoic topos associated with *walking*: namely, that the same class of action (e.g. walking) varies in each actual case of doing.

revelation is distinct to the Son and is properly understood as his
distinctive characteristic or activity. (I call this distinctive revelation
in the Son the 'epistemic' characteristic or activity.)

Having said this Augustine then introduces a new set of questions which further the previous ontological analysis. The original
triadic characteristics Augustine earlier invoked all followed the
pattern of 'All nature or substance [must] . . .'. The first such
characteristic was 'All nature or substance exists [or must exist]'.
The second set of analysis introduced at *Epistle* 11.4 constitutes a
further development of the question 'Does this exist?' The question
of whether something exists implies the question 'What is it?'. The
question 'What is it?' leads to the question of its value. Augustine
remarks that 'all these arguments are inseparably joined together'.
This inseparability is the reason why Augustine introduces the new
analytic categories: to illustrate an important case in which the
three 'moments' which occur in understanding existence are necessarily implied by or 'joined' to one another, even if we move
through each question one at a time and may have to discover or
be taught the existence of the 'next' question and its connection to
the previous question. Indeed, it is not the individual criteria of
being which are of decisive interest, but the fact that they are
inseparably joined and that each leads discursively one to the other.

The discovery, as it were, of the three 'inseparably joined' arguments or characteristics provide the occasion for Augustine to offer
a triad that is in fact analogously descriptive of the Trinity.
Understanding proceeds from the Father, and through the Son
(the character of that understanding in the Son has already been
described by Augustine), and the Holy Spirit produces in the
knower a delight in that knowledge. The distinctive characteristics
of each person of the Trinity are not articulated through an ontological analysis but through an analysis of the epistemological or
soteriological prerequisite for human knowledge of the reality of
the unity of the joint operations of the Trinity. All operations of the
Trinity occur in perfect union, but due to our weakness we have
to be brought to an understanding of this fact. The unity of action
in the Trinity can only be understood (without meaning to be technical about that word) by a human mind that has been properly
trained in right reason, a way of reasoning which, Augustine says,
can best be understood as a way of life.[29] That way of life, revealed

---

[29] This insight of Augustine's will develop and continue to undergird his trini-

in the Son generally and in the Incarnation in a special way, is necessary for the unity of action among the Three to be understood by us in what we might well call an organic way: although the operations of the Three 'occur with the most complete union and inseparability, they none the less have to be proved separately, by reason of our weakness . . .'. Augustine's first triadic account of God is one which describes the joint action of the Trinity in providing humanity with the knowledge necessary in order to understand that life-in-Trinity properly. The common work of the Trinity in providing that knowledge finds its effect in the Incarnation. Augustine has thereby answered Nebridius' question: the Three are all acting in the Incarnation, but the Incarnation must be understood within the context of the Trinity's self-communication. 'First we propose to know on what we may construct an argument and on what ground we may stand. That is why a certain rule and standard of reasoning had first to be proved. This has been accomplished by that dispensation of the Incarnation. . . .' Although *Epistle* 11 pre-dates the beginnings of *de Trinitate* by more than a decade it would be hard to find another summary which better captures the dynamic and motivation of that later work.

I have reviewed *Epistle* 11 in such detail not simply because the letter offers us a revealing, and under-appreciated, view of Augustine's early trinitarian theology, but, more to the overall point of this essay, many of the key doctrinal points which Augustine articulated at this early period remained active throughout his writings on the Trinity. The most obvious (though not necessarily the most significant) example of such a doctrinal 'point' would be Augustine's habit of seeking analogies to the unity of the Trinity. More significant, I think, is the aid *Epistle* 11 can serve in sensitizing the reader to the question of exactly what 'unity' is it that Augustine is trying to explain. In *Epistle* 11 Augustine is seeking to provide an insight into the doctrine of the unity of action

---

tarian theology, thereby proving the practical import for the psychological analogies he will offer in *de Trinitate* and other works. The type of mental life—mapped out within the analogies and elsewhere—that we are to lead is one which purifies the heart and reflects the love which is the root dynamic of the Trinity. Precedents for such a link between 'faith and right conduct' may be observed, for example, in Gregory of Nyssa's *Life of Moses* and in Evagrius' ('Basil of Caesarea') *Ep.* VIII, where the goal of a purified contemplation (identified with the 'kingdom') is intellectual sight of the Lord and the Trinity.

among the three Persons of the Trinity.[30] The notion that the three Persons act inseparably is, for Augustine, the fundamental doctrine of catholic (which is to say Nicene or pro-Nicene) trinitarian theology. What I do not mean to suggest is that already in *Epistle* 11 Augustine's trinitarian theology is mature and well conceived. It is not. Augustine knows that the three Persons act inseparably, but his sense of the logic of that doctrine is not strong, and there is a certain artificiality in his explanation to Nebridius of the doctrine. One can say either that Augustine does not yet really understand the doctrine, or, alternately, one can say that Augustine is, at the time of *Epistle* 11, ignorant of the polemical argument developed (by e.g. Hilary or Ambrose) in support of the doctrine that the three Persons act inseparably. The traditional polemical argument is sophisticated in its use of Scripture and philosophical notions of aetiology, and in the linking of those two resources. Augustine's argument in *Epistle* 11 lacks the sophistication attained nearly forty years earlier by Hilary in *de Trinitate*, VII. Augustine knows what he must believe, he has some interesting ideas in support of those catholic beliefs, but there is much of catholic theology which has not yet begun to play in his thought.

There is one last point to make (again) about *Epistle* 11. As an early (AD 389) work by Augustine, it dates precisely from that period in his life when he is most engaged with neoplatonism, and during which, some scholars have suggested, his thought was largely dominated by neoplatonic categories (to the extent, according to a few influential scholars, he is better understood as a 'convert' to neoplatonism, rather than a convert to Christianity).[31] Over-against this vision of rampant neoplatonism, we find in *Epistle* 11 a treatment of the Incarnation and the unity among the Three expressed in usage clearly informed by Nicene or pro-Nicene doctrine. Moreover, the philosophical categories that are clearly

[30] When in *Sermon* 52. 17 and 18 Augustine introduces the psychological analogy to the Trinity, he is clear that he is searching for an analogy to the inseparable activity. Thus, he says: 'Let us see, then, if I can't find something in creation, by which to show that there are three somethings which can both be separatedly presented and also operate inseparably' (*Sermon* 52. 17, p. 57). And: 'So turn your eyes to the person within. That is where some kind of likeness is rather to be looked for of *three somethings that can be indicated separately but operate inseparably*' (*Sermon* 52. 18, pp. 58–9, emphasis added).

[31] Whatever the later articulations of these judgements, the modern source is probably Otto Scheel, *Die Anschauung Augustins über Christi Person und Werk* (Tübingen: Verlag von J. C. B. Mohr, 1901).

and undeniably in Augustine's account of the unity of the Trinity are not of any clear neoplatonic provenance; in fact, they are most likely drawn from stoic sources. The very authority—du Roy—which is often held to have 'proved' the neoplatonic character of Augustine's trinitarian theology is rather the source for our glimpsing that the triadic usage in *Epistle* 11 may come from a wide variety of sources.

III THE THEOLOGY OF *EIGHTY-THREE DIFFERENT QUESTIONS* NO. 69

The christological focus articulated in *Epistle* 11 can be found again in no. 69 of the collection *Eighty-Three Different Questions* (or *Div. Quaest.*).[32] These 'notes' by Augustine on various topics that arise in his theological reflection (sometimes privately, sometimes in response to a question posed by someone) date from AD 388 to 395/6. *Div. Quaest.* no. 69 is usually dated to 394-6, which means about five years after *Epistle* 11, in that time when Augustine has settled into his life as a cleric, but before he had been consecrated bishop and before he had begun to write the *Confessions*. *Div. Quaest.* no. 69 either slightly pre-dates Augustine's turn to scriptural investigation (particularly the works of Paul), or marks one of our earliest expressions of that well-known turn.[33] The note is, in fact, an exegetical reflection on 1 Corinthians 15: 28, with recurring attention to John 14: 18 and Philippians 2: 5-7. The cause of Augustine's reflection on 1 Corinthians 15: 28 is, as he tells us explicitly (indeed, in the first line of the text), the heretical exegesis some lay upon the passage. These heretics are commonly identified as 'Arians',[34] but the more accurate term is 'Homoians'. The term 'Arian' pushes not simply the origin but the identifying features of such a theology back too far in time, so that a modern

---

[32] David L. Mosher (trans.), *Fathers of the Church* series, vol. 70 (1982).

[33] Augustine wrote *De libero arbitrio* from AD 391-395; the *Usefulness of Belief* was written soon after Augustine became a priest (in AD 391); and the *Letter to Simplicianus* dates from AD 397.

[34] Mosher, the translator of *Eighty-Three Different Questions*, so identifies Augustine's opponents as 'Arians' in his Fathers of the Church translation, vol. 70, p. 167, n. 2. Similarly, G. Bardy, J.-A. Beckaert, and J. Boutet, the editors of the Bibliothèque Augustinienne, *Oeuvres de Saint Augustin*, vol. 10, likewise identify Augustine's opponents as 'Arians' on p. 83 n. 82.

reader imagines the distinctive traits of the theology Augustine opposes to be the specific doctrines expressed by Arius.[35] This is a misleading conclusion, for Augustine's opponents espouse doctrines beyond whatever Arius himself believed. This fact is especially significant—indeed, decisive—if one is to understand Augustine's exegetical strategies, and thus to understand the role of exegesis in the development of Augustine's trinitarian theology.

First Corinthians 15: 28 is a good example of a scriptural text under polemical pressure.[36] We know that in the second half of the fourth century, one way that Latin Homoians articulated their opposition to the trinitarian faith by then associated with Nicaea, AD 325, was through an exegesis of 1 Corinthians 15: 28.[37] In their eyes, this text says that at the end of time the Son will be subject or subordinated to the Father. The fact that we use 'sub-ordination(ism)' as a generic category for a kind of trinitarian or christological doctrine should not desensitize us to the fact that in Latin Homoian theology there is, literally, the attribution of a

[35] Augustine's reasons for using the title 'Arian' have to do with the polemical strategy adopted by Latin Nicene polemicists and those Greek Nicene polemicists who followed Athanasius. Opponents to a theology identified with Nicaea were reduced to, or identified as, followers of Arius and holders of his theology. See my 'The Fourth Century as Trinitarian Canon', in L. Ayres and G. Jones (eds.), *Christian Origins: Theology, Rhetoric and Community* (London and New York: Routledge, 1998), 47–67. Augustine himself understood the difference between doctrines and exegeses which originate directly from Arius, and those which originate with later anti-Nicenes: in *de Trinitate*, for example, he is quite specific in what he attributes to 'Arius', 'Arians', and 'Eunomians', respectively. Modern confusions of the three should not be projected back on to Augustine, whatever rhetorical identifications he may sometimes have employed in his polemics.

[36] In Greek theology of the first half of the fourth century, 1 Cor. 15: 28 figured prominently in the hyper-Nicene (modalist) theology of Marcellus of Ancyra. Augustine seems unaware of the association of the Scripture passage with Marcellus. Evagrius' *Ep.* 8 provides an example of a Greek anti-Homoian (though Evagrius argues against the Greek variety of Homoians) argument for 1 Cor. 15: 28 which focuses exclusively on the Homoian claims on the passage and shows no indication of anti-Marcellan sensitivity. (I cite this letter, erroneously attributed to Basil, because Evagrius is Augustine's almost exact contemporary.) Like Augustine, Evagrius was born in the 350s, and in the 380s witnessed close up, but not as one directly engaged, the confrontation with anti-Nicenes. *Ep.* 8 could have been written anytime from the early 380s to the early 390s (i.e. it is approximately contemporary to Augustine's *Ep.* 11 and *Div. Quaest.* 69).

[37] In the *Acts of the Council of Aquilaea*, no. 39, the Homoian Palladius evidently cites 1 Cor. 15: 28 when he says that the Son is subject to the Father. See Gryson, *Scolies Ariennes sur le Concile d'Aquilée* (SC), vol. 267, p. 359. Some scholars think that this Palladius is the author the *Arian Sermon* Augustine writes a rebuttal of in AD 419.

'subordinate' status to the Son, based, in part, upon exegesis of scriptural texts such as 1 Corinthians 15: 28. Other scriptural passages under polemical pressure from the Homoians include John 14: 28, a text Augustine invokes at the end of his first paragraph of *Div. Quaest.* no. 69 as one which is associated by some with what he considers to be a problematic interpretation of 1 Corinthians 15: 28.

Augustine's refutation of Homoian exegesis begins with the standard Nicene exegetical rule: wherever Scripture speaks of the Son as less than the Father, Scripture is there speaking of the Son's humanity; wherever Scripture speaks of the Son as equal to the Father, Scripture is there speaking of the Son's divinity. This rule provides the basis for a correct understanding of scriptural passages such as John 10: 30, John 1: 1, 14, and Philippians 2: 5–7. However, Augustine recognizes that the Homoians are not arguing for the Son's inferior and different nature simply on the basis of incarnational passages; the Homoians are arguing that some of the scriptural passages which distinguish the persons of the Trinity indicate the Son's inferiority (in short, these passages have nothing to do with Jesus' human weakness). Augustine himself recognizes two kinds of statements in Scripture about the second person: those which distinguish the persons of the Trinity; and those which apply to the assumption of humanity in the Incarnation.

The Homoians read 1 Corinthians 15: 28 to mean either that some things are not now subject to the Son, or that the Son is not now subject to God. The anti-Nicene impetus to saying that 'some things are not now subject to the Son' is fairly obvious, but the polemical weight of suggesting that the Son is not now subject to God is less clear. Interestingly, though, it is this second reading that Augustine treats as the most significant to refute. Augustine is most concerned to reject the suggestion that the status of the Son vis-à-vis the Father will change intrinsically at the end times (i.e. that the Son will become subject to God although he is not now). He is concerned to reject such a suggestion not because Augustine thinks that nothing changes at the end time, but because he has his own very significant and substantial understanding of what 'happens' at the end times, an eschatological dynamic Augustine does not want derailed or confused in our understanding.

Augustine's argument follows this form: the passage 'when he [the Son] will hand the kingdom over to God and the Father' is to be understood following the model of 'Hallowed be thy name'. The line from the Lord's prayer does not mean that God's name is not now holy; rather, the prayer asks that God's name be recognized as holy. Similarly (Augustine argues), 'when he [the Son] will hand the kingdom over' does not mean that the kingdom is not now under the dominion of God; rather, Paul speaks of the time when God's kingdom will be recognized in and through the Son. Or, as Augustine puts it, 'when he [the Son] will show that the Father reigns'. At the end time the Son will 'show' or reveal that the Father reigns as He has always reigned. That dominion has not always been, indeed has never been, *shown*: it has, rather, been believed. What happens at the end times is that the Son will show that the Father reigns, so that what believers have known through belief will be made manifest to them. 'Therefore Christ will hand the kingdom over to God and the Father when through him the Father will be known by sight, for his kingdom consists of those in whom he now reigns through faith.' The meaning of 'the Son will hand the kingdom over' is that `then the Father will be known by sight as He—and the Trinity ("God")—is known now by faith.'

The purpose of this 'handing over of the kingdom', that is, the revealing of the kingdom's existence, is both christological and trinitarian, if we can still use such clumsy categories which are already beginning to crumble under a pressure they cannot bear.[38] The christological and trinitarian *telos* of the 'handing over of the kingdom' is the incarnated Son's leading 'those nourished by faith in his incarnation to the actual seeing of his equality with the Father'.[39] At some future point in time the humanity of Christ, which is now the occasion of our faith, will become perfectly transparent to the divinity of the Son: the vision of that divinity will itself open up into a vision of Trinity. The Son will, 'through

---

[38] We have come now to a key insight into Augustine's 'trinitarian' and 'christ-ological' theology. If the trinitarian axis around which Augustine's theology is structured is the common activity of the Trinity, then the christological axis which equally structures his theology is the Son as revealer of God the Trinity. These two, particularly at the point of intersection of the two axes, map out Augustine's theology; indeed, the intersection of the two is very important in that his theology is one which radically resists the distinctly modern categories of 'trinitarian' and 'christological'. It may indeed be that the widespread modern misreading of Augustine is due, in some substantial way, to an inability to escape the theological violence of the presumed dichotomy between 'trinitarian' and 'christological'.

[39] Mosher (trans.), *Eighty-Three Different Questions*, 175.

himself, the only begotten, cause the Father to be seen by sight. . . . by leading those who now believe in him through faith in his incarnation to the vision of divinity.'[40] That vision is our blessedness, our happiness; of this Augustine is both certain and explicit.[41] In Augustine's theology there is an analogy between the *seen and unseen forms or natures in Christ, and the seen (form or nature) of Christ and the unseen of the Trinity* (an analogy offered with polemical—anti-Homoian—purpose). As the analogy would suggest,[42] the proportionality expresses the equality of the 'unseen' of Christ and the 'unseen' of the Trinity: in each case the 'unseen' is the divine nature. The proportion thus expresses the unity of divinity in Christ with the divinity of the Trinity. Moreover, in different ways over time (beginning with the Incarnation) but nonetheless, what is 'seen of Christ' resolves into (or is the basis for discerning) the 'unseen of Christ' and the 'unseen of the Trinity'. In all cases, the 'unseen' is divinity; in all cases the 'unseen' is the *same* divinity. The dynamic resolution of the 'unseen' in Christ is itself the dynamic resolution of the 'unseen' of the Trinity, and in each case the resolution appears through what will be seen, the 'seen' of Christ.[43]

Augustine's treatment of the trinitarian significance of 1 Corinthians 15: 28 has its climax in book I of *de Trinitate*. In that work Augustine continues the problematic of *Div. Quaest.* no. 69 and makes wholly explicit what was wanting in his earlier argument. The already-present kingdom and the drama (within that kingdom) of the Son 'bringing to God' all humanity[44] is stated pre-

---

[40] Ibid. 175–6. Here again we find an echo of the old question from Nebridius, for Augustine remarks that the decisive faith which recognizes the Son-humbled-as-a-servant properly has the Son as its object, for it is the Son indeed who has undergone this descent 'for one cannot say that the Father either became flesh or was judged or crucified'.

[41] 'For our blessedness is in direct proportion to our enjoyment of God in contemplation' (ibid. 170).

[42] An analogy is, after all, a proportion, which in this case can be expressed: '*the seen of Christ : unseen of Christ :: the seen of Christ : the unseen of the Trinity*'.

[43] A good illustration of this point may be found in Augustine's *Forty-Third Tractate on John* (written sometime between AD 416–420). In sect. 12, in an explicitly anti-Homoian argument, Augustine asserts that the Son, invisible and equal to the Father, made himself visible when he assumed the form of a servant. The Son will show himself again, in the future, when God will be revealed not through a created image (as in the OT), but through the Son.

[44] 'Humanity' here means both the 'humanity' of human nature per se and the 'humanity' of all of us ever alive.

cisely in terms of the epistemic role of the Son as the occasion, the just means,[45] for the revelation of the Trinity (especially in that final revelation), and in terms of the inseparable work of the Trinity. This revelation of the Trinity through the Incarnation Augustine understands both as dependent upon and as the fruition of the real unity that exists between Son and Father. Augustine's description of the epistemic drama of the Incarnation is literally contained, as if by bookends, by assertions of the unity between Father and Son.

We can, in fact, read *de Trinitate*, I. 15–18 as a virtual checklist of references back to issues articulated in the earlier texts. *De Trinitate*, I. 15 begins with Augustine invoking 1 Corinthians 15: 28, and he then cites John 14: 28, the same Scripture passage invoked in *Div. Quaest.* no. 69 in conjunction with 1 Corinthians 15: 28, as examples of texts that are being subjected to Homoian claims. The Homoian claim on John 14: 28 is deflected by the use of Philippians 2: 5–7, the same citation used in the same role it had in *Div. Quaest.* no. 69. As Augustine returns to 1 Corinthians 15: 27–8 and the question of how the 'handing over [of the kingdom]' is to be interpreted, he says that *the Father's and the Son's working are inseparable*, the technical and quasi-credal expression of Nicene orthodoxy which again serves to pivot the discussion into the 'handing over' issue, this time tied to an exegesis of 1 Corinthians 15: 24. The anti-Homoian impetus to this discussion is flagged at the beginning of *de Trinitate*, I. 16 with the reference to (as Hill puts it) the 'cranks' who believe that when the Son 'hands over the kingdom' he deprives himself of it. At this point in his argument Augustine is at a position within which he can direct our attention to the basic question, 'What then does it really mean, "When he hands over the kingdom to God and the Father"?' The answer to this question brings us directly into an articulation by Augustine of the epistemic quality of the drama of the Incarnation, the developing revelation of the Trinity accomplished by and through the Incarnation over time. 'The fact is that the man Christ Jesus, mediator of God and men [1 Tim. 2: 5], now reigning for all the just who live by faith [Heb. 2: 4], is going to bring them to direct sight of God, to the face to face vision. . . . that is what is meant by "When he hands over the kingdom to God and the

---

[45] One can indeed recognize in Augustine a foreshadowing of Thomas's understanding of the Incarnation as 'beautiful' and the paradigmatic work of fine art.

Father," as though to say "When he brings believers to a direct contemplation of God and the Father."' Augustine next returns to the trinitarian issue of the 'inseparable nature in the inseparable works' by citing John 10: 30, a preferred Nicene proof text (since before Nicaea! since Alexander of Alexandria). Augustine then links this revealed unity to one of his favourite narratives of divine unity, the discourse to Thomas in John 14: 8–25. 'In a word, because of this inseparability, it makes no difference whether sometimes the Father alone or sometimes the Son alone is mentioned as the one who is to fill us with delight at his countenance.'[46] This connecting of the trinitarian content of the epistemic event of the Incarnation with a traditional proof text (John 10: 30) for the fundamental unity that exists between Father and Son is repeated again later on in *de Trinitate*, I. 18: 'The actual truth is that "I and the Father are one," and therefore when the Father is shown, the Son who is in him is shown also, and when the Son is shown, the Father who is in him is shown too.'[47]

Augustine's understanding of the soteriological role of the Son locates the Son's mission precisely in the way in which he functions as a kind of epistemic event. Such an epistemological (or revelatory) function is not so much that of revealing what a good human, or even what a good Christian looks like (although he reveals that as well), but rather that the Son, as humbled servant, is the *proper occasion for and proper object of* faith. Already in *Div. Quaest.* no. 69 Augustine uses words which suggest his later argument in *de Trinitate*, XIII that the Son saves not through the 'power game' but through 'the humility game'; Augustine says that 'those believing in him are saved, not through his glory, but through his humility'.[48] The movement from 'form of God'—in which the Son's equality with the Father is evident—to 'form of servant'—in which the Son's equality with the Father is masked (but available in faith)—makes possible a decisive or substantial revelation of God's love, and the unity of that love in action among the Three. The drama of the Incarnation reveals the Three acting in unison in expressing their love; the content of the revelation of the Incarnation is the joint action of love.[49] Stating Augustine's

---

[46] Hill (trans.), *The Trinity*, 77.
[47] Ibid. 79.
[48] Mosher (trans.), *Eighty-Three Different Questions*, 175.
[49] The editor of the critical edition of *de Trinitate*, W. J. Mountain, sees in

theology in this way makes clear the way Nicene/pro-Nicene theology 'controls' his theology of the Incarnation, as well as providing an insight into why Nebridius' question[50] continues to echo throughout Augustine's writings on the Trinity, long after Nebridius' death.[51] The depth of divine love is flattened, with a corresponding vitiation of the revelatory character of the Trinity in the unity of their love, if there is no true, full Incarnation, that is, if Philippians 2: 5-11 does not describe the drama of someone who is fully divine.[52] This fact alone is sufficient to set Augustine on the road to a full engagement with the subordinationist theology of anti-Nicenes. But, more to the point of Augustine's specific understanding of the Son as decisive revelation, Augustine must make it clear—must make it certain and secure—that the very act of

Augustine's articulation of a doctrine of divine inseparability, e.g. at *de Trinitate*, I. 8, signs of Ambrose's doctrine of divine inseparability from *de Fide* IV. 6. 68. (See CCL 50, p. 36, in 22/24.) The parallel is not a precise one, but what may be found there in Ambrose is a doctrine of the inseparability of divine action articulated in terms of the inseparability of divine love. This aspect of Ambrose's treatment comes closest to Augustine's understanding of what is at stake in any trinitarian theology of inseparable or common activity. The NPNF translates Ambrose as: 'Furthermore, to prove to you that it comes of Love, that the Son can do nothing of himself save what he has seen the Father doing, the Apostle has added to the words, "Whatsoever the Father has done, the same thing does the Son also, in like manner," this reason: "For the Father loves the Son" and thus Scripture refers the Son's inability to do, whereof it testifies, to unity in Love that suffers no separation or disagreement' (NPNF, 2nd series, x. p. 270).

[50] Is the Son acting alone, or if not, why do we not say that the Father and Spirit as well were incarnated?

[51] For just one of many more possible examples, see *Sermon* 213.7 (Hill, the English editor/translator, will say only that it was delivered 'before 410'), a sermon on the creed in which Augustine says 'the Son, the Word, became flesh; not the Father, not the Holy Spirit'. But the whole Trinity made the flesh of the Son; the Trinity, you see, works inseparably'. *Augustine's Sermons* (*The Works of St. Augustine* (Hyde Park: New City Press, 1995)), iii/6, p. 144.

[52] Augustine draws upon Phil. 2: 5-7 in virtually every one of his treatments of the Trinity, although the basis for his understanding of the special authority of the scriptural passage is not clear. That a text like *De Fide et Symbolo* (AD 393), which otherwise reveals almost nothing distinctively Augustinian in its theology, still contains frequent appeals to Phil. 2: 5-7 suggests that Augustine's linking of the Philippians passage to a normative understanding of the Trinity may not have been his idea alone, and his claim in *de Trinitate*, II that Phil. 2: 5-7 has a 'canonical' function may not be just Augustine's own idea about the significance of that passage. Both Marius Victorinus and Hilary of Poitiers (see esp. *de Trinitate*, IX. 14-15) give special attention to Phil. 2: 5-7. An initial suggestion of how Phil. 2: 5-7 functions in Augustine's trinitarian theology may be found in Jaroslav Pelikan, 'Canonica regula: The Trinitarian Hermeneutics of Augustine', in *Collectanea Augustiniana*, ed. J. Schnaubelt and F. van Fleteren (New York: Peter Lang, 1990), 329-43.

revelation-in-humiliation is not understood as proof of the impossibility of real union between Father and Son.[53] I am not talking simply of Augustine dealing with—and refuting—a challenge of 'the Son suffers, therefore He is not (really) God'. The debate has widened beyond that point; it was widened when Homoians found in the Old Testament theophanies grounds for doubting the Son's divinity.[54] The Homoians have set the epistemic or revelatory character of the Son against his unity with the Father; Augustine would add that they set the epistemic character of the Son against the unity of divine love in action.

In Augustine's judgement, Homoians misunderstand the revelation of the Incarnation (that is, the way in which the Incarnation functions as revelation); in fact, they misunderstand it twice. The first misunderstanding constitutes their own theology of the Incarnation: the Son's life and death reveals the true God through his obedience to the 'will' of the Father; this obedience is the obedience of a subordinate following the commands of a superior.[55] The second Homoian misunderstanding of the revelation in the Incarnation lies in their understanding of what is the Nicene doctrine of divine revelation in the Incarnation. The Homoians think that Nicenes identify it with the obedience of the Son's body to the divine in the Son. However, this reading is close enough to the truth that Augustine can (as his theological sophistication grows) feel the sting of its criticism.[56] The Nicene 'everything weak

[53] My judgement that with *Eighty-Three Different Questions* no. 69 Augustine's trinitarian concern is for the Son as visible revealer of the Father and of the Trinity itself is, I think, supported by the subject of *Div. Quaest.* no. 74 (written shortly after no. 69). In *Div. Quaest.* no. 74 Augustine's interest turns to Col. 1: 14-15, 'In Whom we have redemption and remission of sins, *who is the image of the invisible God*' (emphasis added). As one would expect from the account I have given, it is precisely the character of the Son as perfect 'image' that concerns Augustine in the later *Question*.

[54] I have mapped out developments in Latin Homoianism criticism of Nicene theology in 'Polemics and Exegesis in the Early Books of *de Trinitate*', forthcoming in *Augustinian Studies*. A portion of that article was presented as the communication, 'Augustine's *de Trinitate* in its Polemical Context: Book I', North American Patristics Society, 1997 annual meeting.

[55] For example, the so-called *Arian Sermon* contains repeated assertions that the Son acted 'at the will and command' of the Father. One such assertion appropriate to quote here reads, 'At the will and command of the Father, he [the Son] came down from heaven and came into this world . . .'. (translated by Roland Teske, SJ, in his select collection of Augustine's writings, *Arianism and Other Heresies* (Hyde Park: New City Press, 1995), *The Works of St. Augustine* i/18, p. 133).

[56] One does not have to believe that Hilary's christology was actually 'docetist'

to the human body, everything glorious to the divine Word' can, improperly nuanced, leave one with a sense that the divine is impervious to the trauma (the 'humiliation') of the Incarnation.[57] Eventually, Augustine will take steps to correct false tendencies in standard Nicene accounts of the Incarnation, just as he will rework the Nicene understanding of the trinitarian significance of 1 Corinthians 1: 24, in both cases developing more and more a pro-Nicene understanding of each doctrine.[58]

IV Conclusion

In modern theology, when works of Augustine's theology of the Trinity are read, they tend to be read with the presumed context of 'neoplatonism'. It is this 'neoplatonic' context which serves to makes sense of that theology of the Trinity, which provides the basis for identifying the key terms or concepts, the underlying logic, and then even the 'historical' milieu of this theology of the Trinity. By contrast, I have offered a reading of Augustine's theology of the Trinity which locates that theology within a more likely and more credible historical context, namely Latin 'catholic' theology of the late fourth and early fifth centuries ('catholic' meaning Latin theology which looked to the reception of Nicaea as normative). In his earliest writing on the Trinity Augustine invokes the doctrines and terminology associated with Nicene theology. I have shown that the fundamental shape and development of Augustine's theology may be found in his attempts to understand or make sense of the key doctrines and terminology of that

to see that it—like Athanasius'—kept any suffering from the divine element in the Incarnated Son. On the other hand, some of what Augustine was interested in articulating would have been expressed in the 'kenosis' categories of theology in the second half of the fourth century.

[57] Augustine says regularly that 'it was the Lord of glory who was crucified'—as at *de Trinitate*, I. 28.

[58] After the early books of *de Trinitate*, Augustine no longer uses 1 Cor. 15: 28 as an occasion to discuss the epistemic character of the Incarnation, rather he treats the passage in line with the questions raised at the beginning of *de Trinitate*, I. 15: does the Son's human nature pass away by being absorbed into divinity at the end time? The fact that Augustine relates 1 Cor. 15: 28 to the same trinitarian/christological issues in *Div. Quaest.* no. 69 and *de Trinitate*, I and II, but ceases thereafter, is one reason why I included *de Trinitate*, I–V in the same chronological set of writings (i.e. 'early') as *Ep.* 12 and *Div. Quaest.* no. 69.

theology within the polemical context of the end of the fourth century. I have proposed that Augustine's theology of the Trinity is centred on divine unity conceived in terms of the inseparable activity of the Three (the traditional Nicene understanding of divine unity), the epistemic character of the Incarnation as the decisive revelation of the Trinity, and the role of faith in leading forward our reflection of the Trinity. These three 'Nicene' features can be documented in Augustine's earliest writing on the Trinity through a reading of those texts which is more credible than the 'neo-platonic' reading in terms of criteria of a bona fide 'historical' reading. Once identified, these three 'Nicene' features can be found in various stages of development throughout Augustine's writings, although admittedly the demonstration (or revelation) of this fact lies outside the scope of this essay. The purpose or use of what I have offered here is not to explain example by example how something which looks 'neoplatonic' is not, but to provide an alternative narrative with which to make sense of Augustine's theology of the Trinity, which provides the basis for identifying the key terms or concepts, the underlying logic, and the 'historical' milieu of this theology of the Trinity.

While many in Systematics today would describe their work as 'post-modern' and thereby marking off a separation from the theological issues and forms of discourse arising out of Enlightenment agendas and sensibilities, the fact remains that the judgements of such theologians of the key moments, figures, and dynamics in the history of Christian theology are still firmly imbedded in the perceptions of Enlightenment Christianity. One can easily name several givens in the 'modern' understanding of doctrinal history which still function as foundational presuppositions in con-temporary—even 'post-modern'—theology: the existence of the 'Cappadocians' and a Cappadocian theology; the presumed integrity of the concept of 'christology'; an ahistorical application of 'oeconomia' usage; the accuracy of de Régnon's paradigm; and the fundamental character of 'Neoplatonic' trinitarianism in Augustine's theology. Each of these thoroughly modern categories for understanding patristic theology is, in fact, an act of self-definition on the part of modern Systematic theology, and needs to be acknowledged (and studied) as such. Conceptual or 'Systematic' claims to the contrary, contemporary efforts at fresh beginnings are really articulated and conceived largely in ecclesiological terms—

how do I believe and articulate something 'new' that my communion (predominantly) does not?—but the terms of reference remain
deeply old-fashioned and unquestioned.[59] My own desire would be
that contemporary theology investigates each of these historical
characterizations for what each reveals about the needs of modern
and contemporary theology. The least I would expect from contemporary theology is that it recognize that its claims to 'post-
modernity' are cheaply won, for its conceptual tender remains that
of the Enlightenment confederacy.

[59] Many contemporary Systematicians like to think—and will say—that they
are doing something new. My phrase '[in] ecclesiological terms' is an attempt to
identify and localize that 'newness': a position sounds new because it has a 'new'
judgement on familiar terms (e.g. the 'Cappadocians', Augustine's neoplatonic trinitarian theology) but in fact the 'new' is just a rearranging of old, worn, and very
familiar presuppositions (e.g. does the Augustine of de Régnon's paradigm and du
Roy's 'triads' violate the oeconomia of Cullmann and Newman?). The 'edge' to the
newness is all ecclesiastical: a new doctrinal fashion-statement within the same old
garment district of historical fabrication.

Systematic Issues

8

Substance and the Trinity

WILLIAM P. ALSTON

I The Programme

My aim in this paper is to examine a certain criticism of classical formulations of the doctrine of the Trinity, viz., that they are defective by reason of being formulated in terms of a 'substance metaphysics'. I will argue that once we appreciate the character of that metaphysics and disentangle it from views with which it is associated by many contemporary theologians, the charge will be seen to be without substance (if you will pardon the expression). Substance metaphysics does not enable us to resolve all the difficulties inherent in the doctrine, but neither does that metaphysics hamper us in our attempts to deal with those difficulties.

Thus I will be sallying forth in defence of a very traditional way of thinking of the Trinity. But I am anxious to avoid being typecast as the worst kind of pre-modern thinker. Though I find the metaphysics utilized in ancient formulations to be innocent of various charges brought against it, I am far from supposing that there is no useful, valuable, and even essential work to be done on the Trinity by contemporary thinkers. I do not suggest that we simply repeat one or another patristic formulation and let it go at that. The Trinity, no less than other articles of the Christian faith, needs re-examination and reformulation for each age, as has happened throughout Christian history. The doctrine provides inexhaustible riches for exploration, a task to which each period brings distinctive skills and perspectives. For example, recent discussions have illustrated ways in which twentieth-century logic can be employed to render threefoldness in unity less mysterious. Again, twentieth-century theologians have made important contributions to the bearing of the Trinity on worship, prayer, and spirituality. Recognizing these and kindred points, the last thing I would want to do, even if I could, is to inhibit creative, imaginative, sensitive reflection on how to think of the Trinity and how to delineate its place in Christian thought and practice. But, as I see it, the usual reaction against a formulation in terms of substance is misconceived; and so far from aiding creative thought about the Trinity, its tendency is rather the opposite. By locating what is needed in the wrong quarter, it diverts attention from avenues along which real progress might be made in rethinking the doctrine and its implications.

When I say that I want to defend 'classical formulations' from the charge that substance metaphysics renders them defective, what formulations do I have in mind? My concern is not with any particular formulation by a patristic or medieval theologian, or any particular creed. I will be citing several formulations that fit the rubric. For my purposes any formulation will suffice that thinks of the divine threeness in oneness in terms such as the following:

The Son is of one *substance* with the Father

The Son is generated from the *substance* of the Father

Father, Son, and Holy Spirit are three different *persons* (*hypostases*)

Rather than presenting at this point some formulations from the Fathers, I will first go back to the fountainhead of substance metaphysics, Aristotle, from whom the Fathers inherited the concepts in terms of which they set out their substantialist formulations. That will provide a useful, indeed essential, background against which to untangle the often knotty aspect these formulations present. I do not suggest that the theologians in question were card-carrying Aristotelians, even to the extent that Augustine was a card-carrying neoplatonist. I am not even assuming that the patristic theologians I quote were familiar with the *Categories* and *Metaphysics* of Aristotle. But Aristotle's philosophy was the original source of the substance terms employed in these formulations. As long as no notice is given to the contrary, we must assume that the best place to find the concepts expressed by these terms is the *Metaphysics* and the *Categories* of Aristotle.

II Aristotle on Substance

Chapter 5 of the *Categories* opens with this statement.

Substance, in the truest and primary and most definite sense of the word, is that which is neither predicable of a subject nor present in a subject; for instance, the individual man or horse. But in a secondary sense those things are called substances within which, as species, the primary substances are included; also those which, as general, include the species. For instance, the individual man is included in the species 'man', and the genus to which the species belongs is 'animal'; these, therefore—that is to say, the species 'man' and the genus 'animal'—are termed secondary substances. (2a 11–18)[1]

What is 'predicable of a substance' is some general property or relation that is true of it, that can be truly predicated of it. What Aristotle calls 'present in a substance' is a particularized property or relation—the colour of this apple or the location of this tree. Leaving aside the fine print, the basic idea is that an individual substance is that which has properties and stands in relations, rather than being itself a property or a relation of something(s) else. This is the common-sense view, enshrined in language, at least Indo-European languages and no doubt many others as well, that there is a fundamental distinction between things that bear or 'stand under' (*substare*) properties, and the properties they bear. Moreover, the bearer, the substance, cannot be identified with the sum of its properties. It is an entity of a different and more fundamental sort. Aristotle holds to this common-sense conviction through all the abstruse twists and turns of his metaphysics.

The other basic feature of individual substances is that they retain their identity through changes of their properties, at least their 'accidental' properties, those that are not necessary for their being the individuals they are. 'The most distinctive mark of substance appears to be that, while remaining numerically one and the same, it is capable of admitting contrary qualities.'[2] This distinguishes substances from events, which do not remain self-identical through change. Unlike events, a substance has no temporal parts. It is wholly present at each moment and temporal

---

[1] R. McKeon (ed.), *The Basic Works of Aristotle*, trans. E. M. Edghill (New York: Random House, 1941).

[2] *Categories*, Ch. 5 (4a, 10–12).

period of its existence; hence it is the same thing at each stage of a change; whereas an event clearly does have temporal parts. The whole of a flight across the Atlantic is not present during each minute of the flight. On the contrary! During the first minute only that (temporal) part of the flight is in existence. Since the whole flight exists only over the whole temporal span it occupies, it is not the same event at each period of the change.

What Aristotle calls 'secondary substances' are better known today as 'natural kinds'. He makes a sharp distinction between the natural kind to which an individual belongs (the 'species' that includes it) and all other general properties that can be predicated of it. He takes it to be an objective metaphysical fact about each individual substance that there is one unique kind to which it belongs in the special sense that membership in that kind constitutes the essence of the individual without which it could not be what it is. This is opposed to the widespread modern view, already enunciated by Locke, that an individual belongs to as many kinds as there are general terms that can be truly predicated of it, and that it is arbitrary to pick out one of these as the 'real essence' of the individual. It is as true to say that a particular human being belongs to the kind *capable of laughter* or the kind *University professor* or the kind *baseball fan*, as to the kind *human being*. Each of these constitutes what Locke calls a 'nominal essence'. Depending on the context, one or another of these will be of more interest than others. But there is no objective basis, metaphysical or otherwise, for picking out one of these as the *essence* of the individual.

Since Aristotle takes it to be an objective fact that each individual belongs to a unique kind, such as *human being, water, horse,* or *maple tree,* which constitutes the essence of those individual substances belonging to it, these kinds can themselves be called 'substance' in a secondary sense. A natural kind is, so to say, 'the substance' of each individual belonging to it. *Being a tree* is 'the substance' of each individual tree.

Aristotle's discussion of substance in the *Metaphysics* is complicated by the oscillation between these two senses—*primary substance*, the concrete individual, and *secondary substance*, that feature of an individual that makes it a substance. Questions are raised such as 'What is substance?', where it is not clear whether he is asking about primary or secondary substance. Nevertheless, a fairly clear position emerges. Corporeal (individual) substances are composites of matter and form, which are related as potentiality and the actualization thereof. This potentiality–actuality distinction (and with it the form–matter distinction) exists on different levels. The proximate matter of a living organism, that which is informed by the essence of the organism (the matter that Aristotle calls 'flesh and bone' when he is thinking of higher animals), is itself a *formed* matter, though less formed than that of which it is matter. Again, the flesh and bone is itself a matter–form composite, with the underlying matter consisting, as we would say nowadays, of certain organic compounds. These in turn involve the informing of more rudimentary matter, their elementary constituents, which in turn. . . . At the bottom of this hierarchy is *prime matter—pure* matter, *pure* potentiality, which is intrinsically informed in no way, the *ultimate substratum* of all substance. Being wholly bereft of forms itself, it cannot exist separately but only as an aspect of corporeal substances. Incorporeal substances, on the other hand, are pure subsisting forms with no matter that they inform.

III Classical Formulations

There are, of course, many components to an exposition of the doctrine of the Trinity, many issues on which it can seek to throw light. Here I will concentrate on only one such issue (without any suggestion that it is the only one, though it is particularly funda-mental), viz., how are we to understand the unity and diversity in the triune God. God is one what and three what's. That is the main point on which the fathers deployed substance metaphysics. A short formulation is that the Father, Son, and Holy Spirit are three persons (individuals, *hypostases*) in one substance. But this decep-tively simple formula conceals many complexities.[3]

The Fathers I will be briefly surveying here—Origen, Tertullian, Basil of Caesarea, Gregory of Nyssa, Augustine, and John of Damascus—all stress, to various degrees, the individual distinct-ness of the 'persons' of the Trinity, sometimes to the point of

---

[3] I am heavily indebted to H. A. Wolfson (*The Philosophy of the Church Fathers* (Cambridge, Mass.: Harvard University Press, 1956)) in providing this patristic neo-phyte guidance in locating passages in the Fathers that are crucial for their uses of substance metaphysics. I have also profited from C. Stead (*Divine Substance* (Oxford: Clarendon Press, 1977)), though his discussion is much more detailed and complex than can be reflected in this paper.

verging on tritheism. Thus, Origen insists that God and the Logos
are real beings and argues against those (modalists) who believe
that the distinction between them is not in number but only
according to ways we think of them.[4] And Tertullian says of the
Son that He is 'to be considered as substantive in reality, by
reason of a property of his substance, in such a way that he may
be regarded as a certain thing and person, and so be able, as being
constituted second to God, to make two, The Father and the Son,
God and the Logos'.[5] Tertullian also refers to each member of the
Trinity as a 'substantive thing' (*substantiva res*).[6] What makes the
persons of the Trinity distinct is the causal relations in which they
stand to each other. According to Basil, the distinguishing property of the Father is that he is ungenerated, of the Son that he is generated,[7] and of the Holy Spirit 'His being sent from God and sustained by the Son'.[8] And according to John of Damascus the Father
is 'without beginning, that is to say, uncaused, for He is from no
one', whereas the Son is 'not without beginning . . . for He is from
the Father', and the Holy Spirit comes 'forth from the Father, not
by filiation but by procession'.[9]

We also find this conviction of the distinct individual character
of each Person in the frequent analogies between the relation of the
Persons of the Trinity to their unity, and the relation of created
individuals of the same species to their common nature or essence.
Thus, Basil, in explaining the unity of the Persons in the divine
nature, compares it with four individuals named Peter, Andrew,
John, and James, who are all one in that they all belong to the
species 'man'.[10] And John of Damascus says that though 'Peter is
seen to be actually distinct from Paul . . . we see that Peter and
Paul are of the same nature and have one common nature, for
each of them is a rational and mortal animal'.[11] As we will see

---

[4] *In Joannem Commentarii*, x. 21, in Allan Menzies (ed.), *The Ante-Nicene Fathers*,
x, Supplement, 5th edn. (Grand Rapids, Mich.: Wm. B. Eerdmans, 1990), 401–2.
[5] *Adversus Praexan*, 13, cited in Wolfson, *Philosophy of the Church Fathers*, 323.
[6] Ibid. 26, 324.
[7] *Ep.* 38, 4, in NPNF, 2nd series, viii. 138–9.
[8] *Adversus Eunomium*, iii. 6, cited in Wolfson, *Philosophy of the Church Fathers*,
340.
[9] *De Fide Orthodoxa*, i. 8, in F. W. Chase (trans.), *Writings of St. John of Damascus*
(New York: Fathers of the Church, Inc., 1958), 187–8.
[10] *Ep.* 38, 2, in NPNF 2nd series, viii. 137.
[11] *de Fide Orthodoxa*, i. 8, in Chase (trans.), *Writings of St. John of Damascus*,
185–6.

later, it is dubious that such analogies do justice to the divine unity. But they clearly show their authors to be dead serious about treating Father, Son, and Holy Spirit as so many different individuals.

If the matter is set up in this way, what account is to be given of the divine unity—three persons but one God. The standard formula is *one substance*. But we already have three different divine substances. How, then, can God be *one* substance?

This confusion goes back to Aristotle's use of *ousia* both for the individual bearer of an essence and properties (*prōtē ousia*) and for the essential nature that makes the individual a substance (*deutera ousia*).[12] The different persons are each said to be a *prōtē ousia*, a subsistent individual. The divine unity, when put in terms of *ousia*, is taken to consist of the common essential (divine) nature which the three persons share. The use of the same term for both was bound to cause trouble and did. In Origen, who wrote before the terminological problems were cleared up, we find *ousia* used in both ways. Thus, he says both that 'The Son is a being (*ousia*) and subject distinct from the Father',[13] and that they are of one *ousia*.[14] Here the first occurrence is Aristotle's 'first *ousia*', the individual substance, and the second is Aristotle's 'second *ousia*', the essence of an individual substance. And because of this ambiguity the crucial statement of the Nicene creed that the Son is '*homoousios* with the Father' is likewise ambiguous. Though it was undoubtedly intended to mean 'of the same essence as the Father', it could be, and was, understood as 'being the same individual as the Father', in which sense it would be denying the numerical distinctness of the persons of the Trinity.

It was the Cappadocian Fathers who put the seal on what

---

[12] One may wonder why Aristotle used a nominalization of a form of the verb 'to be' for either of these senses? Why didn't he use *ousia* to mean something like *being*? The explanation provided by Aristotle himself is that while there are many senses in which something is said to be, the primary sense is that of 'substance'. For any other beings are either properties of substance, relations between substances, affections of substances, and so on. Hence substance *is* being par excellence. In this connection it is interesting to note that in the English translation of the Nicene creed in the latest Episcopal Book of Common Prayer, the more usual translation of *homoousion tō patri* as 'of one substance with the Father' is replaced by 'of one being with the Father'.

[13] *de Oratione*, 15 in R. A. Greer (trans.), *Origen* (New York: Paulist Press, 1979), 112.

[14] *In Joannem Commentarii*, x. 21, in Menzies (ed.), *Ante-Nicene Fathers*, x. 402.

became the standard way in the East of avoiding this confusion. That involved employing the term *hypostasis* for an individual substance, and reserving *ousia* for essence. *Hypostasis* is not prominent in Aristotle's discussion of the metaphysics of substance,[15] even though, ironically enough, it is the etymological twin of *substantia* (substance), which became the standard translation of *ousia* in Latin and many modern languages, including English. Both are derived from roots meaning *standing under*, terms well suited to the Aristotelian conception of an individual substance as that which 'stands under' or 'underlies' properties. In Patristic literature the term is already employed by Origen, who speaks of Christ as *hypostasis*.[16] In criticizing those who deny that the Father and Son are distinct numerically, he says that they deny that Father and Son are 'different in their *hypostases*'.[17] And elsewhere he says of Father and Son that they are 'two considered as *hypostases*'.[18] Plotinus likewise speaks of the members of his trinity, the One, the Nous, and the Soul as *hypostases*. Basil and Gregory of Nyssa consistently mark the distinction between Aristotle's first and second *ousia* by using *hypostasis* for the first and *ousia* for the second. 'The distinction between *ousia* and *hypostasis* is the same as that between the general and the particular; as, for instance, between the animal and the particular man.'[19] And they are followed in this by John of Damascus. ' "*Ousia*" means the common species including the *hypostases* that belong to the same species—as, for example, God, man—while "*hypostasis*" indicates an individual, as Father, Son, Holy Ghost, Peter, Paul.'[20]

This gives us an unambiguous terminology for formulating the Trinity in terms of a substance metaphysics. But the Latin Fathers were faced with a somewhat different situation to which they reacted in a different way. What seems in hindsight a natural move would be to parallel the Greek *ousia–hypostasis* distinction by using *essentia* for what is common to the members of the Trinity, and *sub-*

---

[15] Steve Davis has reminded me that the term is used fairly extensively in Aristotle's scientific works.

[16] *de Principiis*, 1. 2. 2 in A. Roberts and J. Donaldson (eds.), *The Ante-Nicene Fathers*, iv. 246.

[17] *In Joannem Commentarii*, x. 21, in Menzies (ed.), *Ante-Nicene Fathers*, x. 402.

[18] *Contra Celsum*, viii. 12, in Roberts and Donaldson (eds.), *Ante-Nicene Fathers*, iv. 643–4.

[19] Basil, *Ep.* 236, 6, in NPNF, 2nd series, viii. 278.

[20] *de Fide Orthodoxa*, iii. 4, in Chase (trans.), *Writings of St. John of Damascus*, 275.

stantia for each member. That would give us three substances in one essence. But *substantia* was so firmly entrenched as a translation of *ousia* that the way to this solution was barred. What happened instead was that *substantia* was used for Aristotle's second *ousia*, and the individual members of the Trinity were designated as *personae*, thus giving rise to the standard Latin formula of *three persons in one substance*. Of late it has become fashionable to assert that *persona*, as used by the Latin Fathers, had a meaning radically different from our modern term 'person'. I find much of this talk to be misguided and even confused. There is an interesting history of *persona*, and the Greek term *prosopon*, involving masks used by actors and the legal notion of the bearer of certain rights and responsibilities. And since the Greek Fathers made little use of *prosopon* for the members of the Trinity, preferring *hypostasis*, the meaning of their term of choice has no special connection with the modern concept of a person (whatever that is), or any other concept of a person. *Hypostasis* is used for any real individual substance; and its trinitarian employment was chosen for the sake of real individuality, not anything distinctively personal. Nevertheless, and this is the crucial point, the Fathers were quite clear that Father, Son, and Holy Spirit are distinctively personal in possessing knowledge, purposes, and intentions, and in performing intentional actions, including actions vis-à-vis human and other persons. There are, no doubt, connotations and associations that have accrued to the word 'person' in the last few centuries that are not applicable to the persons of the Trinity, such as *autonomy* and *extreme self-enclosedness*. The fact that the persons of the Trinity all together constitute one God inhibits our thinking of them in those terms. But there is a more fundamental notion of a person, as distinct from other types of substances, that would seem to be common to Christian theology and our talk of human persons through the centuries. This is the notion adumbrated by the above reference to distinctively personal attributes and activities. Given all this, I take it that Boethius' famous definition of *persona*, viz., *an individual substance of rational nature*, though it could be further elaborated, captures very well the sense of the term in which it is applied to members of the Trinity by the Latin Fathers. To be sure, we must always remember that terms originally developed for application to creatures cannot, usually, be truly applied to God in exactly the same sense, though that does not prevent a partial univocity such as I believe to hold with respect to 'person' as applied to the members of the Trinity and to human beings.

This brief excursus into person-talk is a detour from the main line of the paper. The question of the sense in which members of the Trinity have been spoken of as 'persons' in Patristic times and at other periods, and the question of the sense in which they can be truly called 'persons', is more specific than the one on which this paper is focused. In Aristotelian metaphysics, persons constitute only one sub-class of individual substances. Hence, the problem of whether the terms of that metaphysics are apt for conceptualizing the Trinity is a more general, and a more basic, one than the question of whether and in what sense 'person' is apt for that purpose.

There is one final resource of substance metaphysics used by the Fathers in formulating the unity and diversity of God. That involves another term that figures importantly in Aristotelian metaphysics, *hypokeimenon*, translated into English as 'substratum' (from Latin *substratus*). The etymology is similar to 'substance' and *hypostasis*, '*lying* under' rather than '*standing* under'. In both cases the metaphor captures the idea that the possessor of properties 'supports' them. But for Aristotle, whereas the emphasis of first *ousia* (substance) is on the concreteness and independent existence (subsistence) of the individual, the emphasis of *hypokeimenon* is on being that which 'receives' and 'supports' properties and can remain the same through change of properties. Thus, 'first *ousia*' is an absolute term. An entity is or is not an individual substance. But *hypokeimenon* is a relative term. X may be a substratum in one relationship but not in another. In particular, an individual substance, for Aristotle, is the substratum of its properties including its essence as well as its accidents. But the individual substance itself, as I pointed out earlier, is a composite of forms and what underlies and possesses them; and this at various levels. The ultimate substratum of all the forms of a material substance is prime matter, that which is intrinsically formless but is the ultimate bearer of all forms.

This is all a prelude to pointing out that some of the Fathers chose to represent the divine unity, not as a matter of the Persons possessing an essence in common, but in terms of their sharing a common *hypokeimenon*, an analogue to a *stuff* or *material* of which they are composed. In Book VII of *de Trinitate*, Augustine presents this substratum construal in opposition to the view that the divine unity consists in the Persons sharing a common species or genus. 'So now we are not talking any more in terms of genus and species, but rather in terms of what you could call the same common material. For example, if three statues were made of the same gold, we would say three statues, one gold; and here we would not be using statue as a specific and gold as a generic term, nor even gold as a specific term and statue as an individual one.'[21]

This is, of course, presented only as an analogy. None of the Fathers thought that God is literally constituted of some stuff or material. With respect to their favourite material analogue, several gold statues all being made of gold, they were at pains to point out that the common divine *hypokeimenon* is not something that is capable of independent existence, as gold can exist unformed into statues. Thus, Augustine writes: 'we do talk about three persons of the same being, or three persons one being; but we do not talk of three persons out of the same being, as though what being is were one thing and what person is another, as we can talk about three statues out of the same gold'.[22]

IV SOME PROBLEMS WITH THESE FORMULATIONS

Although I am concerned in this paper to defend the use of substance metaphysics in patristic trinitarian formulations, I do not claim that all is clear sailing with these formulations. And in saying that, I do not simply mean that they do not represent the Trinity as totally intelligible and free of mystery. That goes without saying. It is rather that in certain respects they fail to deliver what can be reasonably required of a formulation, in particular in their account of the divine unity.

We have seen two ways of using substance metaphysics to do this. Either the unity amounts to the Persons sharing a common essence or nature, or to their sharing a common 'stuff' or 'material'. Either a common (second) *ousia* or a common *hypokeimenon*. These suggestions display different weaknesses. The

[21] *de Trinitate* vii. 11, in St Augustine, *The Trinity*, trans. Edmund Hill (Brooklyn, NY: New City Press, 1991), 229.
[22] Ibid. 230. Notice how Augustine distances himself from the analogy by using 'being' rather than 'substratum' in speaking of the Trinity.

trouble with the second is more glaring but, perhaps, in the end less serious. The basic trouble is that it simply does not seem at all appropriate to think of incorporeal persons being constituted of any material or stuff. As we have seen, Augustine cautions us that this is only an analogy and not to be taken literally. But in the absence of some further indication of just how the analogy is to be understood, some indication of what there is in the divine being that is significantly 'stuff-like', it may well be felt that the analogy is insufficiently illuminating.

With the shared essence view, the problem is quite different. Here there is no difficulty in taking literally the thesis that Father, Son, and Holy Spirit share a common essence or nature. Since they are all divine, that commends itself as an eminently plausible suggestion. The trouble is that this in itself does not constitute a tight enough connection, a sufficiently intimate relationship, to give content to the conviction that all together they constitute one God. How does sharing a common essence amount to that? We have seen Basil comparing the trinitarian situation to four individuals named Peter, Andrew, John, and James, who are all one in that they all belong to the species 'man'. And I cited John of Damascus saying that though 'Peter is seen to be separate from Paul, still Peter and Paul are both of the same nature and have a common nature, for each of them is a rational and mortal animal'. But clearly Peter, Paul, James, and John do not make up one man by virtue of sharing the essence of humanity. How then are we to think of Father, Son, and Holy Spirit making up one God by sharing in the divine essence?

Our authors and their colleagues were not unaware of this difficulty. Apollinaris, in a letter answering the raising of this difficulty by Basil, invokes the distinction between an aggregate of individuals which are not causally connected with one another and a causally connected series of individuals. In the latter case, he says, two or more can be the same in *ousia*, just as all men are Adam, being one with him in *ousia*, since his essence is communicated to us in our generation. And it is in just this way that the Son is the same in *ousia*, as the Father, since He, begotten of the Father, derives that *ousia* from His begetter.[23]

---

[23] See Wolfson, *Philosophy of the Church Fathers*, 342–6. I understand that today the scholarly consensus is that this epistle is spurious. But even so, the suggestion contained therein can be discussed.

The appeal to the idea that all human beings are one in Adam does not answer the difficulty. For surely, according to the doctrine of the Trinity, there is only one God in a much stronger sense than that there is only one man, however the latter is spelled out. Otherwise the charge of tritheism remains on the table. Nor does John of Damascus settle the matter by the point that in the case of Peter and Paul their separation is seen by observation, but their unity is discerned only by 'reason and thought'; whereas for the Trinity, their unity is observed in 'actuality', while their plurality can be perceived only by 'thought'.[24] Though this may be a sound point, it does not seem to advance the question of how the possession of a common nature results in the Persons being one God rather than three Gods.

We find a more promising suggestion in Gregory of Nyssa's treatise 'Not Three Gods'. He makes a number of points there, but the most illuminating is the following. First, no term signifying the divine nature signifies that nature as it is in itself, since that is in principle unknowable to us. Instead it signifies how that nature manifests itself, or the effects that flow from it, or the ways in which it is related to creatures. And so when we confess one God, the specific meaning of this has to do with the divine operations that impinge upon us. He continues:

As we have to a certain extent shown by our statement that the word 'godhead' is not significant of nature but of operation, perhaps one might reasonably allege as a cause why, in the case of men, those who share with one another in the same pursuits are enumerated and spoken of in the plural, while on the other hand the Deity is spoken of in the singular as one God . . . ; men, even if several are engaged in the same form of action work separately each by himself at the task he has undertaken, having no participation in the individual action with others who are engaged in the same occupation. . . . But in the case of the divine nature we do not similarly learn that God does anything by Himself in which the Son does not work conjointly, or again that the Son has any special operation apart from the Holy Spirit; but every operation which extends from God to the Creation . . . has its origin from the Father, and proceeds through the Son, and is perfected in the Holy Spirit. For this reason the name derived from the operation is not divided with regard to the number of those who fulfil it, because the action of each concerning anything is not separate and peculiar, but whatever comes to pass, in reference either

---

[24] *de Fide Orthodoxa*, i. 8, in Chase (trans.), *Writings of St. John of Damascus*, 185-6.

to the acts of His providence for us, or to the government and constitution of the universe, comes to pass by the action of the Three, yet what does come to pass is not three things. . . . From Him, I say, Who is the chief source of gifts, all things which have shared in this grace have obtained their life. When we inquire, then, whence this good gift came to us, we find by the guidance of the Scriptures that it was from the Father, Son, and Holy Spirit. Yet although we set forth Three Persons and three names, we do not consider that we have had bestowed upon us three lives, one from each person separately; but the same life is wrought in us by the Father, and prepared by the Son, and depends on the will of the Holy Spirit. Since then the Holy Trinity fulfils every operation in a manner similar to that of which I have spoken, not by separate action according to the number of Persons, but so that there is one motion and disposition of the good will which is communicated from the Father through the Son to the Spirit . . . neither can we call those who exercise this Divine and superintending power and operation towards ourselves and all creation, conjointly and inseparably, by their mutual action, three Gods.[25]

Here we see Gregory reading the 'economic Trinity' back into the 'immanent Trinity', by virtue of the thesis that all our terms for the latter are based on terms for the former.

But there is also a more general line of which the above is a particular application. It is by virtue of a more intimate interrelationship that the members of the Trinity distinguish themselves from a group of men or other created substances. Another development of this general point is found in the notion of *perichoresis*, or mutual indwelling set forth by various writers. Thus, John of Damascus speaks of the three Persons as being one 'by reason of the co-eternity and identity of *ousia*, operation, and will, and by reason of the agreement in judgment and the identity of power, virtue, and goodness—I did not say *similarity*, but *identity*—and by reason of the one surge of motion'. He further says that this unity of *ousia* and rule is not due to a 'composition' or to a 'blending' whereby they would lose their individual distinctness, but rather a 'circumincession [*perichoresis*] one in the other' of the persons.[26]

Thus, the deficiencies of the notion of a common *ousia*, if taken by itself, are remedied, to some extent, by the introduction of the idea of a mutual *perichoresis*. And both Gregory and John, as well as Basil, take the ontological unity of common *ousia* and the 'eco-

[25] In NPNF, 2nd series, viii. 333-4.
[26] *de Fide Orthodoxa*, I. 8, in Chase (trans.), *Writings of St. John of Damascus*, 186-7.

nomic' unity of joint action as not separate from each other but as two aspects of one situation. It is by virtue of sharing in Godhood, *as they do*, that the Persons of the Trinity so interpenetrate and dwell in each other that the action of one is the action of all.

V CONTEMPORARY DISSATISFACTION WITH SUBSTANTIALIST FORMULATIONS

Although the problems I have just been canvassing are important ones, they are not what worry current theologians about formulations of the Trinity in terms of substance. The dissatisfactions they do express, I will argue, are, for the most part, misguided and do not really tell against the use of categories of substance in construing the Trinity.[27] I will begin the survey with a commentary on a passage in a recent work, *God as Trinity* by Ted Peters.[28] My quotations are taken from a section entitled 'Is the Trinity Tied to Substantialist Metaphysics?'.

When the Niceno-Constantinopolitan Creed was formulated in AD 381 our theologians were quite confident that they could speak about the *being* of God. Whether speaking about the divine *ousia* in Greek or *substantia* in Latin, no one doubted that these terms referred to the divine reality itself. (p. 31)

Peters then says that such a classical commitment 'to a substantialist understanding of God's being' runs into an obstacle in modern thought, viz. 'the denial that we could know God in the Godself' (pp. 31–2).

This, of course, is not a specific objection to a substance metaphysics but a much more general objection to any supposition that we can know 'the being of God' in any terms at all. But the idea that the ancients and other pre-moderns (or is it pre-Kantians?) felt confident in human ability to gain an adequate cognitive grasp of the divine being and nature does not fit the facts. Patristic and

[27] I do not regard all such dissatisfactions to be misguided. For example Pannenberg's suggestion that it is better to think of the divine unity as a unity constituted by the interrelations of the Persons than as a unity of substance (essence) deserves serious consideration. See W. Pannenberg, *Systematic Theology*, i, trans. G. W. Bromiley (Grand Rapids, Mich.: Eerdmans, 1991), ch. 5, sect. 3. Another exception is R. W. Jenson, *The Triune Identity: God According to the Gospel* (Philadelphia: Fortress Press, 1982), which will be briefly touched on below.

[28] (Louisville, Ky.: Westminster/John Knox Press, 1993).

medieval literature is replete with statements that the being and nature of God far outstrips human cognitive capacities and that we are incapable of understanding the divine essence as it is in itself. Nor is this confined to the more mystically inclined like the pseudo-Dionysius. I have just quoted Gregory of Nyssa to the effect that all our terms for God express God's relations to his creation rather than what he is in himself. John of Damascus writes that 'it is impossible to find in creation an image which exactly portrays the manner of the Holy Trinity in Itself'.[29] And to go beyond the Patristic period, do not forget that Aquinas' *Summa Theologiae* announces near the beginning that 'because we cannot know what God is, but rather what He is not, we have no means for considering how God is, but rather how He is not' (Introduction to I. Q. 3). One can hardly get less confident than that of knowing 'God as Godself'! To be sure, what Peters explicitly says these ancients were confident of was that their 'terms referred to the divine reality itself'. But if that is all he is saying, it is no big deal. I can refer to things I have virtually no understanding of at all. I do it all the time. If his contrast with contemporary thought is to have any force, what will have to be attributed to the ancients is a confidence that they could attain an impressively detailed grasp of the divine nature. And on that, the evidence tends in the other direction.[30]

Here are some more specific complaints about substance metaphysics:

What it means for God to be understood in terms of divine substance was spelled out over time. Augustine described God as a substance that is invisible, unchangeable, and eternal. Thomas Aquinas identified God with the fullness of being, as pure act. This excludes such things as becoming and potency. Thus God is immutable and cannot change, because change consists in the transition from potency to act. God in the Godself is unchanging and eternal. The world, in contrast, is temporal and constantly changing in relation to God.

Included in the substantialist presumptions was the distinction between absolute essence and relational attributes. The essence of an entity is absolute, remaining unchanged if identity is to be maintained. Relation-

---

[29] *de Fide Orthodoxa*, i. 8, in Chase (trans.), *Writings of St. John of Damascus*, 183.

[30] Of course, in any period there are disagreements on this as on many other issues. Not all ancient theologians were as modest as John. But then not all twentieth-century theologians are as pessimistic about grasping the divine being as Peters suggests.

ality takes place through the attributes. What could not be countenanced is the notion that the divine essence is contingent upon the relational dimensions of its being. (p. 31)

To these ways of thinking of God, Peters opposes another 'obstacle in modern thought', viz., 'the apparent incompatibility of an eternal unchanging God with the biblical view of a God in relationship to a world he loves'. He goes on to spell this out:

If God is not capable of change or becoming, it would seem that God could not be affected by the world. Even the suffering of its creatures could not elicit divine sympathy. God would be apathetic, unable to feel the pain of others. In addition, human freedom seems to be rendered superfluous because it would make no difference whether I love God or not. How, we might ask, can we reconcile the God of substantialist metaphysics with the portrait of God in Jesus' parable of the prodigal, as a grieving father who goes in search of his lost child? The scriptural story of salvation assumes that God responds to human conditions and actions, and to do so God must be affected by what happens in the world.

Such considerations in recent times have led to an attack against the substantialist metaphysics that are presumed to underlie our idea of God as Trinity . . .; the classical picture of God makes God look aloof, impersonal, unrelated to the world and hence uncaring. To speak of God as a divine substance that is immutable and existing independently of all other things seems to make it impossible for God to love us. To love, one must be affected by the beloved, perhaps even to suffer in loving. This implies change and mutability. (p. 32)

Now Peters, following Hartshorne and Whitehead, has an important point that if God loves us and is concerned for our well-being (and, one might add, even if God just knows about us), then he is related to us, and more generally to his creation, in a way that makes a difference to his being. And hence, unless we are able to scrap any significant relations of God to the world, we cannot think of God as pure act, free of any potentiality, and as unaffected in his being by relations to us, and hence not as purely simple as Augustine and Aquinas would have it. But there is absolutely no justification for saddling substance metaphysics as such with these commitments to timelessness, immutability, pure actuality with no potentiality, and being unaffected by relations to other beings. To see this, we only have to recall that the Aristotelian metaphysics of substance was developed for application to finite created substances, particularly living organisms. And these are far from 'invisible, unchangeable, eternal', pure actuality with no trace of potentiality, and absolutely simple. Quite the contrary! Indeed, as pointed out above, Aristotle takes one of the basic features of substances to be that they retain their identity *through change*. Hence, there is nothing in the category of substance itself that constrains a theologian who applies that category to God to think of God in the ways Peters objects to in the above passages. Moreover, it is particularly ironic to cite Aquinas as one who construes God in these ways *because* he thinks of God as a substance. On the contrary, Thomas was led by his doctrine of divine simplicity—which is the root of his denial of divine potentiality, change, and dependence on creatures for anything—to deny that God is in any genus, including the summum genus of *substance*.

Robert W. Jenson's work, *The Triune Identity*,[31] might seem to be another case of rejecting a substantialist construal of the Trinity on the mistaken supposition that such a construal requires absolute simplicity, timelessness, immutability, and the lack of internal relations to creations. Indeed, Jenson, like Peters, inveighs against those features of classical theological treatments of God. And he plumps for a non-substantialist view of the trinitarian God as an 'event', 'the event between Father, Son, and Spirit' (p. 161). But a closer reading would reveal that Jenson has a much more sophisticated understanding of substance metaphysics than that. In distinguishing his reading of the Cappadocians from the likes of Augustine and Aquinas, he writes:

By distinguishing *ousia* from *hypostasis* in the case of God, Basil and his protégés pushed God's *ousia* unambiguously to the side of the possessed complex of attributes. Their possessor would not have to be either the event of which the Cappadocians predicate 'God', or the hypostases, singly or together. . . . God only *has ousia*; he is not one. (pp. 162–3)

If God is 'one substance', this is a 'substance' with internal relations to other substances. (p. 120)

One could hardly say more clearly than this that applying the category of substance to God does not itself require us to think of God as absolutely simple, impassible, not internally related to creatures, and so on. Thus, Jenson is not, despite first appearances, guilty of underestimating the resources of substance metaphysics. To be sure, he rejects it. He does not want to think of God even as

---

[31] (Philadelphia: Fortress Press, 1982).

a substance with internal relations to other substances. But that rejection is the culmination of a complex argument with many strands, among which are the emphasis on the economic Trinity as *constitutive* of the immanent Trinity and a view of divine infinity as preventing the attribution to God of any fixed set of essential attributes.

Jürgen Moltmann, on the other hand, does base his advocacy of getting away from the 'substantialist unity' of God towards a relational unity in which the divine threeness is given priority, on a overly restrictive view of substantialist unity.

The unity of the three Persons . . . must consequently be understood as a *communicable* unity and as an *open, inviting unity, capable of integration*. The *homogeneity* of the divine substance is hardly conceivable as communicable and open for anything else, because then it would no longer be homogeneous. . . . The at-oneness of the three divine Persons is not presupposed by these Persons as their single substance. . . . The unitedness, the at-oneness, of the triunity is already given with the fellowship of the Father, the Son and the Spirit. It therefore does not need to be additionally secured by a particular doctrine about the unity of the divine substance. . . . It must be perceived in the *perichoresis* of the divine Persons.[32]

But Moltmann is setting up false dichotomies here. As the previous section should make clear, we can recognize that on either interpretation of 'same substance' (second *ousia* or *hypokeimenon*) the 'at-oneness' of the Persons is not sufficiently secured unless we add to this a requirement of a *perichoresis*. Moltmann seems to think that this addition is incompatible with postulating a community of substance. But this view is based either on a gratuitous insistence on a *homogeneity* of substance (gratuitous because not required by the category of substance itself), or on taking the unity of divine substance as an 'addition' to the 'fellowship' of the Father, Son, and Spirit. But the sensible, and sensitive, way to do the doctrine of the Trinity in substance terms is that exemplified by Gregory of Nyssa in the longish quotation in the last section. There the commonality of substance is not an 'addition' to the *perichoresis* but rather its ontological basis, not, indeed, a basis that requires the *perichoresis*, but one that is receptive to it.

My final exhibit of misguided objections to substantialist trini-

---

[32] J. Moltmann, *The Trinity and the Kingdom: The Doctrine of God* (San Francisco: Harper & Row, 1981), 149–50.

tarian formulations is John Macquarrie. In his *Principles of Christian Theology*[33] we find the following:

The Christian community believed that God, who had created heaven and earth, had become incarnate in a particular man and that furthermore he still dwelt with the community and guided it. This, we may say, was the narrative or mythological expression of their faith, and like us, they looked for an alternative interpretative language that would express the same faith in a different way. They came up with the trinitarian formula. (p. 191)

I am sure that both patristic theologians and their non-revisionist successors down to the present day would be surprised to hear that the 'trinitarian formula' was developed as an *alternative* to the belief that God became incarnate in a particular man, one who still dwells with the community and guides it. It certainly seems for all the world as if the 'trinitarian formula' was intended to spell out the ontological presupposition of the incarnation of God and of the continuing life and activity of Jesus Christ, not as a replacement for it. And it has been commonly understood in that way through the centuries. But it is no part of my task here to fight that battle. I include this passage only because it sets the framework within which Macquarrie's objections to substance metaphysics are made.

[T]he formula of one substance and three persons constitutes an interpretation that has ceased to communicate, for it talks the language and moves in the universe of discourse of an obsolete philosophy. This does not mean, however, that the formula is to be rejected. Especially if it does indeed conceal within itself essential Christian insights, what is required is a new act of interpretation that will interpret in a contemporary language this ancient and hallowed formula of the Church, just as it in turn had interpreted the mythological and historical material that lies behind it. (p. 192)

In the part of the book devoted to the Trinity, from which the above passages are taken, Macquarrie does not make explicit just what he finds defective in substantialist metaphysics (except that it is 'obsolete'!). But earlier in the book, in setting out his metaphysics of existence (being) he says things like this.

. . . [T]he attempt to understand the self as substance is really an example of reductionist naturalism at its most abstract. The model or paradigm underlying the notion of substance is that of the solid enduring thing

---

[33] 2nd edn. (New York: Charles Scribner's Sons, 1977).

(like a rock). But thinghood cannot be an enlightening model for selfhood.
. . . This is to reify the self, to treat it as a thing, however refined that
thing may be thought to be. This is at bottom a materialistic understanding of selfhood that cannot do justice to it. The self, as personal existence,
has a dynamism, a complexity, a diversity-in-unity, that can never be
expressed in terms of inert thinghood . . . (p. 72)

He goes on to say that what is needed for 'an understanding of the
self is not substantiality or thinghood but rather temporality, with
its three dimensions of past, present, and future that makes the
kind of being called "existence" possible' (p. 76). Here, of course,
Macquarrie is rejecting the category of substance for *human* selfhood. But he says similar things about an understanding of divine
selfhood. In the course of developing his conception of God as *being*,
he says:

It must also be denied that being can be equated with substance, the
hypokeimenon or substratum sometimes supposed to underlie the phenomenal characteristic of beings. Leaving aside some of the other problems
which the notion of 'substance' raises, it cannot be equated with 'being'
because it is above all a static idea, having thinghood for its model.
(p. 109)

This characterization of substance as 'inert' and 'static' is at least
implicit in some of the quotations from Peters and Moltmann, but
it is much more explicit in Macquarrie. It suffers from the same
defect as the complaints of Peters against immutability and lack of
relation to the world, viz., mistakenly taking features of some
theological uses of substances to be necessarily involved in any
invocation of substance metaphysics. We can see this at the beginning of the last quotation but one, when Macquarrie takes a *rock*
to be the paradigm of a substance. For Aristotle and medieval
Aristotelians, the paradigm was a living organism. Living organisms, though they may be 'solid' are by no means inert or static,
as any dog owner can testify. And when Macquarrie suggests
replacing *substance* with *temporality* as his key notion, he, like
Moltmann, is guilty of posing a false dichotomy. Aristotle's individual substances, most basically organisms, are very much
involved in temporality, in the contrast of past, present, and future.
Hence, if we are to use Aristotelian substance as our basic model
for conceptualizing God, we can think of God as being as *temporal*
as you like. There is no need for a choice here.

Macquarrie does much more by way of developing an alternative metaphysics for theology, and for the Trinity in particular, than Peters or Moltmann (though not than Jenson). In doing this he first follows Aquinas in taking the *essence* of God, that which is shared by the divine persons, to be *Being*. He then spells out a broadly Heideggerian understanding of the sort of Being characteristic of each person:

These three 'persons', however, are . . . 'so to speak' movements within this dynamic yet stable mystery that we call 'Being'. . . . The Father may be called 'primordial' Being. This expression is meant to point to the ultimate act of energy of letting-be, the condition that there should be anything whatsoever, the source not only of whatever is but of all possibilities of being. . . . The second person of the Trinity, the Son, we shall call 'expressive' Being. The energy of primordial Being is poured out through expressive Being and gives rise to the world of particular beings, having an intelligible structure and disposed in space and time. Being mediates itself to us through the beings. . . . We may designate him (the Spirit) 'unitive' being, for it is in the 'unity of the Holy Ghost' that the Church in her liturgy ascribes glory to the Father and the Son, and, more generally, it is the function of the Spirit to maintain, strengthen and, where need be, restore the unity of Being with the beings, a unity which is constantly threatened. (pp. 198–201)

If I had unlimited space in this paper, I would make some critical remarks on this way of conceptualizing the divine and would compare it unfavourably with classical ways that make use of substance metaphysics. But it would be highly unfair to do this on the basis of the above snippets; and I have no space for the more extended treatment. Let me just say that though Macquarrie's ontology is certainly not 'obsolete', it suffers from the more serious disability of obscurity. For example, just how are we to understand 'letting be', and how is it that while the Father is primordial letting be, it is reserved to the Son to 'give rise to the world of particular beings'? Why isn't the latter also a matter of 'letting be'? But leaving all that aside, my central point here is the same as the one I have made about Peters and Moltmann. The things Macquarrie is anxious to get into the picture are simply not, as he supposes, excluded by the use of substance metaphysics. Insofar as I can understand 'letting be' (which may not be very far), I don't see why a (suitably exalted) substance can't be a primordial letter-be. And so for the other notions Macquarrie seeks to utilize *in place of* substance. Once again, the supposition that a certain way of thinking of the Trinity has to be an alternative for a substantialist way stems from arbitrarily saddling substance metaphysics with assumptions to which it need not be committed.

VI Conclusion

Once we get straight as to what is and is not necessarily included in any metaphysics of substance, we will see that most twentieth-century objections to the use of substance metaphysics in formulating the doctrine of the Trinity are based on features of such formulations that are not required by substance metaphysics, rather than on features that are necessarily connected with substance metaphysics as such. Immutability, timelessness, lack of real relations to the world, impassibility, inertness, being static or 'rock-like'—none of these follow just from the employment of the category of substance. The contemporary theologians who object to substantialist formulations on the grounds that features from the above list are objectionable have failed to understand what is essential to substance metaphysics. They have mistaken outer garments that can be donned or discarded at will for the real person wearing those clothes. And so even if they are justified in their strictures against characterizing God as immutable, timeless, impassible, and not really related to creatures, that does not tell against all substantialist formulations of the Trinity. Inveighing against substance on these grounds only serves to divert attention from the real problems in trinitarianism that need addressing.

9

Anti Social Trinitarianism

BRIAN LEFTOW

The Athanasian Creed tells Christians that 'we worship one God in Trinity . . . the Father is God, the Son is God and the Holy Spirit is God. And yet they are not three Gods, but one God.'[1] Such odd arithmetic demands explaining. The explanations I have seen fall into two broad classes. Some begin from the oneness of God, and try to explain just how one God can be three divine Persons. As Boethius, Anselm, and Aquinas pursue this project, let us call it Latin Trinitarianism (LT). Others start from the threeness of the Persons, and try to say just how three Persons can be one God. Some call this theological project Social Trinitarianism (ST). I now try to recommend LT over ST. I now argue that ST cannot be both orthodox and a version of monotheism. I show *en route* that LT does not have ST's problems with monotheism.

I TWO PROBLEMS POSED

In LT, there is just one divine being (or substance), God. God constitutes three Persons, but all three are at bottom just God. Thus, the Creed of the Council of Toledo has it that 'although we profess three persons, we do not profess three substances, but one substance and three persons . . . they are not three gods, he is one God. . . . Each single Person is wholly God in Himself and . . . all three persons together are one God.'[2]

Again, Aquinas writes that 'among creatures, the nature the one generated receives is not numerically identical with the nature the

[1] *The Book of Common Prayer* (New York: Seabury Press, 1979), 864f.

[2] Quoted in Cornelius Plantinga, 'Social Trinity and Tritheism', in Cornelius Plantinga and Ronald Feenstra (eds.), *Trinity, Incarnation and Atonement* (Notre Dame, Ind.: University of Notre Dame Press, 1989), 21.

one generating has. . . . But God begotten receives numerically the same nature God begetting has.'[3]

To make Aquinas' claim perfectly plain, I introduce a technical term, 'trope'. Abel and Cain were both human. So they had the same nature, humanity. Yet each also had his own nature, and Cain's humanity was not identical with Abel's: Abel's humanity perished with Plato, while Aristotle's went marching on. This could be so because though the two had the same nature, they had (speaking technically) distinct tropes of that nature. A trope is an individualized case of an attribute. Their bearers individuate tropes: Cain's humanity is distinct from Abel's just because it is Cain's, not Abel's.

With this term in hand, I now restate Aquinas' claim: while Father and Son instance the divine nature (deity), they have but one trope of deity between them, which is God's.[4] While Abel's humanity ≠ Cain's humanity, the Father's deity = the Son's deity = God's deity. But bearers individuate tropes. If the Father's deity is God's, this is because the Father *just is* God: which last is what Aquinas wants to say.

In LT, then, the numerical unity of God is secure, but one wonders just how the Persons manage to be three. For in LT, the Persons are distinct but not discrete. Instead, LT's Persons have God in common, though not exactly as a common part. In ST, the Persons are distinct and discrete. There is nothing one would be tempted to call a part they have in common. What they share is the generic divine nature, an attribute.

For ST, Father, Son, and Spirit are three individual cases of deity, three divine substances, as Adam, Eve, and Abel are three human substances. For ST, there are in the Trinity three tropes of deity, not one.[5] In most versions of ST, each Person has his own discrete mind and will, and 'the will of God' and 'the mind of God' either are ambiguous or refer to the vector sum of the Persons' thoughts

---

[3] *ST* (Ottawa: Studii Generalis, 1941), Ia. 39. 5 ad 2, 245a. This and all Latin translations mine. See also Edmund Hill, *The Mystery of the Trinity* (London: Geoffrey Chapman, 1985), 103.

[4] For Aquinas, talk of tropes is not strictly appropriate here, since in fact God is identical with the divine nature (so e.g. Aquinas, *ST* Ia. 3. 3). For the nonce this need not concern us.

[5] So e.g. Richard Swinburne, *The Christian God* (New York: Oxford University Press, 1994), 181.

and wills. Like three humans, ST's Persons make up a community. For Plantinga, 'the Holy Trinity is a divine . . . society or community of three fully personal and fully divine entities . . . one divine family or monarchy'.[6] Brown too has it that God names a 'perfect divine society',[7] Layman that 'God is the divine persons in a special relationship'.[8] In some versions of ST, this community is itself at least quasi-personal.[9] And some suggest that the Persons are so intimately entwined, that 'community' and 'society' are almost misleading. Thus, Williams: 'Each of the Persons . . . has knowledge and will of his own, but is entirely open to those of the other, so that each . . . sees with his eyes, as it were. . . . Each speaks with the voice of the others which have become his own voice.'[10] But save for these notes, it is not hard to state ST's version of the Trinity.[11] Nor is it hard to see what motivates ST. Williams, for instance, argues that

if love is God's nature, his love must have an object other than his creation or any part of it: to believe otherwise would be to make God dependent for his innermost activity on something which is not himself. But love is relational, and the relation in question is irreflexive . . ., love in the literal sense requires more than one person. So if God is love, that love must involve the love of one person by another. And if creatures cannot be the only ones who are the object of God's love, there must be a plurality of Persons in the Godhead.[12]

ST claims that its understanding of the Persons' plurality makes best sense of God's inner life. If in God there is just one trope of

[6] Plantinga, 'Social Trinity', 27, 31.

[7] David Brown, 'Trinitarian Personhood and Individuality', in Plantinga and Feenstra (eds.), *Trinity*, 68.

[8] C. Stephen Layman, 'Tritheism and the Trinity', *Faith and Philosophy*, 5 (1988), 295. If we think of the relationship as an ongoing process, we get Jenson's version of ST: 'God is an event. . . . What the event of God happens to is, first, the triune persons. . . . God is what happens between Jesus and his Father in their Spirit' (Robert Jenson, *Systematic Theology*, i (New York: Oxford University Press, 1997), 221).

[9] Brown, 'Trinitarian Personhood', 72–3.

[10] C. J. F. Williams, 'Neither Confounding the Persons nor Dividing the Substance', in Alan Padgett (ed.), *Reason and the Christian Religion* (New York: Oxford University Press, 1994), 240.

[11] Thus, if ST states the doctrine correctly, one has to wonder what all the fuss has been historically: if ST is true, most who have found the Trinity puzzling have just been confused or misled, and the claim that the doctrine is a mystery is misplaced (for the last point, see William Alston, 'Swinburne and Christian Theology', *International Journal for the Philosophy of Religion*, 41 (1997), 56).

[12] Williams, 'Confounding', 238.

deity, the love within the Trinity is one substance's love for himself. Even if there can be such a thing, it is (ST argues[13]) less perfect than love for the genuinely other: and God's love must be perfect love.

There are instead two other hard tasks. One is this. It seems that an individual case of deity is a God, or just is God.[14] This seems so all the more if (as in Swinburne and Bartel[15]) the Social Trinitarian takes pains to explain how the Three can cooperate and avoid frustrating one another's activities. Thus, one hard task for ST is to explain why its three Persons are 'not three Gods, but one God', and do so without transparently misreading the Creed.

Williams argues that ST *must* be a version of monotheism, as the claim that it is polytheist is literally unintelligible. There is one God, Williams tells us, in such a way that 'there is more than one God' or 'there are different Gods' are not false but nonsensical.[16] Consider the claims that

(1) it is not the case that the Father is the same God as the Son,

or

(2) the Father is a different God than the Son.

Phrases of such forms as 'is the same A as' or 'is a different A than' allow only mass- or count-terms as values of 'A'. 'F' is a count-term if its sense carries with it criteria for telling Fs apart, and so (given mastery of number-concepts) for counting Fs. 'Dog' thus is a count-term. Someone who cannot tell where one dog ends and another begins, and thereby count dogs, simply does not understand the term 'dog'. 'F' is a mass-term if there can be such things as a parcel or quantity of F, and one who understands 'F' can sensibly say e.g. that this is not the same parcel of F as that. But (says Williams) 'God' is not a mass- or a count-term, and so cannot substitute for 'A' in the phrase 'is not the same A as'; whatever 'there are three divine Persons' does, it cannot count or sum Gods.[17] Thus while one can say there is one God, one cannot assert

---

[13] Swinburne, *Christian God*, 177–8.

[14] 'A God' sits ill with intuitions that 'God' is a personal name, or the title for an office which can have but one occupant.

[15] Swinburne, *Christian God*, 172–5; Timothy Bartel, 'Could There Be More Than One Almighty?', *Religious Studies*, 29 (1993), 465–95.

[16] Williams, 'Confounding', 235. If this is so, the Creed's 'they are not three Gods' is nonsense on stilts.

[17] Ibid. 236. In this, says Williams, 'God' is unlike 'god'; Williams sees no conceptual problem in counting gods (236 n. 9).

(1) or (2): the claims ST would have to make to be polytheist cannot sensibly be made.[18]

Can we accept all this? Williams is safe in denying that 'God' is a mass-noun.[19] There indeed cannot be a parcel or lump of God. But his case that 'God' is not a count-noun is just that it is part of the concept of God that there cannot be more than one: 'there is no more sense in talk about Gods or "the same God" than in talk about North Poles or "the same North Pole"'.[20] But there is more than one North Pole. We can distinguish the magnetic pole from the pole that lines of longitude determine, and debate which is True North. More to the point, 'one' is a number-word. So while noting that there is just one item in a concept's extension is not a case of counting, it is a case of numbering. If there cannot be more than one God, there cannot be a (correct) count of Gods. But if there is one God, there is a numbering of Gods, and a number of Gods. If 'God' is a number-term, it can substitute for 'A' in the phrases above as well as a count-term. Pike argues—in my eyes plausibly —that 'God is a "title term" like "Caesar"'.[21] There certainly can be many Caesars; the later Roman empire usually had two holding office legitimately at once. So one can very well say, if one wishes, that in ST there are three distinct, discrete Gods.[22] Or if this seems too tendentious, one can surely say that there are three divine beings, each omnipotent, omniscient, etc., and leave to the reader whether this sounds polytheist.

A second hard task for ST is providing an account of what monotheism is which both is intuitively acceptable and lets ST count as monotheist. Monotheists want to say that being a divine being entails being God. In LT, it does. ST must deny this: for ST, there are three divine beings, but there is one God. Intuitively, 'there is one God' tells us how many divine beings there are. In LT, it does.[23] In ST, it does not. Intuitively, 'there is one God' implies

---

[18] Ibid. 236.

[19] Ibid.

[20] Ibid. 237.

[21] Nelson Pike, *God and Timelessness* (New York: Schocken Books, 1970), ch. 1.

[22] As Swinburne once did, writing about the Trinity that 'the first God solemnly vows to the second God in creating him that . . .' ('Could There Be More Than One God?,' *Faith and Philosophy*, 5 (1988), 232). (*The Christian God* avoids such locutions.)

[23] Some Latin Trinitarians deny this—e.g. Aquinas, *ST* Ia. 11. 3 ad 2. But they do so only because they think God immaterial, and as Aristotelians hold that there are quantities or numbers only of material things (ibid.): whence they infer that

that all divine beings are identical. In LT, it does. In ST, it does not. Thus, ST's reading of this claim threatens to be strongly counter-intuitive.

Plantinga suggests three readings of 'there is one God' compatible with ST. As Son and Spirit are in some way *from* the Father, 'there is only one [ultimate] font of divinity, only one Father, only one God in *that* sense of God'.[24] 'God' can also refer to the entire Trinity, and there is only one of these.[25] Finally, there is just one generic divine nature, one set of properties by virtue of which anything qualifies as divine.[26] It is this last, Plantinga suggests, which the Creed mandates: the Creed rules out asserting that there is more than one set of properties by having which something can count as divine.[27] (The Creed is anti-Arian, and the Arians, Plantinga suggests, had taken Christ both as divine and as less so than the Father, thus implying that Christ and the Father have distinct divine natures.) But none of this denies that in ST there are three Gods, if a God is a discrete personal being with the full divine nature. Furthermore, Plantinga's is not the most natural reading of the Creed. Finally, we soon see that each of these readings of 'there is one God' turns out to be problematic for ST. ST's Father is indeed the 'font of divinity', and so alone God in one sense of 'God'. But this (we soon see) creates great inequality among the Persons—perhaps enough to compromise the others' full deity. There is but one Trinity. But if we take the Trinity's claim to be one God seriously, I argue, we wind up downgrading the Persons' deity and/or unorthodox. If we do not, 'the Trinity' is just a convenient way to refer to the three Persons, and talk of the Trinity makes no progress towards monotheism. We soon also see that the moves which most clearly would show ST to be monotheist repeatedly threaten to slide into Plantinga's sort of Arianism, the positing of more than one way to be divine.

---

there is no such thing as how many Gods there are, and that in a technical sense, monotheism is not a matter of number. But they would endorse 'all divine beings are identical', denying that this is just another way to make a number statement.

[24] Plantinga, 'Social Trinity', 31.

[25] Ibid.

[26] Ibid.

[27] Ibid. 34. Thus, while LT takes 'there is one divine substance' as a claim about (in Aristotle's sense) the divine *first* substance, ST takes it as one about (in Aristotle's sense) the divine *secondary* substance. For more on this distinction, see William Alston's paper in this volume.

II THREE SOCIAL STRATEGIES

For ST, it seems that there are three Gods. Thus, ST must explain why it is a sort of monotheism. I now discuss three strategies ST uses to qualify as monotheist.

One contends that while Father, Son, and Spirit are divine, only the Trinity is most properly God. If so, just one thing is most properly God. So Hodgson, reflecting on early Trinitarians: 'It was inconceivable that the Christian Church should ever be other than monotheistic. . . . What was needed was that into the place hitherto held in men's thought by the one God . . . should be put *the Trinity as a whole*.'[28] Let us call this strategy 'Trinity monotheism'.

Some versions of ST claim either that the three divine Persons have but one mind between them, which is God or the mind of the one God, or that they constitute a fourth divine mind, which is most properly God. Let us call this thesis 'group mind monotheism'.

Finally, some friends of ST aver that Father, Son, and Spirit are most properly divine, but *function as* one God. Let us call this the claim that ST is a 'functional monotheism'. As soon emerges, these strategies sometimes overlap.

Trinity Monotheism

Layman, Brown, and Yandell try to strengthen ST's monotheism by focusing on the way the Trinity as a whole is God.[29] Layman speculates that no Person is omnipotent, so that only jointly does their power 'add up to' omnipotence.[30] In this view, the three Persons 'are' one God in the straightforward sense that only when they compose something with a greater degree of what makes an item God than anything else, the Trinity has enough power to

---

[28] Leonard Hodgson, *The Doctrine of the Trinity* (London: Nisbet, 1943), 98, 101.

[29] David Brown, *The Divine Trinity* (London/La Salle, Ill.: Duckworth/Open Court, 1985), 300-1; Layman, 'Tritheism'; Keith Yandell, 'Trinity and Consistency', *Religious Studies*, 30 (1994), 205-6, 216. Yandell calls the Trinity 'an ultimate composite necessarily internally connected individual composed only of essential parts' (205). But his definitions of these terms create problems. According to Yandell, an ultimate individual cannot depend on anything other than itself for existence (205). But every composite depends for its existence on its proper parts, and no composite is identical with any of its proper parts. So it is not clear that the Trinity, as vs. the Persons, really can be an ultimate individual in Yandell's account.

[30] Layman, 'Tritheism', 296-7. Yandell mentions the same thought at 'Trinity and Consistency', 210.

count as divine. Since it would not do to compose God of three non-divine persons, Layman suggests that each Person would nonetheless qualify as divine due to being uncreated, eternal, and morally perfect.[31] For reasons I give below, I am unsure that they *can* all be uncreated.[32] If they cannot, Layman is left with an unacceptably low standard for divinity: for no angel is divine, and yet any number of angels could exist eternally (if God can (as I think) create a universe with an infinite past) and be morally perfect, even by nature. But even if no Person is created, Layman seems to set the bar for deity too low. For one can imagine an uncreated eternal morally perfect feckless simpleton—someone of perfect character who has always been and will always be there, with barely enough knowledge and power to count as a moral agent—but one cannot imagine worshipping such a being. This raises hard questions: how great? why only so great and no more?[33] Why is this limitation compatible with being divine? Why does deity require only this much? Any power and knowledge short of omnipotence and omniscience can be surpassed.[34] Being surpassable in such important respects and being divine do not seem compatible. If the Persons are of large but finite capacity, the Trinity consists of small-g gods; it is a 'divine society' like Olympus. Let us therefore say that no version of Trinity monotheism is acceptable unless its Persons are somehow individually omnipotent and omniscient.

As Brown sees it, the Trinity has a greater degree of what makes an item divine than anything else. While each Person has a *sort* of omnipotence, omniscience, and moral perfection, only the Trinity as a whole has the highest sort.[35] Thus, the Trinity has a better claim to the title 'God' than any one Person: only the Trinity is most properly God, and anything else with any claim to deity is

[31] Layman, 'Tritheism', 296.

[32] Save in the attenuated sense that Son and Spirit are necessary, not contingent products of the Father, and we often reserve the term 'created' for God's contingent products.

[33] So Swinburne: 'That there is an omnipotent God is a simpler hypothesis that there is a God who has such-and-such limited power. . . . A finite limitation cries out for an explanation of why there is just that particular limit, in a way that limitless does not' (Richard Swinburne, *The Existence of God*, 1st edn. (New York: Oxford University Press, 1979), 95).

[34] And in the Layman–Yandell speculation, could even be surpassed by another actual Person.

[35] Brown, *Trinity*, 300-1.

just a contributing part of this one thing. Let us explore this, and first tackle omniscience.

According to Brown, 'omniscience . . . would seem most apposite to . . . the Godhead as a whole . . . though each [Person] would be omniscient to the maximum extent . . . possible for them, their combined knowledge would be greater.'[36] As Brown sees it, some Persons know things others do not: the Son knows first hand what it is to suffer, in a way the Father does not.[37] Plantinga adds that only the Father can say truly 'I am the Father', and only the Son can say truly 'I am the Son'.[38] But neither point is compelling. A version of ST which stresses the Persons' mutual indwelling ('circumincession' or '*perichoresis*') might well let Persons share somehow in other Persons' first-hand knowledge: thus Williams suggests above that each Person 'sees with the other's eyes'. Again, if the Son tokens 'I am the Son', he expresses something true, while if the Father tokens this, he does not. But this does not entail without further ado that there is a truth the Son knows and the Father does not. The latter follows only if 'I am the Son' expresses a private truth, one only the Son can know. For if 'I am the Son' expresses a truth the Father can know, then if the Father is omniscient, He knows it. And the claim that there are private truths is controversial.[39]

But even if we suppose that there are some such items of exclusive knowledge, it does not follow that the Trinity collectively knows more than any one Person does. There are (I think) two basic ways to take the claim that the Trinity knows something. For the Trinity is either *just* a society, a collection of Persons, or something with a mind of its own, however related to the Persons' minds.

Is only the Trinity Omniscient?: The Trinity as Collection
If the Trinity is just a collection, it does not literally know anything. A fortiori it is not omniscient. If the Trinity is a collection,

---

[36] Ibid.

[37] Ibid. 301.

[38] Plantinga, 'Social Trinity', 43. Peter Van Inwagen also notes this ('Not by Confusion of Substance, but by Unity of Person', in Padgett (ed.), *Reason*, 212) but his doing so does not (as far as I can see) commit him to ST.

[39] For discussion, see e.g. Ernest Sosa, 'Consciousness of the Self and of the Present', in James Tomberlin (ed.), *Agent, Language and the Structure of the World* (Indianapolis: Hackett Publishing Co., 1983), 131–45; and John Perry, *The Problem of the Essential Indexical* (New York: Oxford University Press, 1993).

talk of what it knows is in this case just an ellipsis for talk of what all the Persons know, in common or else as a sum. But what the Persons know in common cannot be greater than what any one Person knows, for the intersection of the Persons' bodies of knowledge cannot be larger than any single Person's body of knowledge. And if there is a sum of knowledge greater than that which any Person possesses, but the Trinity is not literally a knower, what still follows from this is not that the Trinity is omniscient but that there is no omniscient knower at all.

The only other sense I can find in talk of a collection having a body of knowledge distinct from its members' runs this way. Each Person has on his own a stock of knowledge. But each supplements his own stock by drawing on the others' stocks. Thus, each has by belonging to the Trinity knowledge he got from another, and so knowledge which in some sense was at first one Person's property becomes in some way a collective possession. Thus, 'the Trinity knows more than the Persons' becomes a colourful way to say 'each Person knows due to being in the Trinity some things he does not known on his own'.[40] But then in parallel, 'on grounds of knowledge, the Trinity has a better claim to the title "God" than any one Person' in turn becomes a colourful way to say:

> (1) Due to being in the Trinity, some of the knowledge by which each Person qualifies as divine is knowledge he does not have on his own, and/or
>
> (2) Some of the knowledge by which each Person qualifies as divine is knowledge he would not have if he were the only divine Person.

If (1) is true, each Person's deity is tied to the others, for each helps the others qualify as divine: the Persons are 'one God' in that they are divine due to the way they are one. (2) is trivial if it entails only that each Persons knows truths which entail the others' existence: *of course* no Person would know such truths if the other Persons did not exist, for then these would not *be* truths. (2) is also trivial if it entails only that each Persons knows truths which would not be true were he the only divine Person. Neither triviality would help us say why the Persons are just one God. For equally,

---

[40] One need not also say '*would* not know on his own', save for the truths which entail the existence of other Persons. This claim, in other words, leaves one able to say: each is fully divine, and so if each were on his own (*per impossibile*), each would still be omniscient—but wholly through himself, not partly through the others.

three Gods would qualify as omniscient (and so Gods) only if they knew all truths, including those entailing the other Gods' existence and some which would not be true were they the sole God. So (2) has punch only if it entails that each Person knows only through the others' aid some truths which would be true even if (*per impossibile*) the others did not exist. (2)'s cost, then, is allowing that each Person, if (*per impossibile*) on his own, would not be omniscient— and so not divine. But this does not entail that the Trinity is composed of non-divine Persons, since it does not entail that the Persons are even possibly on their own, and while I find it troubling to say that divine Persons' being divine depends on anything other than themselves, others may welcome this thought, and say that it expresses precisely the peculiar oneness of the Trinity. For if (2) so read is true, the deity of each Person is tied to the others, for the Persons would not be divine were they not one as they are. If (2) so read is true, then while there are three tropes of deity in the Trinity, it is as if there were but one, for no Person can have his trope unless the others have theirs.

Still, this scenario faces problems. One is just to unpack the way Persons might draw knowledge from other Persons. One does not want to say that some Persons know some things only by other Persons' testimony, or inference from facts about other Persons. True deity seems to require some more perfect mode of knowledge. But anything short of direct access to another Person's mental states would likely involve inference or something equivalent to testimony. If (say) the Father does something to let the Son know that P, this is broadly a sort of testimony. If the Father does nothing to let the Son know that P, but the Son acquires knowledge that P from something about the Father without accessing his mental state itself, and P is not a truth about the Father, the Son learns that P by inference from a fact about the Father.[41] And yet direct access to the contents of other Persons' minds will threaten to undermine the claim that they are *just* that Person's mental contents, and so the basic Social Trinitarian claim that there are three minds in the Trinity.

Again, any Person knows public and (if there are any) private truths. Suppose that each is omniscient on his own with respect to

---

[41] If P were a truth about the Father and the Son learned it just by perceiving something about the Father and without accessing His mental states, P would be a truth the Son acquired on his own.

public truths. Then the only truths for which each might tap the rest's resources are the private ones (if there are any): and knowledge of these is precisely unshareable. So if each Person knows all public truths on his own, it is not in fact the case that each knows due to being in the Trinity some things he does not know on his own. I suppose that the Father (say) might 'share' the Son's private knowledge in the sense of being able to rely on the Son to have it and bring it to bear in the right contexts. But this sort of 'sharing' does not add to the stock of truths to which the Father has cognitive access, give him an extra mode of access to a truth He already knows, or add warrant to any of his beliefs. So it does not provide any literal sense in which being in the Trinity adds to or modifies the Father's knowledge.

Suppose, on the other hand, that no Person has public-truth omniscience on his own. Then we face seemingly unanswerable questions. We must ask just where the line falls in each Person's case between what he knows on his own and what he knows *via* other Persons, and why he knows no more on his own. If the Person can know more on his own, why doesn't he, and if he can't, how is this compatible with deity?

The ideas I have canvassed here may not exhaust the ways ST might claim that the Trinity has on cognitive grounds a better claim to deity than any one person. ST might claim that in some cognitive respect other than sheer amount of knowledge, the Trinity is a whole 'greater than the sum of its parts': say, that the Trinity as a whole has important emergent epistemic properties. Searle explains two sorts of emergent property thus:

Suppose we have a system *S*, made up of elements *a*, *b*, *c*,. . . . For example, *S* might be a stone and the elements might be molecules. In general, there will be features of *S* that are not, or not necessarily, features of *a*, *b*, *c*,. . . . For example, *S* might weigh ten pounds, but the molecules individually do not weigh ten pounds. Let us call such features 'system features'. . . . Some system features can be deduced . . . from the features of *a*, *b*, *c*, . . . just from the ways these are composed or arranged (and sometimes from their relations to the rest of the environment). Examples of these would be shape, weight and velocity. But other system features . . . have to be explained in terms of the causal interaction among the elements. Let's call these 'causally emergent system features.' Solidity, liquidity and transparency are examples of causally emergent system features. . . .

This conception of causal emergence . . . has to be distinguished from a much more adventurous conception (on which a system as a whole) has causal powers that cannot be explained by the interactions of *a*, *b*, *c*, ...[42]

Might the interactions of the Three somehow constitute a whole which while not a mind or a minded thing still has some emergent cognitive perfections? ST's friends have yet to hazard such a view, as far as I know; we must wait on their efforts.

Is Only the Trinity Omniscient?: The Trinity as Mind

Brown may see the Trinity as literally a knower. Brown ascribes

self-consciousness to the social being of God . . . if a society is self-conscious it will also be conscious, that is, aware of itself as a distinct entity over against other actual or possible societies . . . though such self-consciousness . . . exists only . . . in . . . particular individuals. Thus, though in some ways such a society functions just like a person, there remains the most important respect in which it is not a person, namely that it has no existence in itself but only through what are already indisputably persons. (Its) self-consciousness is always a disguised, incomplete function of the form self-in-x consciousness, where x . . . must . . . be filled by some specific person before one has a complete concept capable of instantiation.[43]

Thus, Brown may see the Trinity as a sort of group mind, an agent and knower who while not a fourth Person (i.e. divine substance, or case of deity) is still more than a mere collection of Persons. But if the Trinity *has* a fourth mind, this fourth mind does not know all that each Person knows—in which case there is no clear reason to expect it to know more than any one Person does—or it knows exactly what any Person knows. If there are only public truths about the Persons, each Person and the Trinity will know them all, and if all alike are omniscient about non-divine matters, all will know precisely the same things. If there are private truths about the Persons, the Trinity cannot know them, and so cannot know all that each Person knows. It will instead know all public truths, plus its own private truths. So will each Person. So why should the Trinity know more than any Person?

I thus do not see promise in the claim that the Trinity alone is

---

[42] John Searle, *The Rediscovery of the Mind* (Cambridge, Mass.: MIT Press, 1994), 111–12.

[43] Brown, 'Trinitarian Personhood', 72–3.

fully omniscient, and ST has not yet claimed that the Trinity alone
has other cognitive perfections. Let us now consider the Trinity's
moral attributes.

Is Only the Trinity All-Good?

Brown suggests that only the Trinity as a whole is 'all-loving', all-
just, etc.[44] While he is not wholly explicit, his thought may be that
each Person has his own style of expressing moral perfection, so
that only the Trinity as a whole expresses the whole of divine
goodness. Again, one might read this as a claim about a collection
of Persons, or as involving a group mind somehow distinct from
that of any single Person. But collections are no more agents than
they are knowers. So Brown's real claim, on the first option, is that
the three function as one morally, and their combined action is
somehow better than their individual actions would be. Perhaps
one could argue this thus: the Son, acting alone, gets moral
credit for doing A. If the Son does A in concert with the Father, he
gets that credit *plus* credit for being cooperative with a supremely
good being.

On the first option, then, Brown's move is a version of functional
monotheism—of which more anon. If, on the other hand, there is
a fourth mind in the Godhead, we need to hear more about its
relation to the other three before we can conclude that it will
inherit their virtues, or all of their virtues. Offhand, if the Three
differ in moral 'style', it would seem at least as likely that the mind
they compose would inherit only what they have in common, the
rest cancelling out or somehow composing vector-sum moral
qualities which might be greater than, lesser than, or even incom-
mensurable with the Persons'.

Let us now turn to omnipotence.

Is Only the Trinity Omnipotent?

We want to call each Person omnipotent. If they are, Brown
thinks, they can thwart each other. If they can thwart each other,
they can act only in concert: 'without . . . cooperation, the
individual Persons would in practice have at most the power to
frustrate each other's designs'.[45] But then only the Trinity as a
whole (if it is an agent) is an agent whose intentions no other

---

[44] Brown, *Trinity*, 301.   [45] Ibid. 300.

agent has power enough to frustrate. So the Trinity has a kind of power beyond any Person's. Yet the Persons still qualify as omnipotent. According to Swinburne, this is so because each has power enough on his own to do anything logically possible,[46] and each is such that for all acts A, if he tries to do A, he succeeds.[47] Swinburne's ST preserves the intuition that a divine being cannot fail at anything he tries by claiming that it is not possible that Persons choose to frustrate one another or choose plans which other Persons will frustrate, though they have power enough so to choose.[48] ST, then, can try to combine Swinburne's claim that each Person is omnipotent (and none possibly thwarted) with Brown's thesis that since each Person has power enough to thwart the others, only the Trinity has a power no agent has power enough to thwart.

This argument raises at least four questions. One wonders what it would be to thwart a Person's agency. One wants to know whether even an omnipotent Person truly can thwart an omnipotent Person. Despite Swinburne's definition, one wonders whether a Person whose power someone else has power enough to thwart truly is omnipotent. And one wonders, lastly, in just what sense the Trinity is an agent.

As to the first, let us say that

(1) A thwarts B's bringing it about that P = df. B tries to bring it about that P and A brings it about B fails, and

(2) A brings it about B fails = df. Either A brings it about that though B tries, B cannot contribute toward P's being the case, or A brings it about that though B contributes toward P, B fails to bring it about that P.

Under the second head, some might say that even omnipotence is not power enough to thwart an omnipotent being. For (they might say) it is broadly-logically impossible to thwart an omnipotent being. Not even omnipotence can do the broadly-logically impossible.[49] But consider this.

Both Father and Son can will that some universe exist and that

[46] Swinburne, *Christian God*, 175.
[47] Ibid. 129.
[48] Ibid. 172-5.
[49] Louis Werner, 'Some Omnipotent Beings', in Linwood Urban and Douglas Walton (eds.), *The Power of God* (New York: Oxford University Press, 1978), 94-106.

no universe exist. So suppose that the Father eternally wills that
there be some universe, and the Son eternally wills that there be
none. On pain of contradiction, they cannot both bring about what
they will. If their power is truly equal, it cannot be the case that
one succeeds and the other fails. If (as a 'compromise') the proposition 'some universe exists' comes to lack a truth-value, both fail.
If some other sort of stalemate ensues, then again both try but fail.
So it seems easy to describe cases in which one omnipotent being
thwarts another. Thus, if there are two or more discrete omnipotent beings, as in ST, one must either concede that omnipotence
can be thwarted, deny that the Persons are omnipotent (precisely
because one can thwart another), or hold that the situation just
described is not in fact possible—that for no P can it be the case
that one Person tries to bring about P and another effects it that
the first one fails. The last option is clearly the most attractive
theologically.

Let us distinguish what God has power enough to do from what
God might do.[50] God has power enough to do an act A if and only
if it is the case that if God tried to do it, he might succeed. God
might do A if and only if (*a*) God has power enough to do A,
(*b*) he might try to do A, and (*c*) were he to try to do it, he would
still have power enough to do A. Swinburne argues that for any P,
if one Person has power enough to effect it that P, the others have
power enough to effect it that ¬P, and yet no Person might thwart
another Person, because the Persons necessarily are disposed to
cooperate.[51] This move is appealing. It avoids conceding that
omnipotence can be thwarted, or a deity possibly tries but fails. It
also lets us trace the limits on the Persons' use of their power to a
divine perfection. While Swinburne ties it to the way that their
perfect moral goodness leads them to cooperate, a different sort of
ST might appeal to the Persons' *perichoresis*, or mutual indwelling.
One might cash this out as: the Persons are perfectly joined, inter-
twined, and sympathetic, and *this* perfection rules out attempts to
thwart one another.

Nevertheless, the move still has costs. If neither Father nor Son
can fail, and each can will that P or that ¬P, each has power
enough to restrict the other's agency. For each, by willing ¬P, can

[50] This parallels Swinburne's distinction between God's compatibilist and absolute
power, *Christian God*, 136.
[51] Swinburne, *Christian God*, 171-4.

make it the case that if the other tried to bring about P, he would fail. If the Father wills that ¬P, he makes it the case that if the Son tries to bring about P, the Son tries to make the Father fail. If the Son tried this, he would fail. But the Son cannot fail either. If the Son cannot fail, and it is also the case that if he tried, He would fail, then what prevents his succeeding prevents his trying. So if the Father wills that ¬P, he keeps the Son from trying to use his power to bring about P: given that the Father has willed that ¬P, the Son is unable to try to effect P.⁵² This limits the Son's agency and freedom, and being unable to use one's power sits ill with being divine. In fact, this might leave the Son less effective than we are. Each Person can try only what the others' states of will permit. If the Father wills that the Mississippi flood Louisiana, we can at least try (without avail) to stem the tide. *Because* he cannot fail, the Son cannot even try. Oddly, omnipotence hamstrings him.

Finally, in ST, it seems, the Son's power is intrinsically such as to be able to fail, even if he does not possibly fail. Suppose that the Son can bring about P if the Father permits, but the Father wills that ¬P. In every possible world in which the Father wills that ¬P, it is true that

C. if the Son tried to bring about P, he would fail.

If the Father might permit the Son to bring about P, and the Son can do so if the Father permits, (C)'s antecedent is only contingently false. Thus (C) is not a trivial truth.⁵³ (C) is true partly due to the nature of the Son's power.⁵⁴ If (C) is true in some

---

⁵² A more precise statement of this 'inability': while there may be possible worlds in which the Son tries to bring about P, there are none in which the Father wills that ¬P and the Son tries this. Note that if the Father only contingently wills that ¬P, that the Son cannot then use his power to bring about P does not deprive the Son of that power. It remains possible that the Son bring about P. He could do so if the Father permitted. It is another question, of course, whether Father or Son possibly uses his power to keep the other from trying certain acts.

⁵³ In the standard treatments of counterfactual conditionals, such conditionals are trivially true if their antecedents are necessarily false. See e.g. David Lewis, *Counterfactuals* (Cambridge, Mass.: Harvard University Press, 1973), 24–6; Robert Stalnaker, 'A Theory of Conditionals', in Nicholas Rescher (ed.), *Studies in Logical Theory* (Oxford: Basil Blackwell, 1968), 103–4.

⁵⁴ The rest of what makes it true is that power's environment, the relevant part of which is in this case the Father's having willed that ¬P. But this is nothing unusual. Powers' ranges are always partly set by their environments. If I tried to leap to the top of Everest in one bound, I would fail. This is true due to a limit on my powers. The environment in which I find myself (e.g. the Earth's gravity) is part of the reason my powers are thus limited.

possible world, then even if there is no possible world in which the Son tries to bring about P and fails, the Son's power is intrinsically such as to be able to fail. For there is an act the Son tries in some possible worlds which his power will permit to fail.

Any Person's power would be greater were no conditional of (C)'s form ever true of him. Since we can conceive that this be so, in ST, we can conceive of a greater form of power than any Person of the Trinity has. Further, if Brown's Trinity is a fourth agent, and somehow has at its disposal the Persons' powers (and just how is this supposed to work?), this is the form of power it has.

So Trinity monotheism succeeds all too well at elevating the Trinity's power beyond the Persons'. But it is hard indeed to hold that any divine being has a form or degree of power than which a greater exists, or even than which a greater is conceivable. Further, it seems a reasonable requirement that a genuinely omnipotent power be one whose use no other power is great enough to impede. If this is true, then in ST as here sketched, no Person is omnipotent at all. So the price of Trinity monotheism may include the Persons' individual omnipotence.[55]

Trinity monotheism involves many Gods even in Plantinga's sense. For even if the Persons have the same nature, different natures make the Persons and the Trinity divine: the Trinity is not the kind of thing the Persons are.[56] Further, if the Trinity has more of what makes for deity than any one Person,[57] one wonders why

---

[55] In this line of reasoning, the Persons are at most omnipotent only dispositionally: they would be so if there were no other divine Persons. But it is hard to say even this about them. For orthodoxy, God is necessarily tripersonal—it is not possible that God exist without being triune. If so, then each Person necessarily co-exists with other Persons. But then each Person would be omnipotent only in an impossible circumstance: their 'disposition to be omnipotent' is one which it is impossible that they exercise. Very plausibly there cannot be such a property. If this is so, then if deity requires being omnipotent, only the Trinity as a whole is divine: the Persons are not.

[56] Furthermore, the Layman–Yandell speculation about limited Persons leaves it open that the three Persons each have a different nature.

[57] This winds up so even in Swinburne's version of ST, though he generally parses traits of the Trinity into those of the Persons (as we see below). For Swinburne, each Person exists with 'metaphysical necessity' (*Christian God*, 147–8), but the Trinity as a whole has 'ontological necessity' (ibid. 120–1, 181). What has ontological necessity depends for its existence on nothing which is not part of itself (ibid. 119–20, 181). Each Person, in Swinburne's account, depends for existence on substances which are not part of Himself (ibid. 147–8). Intuitively, ontological necessity is the more impressive property, and the one more appropriate to deity. In fact, it is not clear that Swinburne's version of divine necessity really accords with

it is not more divine than any one Person—demoting the Persons to second-class divinity.

But even if Trinity monotheism avoids talk of degrees of deity, it faces a problem. Either the Trinity is a fourth case of the divine nature, in addition to the Persons, or it is not. If it is, we have too many cases of deity for orthodoxy. If it is not, and yet is divine, there are two ways to be divine—by being a case of deity, and by being a Trinity of such cases. If there is more than one way to be divine, Trinity monotheism becomes Plantingan Arianism. But if there is in fact only one way to be divine, then there are two alter-natives. One is that only the Trinity is God, and God is composed of non-divine Persons. The other is that the sum of all divine Persons is somehow not divine. To accept this last claim would be to give up Trinity monotheism altogether.

I do not see an acceptable alternative here. So I think Trinity monotheism is not a promising strategy for ST.

'Group Mind' Monotheism

Brown may see the Trinity as a sort of group mind. Other versions of ST clearly do.[58] A group mind, if there were one, would be a mind composed of other minds. If the other minds were signifi-cantly simpler than the mind they composed, we might refer to the composing minds as 'sub-minds' and the composed item simply as a mind, but the composed item would be a group mind all the same. In group mind ST, the Trinity has or is a divine mind com-posed of the Persons' minds. There is one God in the sense that there is just one 'minded' being composed of all divine beings.

Groups minds seem at least possible. It may even be that we each have a group mind.

any of the intuitions which lie behind doctrines of divine necessity. These have their roots in the ideas that God is a perfect being and that it is a defect to be insecure in existence, to be such that one's existence depends on factors outside oneself. But on Swinburne's account, at every moment, each Person exists just as each creature exists—only due to some deity's refraining from annihilating him. Classically, doc-trines of divine necessity are ways to express the difference between God and creatures (see e.g. David Burrell, *Knowing the Unknowable God* (Notre Dame, Ind.: University of Notre Dame Press, 1986)). Swinburne's version of ST keeps his doc-trine of divine necessity from doing this.

[58] So e.g. John Champion, *Personality and the Trinity* (New York: Fleming H. Revell Co., 1935), 66–7, and Charles Bartlett, *The Triune God* (New York: American Tract Society, 1937), 81. Hodgson's likening of the Persons' unity to that of a single self (*Doctrine*, 85–96) suggests this as well.

Group Minds by Radio

Our brains somehow subserve our minds. That is, our mental states either just are brain-states or (if minds are immaterial) have important causal ties to brain-states. Our left brain hemisphere receives most of its input from and controls most activity of our bodies' right sides; our right brain hemisphere receives most of its input from and controls most activity of our bodies' left sides. A network of nerves, the cerebral commissures, normally connects the two hemispheres. Imagine that gradually, over a period of months, surgeons replace two brains' cerebral commissures with tiny radio transceivers, so that the hemispheres come to communicate by radio waves, not electrical impulses through nerves.[59] At the end of the process, we have four cerebral hemispheres able to send and receive radio signals, and two unified streams of conscious experience whose unity is preserved by radio. Suppose now that the hemispheres' radio equipment is so tuned that each left hemisphere receives input from both right hemispheres. There are many ways to read the resulting situation. Perhaps we have two (initially baffled) minds, each involving three cerebral hemispheres, each with a stream of conscious experience supported by all three hemispheres. Or perhaps we now have four unshared minds, not two. For perhaps each pairing of a left and a right constitutes a distinct mind, with a conscious stream of experience private to itself. Again, perhaps we have four minds, but just two streams of conscious experience: perhaps, that is, we have two pairs of minds which share numerically the same conscious experiences. Or we could have as many as six minds. Perhaps the four pairings of brain hemispheres each constitute a mind, and the two sharings of conscious experience bring into being further, group minds emerging from the four. We could choose among these alternatives by asking questions and observing the behaviour of those whose brains we have thus connected. Some patterns of answers and actions would favour group-mind hypotheses.[60]

---

[59] I take the thought-experiment which follows from Peter Unger, *Identity, Consciousness and Value* (New York: Oxford University Press, 1990), ch. 6. Unger in turn credits Arnold Zuboff with the basic ideas.

[60] On this, see D. H. M. Brooks, *The Unity of the Mind* (New York: St Martin's Press, 1994), 20–5, 64–7, 143–55.

Cerebral Commissurotomy

One treatment for severe epilepsy involves surgically severing the commissures. Patients receiving this treatment sometimes behave as if their cerebral hemispheres are operating largely independently. Nagel reports experimental results:

if the word 'hat' is flashed on the left, the left hand will retrieve a hat from a group of concealed objects if the person is told to pick out what he has seen. At the same time he will insist verbally that he saw nothing. Or, if two different words are flashed to the two half(-visual) fields (e.g. 'pencil' and 'toothbrush') and the individual is told to retrieve the corresponding object from beneath a screen, with both hands, then the hands will search the collection of objects independently, the right hand picking up the pencil and discarding it while the left hand searches for it, and the left hand similarly rejecting the toothbrush which the right hand lights upon with satisfaction. . . . One particularly poignant example of conflict between the hemispheres is as follows. A pipe is placed out of sight in the patient's left hand, and he is then asked to write with his left hand what he was holding. Very laboriously . . . the left hand writes the letters P and I. Then suddenly the writing speeds up and becomes lighter, the I is converted to an E, and the word is completed as PENCIL. Evidently the left hemisphere has made a guess based on the appearance of the first two letters, and has interfered, with ipsilateral control. But then the right hemisphere takes over control of the hand again, heavily crossing out the letters ENCIL, and draws a crude picture of a pipe.[61]

There is controversy over how to interpret such results.[62] But one very reasonable reading of them is that following the surgery, the patients' hemispheres constitute two distinct functioning minds, which ordinarily so cooperate that the patient is not conscious of the split but can be brought to act independently. If this is the right reading, the next question becomes whether these minds were in fact discrete prior to the surgery—whether, that is, an ordinary human mind is in fact a linking of two in-principle independent subminds, one in each hemisphere, which normally 'fuse' via the cerebral commissures. This is at least a viable hypothesis. If it is true, the ordinary human mind is a group mind.

I suggest, then, that the notion of a group mind makes some

---

[61] Thomas Nagel, 'Brain Bisection and the Unity of Consciousness', in John Perry, (ed.), *Personal Identity* (Berkeley: University of California Press, 1975), 231–2.

[62] See e.g. K. V. Wilkes, *Real People* (New York: Oxford University Press, 1988) and Brooks, *Unity*.

sense. We may each have some first-hand knowledge of what a group mind is like; if we do not, we can at least describe circumstances in which it could be reasonable to believe that a group mind exists. The question, though, is whether the notion of a group mind provides a way for ST to qualify as monotheist.

I see three ways trinitarians might deploy the notion of a group mind. One could hold it to be a fourth divine mind, somehow emergent from the Persons', as Brown seems to do. This is just Trinity monotheism again.

One could instead liken the Trinity's group mind to our own mind, seeing it as the one 'real' divine mind, a single integrated system somehow emerging from sub-minds with no real independence. This certainly gives us a single God in a strong sense. But it denigrates the Persons: is something fully personal if it has only a sub-mind integrated fully into a more encompassing mind, even if the sub-mind has divine capabilities? Certainly something is not fully personal if it cannot refer to itself as 'I', i.e. is not self-aware. But if we have sub-minds, then before (say) commissurotomy renders them independent, they cannot refer to themselves as 'I'.[63] So on this alternative, there is just one 'I' in God—and so no real intra-trinitarian 'sociality' or love. For if we ourselves have discrete sub-minds, then as far as we can tell, they do not keep each other company or love each other. This forfeits one major motivation for ST, the desire to find true, perfect love in God's inner life. Finally, this move also seems to invert orthodoxy, giving us not three Persons in one substance but one Person in three substances.[64]

If there are four minds in God, Trinitarian monotheism looms. If there is but one, the Trinity is unsocial. Williams may try to slide between these alternatives.[65] Perhaps (he speculates) the Persons' minds are wholly open to one another, as if by telepathy. Perhaps their minds so mingle that though they are three, there is literally but one thought between them, and when they act, there are not three cooperating actions, but one action: the Persons literally 'will the same thing with the same will (and) act in one and the same act . . . the wills of the divine Persons are . . . a unanimity which is actually a unity . . . the will of the lover and the beloved coincide so completely that there is a single act of willing.'[66]

---

[63] I do not know whether they can do so afterward.
[64] I owe this phrasing to the counsel of Trent Merricks.
[65] Williams, 'Confounding'.   [66] Ibid. 242.

In this scenario, no fourth mind emerges from three. Nor (it may be) do the Persons' minds collapse into one.[67] Instead, there are three minds in the Trinity, but there is just one set of divine mental states, with three subjects. This violates our ordinary ways of individuating mental states, but then we expect the doctrine of the Trinity to be unusual in some way. Perhaps for Williams, each Person has his own mind, but there is but one content of consciousness between the three, and it depends equally on the thinking activity of all. Suppose one wires a light bulb to two power sources, either sufficient to light the bulb alone. One trips the switches, and electricity from the two reaches the bulb precisely at once. What then powers the bulb? It is not either power source alone. All we can say is that the two together overdetermine the bulb's lighting up. In such cases, the joint effect has not two individual causes, but a single joint cause, the compound of the two. So too, perhaps the Persons' mental states and thought-contents literally belong only to the Trinity as a whole, not to the individual Persons as such—in which case perhaps their intentions and acts do as well.

If this is Williams's view, it raises a puzzle and a nest of problems. The puzzle is this. We can make sense of commingled human minds remaining distinct, even if they somehow partake in the same consciousness, because we can associate them with different (groupings of) brain hemispheres. But what would keep Williams's discarnate minds distinct? If they do not differ in mental state, presumably their non-identity rests on or involves their not sharing some other, non-mental sort of state. But we do not know what kind of non-mental states discarnate minds have. So we really have no way to fill out Williams's picture. We do not know whether what he describes is possible or not.

The other puzzle concerns first-person mental states. If three minds share one such state—say, a tokening of 'I am'—to whom or what does its 'I' refer? 'I' always refers to its own tokener. For Williams, the Persons, not the Trinity, do the tokening. The Trinity is not identical with any one Person. So no Person's 'I' can refer to the Trinity. Nor then can the 'I' they share. That the Persons token 'I' as one, as a Trinity, does not affect this point. For it does

---

[67] I am not sure this is the right way to read Williams; 'the same will' suggests the one-mind option. But taking Williams this way at least gets one more idea on the table.

not alter the fact that *they* token it. But if the Persons have just
one mental state among them, it is unclear how any one Person
could refer just to himself. What would the 'I' in their common
state refer (say) to the Son rather than the Spirit? If their common
state's 'I' does not refer to just one Person or to the Trinity, the
last alternative (it seems) is that it refers to all three Persons. But
a token of 'I' cannot refer to many speakers. Doing so is the job of
'we', not 'I'. The 'I' puzzle opens out into many more. For instance,
the Son willed to become incarnate. When he willed that, did the
whole Trinity will 'I shall become incarnate'? If it did, not just the
Son but the whole Trinity became incarnate.[68] Or did the whole
Trinity will 'the Son shall become incarnate'? The Son could not
learn from that that *he* would become incarnate unless he could
also think to himself, in effect, 'I am the Son, so *I* shall become
incarnate'.[69] But in Williams's account, it is hard to see how the
Son could do so.

The problems come with the claim that all thoughts, intentions,
and actions of God belong to the Trinity as a whole. For then it
seems the Trinity, not the Second Person, does all that Christ does.
But if the whole Trinity, not the Son, does the act of becoming
incarnate, then not only the Son but the whole Trinity becomes
incarnate. This is theologically unacceptable. Again, if the Father
as well as the Son is the subject of all mental states involved in
Christ's being on the Cross, not just the Son but the Father 1st-
person feels the nails go in, the thorns dig into Jesus' brow, and so
on. So Williams's view seems to commit him to Patripassianism.
Again, orthodoxy has it that the Father begets the Son. In
Williams's proposal, not just the Father but the Son does the begetting—and so the Son brings himself to be. Further, presumably the
Father begets the Son intentionally.[70] So the Father intends to
beget the Son, and so in Williams's proposal, the Son intends this
too—causally before he exists.[71] Williams can avoid this and like

---

[68] I am indebted for this point to a similar one by Bartel (T. W. Bartel, 'Could
There Be More Than One Lord?,' *Faith and Philosophy*, 11 (1994), 367–8).

[69] For the difference between such indexical self-knowledge and anything which
can be expressed in such third-person forms as 'the Son shall . . .', see John Perry,
'The Problem of the Essential Indexical', in Perry, *Essential Indexical*, 33–50.

[70] 'Intentionally' and 'by nature' are compatible, because not everything one
intends to do is something one chooses to do. See e.g. *ST* Ia. 41. 2 ad 3.

[71] One might ask: couldn't it be that first the Father alone has this intention, and
it comes to belong to the Son only once he exists? This requires us to say that one

impossibilities only by denying the trinitarian processions. So his view is either impossible or (again) theologically unacceptable. Finally, Williams's view entails threefold overdetermination of every divine act *ad extra*, i.e. that in each divine act, each Person individually does enough that if the other two did not act, the act's effect would take place just as it actually does. It is not clear how to square this with the Incarnation. For it is surely not true that if the Son did not act at all, the Son would become incarnate just as he actually did.

Functional Monotheism

Group mind monotheism seems unpromising. Trinity monotheism runs into trouble (I have argued) by trying to make the Trinity more properly divine than the Persons. Swinburne takes the opposite tack, contending that the Persons are more properly divine than the Trinity, as it is they 'who to speak strictly . . . have the divine properties of omnipotence, omniscience, etc., though . . . if all members of a group know something the group itself, by a very natural extension of use, can be said to know that thing, and so on'.[72] 'Extension' of use indeed. Collections do not literally have knowledge at all. So saying that the collective has knowledge can only be a way to say that its members do. Swinburne suggests that we so treat all the Trinity's divinizing attributes. So for him, the Trinity's being divine is just the Persons', i.e. talk of the Trinity being divine is just elliptical for talk of the Persons' being so. The Trinity as a distinct *locus* of divinity drops out altogether. For Swinburne, 'the Trinity' is not a singular term referring to something divine. If it is a singular term, it refers to a 'group' (above) or 'collective' (below)—a set, or perhaps a mereological sum. No set is divine, and if the Persons have a sum, this by itself no more makes them 'really' one divine being than having a mereological sum makes all trout 'really' one trout. For Swinburne, 'the Trinity' may really be a plural term (like 'Bob and Carol and Ted'), referring to three divine things without treating them as one of anything. Whether the term be singular or plural, in Swinburne's account, use of 'the Trinity' makes ST no more monotheistic than

and the same mental state first has one subject, and then has two. I am not sure this makes sense.

[72] Swinburne, *Christian God*, 181.

ST would be if we eschewed such use, and instead used only 'the three Persons'.

For Swinburne, ST is monotheistic because

the three divine individuals . . . form a collective source of the being of all other things (and are) totally mutually dependent and necessarily jointly behind each other's acts. This collective (is) indivisible in its being for logical reasons—that is . . . each of its members is necessarily everlasting and would not have existed unless it had brought about or been brought about by the others. The collective (is) also . . . indivisible in its causal action in the sense that each (backs) totally the causal action of the others . . . this very strong unity of the collective would make it, as well as its individual members, an appropriate object of worship. The claim that 'there is only one God' is to be read as the claim that the source of being of all other things has to it this kind of indivisible unity.[73]

One who worships addresses someone. So worship makes sense only if directed to someone who can be aware of being addressed. Collections are not conscious, nor are mereological sums conscious as such.[74] So one cannot really appropriately worship Swinburne's collective, save as a way to worship its members. But Swinburne's meaning is plain. As he sees it, 'there is one God' is really a transform of 'God is one', and 'God is one' states not the quantity but the quality of divine things. It asserts that the Persons exhibit unity, i.e. that they always function *ad extra* as one.[75] For Swinburne, then, ST is a *functional* monotheism.

How unified are the Persons of functional-monotheist ST? They all instance the same nature. They all have almost the same almost-omniscient knowledge. This includes all morally relevant knowledge, and so (one presumes) all concrete moral perceptions. They share the same perfect moral character, ideal wisdom, and rationality, and the same great inclinations to love and faithfulness.

---

[73] Ibid. 181. But again, the Persons would be 'totally mutually dependent and necessarily jointly behind each other's acts' even if they hated each other and were constantly at odds. If such Persons had the power to destroy each other, they would depend on one another's forbearance even to continue in being. If they did not, then still, for reasons already sketched, any one could achieve what He purposed only to the extent that the others permitted, and so any act one did would necessarily have the others 'behind it' as well.

[74] A sum of conscious beings is not a conscious being *just because* it is a sum of conscious beings: the sum of all humans is not conscious. If a group mind is both a sum of minds and itself a conscious mind, it is conscious not because it is a sum but because of other relations between the minds it combines.

[75] So *Christian God*, 181; see also Hodgson, *Doctrine*, 94, 105.

Thus, Plantinga infers that the Persons are by nature mutually loyal and loving—as absolutely so, one may add, as their moral perfection dictates.[76] There is in addition something like a family relation between them, if one takes seriously credal claims that the Father 'begets' the Son, and the two together bring the Spirit to be.[77] So one can reasonably expect the Three to share not only an essence (as any three humans do) but such contingent properties as family members share: and surely the omnipotent Father will do far better in imprinting traits harmonious with his one Son and Spirit than parents do in moulding their offspring in their likeness. Again, genetically identical human twins may differ in personality if brought up differently, but there is *in divinis* nothing like upbringing to account for this. In fact, the Three are never separated in any way, as human parents and offspring are. Instead they somehow eternally 'interpenetrate' one another.[78] So it is not clear that ST's Persons could differ in personality, and Persons so perfectly alike might never (one may think) hatch different plans of action. But even if ST's Persons did somehow form different goals, the factors just listed doubtlessly would make them try to work them out as not to impede the others' projects. Swinburne speculates that a further moral tie might bind the Persons: if the Father is the Son and Spirit's ultimate source of being, He would have the moral right to set terms for the Three's cooperation, and Son and Spirit would respect these out of love, gratitude, and moral acknowledgement of their indebtedness.[79] Thus, the ST's Persons act as one *ad extra* by perfect cooperation flowing from their internal relations. If the Persons are a plurality or family of Gods, they are far from the sort of strife that gave the Olympian family a bad name.

Still, even perfect cooperation is cooperation. This introduces a kind of conflict within each individual divine Person, though not between them—at least in versions of ST in which the Persons cooperate. For each obtains the good of the others' society at the cost of having henceforth so to act as to avoid conflict with what

[76] Plantinga, 'Social Trinity', 36.
[77] Ibid. 28–9. For Western Christendom, Son and Father jointly 'breathe' the Spirit. For the East, this is false, but the Spirit proceeds from the Father through the Son.
[78] Again, this is the doctrine of *perichoresis*. For discussion and references to Gregory of Nyssa, see Sarah Coakley's paper in this volume.
[79] Swinburne, *Christian God*, 171–5.

the others do: the good of sharing in love has a price in terms of the good of freedom of action. This is particularly clear in Swinburne's version of ST, in which Persons cede each other distinct spheres of influence.[80]

I now point out a number of oddities that follow if the Persons are one only functionally. I then try to press functional mono-theism towards making clear what I think is in fact its basic claim, that a religion's number of divine beings is irrelevant to 'what really matters' about being monotheist. Once this claim is on the table, I try to show against it that sheer number does not count. This brings me to the end of my campaign specifically against the functional-monotheist move. I then raise two sorts of problem that apply to any version of ST.

Some Oddities

For Swinburne, we call the Trinity 'God' only by 'extension of use'.[81] But this is an awkward claim. If it is true, those who use 'God' to address a prayer to its hearer err as one would who addressed the holders of a joint Presidency as 'Mr. President'[82]—or else unknowingly address only one of the Three. So too, the voice from the burning bush should have introduced itself as 'We Are', not 'I Am'—or else we should enquire which of the Three spoke there, or conclude that the 'I' of 'I am' is ambiguous. All this is quite unintuitive, as it is to suppose that the Old Testament prophets who thundered that God is one (and whose monotheism Christians inherit) meant only that pagans preached a few too many divine beings, and did not know how alike, akin, and in accord all divine beings truly are.

---

[80] Ibid. 174. In versions of ST which more deeply stress *perichoresis*, e.g. Williams's or perhaps Gregory of Nyssa's, talk of cooperation is out of place, and this point would not apply.

[81] Aquinas called 'God' a *nomen naturae*, a name for an individual which signifies a kind-nature in the item to which it applies (*ST* Ia. 13. 9 ad 2). Perhaps 'God' in 'the Father is God' is such a term. But in ST, this cannot be how 'God' functions in 'the Trinity is God'. For ST's Trinity is not a fourth case of the divine nature alongside the Persons.

[82] Particularly given Pike's attractive thesis that 'God' has the logic of a 'title term' (Nelson Pike, *God and Timelessness* (New York: Schocken Books, 1970), ch. 1). ST clashes with the linguistic evidence which favours Pike's thesis, for one can use a title-term to address the holder of an office whose title the term gives ('Caesar, we beseech you'). For discussion of the logic of 'God', see Michael Durrant, *The Logical Status of 'God'* (London: Macmillan, 1969).

In Swinburne's view, the Creed's 'the Father is God' and 'they are . . . one God' use 'God' in different senses. 'The Father is God' tells us what kind of thing the Father is, and that the Father instances deity. 'They are . . . one God' does not say that the three instance deity, or say what kind of thing they are. The Three collectively are *not* anything which instances deity (though they are a collection of items instancing deity). Instead, 'they are . . . one God' tells us how the Three act. But the Creed's 'and yet they are not three Gods, but one God' suggests otherwise. If 'God' does not occur in the same sense in 'the Father is God' (etc.) and 'they are . . . one God', why the 'and yet . . . but'?[83] Moreover, 'and yet they are . . . one God' strongly suggests that 'one' occurs in a sense which contradicts 'three'. But 'three' gives the quantity of Persons. So being 'not three Gods' also seems a matter of quantity—in which case being one God is too.

Swinburne suggests that the Creed 'in denying . . . that there are three Gods (denies) that there (are) three *independent* divine beings, any of which could exist without the other, or which could act independently of each other.'[84] Can this be what the Creed means? If the Persons have non-overlapping ranges of power, then they *can* act independently of one another: that is, none can block or undo anything the others can do. So if the Persons cannot act independent of one another, their ranges of power overlap: some can block or undo what the others do. But if some can block or undo what the others do, that none can act independently of the rest is trivially true. For none can effect what he wishes unless the others do not block or undo it. Each depends for success on the others' restraint, just because all are omnipotent. In fact, if all are omnipotent, then (*per* our earlier treatment of thwarting omnipotence) none can even try to act unless the others' states of will permit it.

The Persons thus would be 'not three Gods', on Swinburne's account, even if in fact most of their purposes were always opposed. For all that would follow from this would be that each has many purposes he cannot even try to achieve (or, if the treatment of thwarting omnipotence was not sound, at least that some acts some of them try do not succeed), and that each achieves some subset of his purposes on which the Three agree. If this is right,

<hr />

[83] One can also ask this of Yandell, who suggests taking 'the Father is God' (etc.) as 'the Father is part of God', etc. ('Trinity and Consistency', 211).

[84] Swinburne, *Christian God*, 180.

then an omnipotent Zeus, Hera, and Venus, constantly at odds, would satisfy one clause of the 'not three Gods' condition. Further, were Zeus *et al.* necessary beings, they would satisfy the full condition. But it is not plausible that one can make Greek paganism a belief in 'not many gods, but one' by adding to it the claims that the gods are omnipotent and necessary.

Monotheist Paganism?

Let us consider paganism further. For Christian orthodoxy, the Father 'begets' the Son and 'breathes' the Spirit.[85] So on the functional-monotheist account, the reason the Persons are one God and the Olympians are not is that the Persons are far more alike than Zeus and his brood, far more cooperative, and linked by procession. But it is hardly plausible that Greek paganism would have been a form of monotheism had Zeus & Co. been more alike, better behaved, and linked by the right causal relations. Suppose that Zeus, frustrated with his Olympian cohorts, wipes them out one by one and gradually replaces them with gods qualitatively just like himself, begotten out of his own substance (from his forehead, as with Athena) and sustained by his power. In the end, we have a Greek religion in which Zeus is king of the gods, Zeus-2 is god of war, Zeus-3 is god of metallurgy, etc. Has Greek religion now become monotheist? Surely not. Or—if one insists that gods with temporal beginnings cannot count as Gods—vary the picture, so that for any time, before that time Zeus had begotten all his doubles. The result is the same.

Perhaps (a friend of ST may say) the reason even *this* modified paganism does not seem monotheist is that it worships gods, not Gods. Now even if we accept this explanation, there is still this point: if Swinburne's are the right conditions for a religion's having just one God, parallel conditions should entail that Greek religion has just one god. But I am not sure the gods/Gods explanation holds up. A religion which acknowledged only one god, Zeus, would seem monotheist to me; if this is right, gods vs. Gods is not a relevant difference. Further, the gods/Gods reply entails that we should be able to make the beliefs of our modified paganism monotheist by stipulating that Zeus and his doubles are omnipotent, exist with an appropriate sort of necessity, and have

---

[85] Again, orthodoxy also assigns the Son some role in the Spirit's existing.

the rest of Swinburne's deifying attributes. My own intuition is that we cannot. If we make these last changes in paganism, it may become 'functionally monotheist'. In fact, it might look just like Swinburnean ST with the number of Persons expanded to equal the number of Olympians. But to me, at least, there seems a gap between this and being monotheist *simpliciter*: if we started with polytheism, we have it still. It does not seem that we can make a religion monotheist merely by altering its gods' *nature*. If a notion as recondite as 'monotheism' has an intuitive content, that content seems to have something to do with the bare number of a religion's deities. And if there is an upper numerical bound for being monotheist *simpliciter*, one wonders why three instances of deity are not too many.

Again, suppose that Christianity counts as monotheist by meeting conditions on the Persons' links of origin, necessity of existence, likeness of nature, and agreement in action. Then if it failed one of these conditions, Christianity would not be monotheist. Thus, Swinburne's account entails that since Father and Son always agree, Christianity is monotheist, but if they disagreed (and how much?), it would not be. This is not plausible. Deities' conduct does not seem the sort of thing that makes a religion monotheist. If it were, there would have to be good answers to such questions as these: why must gods disagree, rather than just differ in will, to make a religion polytheist? Just how much divine disagreement makes a religion polytheist? Is there a sharp cutoff point for monotheism? (If there is not, then there can be religions which are neither mono- nor poly-theist, since of course there is a continuous scale of degrees of divine likeness and behavioural conformity.) Where does it come? Why just there? These do not look like questions with plausible answers.

A Question of Number
Either there is or there is not a maximum number of Gods a religion can tolerate while being monotheist. If two other cases of deity proceed from the Father and yet there is one God (in the Creed's sense), would there be just one God if a million did? It is no reply to say, 'the Father necessarily gives rise only to the Son and the Spirit, and so we can ignore the conditional

    1. were the Father to give rise to a million deities just as he does the Son, there would be one God (in the sense of the Creed).

due to its impossible antecedent'. Some such conditionals express important theological truths, and can be subjects of genuine controversy. Consider the claims

were God to try to destroy himself, he would succeed,
were God to try to destroy himself, he would fail,
were God to try to sin, he would succeed, and
were God to try to sin, he would fail.

Intuitively, not all are true;[86] and intuitively, a full Christian theology cannot ignore the question of which ones are true. (1), I suggest, is a conditional that discussions of ST cannot ignore. Further, (1) has a relative with a quite possible antecedent,

> 1a. were Christianity to hold that the Father gives rise to a million deities just as he does the Son in ST, Christianity would be monotheistic.

(1a) seems implausible to me.

If there is no upper bound on the number of Gods a religion can tolerate and yet be monotheist, then a religion with an infinity of Gods could be monotheist. But I for one baulk at this. It is not all that intuitive wholly to separate functional and numerical monotheism. One is nagged by a sense that a religion of infinite Gods could not be any sort of monotheism, howsoever much they spoke as one. If an infinity of Gods will not do, there is an upper numerical bound on monotheism, be it sharp or vague. If the maximum for monotheism is not one God, this demands explaining (just what in the concept of monotheism would set a bound other than 'one'?), as do such claims as that there is a bound at all if it is not one, that it is just the number that it is, and that three Gods are not too many. If there is a maximum number of divine beings a monotheist religion can tolerate, and it is one, then (of course) ST is not a version of monotheism.

---

[86] True, most writers follow Stalnaker and Lewis in calling all such conditionals true. But few if any are sure that they are *right* to do so. Lewis himself, for one, is quite diffident on this (see Lewis, *Counterfactuals*, 25–6). Furthermore, it is not hard to see why such conditionals involving God might be an exception to this rule; see e.g. my 'God and Abstract Entities', *Faith and Philosophy*, 7 (1990), 193–217. Finally, even if we accepted that all such conditionals are true, still some might have their truth overdetermined, with both a general semantic theory and some specific theological truths as sufficient grounds for truth—and this could itself constitute a significant difference between some of them.

The Obvious Comeback

The last two sections have tried, *inter alia*, to elicit and strengthen one intuition, that there is more to monotheism than functional monotheism—or, put elsewise, that whether a religion is monotheist has something to do with the number of deities it acknowledges. At this point, the friend of ST may ask just why sheer number of Gods should matter. If one's Gods act as one, if it is not possible that two Gods place one under conflicting obligations, if there can be no conceivable situation in which loyalty to one conflicts with loyalty to all, surely (ST will argue) that is the main thing. The claim that all cases of deity are identical is worth making only because it is an obvious way to assure all this. Assure the religious consequences of monotheism without identifying all cases of deity—assure qualitative monotheism without quantitative—and there is no further reason to care whether all cases of deity are identical. 'What matters' about monotheism really has nothing to do with number.[87] I think this may be the root thought of the 'functional monotheist' move. Functional-monotheist ST may assert it directly, or may do so by redefining polytheism functionally, taking it as 'really' the view that the gods or Gods may disagree, or even (with Yandell) as 'the view that . . . there are various divine or quasi-divine beings all of whom lack omnipotence, omniscience, full creatorhood and full providentiality; they divide the world between themselves with each taking care of part of it . . . or the like.'[88]

In reply, I now try to show that sheer number does matter, at least in Christianity.

Why Number Matters: The Law and the Prophets

The Law tells us to 'hear, O Israel: the Lord our God is one' (Deut. 6: 4). Jesus tells us that He came not to destroy but to complete, perfect, or fulfil the Law (Matt. 5: 17).[89] I think this lays down a condition Christian theology must meet: the Christian version of monotheism should complete, perfect, or fulfil its Jewish version. It should be a monotheism a Jew could accept as monotheistic, and

---

[87] So e.g. Layman, 'Tritheism', 294, and Thomas Morris, *The Logic of God Incarnate* (Ithaca, NY: Cornell University Press, 1986), 214.

[88] Yandell, 'Trinity and Consistency', 216.

[89] Jesus specifically endorses the *shema* at Mark 12: 29. See also 1 Cor. 8: 6.

a completion of Jewish monotheism.[90] Failing that, it should come as close to this as trinitarian orthodoxy permits. Being monotheist both qualitatively and quantitatively is closer than just being monotheist only qualitatively.

Again, a proper successor to Jewish monotheism ought to be such that a religious allegiance divided between the Persons makes no sense. That is, its God ought to be one in such a way that divided allegiance is as conceptually incoherent as a divided allegiance to the God of Judaism would be. This is clearly not so in ST's case. It may be that ST's Persons would never demand exclusive loyalty, and would even demand that one's loyalty be to all alike. But still, if Father, Son and Spirit are discrete substances, there is conceptual space to think of being loyal to just one. Were there not, one could not so much as discuss why this would never actually be a problem. LT does not allow such conceptual space. For LT, being loyal to any Person is *just* one way to be loyal to the same divine being. There is no second discrete divine being to whom loyalty might be directed.

Why Number Matters: Power

As we have seen, if there is more than one discrete being with the full divine nature, each such being suffers restrictions of freedom, agency, and power. The question also arises of how and to what extent their actions are coordinated. The three either do or do not restrict one another's ranges of action etc. equally. If they do not, this is a substantive inequality between them, threatening degrees and distinct kinds of deity. If they do, one must say why, since it is not an especially likely result. Swinburne suggests that the Father lays down the conditions which coordinate the Three.[91] But if any one Person does this, it constitutes (again) a serious inequality among the Three. If no one Person does this, there is no guarantee that the Three wind up placing equal restrictions on one another.[92]

---

[90] Clark notes that this should also affect how we read the Church's intent in its early Creeds (Kelly Clark, 'Trinity or Tritheism?,' *Religious Studies*, 32 (1996), 473).

[91] Swinburne, *Christian God*, 174.

[92] Clark speculates that discrete, equally-omniscient, and perfectly good deities might each just freely will, in accord with a commonly held moral theory, to do a good-optimizing act complementary to whatever acts the other chose (Clark, 'Tritheism?,' 469). But there is no guarantee that Persons will in fact adopt the same moral theory (though their likeness of mind makes this very likely). More

Why Number Matters: Action

Again, in the Three's acts *ad extra,* either each Person has a distinct sphere of activity, in which the others do not act, or their agency overlaps. But talk of distinct spheres of activity yields an uncomfortably Olympian model of life within the Trinity. If (say) the Son alone rules the weather, it seems to follow that the Son is more specially the God of weather than other Persons, and that those who depend especially on the weather owe the Son more worship than they owe the others. This is not what the tradition makes of apparent acts of just one Person—say, the Son's incarnation. Traditionally, in these acts, the other Persons support the one in the foreground: the Father sends and the Spirit empowers the Son. So traditionally, it is not the case that the Son is the (sole) God of salvation.

Yet—to digress a moment—it is hard to see how ST can avoid at least a soupçon of Olympus. If the Persons are discrete, and only the Son died for our sins, then however much the Father and Spirit helped out, it seems that the Son did more for us than the other two, who neither bled nor suffered. If the others shared the Son's experience so completely as to make the claim that they bled appropriate, it would be hard to say why it is not the case that not just the Son but all three Persons were incarnate. So it is hard to see how we could fail to owe the Son more than we owe the other two. This issue arises solely because ST's Persons are three discrete substances. If so, LT faces nothing like this issue. For in LT, there is just one substance to whom we owe anything for our salvation, God. There can be a question of unequal loyalty or debt to two discrete divine substances. There cannot be a question of unequal loyalty or debt to one and the same substance.

Back to the main track. If we do not wish to assign the Persons fields of sole agency, we must consider how three discrete divine Persons might participate in one divine activity. There are four ways this might occur. It could be that one Person makes the

importantly, if they are all on an equal footing, and none has more right to 'go first' than any of the others, and all are equally good (and so respectful of one another's rights and prerogatives), why would any single Person 'go first' and make the others conform their actions to his initiatives? (Swinburne's answer, that the Father has the moral right to do so because he is the others' ultimate source, creates problems of inequality—of which more anon.) Further, whether or not some Person would 'go first', there is no guarantee that one Person's range of complementary acts will not wind up more restricted than some other's does.

largest contribution, with the others merely supporting or co-operating.[93] It could be that all three Persons contribute partly but equally. It could be that the Three overdetermine the divine action, each of them contributing enough on his own to fully account for the divine effect. Or, as in Williams, it could be that the three Persons together just are one agent, in the sense they make not three distinct contributions, however related, but just one contribution among them. So to say: the Father acts, the Son acts and the Spirit acts, and yet there are not in any sense three acts, but one act. Any act-token which is the Father's is equally and fully the Son's and Spirit's, without overdetermination, partial contribution, etc.

We rejected the last two options above. Equal or unequal partial responsibility for a divine effect could mean that each Person causes an equal or unequal part of the effect. Or it could mean that while no part of the effect is assignable to any one Person alone, the three Persons together account for the whole of a single effect, so acting in such a way that none individually would have sufficed to cause it and all together just suffice to cause it.

The options which say that each Person causes some discrete part of the divine effect give us just another variant of the Olympian problem. If (say) the Father makes the left third of the rainbow, the Son its middle, and the Spirit its right, whom to thank for it (or thank most for it[94]) depends on which part you have in mind. Things differ given LT. In LT, the Son is not *discrete* from the other Persons. For the Son to be in the forefront of an act is just for God to be more prominent in one role (or state, etc.) than he is in others. So thanking the Son is thanking the same individual God who is Father and Spirit. We cannot owe God more thanks than we owe God.

It is hard to make sense of the second version of the partial responsibility options. Consider God declaring '*fiat lux*' and having *lux* shine, or parting the Red Sea. Just what could a one-third-of-sufficient contribution to either *be*? After all, it is not as if God parts the Sea by pushing, so that each Person can contribute one-third of the total force needed. God parts the Sea by deciding that it shall

---

[93] This seems to be Swinburne's choice, assuming that the divine being who initiates an act has somewhat more responsibility for it than the divine beings who merely support it; see *Christian God*, 174, 178.

[94] If, say, one Person could not act unless the others let Him.

be parted. One may well wonder how a Person could make a one-third contribution to a mental event of deciding. As acts of LT's Persons are just acts of God, LT need not try to make sense of this.

Still, there may be a kind of ST which can make sense of this, and that is a group mind ST in which the Persons are or have fully submerged sub-systems or sub-minds composing a fully integrated mind which belongs to the Trinity—one in which the Trinity's group mind is like a single human mind. But this move has a steep theological price. If every Person makes just some less-than-full contribution to a trinitarian mental act, no individual Person ever accounts fully for any mental act—none ever individually makes a full decision, or has a full thought, or does a full action. If so, none is ever fully a person, for none has a full mind. So this move's price would be the Persons' full personhood. It would be hard to square this with the Persons' full deity and perfection, or (again) the 'social' note of ST.

Why Number Matters: The 'Why this many' Question

The question 'why does deity have the number of cases it has?' is live for ST in a way it is not for LT. For LT, there is just one case of deity. Told that there is just one, we do not feel a need to ask why there are not more. Nor (if we did ask) would this be hard to explain. For if a being is a case of deity, nothing distinct from that being exists unless that being creates it, and (we think) one cannot create cases of deity. To ask why there are not fewer cases of deity would be to ask why there is a God, rather than none. Theists are near unanimous that this question does not arise, that the existence of God is a truly adequate stopping-point for explanation.[95] One might also ask 'well, let's not suppose that there is one God. *A priori*, there might be any number of Gods. So why should there be just one, not more?' In answer, LT can argue in many ways that there simply cannot be many cases of deity.[96]

In ST, none of this holds. Given that there are three cases of deity, we do wonder why just three, not more. Nor (I argue below) can ST reply with an argument that cases of deity cannot be

---

[95] Some theists (e.g. Leibniz) say that God exists because it is his nature to do so. It is not clear, though, that this does or means to trace God's existence back to some more basic fact.

[96] See e.g. William Wainwright, 'Monotheism', in Robert Audi and William Wainwright (eds.), *Rationality, Religious Belief and Moral Commitment* (Ithaca, NY: Cornell University Press, 1986), 289–314.

created: unless ST denies the other Persons' procession from the Father, in which case the arbitrariness of there eternally, necessarily being three wholly independent cases of deity becomes all the sharper. Nor can ST answer the *a priori* number-question with arguments that there cannot be many cases of deity.[97] Finally, in ST, the 'why not fewer?' question is wholly legitimate. For it can have the sense 'does anything about deity dictate having more than two instances, and if not, does anything *else* explain this?'

As far as I know, only Swinburne among ST's friends tries to say why there should be just three cases of deity—strictly, why given at least one, there should be just three. Swinburne thinks that what drives the production of Persons is that God is perfectly loving by nature:

Love is a supreme good. Love involves sharing . . . and love involves co-operating with another to benefit third parties. There would be something deeply unsatisfactory (even if for inadequate humans sometimes unavoidable) about a marriage in which the parties were concerned solely with each other and did not use their mutual love to bring forth good to others.[98]

Perfect love, Swinburne thinks, requires three but does not require four:

The reason why it was an overall good that the first divine individual should bring about the second was that otherwise there would be none with whom to co-operate in sharing totally; and the reason why it was an overall good that the first and second divine individuals should bring about a third was that otherwise there would be no one with whom to co-operate in sharing totally. . . . My ethical intuitions are inevitably highly fallible here, but it seems to me that co-operating with two others in sharing is not essential to the manifestation of love so long as co-operation with one in sharing is going on. There is a qualitative difference between sharing and co-operating in sharing . . . but, as it seems to me, no similar qualitative difference between co-operating with one in sharing and co-operating with two.[99]

---

[97] Thus, ST is in Swinburne's sense relevantly more complex than non-Social Trinitarianism—and so Swinburne ought to grant that LT explains those facts about the world which call for theistic explanation better than ST. If a non-Social view is relevantly simpler than ST, and (as Swinburne argues) the simpler theory is *a priori* more probable, Swinburnean natural theology confirms some non-Social view more than ST.

[98] Swinburne, *Christian God*, 177–8.

[99] Ibid. 179.

Swinburne concludes that if perfect love does not require four, then deity does not require it, and it is impossible to bring about a divine individual other than by nature.[100] Yet many parents expand their families beyond a single child because forms of love become possible with greater complexity which are not possible given only one child, or because there is something very good about a child having a sibling, and about together teaching that child to share in love for that sibling, or because there are peculiar joys to (say) taking a large brood rather than an only child on a family vacation or involving a bigger band in family chores. If marital and familial analogies have a place in thinking about the inner life of God, why shouldn't this one? Cooperating with two to love yet another is a greater 'balancing act' than cooperating with one to love yet another. It requires kinds of diplomacy and interaction which cooperation with one does not. It has its own unique values. Why would these values not matter as much as those unique to the three-membered relation? And why would the point that a 'love unit' is less than perfect if it remains wholly self-absorbed apply to pairs but not trios, or apply less forcefully to a trio?[101]

Since the present question is a live one for ST, one cannot but applaud Swinburne for tackling it. But it still seems to me that trinitarians should prefer LT, in which 'why this many' questions either do not arise or have better answers.

Such, then, is my case against the third of our strategies for showing ST monotheist. I now turn to problems facing not just the functional monotheist, but any version of ST.

III A CREATED GOD?

The Nicene Creed requires Christians to hold that the Son is 'begotten of the Father, God from God, light from light, true God from true God'. If Father and Son are distinct substances, there are

---

[100] Ibid.

[101] Swinburne is right that the qualitative difference between cooperating with one and cooperating with two is not as great as that between sharing and cooperating in sharing. But one cannot help thinking that with the absent pre-given theological conviction that there are in fact just three Persons, the difference to which Swinburne points is not a satisfying answer to 'why just three?' (as vs. 'why at least three?').

only two ways to understand this.[102] One would be to say that the Father separates off some portion of His own substance and forms the Son from it.[103] But as the Father is not made of any stuff, this cannot be true. The other is to say that the Father creates the Son *ex nihilo*. Thus, Swinburne, in his first account of the Trinity, wrote that

there is overriding reason for a first God to create a second God and with him to create a third God;[104]

unity of action could be secured if the first God solemnly vows to the second God in creating him that he will not frustrate any action of his. . . . The creation of the second God by the first of which I am speaking is an everlasting creation; at each moment of endless time the first God keeps in being the second God.[105]

It is hard to see how ST which includes divine 'begetting' can avoid the claim that the Father creates the Son *ex nihilo*. For in ST, the Son comes to exist as one more instance of a nature which pre-exists Him. (The Father bears it logically or causally if not temporally before the Son does.) We do not hesitate to call anything else of which this is true a creature; Thomists would say that any such item has a nature 'really composed' with its existence, and that this is the mark of createdness.[106] If the Father creates the Son, Arius was right in at least one particular: the Son is a creature (though one nearer the Father in status than any other).[107] The Creed's

---

[102] All that follows could be also said of the Father (and in Western trinitarianism the Son) in relation to the Spirit.

[103] So Swinburne: 'he divides himself . . . he creates as a separate God what but for his creative action would be himself' ('Could There Be?,' 232). In *The Christian God*, Swinburne drops this claim.

[104] Swinburne, 'Could There Be?,' 233.

[105] Ibid. 232. Swinburne goes on to deny that this is creation *ex nihilo*, because the second God does not exist contingently, and that this 'creation' amounts to a self-division by the first God: 'he divides himself' (ibid.). In *The Christian God*, Swinburne carefully avoids calling the Father's begetting the Son a case of creating, to stress the distinction between the Father's producing what we ordinarily call creatures, contingently, and his producing the Son and Spirit, necessarily. But if the Son and Spirit are discrete substances, and their appearings are in no sense the Father's 'dividing Himself', they do not literally come from 'the stuff of' the Father. So they can only be appearing *ex nihilo*, i.e. not from any stuff, even if they appear necessarily.

[106] So Burrell, *Knowing*. By contrast, the Father is unique either in having no source for his nature, or perhaps being somehow the source of his own nature.

[107] Not, of course, in all. For instance, nothing in ST requires one to say that 'there was a time when the Son was not' (see J. N. D. Kelly, *Early Christian Doctrines*, rev. edn. (San Francisco: Harper, 1978), 228).

'begotten, not made', must for ST have the sense 'not only made, but begotten'.

Further, 'created God' is at best an oxymoron.[108] It may be worse. For we tend to see the line between the divine and the non- as that which separates the uncreated and the created.[109] Again, particularly when cosmological arguments for God's existence are in view, we tend to mean by 'God' (or at least use to fix its reference) something like 'uncreated creator of all else'. But if two members of a collection are created, the collection as a whole is created: it comes to exist only once all its members come to exist. So if the Trinity has created members, it is itself a creature, not in this sense God, and *not* the uncreated creator of all else.

One 'fix' for this would be to see cosmological arguments as inferring the existence only of the Father, the uncreated God, rather than the full Trinity, or more generally to see creation as primarily the Father's work. Swinburne may have this in mind when he writes that Christians hold that 'our . . . universe derived its being from a single personal source of being, possessed of all perfection',[110] for on his showing, the Trinity is not a *personal* source of being, but instead a '*collective* source of the being of all other things'.[111] Again, Swinburne relates *a posteriori* arguments for God's existence to the doctrine of the Trinity thus: 'the data which suggest that there is a God suggest that the most probable kind of God . . . inevitably . . . becomes tripersonal . . . the doctrine of the Trinity is not a more complicated hypothesis than the hypothesis of a sole divine individual; the simplest sort of God to whom arguments lead inevitably tripersonalizes.'[112] The God who

---

[108] Orthodox Chalcedonian christology avoids this. Jesus Christ consists exhaustively of the second Person of the Trinity, a human body and a human soul (or mind). None of these is both created and divine. Thus, Christ is both human and divine without there being a created God.

[109] Thus, the drive, across a millennium of Christian Platonism, to construe the Forms either as not distinct from God or as created.

[110] *The Christian God*, 190.

[111] Ibid. 180, my emphasis. Swinburne writes that 'it surely must be that if there are two divine individuals, one is the ultimate source of being . . . arguments to the existence of God derive their force from their ability to explain the orderly complexity of our world as deriving from a single source of being. To suppose that there were two or more ultimate sources of being, neither of which was dependent on the other, would be to make a suggestion contrary to what is indicated by arguments for the existence of a God' (173). In this passage, is it the Trinity (though not under that description) to which natural theology concludes, or only the Father?

[112] Swinburne, *Christian God*, 191.

'becomes tripersonal' is for Swinburne the Father, for prior to the Son and Spirit's existing (God's 'tripersonalizing'), deity exists only in the Father. So the picture one gets here is that natural theology infers the Father's existence, and further reasoning shows that the Son and Spirit also exist. But Colossians 1: 16–17 and Hebrews 1: 2–3 give the Son as full a share as the Father in creation and sustaining.[113] So a Christian would expect natural theology to conclude to an acting God who is all three Persons (though not under that description)—as it does in LT.

The created-God problem does not arise for LT. For in LT, one single substance, God, underlies the three Persons. And nothing in the models requires us to say that this one God creates Himself.

IV AN INEQUALITY PROBLEM

In the models of LT I have given, if the Father did not beget the Son, there would be neither Son nor Father, but only God. In ST, it seems, if *per impossibile* the Father did not beget and spirate the Son and Spirit, the Father would exist, and deity would exist only in Him. For ST, that is, were there no Trinity, the Father would be identical with God. This conditional has a necessarily false antecedent, according to Christians, but I would argue that it is all the same not a trivial truth,[114] and it makes the Son's and Spirit's existence less intrinsic to God's than the Father's. So even if ST somehow dodges the problem of created Gods, it is left with a substantive inequality between the Persons. By contrast, in LT, were there no processions, there would be no Persons, but simply God. The Persons are wholly equal: as ought to be so if they are equally divine. And yet on the accounts above, the Father does have a relevant priority. For given that there *are* Persons, the others exist because the Father does.

Still other things point to the inequality of ST's Persons.

The Father's unique causal role seems a relevant respect in which he is greater than the Son and Spirit, if they are discrete

---

[113] Such texts as John 1: 3 and Rom. 11: 36 suggest that creation is from the Father through the Son. But this does not deny that the Son exercises causality. It merely suggests how Father's and Son's causality are related.

[114] For the contrary claim that all such conditionals are vacuously true, see Lewis, *Counterfactuals*, 24–6, and Stalnaker, 'Theory', 103, 104.

substances. For if it makes God (as a whole) greater than the world to be its total and sustaining source, and to be causally 'before it', then being their total and sustaining source and causally before them makes the Father greater than the other Persons.[115] Further, this seems relevant to being divine. So ST's Father seems to have more of what makes for divinity than the other two Persons.

Again, as noted earlier, we tend to think that part of what makes God divine is not being created: we tend, that is, to see being uncreated as a deifying attribute. If it is, then if the Father is un-created while Son is created, the Son lacks a deifying attribute the Father has. The Son may be eternal, omnipotent, omniscient, etc. But still there is real reason to say that the Father has more of what makes an item divine than the Son.

Again, one can make a strong case that ultimacy—being absolutely the first being—is itself a deifying attribute.[116] If it is, this too is a deifying attribute the Father has and the Son lacks.

To see another relevant respect of greatness, we must consider the concept of deity. God is divine just in case he satisfies the con-cept of deity. You may ask, whose concept of deity? I will beg many questions and answer, the right one. The right concept of deity (as it were) embodies the standards by which one would judge correctly what things are divine. It tells one what a thing ought to be if it aspires to deity. Let us now ask an odd, abstract question. What sets the content of the right concept of deity? How is it deter-mined what an item must be to count as truly divine?

There are just two answers to this question. The content might somehow be set independent of God. Or the content might some-how depend on God.

Theists will not tolerate the first answer. For on it, there is an

---

[115] Swinburne allows for the possibility that another Person, once existing, might not be sustained by the Father, but go on 'under its own steam' (*Christian God*, 119) and claims that once the others exist, the Father also in a way depends on them, since he depends for his continued existence on their not annihilating him (ibid. 173). Even if we grant Swinburne all this, there still remains a real, important asymmetry between the Persons. The Father was at some time the active cause of the others. The others were never at any time active causes of the Father (see esp. ibid. 177, 185 and for a careful treatment of all this, Alston, 'Swinburne and Christian Theology', 35-57). So even if we grant Swinburne all his claims, the Father remains roughly a 'Deist creator' vis-à-vis the others (save that a Deist God does not exist at the good pleasure of the universe)—still a significantly greater position than theirs.

[116] See my 'Is God an Abstract Object?,' *Nous*, 24 (1990), 581-98, and 'Concepts of God', *The Encyclopedia of Philosophy* (New York: Routledge, 1998).

abstract template, independent of God, to which God must conform to count as divine. God has no say as to what something ought to be to count as divine. God must measure up to a set of requirements he in no way determines. Something beyond him tells him what he ought to be. Theists will baulk at this, and rejoin: surely what God is determines what it is to be divine. There is no independent standard of deity; all the concept of deity can do is reflect the nature of the one real God there ever could be. This claim makes sense. Aristotelian theories of attributes embody something like it: compare 'what dogs *are* determine what it is to be a dog'.

In ST (but for obvious reasons not in LT), this cannot be the end of the story, though. For one then must ask *which* divine being(s) set the content of the concept of deity. And if the Father is causally prior to the other Persons, and is fully divine causally before they exist, there can be only one answer. The Father sets the concept's content. The Father's nature sets what it is to be divine. And the Father then shares his nature with the other Persons. If the Father determines what it is to be divine, and then passes this nature along to the Son and Spirit, it seems that they share in what is first and foremost *the Father*'s nature: the Father determines the other Persons' very natures. They do not in turn determine his. The Father is prior and the Son and Spirit posterior to the concept of deity. This seems again to make the Father more divine than the other two—*a fortiori* because it makes him more ultimate than they.

One could avoid this consequence only by holding that the Father does not determine what it is to be divine, and so all Persons equally do not determine this, or that all Persons equally determine this. The first (I have argued) is unacceptable. The second is true only if (counter to orthodoxy) the other Persons do not in fact proceed from the Father. So the best an orthodox ST can do is accept this further respect of inequality among the Persons.

If ST holds that what explains the universe's existing is the Trinity as a whole, still its Trinity is a composite, a whole consisting of three divine parts. As Aquinas reminds us, for any composite, one can ask what puts its parts together, and how.[117] In ST,

---

[117] *Summa Contra Gentiles*, I. 18. It is because he appreciates this that Williams argues that ST provides a good terminus for natural-theological arguments only if its three Persons have but one act and will among them (Williams, 'Confounding', 230, 242)—for if this is so, then *qua* explainer, the Trinity is not composite.

there is a clear answer for this: the Father is the other parts' source, and determines their natures and modes of interaction. If so, the Father determines the real nature and direction of the Trinity's causation *ad extra*: he is the world's most ultimate source, and so its source in a way the Trinity as a whole is not. He is wholly so if the Son and Spirit act only as he directs. If they do not, and do act independently of the Father—as on Swinburne's suggestion that the Father graciously leaves them some scope for independent operation within his overall direction[118]—the Trinity seems ever more like a family of well-behaved Olympians. In either case, it is fair to call the Father the 'God before God', using 'God' the first time in the sense proper to the Father (Plantinga) and the second in the sense proper to the Trinity. If the Father pre-existed the Trinity (causally if not temporally), determined its nature and composition and set the conditions under which its components relate to each other, he seems in some ways superior to the Trinity. But how can anything be in any way superior to the sum of all divine beings?

In any event, there is no question that ST's Father is greater and has more of what makes for divinity than the other Persons. Now I know of no obvious truth which *entails* that what has more of what makes for divinity (or *enough* more of it) is more divine. Perhaps deity is a 'pass/fail' attribute—perhaps higher passing grades on the qualifying exam do not translate into a higher grade *simpliciter*, i.e. perhaps whoever has certain properties is fully divine, but some full divinities exceed the minimum requisites. But still, it seems to me very intuitive that ST's Father is so much greater than the Son and Spirit that he is more divine than they: a point Plantinga verges on conceding when he notes that there is a sense of 'God', tied to being the 'ultimate font' of 'divinity'and so of all else, in which the Father alone is God.[119] Further, the inequalities between Persons which I have pointed out are large enough to be themselves further reasons to say that ST's Persons are divine in different ways, i.e. have non-identical divine natures. If they are, they are further reason to say that ST is Arian in even Plantinga's sense—and so polytheist.[120]

---

[118] *The Christian God*, 174-5.

[119] Plantinga, 'Social Trinity', 31.

[120] If some cases of deity are greater than others, then being divine (i.e. being a case of deity) does not entail being the greatest thing there is, let alone the

There is no inequality problem for LT. In LT, all deifying attributes primarily belong to God, the sole substance of the Trinity. God is equally the 'substrate' of all Persons he constitutes or all events of his cognitive and affective life. So his deifying attributes exist equally in all three Persons.

A Glance at Unorthodoxy

Of course, ST can avoid the problems of created Gods, and perhaps that of inequality, by denying that the Father begets the Son, claiming perhaps with Brown that this is an illicit transfer to the Godhead of the relation between the Father and Christ's human nature.[121] But to do so would flout orthodoxy. It would also raise difficult questions. One would then wonder, for instance, why there are no less or more than three Gods.[122] Again, if no divine being derives from any other, one wonders why all have just the same nature, or at least natures so congruent as to assure their cooperation. Is it really credible that there be three deities of precisely the same nature with no causal connection among them? We would not find it credible to say that in the course of evolution, by cosmic coincidence, there appeared at once three animals with the precise genetic make-up of lions and no common ancestry. Most basically, if no divine being derives from any other, if all are equally uncreated and ultimate, then even if their actions always coordinate (due perhaps to their all being omnipotent and so cancelling out one another's tendencies to discordant volitions), one wonders whether we have not finally passed over to full tritheism. In any event, I do not think unorthodoxy acceptable if LT is remotely viable. Historic Christian orthodoxy represents the best effort of nearly 2,000 years of Christian minds to plumb God's nature. It is possible that they have all been wrong, even fundamentally wrong. But it would be hubris for a twentieth-century

greatest *possible* being, and some Persons have perfections which accrue to them other than by being divine (in which they are all equal) or by their actions (in which all partake equally). Rather, at most, being divine entails belonging to a kind each of whose members must be greater than any non-member. And the title 'greatest possible being' can apply (if at all) only to the Father or to the Trinity as a whole. Thus, ST has implications for perfect being theology.

[121] Brown, *Trinity*, 283. This is Bartel's move, 'More Than One Almighty?,' 472–3.

[122] More orthodox ST can appeal to the Father's action and nature here.

trinitarian to conclude this so long as any orthodox approach is not utterly exhausted.[123] So if ST's prospects do not look good, the moral one ought to draw is that it is time to reconsider LT.

Taking Stock

I have suggested that one basic problem for ST is showing that it is a form of monotheism, and I have examined three broad ways ST's friends have tried to show this. 'Trinity' and 'group mind' monotheist moves try to treat the sum of the Persons as the 'one God' of the Creed. I have argued that these moves denigrate the Persons or are unorthodox even on ST's reading of the Creed.[124] ST's third strategy is functional monotheism. I have raised a variety of problems for this; my overall claim has been that merely functional monotheism is not enough for Christian purposes. So if my arguments are sound, it is not clear that ST can be orthodox or truly monotheist.

---

[123] Here I am indebted to some recent remarks by Eleonore Stump.
[124] 'Or' here is not an exclusive disjunction.

10

John Hick on Incarnation and Trinity

STEPHEN T. DAVIS

I

This paper is a critique of John Hick's recent arguments against the orthodox Christian notion of incarnation, and by implication his understanding of the Trinity. Hick's career as a scholar has spanned some forty years, and many of his opinions have changed and developed during that time. This is certainly true of his christological views. I will concentrate on recent writings that surely contain the views on christology for which Hick will be remembered.[1]

As is well known, Hick rejects orthodox or Chalcedonian christology. Briefly, this is the claim that Jesus Christ is 'truly God and truly human' and is 'one person in two natures'. Let us call this claim the 'classic doctrine' of the incarnation. Hick has three main criticisms of it. First, Jesus himself did not teach it. Second, Christian belief in it has had dire historical consequences. Third, it has never been spelled out in a way that is both philosophically coherent and religiously acceptable. Unable for these reasons to accept the classic doctrine, Hick argues in favour of understanding incarnation metaphorically rather than literally, i.e. as a way of pointing to Jesus as one who was radically open and responsive to God and who 'embodied a love which is a human reflection of the divine love'.[2]

In this paper I want to comment on all three of Hick's criticisms, on his specific objections to kenotic versions of orthodox christ-

---

[1] My main sources will be John Hick, *The Metaphor of God Incarnate: Christ and Christology in a Pluralistic Age* (Louisville, Ky.: Westminister/John Knox Press, 1993), and part II ('Christ and Christology') of John Hick, *Disputed Questions in Theology and the Philosophy of Religion* (New Haven: Yale University Press, 1993).

[2] *MGI*, ix.

ology, on the positive christology that he suggests in place of the classic doctrine, and on his implicit notion of the Trinity. To lay my cards on the table, I see myself as a defender of the classic doctrine, and hence as a critic of Hick's overall christological and trinitarian programme.

II

Did Jesus accept orthodox christology? Hick says no; he argues that the historical Jesus did not regard himself as God incarnate. But what exactly is Hick denying? Perhaps his argument amounts to the claim that Jesus himself did not teach the classic doctrine that the church codified centuries later at Nicea (AD 325), Constantinople (AD 381), and Chalcedon (AD 451).[3] If so, Hick is of course correct. In Jesus' teachings, we find nothing like the technical metaphysical concepts of *hypostasis*, *physis*, *ousia*, or even *person* which the church used to express the doctrine. But it is unclear why Hick would stress this point, since I am aware of no scholar who attributes to Jesus himself the 'one person in two natures' doctrine.

But perhaps Hick is making the more controversial point that, quite apart from the concepts used in the creeds, Jesus did not regard himself as divine.[4] He suggests that the historical Jesus would probably have considered any suggestion that he was divine as blasphemous. But when it is understood in this way, it is possible for a defender of orthodox christology happily to grant much of Hick's point. Although I myself do hold that Jesus in effect or implicitly claimed to be divine,[5] I certainly do not argue that he went about saying, 'I am God' or even 'I am the Son of God'.

The rub comes at the point where Hick tries to combat the view just noted, the theory that most orthodox christologists today accept.[6] They claim that by his words and deeds Jesus *implicitly*

---

[3] Thus, Hick says: 'Jesus himself did not teach what was to become the orthodox Christian understanding of him' (*MGI*, ix).

[4] Thus, Hick says: 'the historical Jesus did not . . . understand himself to be God, or God the Son, incarnate' (*MGI*, 27).

[5] See Stephen T. Davis, *Encountering Jesus: A Debate on Christology* (Atlanta: John Knox Press, 1988), 47–9.

[6] See C. F. D. Moule, *The Origin of Christology* (Cambridge: Cambridge University Press, 1977), 4; Gerald O'Collins, SJ, *Interpreting Jesus* (Mahwah, NJ: Paulist Press,

understood himself as divine, and that accordingly the church's 'high' christology of the late first century and of the creeds was an appropriate theological response to Jesus' own life, teachings, death, and resurrection, to his own sense of who he was, and to associated events like the giving of the Holy Spirit. And in combating this view Hick is less persuasive.

The claim that Jesus implicitly viewed himself as divine revolves around such assertions as: (1) Jesus understood himself as uniquely filially related to God, as is evidenced (among other things) by his referring to God with the intimate and highly unusual term, *Abba* (which many scholars translate as something like 'Daddy'); and (2) Jesus, in three ways, took upon himself divine prerogatives: in assuming for himself authority to forgive sins, in teachings that in effect superseded the Mosaic law, and in presenting himself as the Son of Man to come in judgement.

In opposition to these points, Hick argues: (1) that *Abba* was fairly commonly used of God by first-century Jews, that it meant simply 'father',[7] and that while Jesus certainly sensed that God was his loving father, this had nothing to do with thinking of himself as the Son of God incarnate. (2) Jesus did not abrogate the Torah. Hick notes that there is room for scholarly disagreement on this point, and he cites E. P. Sanders's opinion that only once did Jesus demand transgression of the law. (This was in his command to the man whose father had died, 'Follow me, and leave the dead to bury the dead' (Matt. 8: 22).) (3) Jesus did not usurp God's prerogative to forgive sins but only (again Hick is quoting Sanders) 'pronounced forgiveness, which is not the prerogative of God, but of the priesthood'.[8]

Hick admits that christologically orthodox scholars can 'reasonably interpret some of Jesus' words and actions, as presented by the Gospel writers, as implicitly supporting [the classic doctrine]'[9]— although he also insists that the texts can more sensibly be read in

---

1983), 184–5; James Dunn, *Christology in the Making* (Philadelphia: Westminster Press, 1980), 60.

[7] Here Hick is following James Barr. See Barr's 'Abba Isn't "Daddy"', *JTS* 39 (1988), and 'Abba, Father', *Theology*, 91, no. 741 (1988). For a response to Barr, see Gordon D. Fee, *God's Empowering Presence: The Holy Spirit in the Letters of Paul* (Peabody, Mass.: Hendrickson Publishers, 1995), 408–12.

[8] See *MGI*, 32; the citations from Sanders are from E. P. Sanders, *Jesus and Judaism* (Philadelphia: Fortress Press, 1985), 240.

[9] *MGI*, 33.

his way. But the main point he wants to make is that given the scholarly disagreement about these points, 'it is hazardous to rest a faith in the deity of Jesus on the historical judgment that he implicitly claimed this'.[10]

It is certainly true that there is scholarly disagreement about these items, and Hick is also correct that there is a kind of circularity here, with scholars interpreting the gospel texts in ways that agree with their already-formed christological convictions. For reasons of space, I will not dispute everything that Hick says on this point, but I do want to note the weakness, given an open-minded reading of the relevant texts, of the Sanders–Hick thesis that in forgiving sins Jesus was simply doing what levitical priests did.

There are some texts where Hick and Sanders could conceivably be correct. In Luke 7: 36–50, for example, Jesus declares a woman who was a sinner forgiven after she anointed his feet with her tears and dried them with her hair. The woman's tears can possibly be read as expressing sorrow for her sins and perhaps even repentance. So perhaps when Jesus said to her, 'Your sins are forgiven,' this amounted to no more than Jesus performing the role that priests performed—declaring that a sinner who had fulfilled all the religious requisites for forgiveness was indeed forgiven by God.[11]

But notice that the paralytic in Mark 2: 1–12 had done none of the religious acts that are normally requisite to receiving forgiveness. There is no evidence of sorrow for his sins, confession of them, repentance from them, nor of any sacrificial act at the temple or elsewhere. Doubtless this is why the scribes in the story were so incensed when Jesus said to the paralytic, 'Son, your sins are forgiven'. They said, 'Why does this fellow speak in this way? Who can forgive sins but God alone?' The violent reaction of the scribes seems to me to preclude the Sanders–Hick interpretation of this text.[12]

Perhaps Hick would argue that I am interpreting these texts

[10] Ibid.

[11] But even if the Sanders–Hick thesis is true, large questions about Jesus' person and status still loom. What qualified Jesus to function as a levitical priest? What made others accept the idea that he had the priestly authority to forgive sins? And how did Jesus himself come to this understanding?

[12] The same sorts of points could be made about Jesus' forgiveness of or (since the word 'forgive' is not used in the pericope) at least leniency towards the woman taken in adultery in John 8: 2–11.

incorrectly, or that they reflect the view of Jesus held by the church in the 70s, 80s, and 90s, rather than events that actually happened to Jesus in the late 20s. But of course such claims will have to be argued for and not just made. It certainly seems that, on his own initiative (so to speak), Jesus was forgiving sins. And of course all human beings have the right to forgive sins that have been committed *against them*, but only God has the right to forgive sins *simpliciter*.[13]

I conclude that Hick has not refuted the claim that Jesus implicitly thought of himself as divine. I agree that defenders of the classic doctrine ought not to base their case entirely on attempts to reconstruct the self-consciousness of Jesus.[14] Still, I think such evidence about the self-consciousness of Jesus can constitute a valid part of a compelling case for the classic doctrine.

III

Hick's second argument is that belief in the classic doctrine has had dire historical consequences, i.e. it has been used at various times by Christians to justify or sanction terrible evils. The specific evils that he has in mind are: anti-Semitism, colonial exploitation of the Third World, oppression of women, and the Christian sense of superiority over other religions. Hick knows, of course, that even if his charge is true, that does not falsify the classic doctrine. But what his argument ought to do, he says, is cause us to take a second look at the doctrine to see if it really is essential to Christianity.

Here it would be helpful to make a distinction. Some evils probably are directly caused by commitment to a certain ideology. For

[13] Hick's own view (in a letter of 3 March 1997) is that 'anyone who is a "friend of God" or (in the Hebrew sense) a "son of God" can declare God's forgiving love to one who needs to know of it'. With that point, I fully concur. But (1) to 'declare God's forgiving love' is not quite the same thing as declaring, 'You are forgiven'; and (2) the real issue is not whether Hick and others can agree on the theological point Hick makes in the above quotation but whether first-century Judaism could accept Jesus' declarations of forgiveness. The extreme reaction of the scribes in the Mark 2: 1–12 pericope (among other things) makes me doubt it.

[14] Indeed, one can find scholars on all sides of the theological spectrum presupposing something that in my opinion ought to be viewed with suspicion, viz., that if a given claim about Jesus cannot be proved from the synoptic gospels, it ought to be rejected.

example, those people who are committed to an ideology of anti-Semitism are typically led by that very commitment to disrespect or even oppress Jews. Hick is not claiming that the classic doctrine directly, in this sense, produced evil. His point is more like this: some folk who are committed to a certain ideology tend to justify or defend certain evils by reference to that ideology. This is what Hick thinks the classic doctrine has done. It is inherently liable to be misused by evil people, and has been misused throughout history to sanction the injustices mentioned.

Now it is undeniable that Christians have been implicated in the evils that Hick mentions, as well as in others. And some Christians have used the doctrine of the incarnation as a way of validating certain evils. This is especially true of anti-Semitism, which has at times been rationalized by the charge that the Jews who were responsible for Jesus' death committed deicide. But of course anti-Semitism might well have existed among Christians even if the church had adopted a much more minimalist christology than the classic doctrine. 'The Jews killed the messiah' or even 'the Jews killed our founding guru', could have been the way anti-Semitism would then have been justified. In other words, I do not see that the real culprit in the history of Christian anti-Semitism is the classic doctrine of the incarnation. Like most human evils, anti-Semitism is a perverse attitude of the heart that, when present in a person, will cause that person to look for and find some intellectual justification or other.

Moreover, it seems that almost any ideology or theology can be used by confused or perverse people to justify evil. Take Hick's own metaphorical christology. I am not saying that it has been used to justify evil; obviously, this is because that theology has never been widely adopted. But I see no reason why it could not have been so used had it been widely adopted. Hick cites the argument that oppresses women which says, 'God the Son, being male, became incarnate as a man, not as a woman, and therefore only men can be God's priestly representatives on earth'.[15] But had Hick's christology been widely accepted from the earliest Christian era, I fail to see why it could not have been used as the basis of an equally muddled argument for the same conclusion: 'Jesus, a man who was radically open to God and whose life revealed the love of God,

---

[15] *MGI*, 86.

and who was metaphorically the Son of God, was male not female, and therefore . . .'.[16]

My conclusion is that Hick is probably correct that the classic doctrine has been misused in the indicated ways. But this is a frail reed on which to hang a case for dumping it. It seems that any ideology or doctrine, no matter how inclusive or congenial, can be used for evil if perverse people are clever enough.

IV

Let us turn now to Hick's third and most important criticism of the classic doctrine, viz., that it has never been stated in such a way as to be both philosophically coherent and religiously adequate. Hick admits that with enough logical and metaphysical dexterity (e.g. by insisting on certain definitions of certain key concepts like 'human nature'), it is possible to produce philosophically coherent ways of understanding incarnation.[17] But what always happens, he says, is that the resulting understanding will be religiously inadequate.[18] He illustrates his point by offering a detailed critique of two versions of the classic doctrine that have recently been defended by christologically orthodox scholars, viz., the 'two minds' theory of Tom Morris,[19] and the 'kenotic' option.[20] Hick concludes that no one has ever offered an understanding of the classic doctrine that is 'intelligible in a religiously valuable way'.[21]

At this point let me say a few words about the notion of paradox in christology. I do so because Hick claims that the classic doctrine has never been given a satisfactory literal sense, and that since this is true, defenders of incarnation always end up (1) admit-

[16] Perhaps Hick believes that the higher the christology, the more harm it can do when misused. The idea might then be that those who view Jesus as God incarnate have a stronger available justification for anti-Semitism than do those who accept Hick-like christologies. If there is a plausible argument in the neighbourhood here somewhere (which I doubt), I will leave it to Hick to find it.

[17] This represents a more sophisticated criticism of the incarnation than Hick had offered before. Earlier in his career, he at least seemed to be accusing the classic doctrine of flat-out incoherence. See John Hick (ed.), *The Myth of God Incarnate* (Philadelphia: Westminster Press, 1977), 178.

[18] See *MGI*, ix, 12, 45–6, 48.

[19] See *MGI*, 49–60. Morris's theory is found in Thomas V. Morris, *The Logic of God Incarnate* (Ithaca, NY: Cornell University Press, 1986).

[20] See *MGI*, 61–79.

[21] *MGI*, 46.

ting that the doctrine is paradoxical and (2) arguing that it ought to be accepted nonetheless. Indeed, Hick says of defenders of kenosis that 'all they can do is offer analogies which fail to reach the key issue, and then appeal to mystery'.[22]

The first point I want to make is that virtually every theologian who has ever defended the classic doctrine has emphasized that there is an element of mystery or paradox about it. To give just one example, Thomas Aquinas, speaking of the unity of the divine and the human natures of Christ, says: 'To explain this union perfectly is beyond man's strength'.[23] And this is just what we ought to expect, since the doctrine claims that one person, Jesus Christ, was fully and truly divine and fully and truly human. So the fact that the classic doctrine is paradoxical is hardly a discovery made by Hick.

As we have seen, Hick no longer accuses the classic doctrine of being plainly contradictory. Still, my second point is that it is possible to distinguish between a claim that is contradictory (and thus should not be believed by any sensible person) and a claim that is mysterious or paradoxical (which can be sensibly believed in certain circumstances).

A *contradiction*, let us say, is a statement that is a substitution-instance of the form '*p* and not-*p*', where there is no suggested or available explanation of the statement that shows the inconsistency to be only apparent. Take the apparently contradictory statement, 'Mary, Joseph, and Jesus are one thing, and Mary, Joseph, and Jesus are separate things'. The air of contradiction is dispelled once it is realized that what is meant is this: they are separate things as *persons* and one thing as *family*. But with a genuine contradiction, there is no such explanation that resolves the difficulty. I take it that it is never rational under any circumstance to believe a contradiction.

A *mystery*, on the other hand, is an apparent contradiction that there is good reason to believe. Religious mysteries are paradoxical religious claims that typically stretch the mind and are difficult or even impossible (given human cognitive weaknesses) to comprehend, but which (it is claimed) there is good reason to believe. The 'good reason' that is usually adduced for believing a mysterious

---

[22] *MGI*, 62.
[23] Thomas Aquinas, *Summa Contra Gentiles* (Notre Dame, Ind.: University of Notre Dame Press, 1975), IV, 41, 8.

proposition *p* is a further claim to the effect that *p* has been revealed by God or is entailed by what has been revealed. This is the reason that religious mysteries, like the incarnation and the Trinity in Christianity, are said to be such that no human being could ever arrive at them or fully understand them by human reasoning power alone. In order for us to know them, they must be revealed.

Now my next point has something of an *ad hominem* quality about it, but I do not think the objection unfair. Hick strongly criticizes defenders of the classic doctrine for their appeals to mystery, yet there are below-the-surface paradoxes in Hick's system too. Let me mention two of them.

First, Hick has no trouble accepting theologian Donald Baillie's celebrated 'paradox of grace'. Baillie argues that it is important for Christians to accept the point that 'Some actions performed by human persons are both done freely and responsibly by those persons, and by God's grace acting through them'.[24] Is this paradox less paradoxical and more acceptable than the classic doctrine? According to Hick, apparently so. I still believe (as I did in 1988[25]), that if Hick tried hard enough, he could find a way to render the paradox of the incarnation acceptable. But the real problem with the incarnation from Hick's point of view is that it, unlike the paradox of grace, entails what Hick considers untoward conclusions in the area of religious exclusivism.

Hick will doubtless respond to my criticism by claiming that the paradox of grace, unlike the paradox of the incarnation, is something that Christians experience. We may not understand it; but we *know* that it happens; we know that we do things both freely on our own and as enabled by God's grace.[26] But this is not quite correct. Virtually all human beings have the sense that they do certain things freely, but that fact proves almost nothing. There is a whole group of people—determinists of every stripe—who not only deny the claim but typically propose explanations as to why people (mistakenly) feel that they are free when they are not. Again, certain people sense that they are enabled to do the things

---

[24] See Donald M. Baillie, *God Was in Christ: An Essay on Incarnation and Atonement* (New York: Scribner's, 1948), 114–18. Hick's discussion of Baillie's paradox is found in *MGI*, 106–8, and in *Disputed Questions*, 51–2.

[25] See Davis, *Encountering Jesus*, 24.

[26] At least this was Hick's response to the criticism in 1988. See *Encountering Jesus*, 34.

that they do by God's grace, but that fact too proves almost nothing. Lots of people think that God does not even exist, and others who do believe in God have no sense of God's grace. Since both halves of the paradox of grace are in dispute, it is surely at least as paradoxical as the paradox of the incarnation. Few people want to deny that half of the paradox of the incarnation which asserts that Jesus was truly human.

Second, Hick's theory of religious pluralism has a paradoxical aspect. Suppose someone were to say, borrowing Kantian language, that two things, x and y, are different phenomenal apprehensions of the same one noumenon. In some cases, there is no mystery or even serious problem here. To borrow a philosophically well-worn example, suppose someone were to suggest that what we call 'the morning star' and what we call 'the evening star' are two different descriptions of one and the same thing, viz., the planet Venus.[27] There is no big paradox here because we have a way of understanding how, and in what circumstances, the planet Venus might appear as the morning star on some occasions, and as the evening star on others. But suppose I were seriously to claim that (1) my wristwatch and (2) Mount Everest are two different phenomenal apprehensions of one and the same noumenon. Such a claim would be altogether paradoxical because we have no such way of understanding how this could be possible.

To turn to Hick's theory of religion,[28] in some cases the theory may well be true. Take the God of Judaism and the God of Christianity. The claim that they are phenomenal apprehensions of the same noumenal reality is not hard to accept because: first, Christians hold that the God whom they worship is the same being as the God of the Jews; and second, with the exception of the Christian notion of the Trinity (which Jews reject), the properties the two Gods are said to have are remarkably similar. But notice that it is also part of Hick's theory that (1) the God of Judaism and (2) the impersonal 'voidness' spoken of in Mahayana Buddhism are two different phenomenal apprehensions of the same noumenon. And here I must insist that the two notions are far too different; I would argue that they are even more different from each other

[27] This is not precisely analogous to the claim that Hick makes in the area of religious pluralism, because the planet Venus is a phenomenon too; still, the analogy is close enough to illustrate the point I am making.

[28] It is expounded definitively in John Hick, *An Interpretation of Religion: Human Responses to the Transcendent* (London: Macmillan, 1989).

than are my wristwatch and Mount Everest. It is extremely difficult to see how they can be phenomenal apprehensions of the same noumenal reality.

Now I am not saying that Hick claims that 'God' and 'voidness' are phenomenally identical. But his theory requires that he assert that they be two different phenomenal apprehensions of the same noumenon, which he calls the Real.[29] And that claim, I say, is paradoxical. Now I have not even raised the question of *evidence* in favour of Hick's thesis, nor the question of whether Hick is able to explain the thesis in such a way as to avoid any suggestion of sheer contradiction. I only assert (1) that anybody who like Hick makes the above claim about 'God' and 'voidness' is making what is at the very least a patently paradoxical and mysterious claim, and (2) Hick is accordingly the wrong person to condemn other theologians for appealing to paradox.

V

In *The Metaphor of God Incarnate*, Hick specifically criticizes a kenotic version of orthodox christology that I once proposed. So I had best say some things in my own defence. But first let me point out that I am not committed to kenoticism as the only or even best way of understanding the classic doctrine. Kenotic theory is attractive to me. Since I first heard, at about age 17, that Christ was 'truly human and truly divine', somehow I have found myself naturally thinking along kenotic lines. I still want to try to see if kenoticism turns out to be a sensible way of understanding and defending the classic doctrine. But from the sidelines, so to speak, I consider myself a supporter of efforts by Tom Morris, Richard Swinburne, Gerald O'Collins, and others to defend more traditional versions of the classic doctrine.

The kenotic theory is loosely based on the notion of the self-emptying of Christ Jesus in Philippians 2: 5-11. It was first suggested in the nineteenth century, although some of its early defenders seemed to view it as an alternative to, rather than a way

---

[29] The two notions arise, Hick says, 'at the interface between the transcendent Real and a human religious mentality, and is a joint product of human projection and transcendent presence'. John Hick, 'Response', in Linda J. Terrier (ed.), *Concepts of the Ultimate* (London: Macmillan, 1989), 173.

of defending, the classic doctrine. Now I am not going to present here a full-blown kenotic theory, but I do need to explain enough of it to make Hick's criticisms understandable.

Kenosis is the notion that during the thirty or so years of Jesus' life on earth, the Logos (Second Person of the Trinity) gave up or divested itself of those divine properties that are inconsistent with being truly human. And both before and after those thirty or so years, the Logos did not possess those human properties that are inconsistent with being truly divine.[30]

This picture depends, of course, on these divested properties being contingent rather than necessary properties of God. A contingent property of x is a property that x has but can fail to have and still be x. Being a philosopher is a contingent property of mine—I could still be the person who I am even if I stopped being a philosopher and became a mechanic. A necessary property of x is a property that x has and cannot lose without ceasing to be x. Three-sidedness, for example, is a necessary property of triangles; if a given triangle lost its three-sidedness, it would no longer be the thing that it is.

The whole kenotic scheme also depends on there not being any necessary divine properties that a human being cannot have and on there not being any necessary human properties that God cannot have. And following a suggestion from Tom Morris,[31] a coherent kenotic theory of the incarnation will doubtless hold that what is necessary to God is not, for example, omniscience, but the more complex property of being omniscient-unless-freely-and-temporarily-choosing-to-be-otherwise. The same point will then be made with such other divine properties as omnipotence, omnipresence, etc.[32]

Now Hick virtually admits that kenoticism might well be logically coherent as a theory of incarnation. If you have got sufficient logical dexterity and are willing to define certain key terms in

---

[30] For a helpful analysis of different senses of kenosis, see Sarah Coakley, '*Kenosis and Subversion: On the Repression of "Vulnerability" in Christian Feminist Writing*', in Daphne Hamson (ed.), *Swallowing a Fishbone? Feminist Theologians Debate Christianity* (London: SPCK, 1996).

[31] *The Logic of God Incarnate*, 75. Morris is not, however, a defender of kenosis.

[32] It may well be logically impossible for me—and, presumably all other human beings except Jesus Christ—to have the property of being omniscient-unless-freely-and-temporarily-choosing-to-be-otherwise, because God has not chosen to be incarnate in us.

certain ways, you can find a way of understanding incarnation that is logically possible. But, he insists, what always happens in such cases is that you end up with a theory that is religiously unacceptable or theologically unattractive. This is Hick's criticism of kenosis. He argues that in making conceptual room for divine incarnation, kenoticists have to reject much of the traditional Christian understanding of God. What Hick has specifically in mind here are such notions as divine immutability and aseity, which he thinks are inconsistent with kenosis.

One's first reaction to this argument (an unfair reaction, I admit) is that John Hick is hardly the one to argue against a theological claim on the grounds that it is non-traditional. There are few items in the Christian theological curriculum, including the doctrine of God, where Hick has not proved himself to be quite theologically iconoclastic. But the reason I will go no further with this point (the reason I called it unfair) is that there is another way to understand Hick's criticism. Perhaps he is simply pointing out that those who see themselves as christologically orthodox (and presumably orthodox on other theological points as well), and who make use of the kenotic theory, will end up with a view of God that is unacceptable *on their own terms*.

But is this true? Let us consider immutability first. It is certainly true that in the tradition we can find notions of divine immutability that are inconsistent with kenosis. For example, if someone were to insist that divine immutability means that it is not possible for God to have a certain property—any property—at a certain time and not have it at another time, such a person would surely not be attracted to the kenotic theory of the incarnation. (In fact, however, nobody holds such a theory of immutability; a stock refutation of it in the medieval period was the property, 'is loved by Augustine'. It seems that this relational property was not possessed by God prior to Augustine's conversion and was possessed by God after Augustine's conversion.[33])

But what if divine immutability is understood in some such way as this: God is not fickle, capricious, mercurial, or moody; God's holy and benevolent nature remains ever and eternally the same; God is faithful in keeping God's promises; God's aims and inten-

---

[33] Obviously, there is much more than this that can be said about immutability and even about such properties as 'is loved by Augustine'. For discussion, see Stephen T. Davis, *Logic and the Nature of God* (London: Macmillan, 1983), 41–51.

tions for human beings and human history do not change? Now I have no idea whether Hick would call such a view of divine immutability theologically attractive, but I would; and it is a view that is perfectly consistent with kenosis. One can consistently affirm divine immutability, understood in some such sense as this, and understand the incarnation kenotically.

What about divine aseity? This is the property of being ontologically self-sufficient, of existing necessarily, of depending for one's existence on no other thing. Now since Jesus was born and died, it seems to follow that Jesus did not possess aseity. So if aseity is a necessary property of God, it follows that Jesus was not divine. That is presumably the argument that Hick has in mind. All kenotic theoretic explanations of the incarnation must deny divine aseity.

But again this is misleading. Obviously some things are going to be true of the Logos-as-kenotically-incarnate that are not true of the Logos-as-not-kenotically-incarnate, or as not-yet-kenotically-incarnate, e.g. having a human body.[34] Kenotic theorists make use of what are called reduplicative or 'as' propositions to express these sorts of points. Their notion would be something like this: God, as non-kenotically incarnate, possessed aseity; God, as kenotically incarnate for some thirty years, did not possess aseity. This is not a logical trick invented by kenoticists to save their theory. The Chalcedonian definition itself seems to imply something of the sort: it says that Jesus Christ was 'of one substance with the Father *as regards his Godhead*, and at the same time of one substance with us *as regards his manhood*'.[35] Now I have not dealt with all the logical and theological difficulties that can be raised against kenosis (perhaps on another occasion I will try to do that).[36] My only purpose was to show that defenders of kenosis can affirm divine aseity, as I in fact do.

But my basic complaint about Hick's criticism of kenosis is its

[34] This is not to deny the traditional notion of the eternal incarnation of the Logos. My own view would be that the incarnation is eternal but the kenosis lasted only for some thirty years. This is one reason I consider myself a friend of non-kenotic explanations of the incarnation; they must be invoked to explain the incarnation of the Logos at all moments, and not merely the moments of Jesus' earthly life.

[35] Henry Bettenson (ed.), *Documents of the Christian Church*, 2nd edn. (London: Oxford University Press, 1960), 73. Emphasis added.

[36] Some are discussed in *Encountering Jesus*, 52–7.

claim that kenotic theory 'clashes with any traditionally orthodox understanding of God'.[37] Indeed, he says:

But what is it to be divine? Part of the traditional answer is that being divine consists in being the eternal, omnipotent, omniscient, omnipresent and self-existent creator of everything that exists, other than God. But all these attributes have been set aside by Davis as accidental, since the historical Jesus did not possess them. Thus in making conceptual space for divine incarnation, Davis has had to reject much of the traditional Christian understanding of God.[38]

But this gives the impression that to claim that a given property of a given being is contingent is to claim that the being does not have that property. On the contrary, if I were to claim that omniscience is a contingent property of God, i.e. that God could still be God even if there were some one fact that God does not know, that would be to affirm, not deny (or 'set aside', as Hick says), that God is omniscient. Indeed, I do affirm it.

There are people in the Christian theological tradition who affirm that God has the property of omniscience necessarily. Indeed, there are people who affirm that *all* of God's properties are necessary properties. But I do not consider these views part of the 'traditional Christian understanding of God'. What is part of that understanding is that God is omniscient, and kenoticists can consistently affirm that, as I certainly do.

I conclude that Hick's criticisms of the kenotic theory are inconclusive. So far as his criticisms are concerned, kenosis remains a viable option for defenders of orthodox christology.

VI

Let us now consider the positive christology that Hick recommends in *The Metaphor of God Incarnate*. There are two main points to be noted here. First, as we have seen, Hick denies the claim that Jesus Christ was literally the Son of God incarnate, but he holds that it is still appropriate for Christians to affirm the incarnation as long as it is understood metaphorically. And exactly what is that metaphorical sense? This is Hick's second point. 'Jesus embodied, or incarnated, the ideal of human life lived in faithful response to

---

[37] *MGI*, 75.   [38] *MGI*, 73.

God, so that God was able to act through him, and he accordingly embodied a love which is a human reflection of the divine love.'[39]

An important corollary of Hick's christology is that it allows for religious pluralism. If Jesus is literally the Son of God incarnate, Hick says, it follows that Christianity is unique among the religions of the world in having been directly founded by God; Christianity is superior to all the others. But avoiding this result is one of Hick's strongest *desiderata* in theology. Thus, he says that his metaphorical christology 'can see itself as one among a number of different human responses to the ultimate transcendent Reality that we call God, and can better serve the development of world community and world peace than [the classic doctrine]'.[40] One suspects, then, that Hick's deepest argument against incarnation can be spelled out by *modus tollens*:

(*a*) The classic doctrine entails Christian exclusivism;
(*b*) Christian exclusivism is false;
(*c*) Therefore, the classic doctrine is false.

Let us spell out a bit more completely what Hick wants to say about Jesus. The overall rubric is that Jesus is metaphorically the Son of God incarnate. When understood properly, Hick says, this is an appropriate and illuminating metaphor. But what does it mean? It means that these points are literally true:

(1) Jesus was a man who was extraordinarily aware of God, and responsive to God's influence.
(2) God was accordingly able to act through Jesus; Jesus was an agent of God on earth.
(3) Jesus embodied in his life a self-giving love which was a finite reflection of the infinite divine love; accordingly, Jesus incarnated the ideal of human life as lived in faithful response to God; Jesus makes God real to us.
(4) Jesus' teachings challenge us to live in God's presence.
(5) Understood in this way, Christians can appropriately take Jesus as their Lord (spiritual guide, leader, guru, exemplar, teacher).[41]

Hick makes it clear that, thus understood, Jesus is not unique. There are other religious founders, prophets, gurus, and teachers

---

[39] *MGI*, ix.
[40] Ibid.
[41] On these points, see *MGI*, ix, 12, 105–7, 162–3.

who constitute for Buddhists, Hindus, Muslims, etc., something like what Jesus is for Christians.

Is this an acceptable christology? Let me make two points in response to this question. The first is simply the expression of a puzzle. As we have seen, Hick affirms the incarnation as metaphorically true, and my puzzle is that I do not understand why he wants to affirm the incarnation in any sense. In the picture of Jesus painted in *The Metaphor of God Incarnate* (summarized in points (1)-(5) above) we understand pretty clearly the kind of Jesus that Hick has in mind. Why is the idea of incarnation of God in the form of a human being needed—even as metaphor—to say what Hick wants to say about Jesus? Why not just make points (1)-(5) and leave it at that?

My second point is that Hick's christology says too little. So far as they go, I have little trouble with points (1)-(5). My problem is that they do not say nearly enough. Too much that is crucial is omitted. When all notions of uniqueness, ultimacy, and finality are missing, I question whether the christology under discussion, if it were widely adopted, would be able to carry the Christian community through the next two thousand years, or even the next hundred.[42] Of course I recommend the classic doctrine because I think it is *true* and not just *useful*. Still, it seems to me entirely possible that Christians some day will constitute, in the face of rising secularism, a tiny minority or, in the face of oppressive political regimes, even a persecuted minority. Christianity will survive such scenarios, in my opinion, only if it keeps its distinctives, including the classic doctrine.

Note that Hick's Jesus is essentially a guru rather than a saviour. And I think it has been the unanimous testimony of Christians throughout history that what is needed is a saviour. We are incapable of saving ourselves. If we are to be forgiven, God must forgive us; if we are to be reconciled to God, God must do the reconciling; if we are to escape death's clutches, God must overcome death. If Jesus were a mere human being, he would in the end amount to nothing more than a great religious teacher or spiritual guide like all the others. The only reasons to listen to one guru rather than another are subjective ones ('My guru speaks powerfully to me; yours leaves me cold'). Some gurus speak the

---

[42] Hick discusses this sort of point on *MGI*, 163 f., but my concerns are still intact.

truth and are worth hearing, but what they teach is a truth that is not essentially connected to their own persons or personal authority. As Hick recognizes, if Jesus is God incarnate, there is an undeniable finality about him and his teachings.

Suppose that Christianity were, at heart, a spiritual-ethical system in which it is possible, by hard spiritual effort, for human beings to save themselves. Then christologies like Hick's would suffice. Indeed, I suspect that Hick holds that human beings are capable of saving themselves, especially given the series of lives that he postulates after death.[43] But Christianity is not primarily an ethical-spiritual system. It involves an ethic, to be sure, just as it involves spiritual practices and goals. But at heart it is a set of beliefs and practices that form our feeble and halting response to a surprising and quite undeserved act of infinite love that God has performed on our behalf through Jesus Christ.

We do, of course, desperately need spiritual guides and exemplars of openness to God. Hick's christology provides both. But it does not provide a saviour from our bondage to pride, self-centredness, lust, and violence. Hick's Jesus is not a redeemer from bondage. What we most desperately need is not a guru but a saviour. The classic doctrine, recognizing as it does that we are enslaved to sin and can only be saved through the grace of God, gratefully points to a saviour.[44]

VII

Since he denies the classic doctrine, Hick can hardly count as a believer in the Trinity.[45] And although he does not say much about the Trinity in *The Metaphor of God Incarnate*, it is clear that he does deny the orthodox understanding of it. The claim that the one and only God exists as three unconfused and co-equal persons is one

[43] See John Hick, *Death and Eternal Life* (New York: Harper and Row, 1976), 399–466.

[44] In fairness it must be pointed out that the argument of the last four paragraphs presupposes a fairly traditional Christian notion of salvation in terms of forgiveness and acceptance by God. I am prepared to argue for that notion, but not on this occasion. On Hick's own notion of salvation—transformation from self-centredness to centredness in the Real—my argument would not go through.

[45] 'To question the idea of Jesus as literally God incarnate is also, by implication, to question the idea of God as literally three persons in one. For the doctrine of the Trinity is derived from the doctrine of the incarnation' (*MGI*, 152).

that Hick does not make. First, let us look at what he actually says about the Trinity in *The Metaphor of God Incarnate*; then I want to ask what his pluralist theory *should* allow him to say. The two are not quite the same

Hick does endorse a version of the Trinity, one that seems to amount to what is usually called modalism.

It would be a better use of theological time and energy, in my opinion, to develop forms of trinitarian, christological and soteriological doctrine that are compatible with our awareness of the independent salvific authenticity of the other great world faiths. Such forms are already available in principle in conceptions of the Trinity, not as ontologically three but as three ways in which the one God is humanly thought and experienced.[46]

But for a non-traditional form of Christianity the trinitarian symbol does not refer to three centres of consciousness and will but to three ways in which one God is humanly known—as creator, as transformer, and as inner spirit. We do not need to reify these ways as three distinct persons.[47]

Now modalism has (no pun intended) two faces. In its less radical form, it is a slightly askew version of the orthodox doctrine of the Trinity, one that explains the threeness of the Trinity in a certain way, and affirms threeness but stresses the oneness over the threeness. Certain theologians, notably Karl Barth, tend towards modalism but are still safely orthodox. Modalism in this sense has always struck me as the least egregious of the Trinitarian heresies. The other and more radical face of modalism denies any ontological threeness at all, and is accordingly not orthodox. The threeness is only an appearance; there is no real threeness in the Godhead. Hick's version clearly fits into this category.

I am not going to argue here against modalism and in favour of the orthodox notion of Trinity. What I do want to do is compare what Hick the Christian theologian (the Hick of such works as *The Metaphor of God Incarnate*) says about God with what Hick the global theologian (the Hick of such works as *An Interpretation of Religion*) says about the Real. The evident disjunct between the two constitutes a problem.

The official doctrine of Hick's religious pluralism, crucially based as it is on Kant's distinction between noumena and phenomena, is that there are only two things that we can say about the Real:

[46] *MGI*, 149.   [47] *MGI*, 152–3.

(1) it exists; and (2) it is the ground of religious experience. There are many passages that could be quoted from Hick; here is one:

we cannot apply to the Real *an sich* the characteristics encountered in its *personae* and *impersonae*. Thus it cannot be said to be one or many, person or thing, conscious or unconscious, purposive or non-purposive, substance or process, good or evil, loving or hating. None of the descriptive terms that apply within the realm of human experience can apply literally to the unexperienceable reality that underlies that realm. All that we can say is that we postulate the Real *an sich* as the ultimate ground of the intentional objects of the different forms of religious thought-and-experience.[48]

Now the intentional object of Christian religious experience is of course God. But on Hick's pluralist theory, the God of Christianity, like the various personal Gods (Yahweh, Allah, Shiva, etc.) and impersonal ultimates (voidness, the Dharmakaya, Brahman, etc.) of the world's religions, is a phenomenal manifestation of the noumenon that Hick calls the Real. And, as we have seen, we can say very little about the Real in itself.

But Hick the Christian theologian says much more than this. After arguing that the doctrines of the incarnation and Trinity 'are in fact incomprehensible to most people', Hick asks us to consider this belief, which he appears to be recommending, and which clearly concerns the religious noumenon:

that there is an ultimate transcendent Reality which is the source and ground of everything; that this Reality is benign in relation to human life; that the universal presence of this Reality is reflected ('incarnated') in human terms in the lives of the world's great spiritual leaders.[49]

Given Hick's pluralistic theory, one naturally wonders how it is possible to know or rationally believe that the 'reality' of which he speaks is 'benign in relation to human life'. As we have seen, Hick also asserts that God is one (and not three) and that 'Jesus embodied a love which is a reflection of the divine love'.[50] He even calls that love infinite. So it seems that Hick the Christian theologian makes certain assertions about the Real and God—that reality is benign, that God is one, that God is loving, that God is personal—which Hick the global theologian says that we cannot make about the Real (which is of course the noumenal reality of which 'God' is a manifestation).

[48] *An Interpretation of Religion*, 350.
[49] *MGI*, 163.   [50] *MGI*, ix.

As I understand it, Hick's way of dealing with this problem is as follows. He makes a firm distinction between statements about the various *manifestations of the Real* (e.g. Yahweh, Allah, Brahman, the Tao) and statements about *the Real itself*. Statements about a given manifestation of the Real can be literally or analogically true of it, Hick says; statements about the Real itself are only mytho-logically[51] or metaphorically true. But of course this does not solve the problem, since on Hick's view the various manifestations of the Real do not in fact exist in themselves (i.e. as noumena) and thus do not actually possess—they only appear to possess—the proper-ties his theory allows us literally or analogically to attribute to them. How can the statement, 'Atman is Brahman' be literally or even analogically true since on Hick's theory Brahman is a mani-festation of the Real rather than something that exists in and of itself? All his theory will allow is some such statement as, 'Atman is the same phenomenal manifestation as Brahman'.

Perhaps Hick can again appeal to metaphor. All the things that Hick the Christian theologian is willing to say about God are, like the incarnation, not literally but metaphorically true about God. Although Hick does not say so, it seems that his phrase, 'the divine love',[52] must be taken metaphorically too, since (as noted) Hick's view of the Real limits what we can say about it to an affirmation of (1) its existence and (2) its status as the ground of religious experience. We cannot say that the Real is loving.

Of course metaphors can be powerful linguistic tools, as Hick argues. The question to ask of a metaphor is not whether it is literally true (that is part of what is being excluded) but whether it is appropriate or illuminating. So on this interpretation of Hick's overall programme, the oneness of God, the personalness of God, the fact that reality is benign towards humankind, and the love of God are all metaphorical statements about the Real. It is not liter-ally true that the God is one, personal, benign, and loving, because the personal being that Christians call 'God' does not so much as exist in itself.[53] Nor is it literally true that the Real, which *does* exist, is one, personal, benign, and loving. Or at least there is no possible way to know or even rationally believe that it is.

---

[51] See *An Interpretation of Religion*, 347–60, for Hick's intended notion of 'mytho-logical'.   [52] *MGI*, ix.

[53] I am not claiming that Hick 'denies the existence of God' in the same sense that, say, Bertrand Russell did. Although Hick does not affirm the existence of 'God', he is not an atheist.

But even here Hick faces a problem: in precisely what sense is the statement, 'God is loving', appropriate or illuminating *given the fact that we know that it is not true* or at least *do not know that it is true* (if we accept Hick's pluralism)? Of course it is sometimes fitting to accept the metaphorical truth of (i.e. consider appropriate or illuminating) a statement that we know to be literally false, e.g. 'It's raining cats and dogs'. But what exactly does, 'God is loving', appropriately express or exactly how is it illuminating, if it is not literally true of something that exists in itself? (Indeed, the statement, 'God is loving' is, on Hick's view, simply false; what is true is something like, 'The Real, appearing as God, appears as loving'.) I am not able to answer this question on Hick's behalf.

And if this is the route we are to follow, then Hick's modalistic claims about the Trinity are to be taken as metaphor too. And again we will wonder: in what sense is Hick's statement, 'The trinitarian symbol . . . refer[s] to three ways in which one God is humanly known',[54] appropriate or illuminating given our knowledge of the fact that it is not literally true of anything that exists in itself? In fact, if Hick is right, there is no existing Trinity (of any sort, modal or ontological); indeed, except as an appearance, there is no 'God'.

These are deep questions that Hick must answer. This especially since he wants to be seen not just as a global philosopher of religion but as a Christian theologian.

VIII

I conclude that Hick has not succeeded in overturning the classic doctrine of the incarnation; that the positive christology that he proposes is flawed; and that his discussion of the Trinity reveals deep fault lines in his thought. It is not clear, at least to me, how to connect what he says about the Real with the theological proposals that he wants to make to Christians.[55]

[54] *MGI*, 152–3.

[55] I would like to thank William P. Alston, Avery Fouts, Doug Geivett, John Hick, Brian Leftow, Anselm Min, Alan Padgett, Gerald O'Collins, SJ, and Frans Jozef van Beeck, SJ, for their helpful comments on earlier drafts of this essay.

11

Trinitarian Speculation and the Forms of Divine Disclosure

DAVID TRACY

I Introduction: The Fatal Separations of Modernity

In trying to help our contemporaries appreciate and understand the vitality of trinitarian reflection we may be failing to consider how three great separations of modern Western culture have damaged many modern intellectuals' ability to understand the achievements of pre-modern thought, especially trinitarian theology. These three fatal modern separations are: the separation of feeling and thought; the separation of theory and practice; the separation of form and content. All three of these peculiarly modern separations are related to one another. Moreover, each is based on an originally helpful scholastic distinction that became, in modernity, a separation. Let us recall the original distinctions and their modern separations in our attempt to turn these separations back into distinctions.

The modern separations contrast sharply with the relative ease with which either the ancients (see the work of Pierre Hadot) or the medievals (see the work of Jean Leclercq on the monastic schools and Marie-Dominique Chenu on the scholastics) developed, in their different contexts and schools, valuable distinctions that they all insisted must not be made into separations: the distinctions of feeling and thought, practice and theory, form and content.

I will not discuss in this essay the first two distinctions which became separations: feeling and thought; and practice and theory. In contemporary theology, the separation of feeling and thought has been the most 'healed'—i.e. rendered into a useful distinction, and no longer a separation. Consider the many discussions of experience (both personal, communal and ecclesial) as a 'source' for contemporary theology. One may note especially the new contextual theologies around the globe as practice of sustained critical reflection on a people's or culture's experience. Each of these contextual theologies (especially but not solely liberation, political, and feminist-womanist-mujerista theologies) distinguish but never separate feeling and thought, or 'experience' and 'reflection'.

There is, of course, need for further analysis of this first separation allied to the second separation, that between practice and theory or between spirituality and theology. The distinction of practice and theory—indeed theory itself as a distinct practice—was a natural distinction (never separation) to all the ancient and medieval schools, including the great Scholastics. This distinction, rendered a separation in the fourteenth-century nominalist crisis and in most of modern neo-Scholasticism, was still only a distinction for the great Renaissance humanists (e.g. Erasmus, Colet, Ficino) as well as the great reformers (Luther, Calvin, Ignatius, Teresa, Las Casas, and their contemporaries).

The third distinction—between form and content—was crucial in the reflection of all the ancients even if casually set aside by so many modern theologians and philosophers. As the least reflected upon of the three separations in modern thought, it is the most needing reflection by theologians.

II Form and Forms

What Hans Urs von Balthasar argued, on theological grounds, for theology, Louis Dupré argues for philosophy: no interpreter can understand the Western intellectual tradition without focusing on the phenomenon of form from its beginning to its present crisis. Indeed the central ideal of Western thought from its beginning in Greece (or even, before classical Greece as argued by Mircea Eliade in his studies of archaic religious manifestations) was the idea of the real as, in essence, its appearance in form. As Dupré interprets this centrality of form (the principal leitmotif of his study of modernity), form grounds the ancient and medieval ontotheological synthesis. For the ancients, the essence of the real and our knowledge of it consists ultimately of form. Form, moreover, shows forth the real in harmonious appearance: whether in sensuous image as in Greek sculpture; in mathematics as in Pythagoras; in the forms of tragedy which bring some aesthetic harmony even to chaos and strife; above all, in the ancient philosophical turn to reflective form in the soul or mind. For the ancients the essence of the real and our knowledge of it consists ultimately of form. The real appears in an orderly way and thus becomes (even in tragedy) harmonious appearance. This aesthetic, i.e. form-focused understanding of the real, provided the ancients with the ultimate grounding for any harmonious synthesis of the cosmic, the divine, and the human realms. It is difficult for us late twentieth-century heirs of the fragmentation of all syntheses to comprehend this. The task is made even more difficult for us as inheritors of a hermeneutics of suspicion that every form may merely mask indeterminacy and every appearance or manifestation may always hide a strife involving both disclosure and concealment.

Nevertheless, both critics and proponents of classical, medieval, and much modern thought (Bruno to Hegel) cannot grasp Western thought without dwelling on the centrality of form. For the premoderns, what appears or manifests itself through form is not our subjective construction, but the very showing forth, through form, of the real. For the Greeks real being begins with intelligible form: i.e. with a multiplicity, chaos, strife rendered somehow orderly and harmonious through form. The Jewish and Christian thinkers accepted the centrality of form but could not accept the necessity of form in Greek and Roman thought. The Greek gods need the form principle; indeed the form is divine and the divine is form for the Greeks. For the Jew, Christian, and Muslim, God creates form. But as long as God is not understood to be a purely transcendent will and as long as God's actions are not read exclusively through efficient causality, form survives, indeed prevails: now through the Creator-God's formal, immanent causality and the trinitarian God's relationality in-and-through form. For Christian thought, moreover, the doctrine of the Word grounded this reality of form in the central Christian doctrines of christology and Trinity.

This principle of reality manifested *as real* in and through harmonious form in-formed the Western philosophical ontotheological tradition from Plato through Hegel. For Plato, with all his constant rethinking of 'form', especially in *Parmenides*, form in some manner resided within the appearing objects of which it constituted the intelligible essence. As determining that intelligibility (and thereby reality) form also went beyond the objects. In all Greek philosophy (including Aristotle, despite his critique of Plato on form) being is defined in terms of form. Moreover, form's dependence is to be understood primarily, not exclusively, in terms of participation. The same is also true, it might be added, of archaic and Greek religion as manifestation (Eliade) or, as Hegel nicely named Greek religion, the religion of beauty. The same centrality of form, as Balthasar brilliantly shows, is true of any form of Christianity faithful to the incarnational principle and to a properly theological understanding of Word as Logos: i.e. manifestation in and through form and thereby God in and through trinitarian form. Indeed, even for Hegel (that strange modern speculative trinitarian—see below) all content attains its truth in and through form.

In my judgement, we can render this new interest in form explicitly hermeneutical in philosophy and theology. The ancients hold that truth needs 'to be justified' (as for the moderns), but that justification can be found principally in the sense that truth means participation in being (not construction of it) as manifested through form. This ancient sense is also argued by modern hermeneutics: first by Gadamer with his insistence in *Truth and Method* that truth is fundamentally disclosure and is best rendered through form (*Darstellung*, not *Vor-stellung*); second, and most carefully, by Ricoeur in his contemporary argument that truth is primordially manifestation, and only derivatively correspondence or even coherence. Any philosopher who argues, on contemporary grounds, in favour of a hermeneutical understanding of truth as primordially manifestation through some form (as I also have in other writing) cannot but be heartened by the new emphasis on the centrality of form in contemporary philosophy and theology. Indeed, in terms of contemporary hermeneutics truth is primordially manifestation through form.

Since the critiques of Heidegger and Derrida, there have been few more pejorative words in contemporary thought than the word 'ontotheology'. It is no small part of the trinitarian recovery in contemporary theology that we may restore one fully positive meaning to this word. For now we find subtle and rich studies of how the ancient as well as the Jewish–Christian medieval synthesis of the cosmos, the divine, and the human rendered Western thought into a whole, in all its principal and very different religious, cultural, philosophical, and theological forms. The ancient organic Greek and Roman unity was, of course, originally threatened by the Jewish–Christian notion of a Creator-God transcendent to the cosmos (unlike the 'gods'). Indeed the greatest and, on the whole, most successful accomplishment of the Jewish, Christian, and Islamic medieval thinkers was the development of new syntheses designed to maintain the transcendent Creator-God's profound immanence in the cosmos and in humanity (through wisdom and grace). This was most clearly achieved in the trinitarian theologies of Bonaventure wherein a new Christian ontotheology was formed. This medieval achievement has been recovered in several contemporary trinitarian theologies.

III The Turn to the Other and to a Trinitarian
Form in Christian Theology

The turn to the other takes many forms in post-modernity. Every form interrupts the role of the same, more often understood as the reign of the modern. Interruption itself takes many forms. Sometimes it comes as sheer interruptive event, power, gift. At other times it comes as revelation and grace. Where transgression often serves as the first sign of a post-modern arrival, the reality of gift and its economy are often a second and more explicitly theological sign of the presence of post-modernity. As with the early dialectical theologians (especially Karl Barth), if for very different reasons, both event-language and revelation-language have returned to theology. Both now return not so much to retrieve some aspect of pre-modernity (although that too becomes a real possibility) but rather to disrupt or interrupt the continuities and similarities masking the increasingly deadening sameness of the modern worldview. 'Event' is that which cannot be accounted for in the present order but disrupts it by happening. 'Gift' transgresses the present economy and calls it into question. Revelation is the event-gift of the Other's self-manifestation. Revelation disrupts the continuities, the similarities, the communalities of modern 'religion'.

Many forms of philosophy and theology partake of such otherness. With the fine exception of that form of analytical philosophy naming itself 'Christian philosophy' (and thereby, considering 'revelation' to be not only 'religion'), much philosophy of religion seems capable only of further scholasticism or of the relatively untroubled, not to say relaxed post-modernity of Richard Rorty. Moreover, most forms of 'philosophy of religion' (a discipline invented in and for modernity) are far too caught in their own disciplinary modernism to even consider the otherness of revelation as worthy of their attention. On the other hand, all those forms of philosophy in which 'otherness' and 'difference' have become central categories now find modernity more a problematic concept than a ready solution. These philosophies of otherness and difference have become, in fact if not in name, 'post-modern'. Often this occurs through a self-conscious recovery of the non-Enlightenment, even at times the non-Greek resources of Western culture itself: witness Emmanuel Lévinas's brilliant recovery of ethics as first philosophy partly made possible by his recovery of the Judaic strands of our culture; witness Pierre Hadot's and Martha Nussbaum's distinct recoveries of the pluralistic, 'literary' (Nussbaum), and 'spiritual exercises' (Hadot) aspects of pluralistic Hellenistic rather than merely classical Hellenic culture; witness Jean Luc Marion's brilliant recovery of Pseudo-Dionysius or Julia Kristeva's recovery of the love mystics; witness Jacques Derrida's interest in (and critique of) the traditions of apophatic theology; witness John Caputo's recent Judaeo-Christian philosophical critique of Heidegger's obsession with the 'Greeks'; witness, above all, how many modern Christian trinitarian theologians (e.g. Moltmann, von Balthasar, LaCugna, Coakley, R. Williams, *et al.*) have rediscovered the import of the form(s) of the liturgy in the great Eastern Orthodox traditions to complement and critique the contemporary (especially post-modern) love of and retrieval of the apophatic traditions. Indeed contemporary Orthodox theology (Lossky, Zizioulas, Yannaras) have led the way for all of us in sustained attempts to honour a Christian theology of God incorporating both apophaticism and trinitarianism.

The list of genuinely post-modern philosophical exercises could easily be expanded. Some (as, curiously, with the ancients) make it difficult to distinguish a philosophical from a theological position any longer: recall Mark C. Taylor, Robert Scharlemann, or Edith Wyschogrod. Others especially in French philosophy deliver their descriptions of the Other in more familiar theological terms—the gift is explicitly named 'grace'; the 'event' of the Other is named the 'revelation' event of the Other's self-manifestation. Indeed those new post-modern theological options have exploded in a hundred new cultural and theological forms.

Surely the very question of form itself is what should most command our attention. My own belief is that across the Christian theological spectrum there is occurring an event of major import: the attempt to free Christian theology from the now smothering embrace of modernity—an event which is as difficult, as conflictual, and as painful as the earlier (equally necessary) attempt in early modernity to free theology from the suffocating embrace of pre-modern modes of thought. Some moderns have now become, in every intellectual discipline, including theology, the most defensive and troubled thinkers of all. They always seem to be searching for one more round of pre-modern vs. modern debate in order to display their honest modern scruples and arguments one more time. Fortunately for them, there are more than enough fundamentalist groups (that curious 'underside' of the modern dilemma) to allow the 'modern' debate to continue.

Unfortunately for the moderns, however, the more serious debate has shifted to one they continue to avoid: the debate on the 'unthought' aspects of modernity itself. Was the modern turn to the subject also a turn to the same? Was the 'religionizing' of all theology more of that same? Is the modern form of argument adequate to understand genuine otherness and difference? Was trinitarian theology far too marginalized in Catholic neo-Scholastic theologies' distinction (and sometimes separation) of the tract *De Deo Uno* and *De Deo Trino*? Was modern liberal theologies' 'quiet funeral' (C. Welch) for a Christian trinitarian understanding of God radical by impoverishing the properly Christian understanding in favour of some modern version of a non-trinitarian monotheism? Is not modern liberal thought far more engendered, colonialist, even at times, racist, classist, and above all Eurocentric than it seems capable of acknowledging? These questions begin to haunt the modern conscience like a guilty romance. For some philosophers and theologians the only honest option is to find better ways to honour otherness and difference by transgressing the modern liberal pieties when necessary, in order to honour in thought as in life the otherness manifested in Jesus Christ and (through Christ) in the radical otherness-as-radical relationality in a Christian trinitarian understanding of God.

The question of form itself, I repeat, is one way to begin to address these new theological questions with new resources for thought and action. Christian theology should never be formless. Christian theology should always be determined in its understanding of God and humanity by its belief in the form-of-forms, the divine-human form, Jesus Christ—that form which must inform all Christian understanding of God as trinitarian and transform all Christian understanding of human possibility for relational thought and social, political action.

There is no serious form of *Christian* theology that is not Christomorphic. This is a more accurate designation of the christological issue, I believe, than the more familiar but confusing word 'Christo-centric'. For theology is not christocentric but theo-centric, although it is so only by means of its christo-morphism. In sum, Christian theology, precisely as Christo-morphic, should always be a trinitarian theo-centrism.

IV CHRISTIAN MONOTHEISM: REALISTIC FORMS AND THE TRINITARIAN FORM FOR UNDERSTANDING GOD

A. *Monotheism and its Different Meanings*

The first problem with monotheism is the word itself. Although its basic meaning is clear (mono - theos: the one - God), that meaning changes into a surprising multiplicity as the horizon for understanding the word 'monotheism' shifts. Wittgenstein's insistence that the meaning is not an abstract property of words but is discovered by noting the use of a word in context is nowhere more true than in a case like the word 'monotheism'. It is the ever-shifting contexts that change the meaning.

At least three contexts are worth noting here. First, 'monotheism' is a modern philosophical word meaning an abstract property (oneness) that belongs to God alone. More exactly, 'monotheism' is an Enlightenment invention (H. More, D. Hume) that bears all the marks of Enlightenment rationalism. Monotheism, in this not so secretly evolutionary view, is a contrast word to 'polytheism': i.e. (by Enlightenment standards) monotheism is a more rational understanding of the logic of the divine as implying a unicity of divine power, not a dispersal of that power into many gods and goddesses. Like the other famous 'isms' of the Enlightenment (deism, pantheism, theism, panentheism), modern philosophical 'monotheism' is, above all, 'rational' and 'ethical'. The relationship of this Enlightenment notion of monotheism to the historical religions (especially but not solely Judaism, Christianity, and Islam) is often obscured by Enlightenment prejudice against 'positive' (i.e. historical) religions in contrast to 'natural religion'. Unfortunately, most philosophical and even many theological uses of the word 'monotheism' still bear this dehistoricized and decontextualized Enlightenment meaning.

A second context also presents itself for understanding the word monotheism—history of religions. In a history of religions' context 'monotheism' describes the 'family resemblances' among different religious phenomena: the 'high gods' of some primal traditions (e.g. the *deus otiosus* traditions in Africa); the philosophical reflections of the logic of unicity among the Greek thinkers from Xenophanes to Aristotle; a possible name for some Indian thinkers (especially Ramanujan); a clear name for such religions as Sikhism and Zoroastrianism; the revisionary monotheism of the reforming pharaoh Akhenaton; above all, of course, the three classical 'religions of the book' or, in the history of religions' terms, the historical, ethical, prophetic monotheism of Judaism, Christianity, and Islam. Clearly such history of religions' reflections have influenced modern scholarship on the history of ancient Israel as well as on the history of early Islam. Many scholarly studies show the final emergence of radical monotheism in the 'Yahweh alone' prophets (especially Amos, Elijah, and Hosea). This movement culminated in the prophet of the Babylonian exile (Deutero-Isaiah). There Yahweh is clearly not only the God of Israel but also both creator of the whole world and the one and only God who determines not only Israel's history but all history: recall Deutero-Isaiah's reading of the Persian king Cyrus as the 'Messiah' appointed by Yahweh. It is the Deuteronomic reading of Yahweh which will influence the theological—i.e. radical monotheistic reading of Israel's history in the Bible. From that point on, the central religious affirmation of Judaism, Christianity, and Islam will be the classic *shema Yisrael* of Deuteronomy 6: 4–5: 'Hear, O Israel! The Lord our God is one Lord; and you shall love the Lord your God with all your heart, and with all your soul, and with all your might!'

The route to this radical monotheism, however, was a long and complex one whose many twists and turns are still debated among scholars. Indeed, there are few more fascinating debates in the history of religion than the conflict of interpretations among scholars of ancient Israel on the most likely history of the emergence of radical monotheism from polytheism, henotheism, monarchic monotheism, and monolatry. There can be little doubt that, in the emergence of radical monotheism in ancient Israel, there have been as many forms for the divine reality as there were names for the divine power(s). In strictly historical terms, radical monotheism is a relatively late arrival in the founding history of ancient Israel. But the principal theological question today for Jews, Christians, and Muslims is not so much the theological implications of the fascinating history of the earlier different names and forms for the divine in the complex history of ancient Israel but rather the still contemporary theological question of the different *forms* for experiencing, naming, and understanding divine reality since the prophetic and Deuteronomic emergence of radical monotheism.

Hence, the third, and for present purposes, the principal context for understanding the word monotheism is the strictly theological context of the category for monotheistic Judaism, Christianity, and Islam. For the purpose of clarity, this theological-soteriological understanding of historical, ethical monotheism bears the following characteristics:

(1) God is one: an individual distinct from all the rest of reality;
(2) God is the origin, sustainer, and end of all reality;
(3) God, therefore, is the One with the person-like characteristics of individuality, intelligence, and love;
(4) God, and God alone, is related to *all* reality. Indeed God is Creator of all reality, both natural and historical;
(5) In sum, God, and God alone as the Wholly Other One, is both transcendent to all reality and totally immanent in all reality;
(6) God discloses Godself in chosen prophets, historical events, and scriptures.

B. *Christian Trinitarian Monotheism: The Import of Christian Realism in the Forms of Narrative, Doctrine, Liturgy*

To understand the many faces of the divine in Christianity means to understand who God is in and through the revelatory event which is, for the Christian, the decisive mediation, as self-revelation, of God: the person of Jesus Christ. A Christian understanding of God becomes the question of the identity of God: Who is God? For the Christian, God is the One who revealed Godself in the ministry and message, the cross and resurrection of Jesus Christ. A Christian theological understanding of God cannot ultimately be divorced from this revelation of God in Jesus Christ: neither through solely philosophical understandings of 'monotheism' (although these philosophical arguments are, of course, relevant for questions of intelligibility); nor through historical-critical reconstruction of 'the historical Jesus' (although these reconstructions, even if never constitutive of Christian self-understanding, are relevant as correcting such recurrent views as Docetic and Monophysite christologies). The full Christian doctrine of God discloses the trinitarian form of divine reality that must inform every symbol and doctrine, just as the trinitarian doctrine of God is informed in its many formulations (East and West, pre-modern and contemporary) by every symbol and doctrine (creation-redemption, eschatology, church, spirit, sacrament, revelation, and especially christology). A theological insistence on the interconnection of the central mysteries of the faith is true, of course, of the understanding of every great symbol of Christian faith, but is especially crucial on the question of the trinitarian God. Christian theology must always be radically theocentric so that no single symbol or doctrine in the whole system of doctrines can be adequately understood without explicitly relating that symbol to the reality of God as disclosed in Jesus Christ.

The best initial way to understand Christian realism as a trinitarian understanding of God is to recall how all three principal forms of realism in Christian thought and life—the realistic forms of narrative, doctrine, and liturgy—demand a trinitarian understanding of God even when that trinitarian understanding yields to the development of more speculative (both cataphatic and apophatic) namings of the trinitarian God (the Cappadocians, especially Gregory of Nyssa, Dionysius the Areopagite, Gregory Palamas, Augustine, Aquinas, B. Lonergan, K. Rahner, Bonaventure, Dante, H. U. von Balthasar, Luther, Calvin, E. Jüngel, J. Moltmann; C. LaCugna, M. Suchocki, E. Johnson; G. Gutierrez, J. B. Metz, L. Boff, V. Lossky, J. Zizioulas, C. Yannaras).

The passion narratives, nicely described by H. Frei as 'history-like' and 'realistic', disclose the most basic realistic form of Christian understanding not only of the identity of Jesus Christ but, in and through that identity, of the identity of the God who acts with the 'face' of the Divine Agent in and through the actions and sufferings of Jesus of Nazareth. As in any realistic narrative, so too in the passion narrative an identity is rendered through the plotted interactions of an unsubstitutable character (Jesus) and the unique events (betrayal, cross, resurrection) which Jesus both performs and suffers. The fact that the Christian understanding of the one God is grounded not in a general philosophical theory of monotheism but in this concrete passion-narrative history of God's self-disclosure as agent in the cross and resurrection of Jesus of Nazareth provides the primary theological foundation for all properly Christian trinitarian understandings of God. This is what contemporary Lutheran and Reformed trinitarian theologies (Barth, Moltmann, Jüngel, Frei, Lindbeck) see so clearly in their close attention to the details of the realistic biblical narratives (not, it is important to recall for any of these trinitarian theologies, in the historically reconstructed narratives).

The central passion narrative, moreover, should not remain isolated from the rest of the scriptures nor from the later creeds. Rather, the passion narrative, as foundation and focus of all properly Christian understanding of God, should open up to the larger gospel narratives (on the message and ministry of Jesus), the theologies of Paul and John, the Pastorals, the Book of Revelation, and all the rest of the New Testament. The many faces of God, for the Christian, are found, therefore, not only in the foundational insight into God as principal agent in the passion narratives of Jesus the Christ. God is also disclosed through the pre-passion actions of the ministry and message of Jesus of Nazareth as they are rendered in importantly different ways by the four gospels. The typical speech of Jesus, for example, becomes part of the way through which Christians understand the many faces of God: the parabolic discourse on the Reign of God discloses God's face as an excess of both power and love (e.g. the Prodigal Son); the typical word of Jesus for God, 'Abba', becomes crucial for any Christian understanding of the Power ('Lord') and Mercy (Father) of the mysterious face of God disclosed through Jesus; the centrality of the cross in the apocalyptic tale told by Mark and the dialectical language of Paul also opens later Christians to the *tremendum et fascinans* face of God disclosed in the hidden-revealed trinitarian God of Luther, Calvin, and Pascal; the intrinsic link of Jesus' actions to the poor, the oppressed, and the marginal, especially in Luke and Mark, open many Christians to discovering the face of God above all in the faces of the victims of history and all those involved in the prophetic struggle against all oppression.

At the same time, as focused and grounded in the understanding of God's agency in the passion narrative, the Christian understanding of God should also be open to the complex and profound disclosures of God's identity in the history of Israel rendered in the many genres and forms (narrative, law, praise, lamentation, wisdom) of the Old Testament. This is clearly not the place to review and interpret the extraordinary complexity of a full scriptural understanding of the many faces of God disclosed in the many scriptural genres naming God. This much, however, does need to be affirmed: for the Christian, God is above all the One who disclosed the authentic face of God in raising Jesus of Israel from the dead. God, for the Christian, is the One who revealed decisively who God is in and through the message and ministry, the incarnation, cross, and resurrection of none other than Jesus the Christ. The most profound Christian metaphor for the true face of God remains the metaphor of First John: 'God is love' (1 John 4: 16). To understand that metaphor (which occurs, let us note, in the first theological commentary on the most theological and meditative of the four gospels), is to understand, on inner-Christian terms, what has been revealed by God of God's agent identity as the very face of Love in the ministry, the message, the incarnation, cross, and resurrection of Jesus Christ.

The answer to the question 'who is God?' is therefore, for the Christian faithful to the self-disclosure of God in Jesus Christ, 'God is love' and Christians are those agents commanded and empowered by God to love. However, if this classic Johannine metaphor 'God is love' is not grounded and thereby interpreted by means of the harsh and demanding reality of the message and ministry, the cross and resurrection of this unsubstitutable Jesus who, as the Christ, disclosed God's face turned to us as Love, then Christians may be tempted to sentimentalize the metaphor by reversing it into 'Love is God'. But this great reversal, on inner-Christian terms, is hermeneutically impossible. 'God is love': this identity of God the Christian experiences in and through the history of God's actions and self-disclosure as the God who is Love in Jesus Christ, the parable and face of God.

To affirm that 'God is love' is also to affirm, now, in the necessarily more abstract terms proper to post-scriptural metaphysical theologies, that the radically monotheistic God, the origin, sustainer, and end of all reality, is characterized by the kind of relationality proper to that most relational of all categories, love. God, the One Christians trust, worship, and have loyalty to, should be construed as the radically relational (and, therefore, personal) origin, sustainer, and end of all reality.

To affirm that the Christian understanding of God refers to the One whom Christians worship, trust, and are loyal to is also to 'place' this Christian understanding on the language-map of radical monotheism (shared by Judaism and Islam). To affirm, with First John, in and through the gospel narrative and the realistic ecclesial confession and doctrines (B. Lonergan) of the incarnation, cross, and resurrection of Jesus Christ, that 'God is love' is further to affirm the radical relationality of God's nature as ultimately mysterious yet person-like (i.e. characterized by intelligence and love). The latter affirmation, moreover, both grounds a theological understanding of the economic Trinity in the primary Christian confession of Jesus Christ and also suggests how the immanent Trinity can be partly, analogously but really understood in and through the economic Trinity. Christian monotheism is a trinitarian monotheism as the realistic Christian narratives, doctrines, and liturgy all witness. For the trinitarian understanding of God is the fullest Christian theological understanding of the radical, relational, loving, kenotic God who revealed Godself in and through the incarnation, the ministry (healing, preaching, actions), the name 'Abba' for God, the parables on the 'Reign of God', the fate of the cross and the vindication by resurrection of Jesus of Nazareth, and the disclosure of this Jesus as the Christ through the power and activity of the Spirit as proclaimed in Word and celebrated in sacrament, especially the context of the explicitly trinitarian sacraments of Baptism and Eucharist (to the Father through the Son in the Spirit). It is impossible to separate trinitarian theo-logy and christology. In the same sense, the Christian understanding of the 'existence' and 'nature' of the radically monotheistic God must be grounded in the 'identity' of the God disclosed in the history and effects of Jesus Christ; i.e. in the confession of trinitarian monotheism.

V IN DEFENCE OF THE SPECULATIVE FORM OF TRINITARIAN THEOLOGY

Although Christian reflection on the trinitarian reality of God is initiated by and grounded in the realism intrinsic to the three classic forms of Christian life and thought—narrative, doctrine, liturgy—it is also open to the form of speculation. In most instances of speculative trinitarian thought there is a move from the economic Trinity discussion with its affinities to realistic forms to more conceptual and abstract forms of trinitarian reflection and its affinities to speculative forms for reflection on the 'immanent Trinity'. Karl Rahner's and Karl Barth's distinct insistences on the priority of the economic Trinity for any speculation on the immanent Trinity can also be read (by concentrating on the issue of form and content) as the priority (chronologically and ontologically) of realism in the forms of narrative, doctrine, and liturgy as always grounding any speculation on the immanent Trinity (as narrative does for Barth, doctrine for Rahner, drama for von Balthasar, and liturgy for most Orthodox trinitarian theologians). When that grounding is lost, we have Hegel's conceptual (the form of absolute knowledge—the *Begriff*), speculative, and indeed dialectically necessary trinitarian theology (still grounded if the realism of the *Aufhebung* by the Absolute *Begriff* of all earlier forms of the *Phenomenology* works; not grounded if it does not).

I continue to believe that the brilliant use of the analogies of intelligence and love by the Western trinitarian theologies of Augustine, Aquinas, and Lonergan are splendid, plausible, and modestly speculative forms for reflection on the immanent Trinity without any loss of a grounding in the realistic forms (here especially doctrine and confession) of articulating the economic Trinity. Even in less modest and more daring trinitarian speculative theologies that realistic grounding can reappear at the heart of speculation itself. This is especially the case with the relationship of radical apophaticism to trinitarian theology. That relationship—so central to our own period's recovery of both the apophatic tradition and the trinitarian tradition—is, of course, central to most contemporary Orthodox trinitarian reflection. It also occurs in Western theology more frequently than many histories of the Western doctrine of the Trinity seem to admit. Hence the need today to return to classic Western medieval instances of speculative trinitarian theology and its relationship to radical apophaticism: the work of Eckhart and Ruusbroec.

The complexities of Eckhart's position continue to puzzle interpreters. Indeed, the complexities are such that Rudolf Otto could compare Eckhart to Shankara while D. T. Suzuki found the more apt comparison to be Nagarjuna. There remains, as well, continuing debates over the accuracy of the posthumous papal condemnation of some propositions of Eckhart in the bull *In Agro Dominico*. Moreover, in philosophy and Christian theology, some recent readings of Eckhart tend to compare his position to the more radical—that is, apophatic—side of Heidegger (Caputo and Schurmann), while other interpreters (McGinn and Colledge) argue for the importance not only of the more apophatic of his vernacular sermons but also of the scholastic categories of his more systematic Latin works.

I cannot presume to resolve the conflicts between expert interpreters. Fortunately, for the present limited purposes, that is unnecessary. Rather, informed by my own reading of the relevant texts and some principal interpreters, I shall confine my comments on Eckhart to two principal questions relevant for the discussion of the relationship of apophatic and trinitarian theology. The first issue may be called one of spirituality. What strikes a reader most about Eckhart's texts is a spirituality marked, above all, by two characteristics: intellectualism and radical detachment. Here a rigorous intellectualism not only is not divorced from spirituality but is a central element in it. For Eckhart, this shows, of course, his fidelity to his Dominican tradition in contrast to the greater love orientation of Bernard of Clairvaux and the Franciscans. This intellectualism, in turn, leads to a spirituality of radical detachment that bears remarkable resemblances to the non-attachment, non-clinging spirituality of many forms of Buddhism. Like the Buddhists and unlike the love-mystics, Eckhart sometimes seems to accord a 'higher' spiritual role to radical detachment than to Christian love. This has serious consequences in his theology. Unlike some Christian mystics, Eckhart is not interested in such intense experiences as rapture or ecstasy but, like Zen Buddhists, far more interested in illuminating our true awareness of the everyday. In the Buddhist case, nirvana and samsara are one. In Eckhart's case, the disclosure of the Godhead beyond God is, at the same time, the disclosure of our release for everyday life of activity-in-the-world. Eckhart's remarkable reading of the Martha–Mary story highlights the active-contemplative Martha and not (as for many Christian contemplatives) the purely contemplative Mary who illustrates the Christian contemplative's life as a life-in-the-world 'without a why'.

These affinities (not *identities*) between the spiritual awareness of Eckhart and Zen explain the enormous appeal of Eckhart to so many Buddhist thinkers. This spirituality of detachment and intellectualism leads to some of the more radically apophatic conceptualities of Eckhart, especially his famous insistence on the 'Godhead beyond God', wherein even the names of Father, Son, and Spirit are seemingly no longer relevant. For Eckhart, 'nothingness' receives an unusual radicality for a Christian thinker. To be sure, as Buddhist thinkers have been quick to note, even Eckhart's 'nothingness' is not the 'absolute nothingness' of Zen thought.

However radically apophatic Eckhart is for a Christian thinker, he remains a God-obsessed thinker who constantly shifts, in different contexts, his language of transcendentals for both God and the Godhead beyond God. Not only Nothingness but also One, Intelligence, and *Esse* seem to him appropriate if always inadequate analogical language. Whether all Eckhart's language can be rendered coherent without losing all *Christian* trinitarian God-language or without reducing his position to some more familiar Christian understanding of God remains the principal question still under dispute, despite *In Agro Dominico*. What is relatively clear, however, especially but not solely in the Latin texts, as McGinn argues, is Eckhart's unique use of the languages of predication, analogy, and dialectic.

The dialectical language of Eckhart invites reflection. All Eckhart's dialectical language for the Godhead and God can occur only after the possibilities and limits of predication and analogy have been tried. What is striking about Eckhart's use of analogy is its difference from his Dominican predecessor, Thomas Aquinas. Eckhart, however faithful to Aquinas' language of analogy, totally reverses its meaning: only God can provide the proper analogy. Indeed, this is true for Eckhart to the point where we are left with 'extrinsic attribution language' rather than with Thomist 'intrinsic' attribution or 'proportionality'.

But lest one think that Eckhart is an early proponent of Barth's *analogia fidei* against *analogia entis*, one must note that this 'failure' of traditional analogical language (and, before it, of traditional predication) becomes, for Eckhart, an occasion to note the need for a radically dialectical language. Here is where Eckhart makes his most original moves—for the Godhead as One is indistinct, and precisely as such is distinct from all reality (and vice versa). This radically dialectical understanding of indistinction and distinction, of immanence and transcendence, allows Eckhart to interpret the *bullitio* of the emergence of the divine relations within the Trinity, while still, in a final dialectical speculative apophatic negation, claiming to 'break through' to the 'Godhead beyond God'. Thus Eckhart, in a final paradox, can *pray* to God to free him *from* God.

Even in the abbreviated form given above, one cannot but find Eckhart's intellectual-spiritual journey a remarkable one for a Christian. He can even be said to go a long way—although not all the way—with a Buddhist. But Eckhart's dialectic nonetheless demands a move which Buddhism does not: it is a trinitarian move—the self-manifestation of the Godhead in the distinct *bullitio* as the Trinity and the *ebullitio* of the creature. To be more exact, a Buddhist dialectic of dynamic *sunyata* may have a similar self-manifestation character, insofar as dynamic *sunyata* manifests itself as wisdom and as compassion to the enlightened one. But this is still unlike Eckhart's explicit revision of neo-Platonic 'emanation' language into the more radically dialectical language of *bullitio* and *ebullitio* (and, allied to that, on the human side of awareness, the birth of the Word in the soul and the 'breakthrough' of the soul to the Godhead).

Nevertheless, I remain puzzled whether the Christian trinitarian understanding of God can receive as radically an apophatic character as Eckhart sometimes insists upon. I say this not to doubt the greater need to recover the apophatic tradition in Christian theology nor to doubt that no-thingness needs to be examined seriously in that tradition in relationship to such tradition (but difficult!) language as One, Intelligence, Being, or Creativity.

It is possible (I suspect, but do not yet know) that Eckhart's 'Godhead beyond God' language may be appropriate Christian theological language—not merely in the relatively easy sense of one way to acknowledge the radical inadequacy of all our God-language, but in the more difficult dialectical sense of a more adequate trinitarian naming of what Christians call God. For that reason, at this time and prior to further reflection I find myself, in Christian theological terms, more with Jan Ruusbroec than with Meister Eckhart. To continue the parallel with Eckhart, one may furnish the Christian theological reasons to move in Ruusbroec's direction for understanding the Christian God in terms of both spirituality and theology. In the Christian spiritual life (here Merton in his famous dialogue with Suzuki clearly agrees with Ruusbroec), the move to radical negation and nothingness is construed by the Christian as one of the important moments of awareness in the larger sphere of awareness of the fuller Christian life. Even Eckhart, with his language of *bullitio* and *ebullitio* may agree here.

In the Christian construal, the most radical negation of the cloud of unknowing and the acknowledgement of nothingness must, through their own power of awareness, yield to the self-manifestation (emanation, *bullitio–ebullitio*, revelation) of the Divine Reality (whether named Godhead or God).

Theologically, this means, as Ruusbroec clearly sees, that the radical indistinction, the no-thingness of Eckhart's Godhead-beyond-God, will necessarily manifest itself in the Christian life as the self-manifesting Father–Son–Spirit. Where Eckhart is unclear in his language about applying his diverse transcendental terms (One, *Esse*, Intelligence), sometimes to the Godhead and sometimes to the Father-Source, Ruusbroec is clear. In Christian terms, all our language for God is inadequate. The radical negations of the spiritual life demand radical negations of all our names for God. And yet the Christian experience (especially liturgical experience) and thereby awareness of God's wisdom in the Logos and God's love in the Spirit remain our central clues to the reality we hesitantly name God. Insofar as Christians experience Godself as Source, Logos, and Spirit, they find their central insight into God's own reality as always self-manifesting. That self-manifestation of the Father as Logos-Image is the Son. That relationship of divine self-manifestation is the Spirit. Christians find these conceptualities for understanding the divine reality through their very experience and awareness of wisdom and love (Augustine, Aquinas, Lonergan). These clues to the source, order, and end of all reality allow them to name God as an always self-manifesting God—as Father–Son–Spirit (or Source–Logos–Spirit).

In traditional theological terms, the 'economic' Trinity grounds all talk of the immanent Trinity of God's own reality. Nor need one fear that there will always be a 'fourth'—the divine essence in all Christian trinitarian understanding of God—insofar as one grasps, as Ruusbroec clearly does, that God's essence is dialectically self-manifesting and thereby is necessarily Father–Son–Spirit.

I believe, furthermore, that Macquarrie is correct to state that this Christian insight implies that 'natural theology' should also feel obliged to show the intrinsically incarnational and relational trinitarian structure of all reality. Unlike not only the Barthians but also the Thomists (with their distinction between 'natural' mysteries and 'supernatural' mysteries), the neo-Platonists (including, here, some Hegelians and some Whiteheadians, Rahnerians, and Tillichians) develop philosophical positions that attempt to show, minimally, the reasonableness of an incarnational, relational, and trinitarian understanding of all reality. Such an enterprise, to be sure, demands a full incarnational metaphysics of relationality.

In the meantime, precisely the Christian trinitarian (self-manifesting, radically relational) understanding of the Divine Reality so well expressed by Ruusbroec may suggest that even the most radically speculative form for trinitarian theology of the immanent Trinity can cohere with the realistic forms (narrative, doctrine, liturgy) for the economic Trinity. Even more important is the contemporary rediscovery of the importance of radical apophaticism for all naming of God—including an adequate trinitarian economic and immanent naming—as well as for trinitarian reflection in the analogical (and thereby also partly apophatic) theologies of Augustine, Aquinas, and Lonergan, and even for the more radical apophaticism of Ruusbroec and possibly Eckhart. Some further attention by trinitarian theologians to form–content relationships here could significantly aid what is for me a central question for all trinitarian theology: the relationship of trinitarian language to apophaticism. The key to that relationship is the relationship for form and content.

Bibliographical Suggestions for Parts I–III

On hermeneutics: see Hans-Georg Gadamer, *Truth and Method*, rev. trans. J. Weinsheimer and D. G. Marshall, 2nd rev. edn. (New York: Continuum, 1994); Martin Heidegger, *Zur Sache des Denkens*

(Tübingen: Max Niemeyer Verlag, 1969); Paul Ricoeur, *Hermeneutics and the Human Sciences* (Cambridge: Cambridge University Press, 1981); Hans Robert Jauss, *Toward an Aesthetics of Reception* (Minneapolis: University of Minnesota, 1982).

For pre-modern sources in modernity, see Louis Dupré, *Passage to Modernity* (New Haven: Yale University Press, 1993); Pierre Hadot, *Exercises spirituels et philosophie antique* (Paris: Études Augustiniennes, 1987); and my *The Analogical Imagination* (New York: Crossroad, 1982).

BIBLIOGRAPHICAL SUGGESTIONS FOR PART IV

Concilium, vol. 177, *Monotheism*, ed. Claude Geffré and Jean-Pierre Jossua, 1985.
Hans Frei, *The Identity of Jesus Christ* (Philadelphia: Fortress Press, 1975).
Bernard-Henri Lévy, *La Testament de Dieu* (Paris: B. Grasset, 1979).
Theodore M. Ludwig, 'Monotheism', in *The Encyclopedia of Religion*, ed. Mircea Eliade, vol. x (New York: Macmillan, 1987), 36-66.
Jürgen Moltmann, *The Trinity and the Kingdom: The Doctine of God* (London: SCM Press, 1981).
H. Richard Niebuhr, *Radical Monotheism and Western Civilization* (New York: Harper, 1960).

BIBLIOGRAPHICAL SUGGESTIONS FOR PART V

Edmond Colledge and Bernard McGinn, translators and editors, *Meister Eckhart: The Essential Sermons, Commentaries, Treatises, and Defense,* (New York: Paulist, 1981).
Louis Dupré, *The Common Life* (New York: Crossroad, 1984), a study of Ruusbroec.
Bernard McGinn, 'The God Beyond God: Theology and Mysticism in Meister Eckhart', *Journal of Religion*, 61 (1981), 1-19.
id., *Meister Eckhart: Teacher and Preacher* (New York: Paulist, 1986).
James Wiseman (ed.), *John Ruusbroec: The Spiritual Espousals and Other Works* (New York: Paulist, 1985).

12

Trinitarian Theology as Participation

FRANS JOZEF VAN BEECK, SJ

I FROM DIDACTIC DOGMATICS TO INQUIRING HERMENEUTICS

Let us open with a statement of fact: of late, theology (I mean the art of pursuing and clarifying the Christian understanding of God and things divine with scholarly integrity) has become far less didactic and far more hermeneutical, and *consciously* so.

Theology has greatly profited from this. By way of examples, let me mention Eberhard Jüngel's *Gott als Geheimnis der Welt: Zur Begründung der Theologie des Gekreuzigten im Streit zwischen Theismus und Atheismus*,[1] Michael Buckley's *At the Origins of Modern Atheism*,[2] and Louis Dupré's *Passage to Modernity: An Essay in the Hermeneutics of Nature and Culture*.[3]

A passage from Vatican I can help us put this in perspective. The Council demands that in the construal and elucidation of doctrine, biblical interpretation should respect the true sense of Scripture, which the Church has always held and still holds. It equally firmly insists that Catholic dogmas are to be understood to mean what Holy Mother Church has once and for all declared them to mean.[4] Still, instead of ordering theologians to *reiterate* the doctrinal tradition, it urges them to *study* it *as a complex of mysteries*, as follows:

if reason, illumined by faith, inquires in an earnest, pious and sober manner (cf. Tit 2, 12), it acquires by God's grace a certain—and most fruitful—understanding of the mysteries, both *by analogies drawn from what*

---

[1] (Tübingen: J. C. B. Mohr (Paul Siebeck), 1978); ET *God as the Mystery of the World: On the Foundation of the Theology of the Crucified One in the Dispute between Theism and Atheism* (Grand Rapids, Mich.: William B. Eerdmans, 1983).

[2] (New Haven and London: Yale University Press, 1987).

[3] (New Haven and London: Yale University Press, 1993).

[4] DS 3007, 3020, 3043.

it *naturally knows, and from the mysteries' connectedness among themselves and [their connectedness] with humanity's ultimate end.*[5]

Thus, in upholding the tradition, Vatican I did not forsake that very catholic thing: the theological appreciation (i.e. *interpretation*) of the history of doctrine. And what moves theologians to interpret the tradition and teach it reliably is *participation in the church's present faith-experience.*

So, no contemporary theology without hermeneutics and without the *participative knowledge* that must lie at the root of hermeneutics. But then again, no hermeneutics without imagination either. This essay is about trinitarian theology as participation, but let us start by imagining.

One more preliminary remark. Much of this essay is an exercise in *fundamental theology.* It seeks to lay bare basic philosophical/ theological foundations for the development of trinitarian theology viewed and undertaken as a 'positive', 'doctrinal', 'constructive' pursuit.

II Intentionality, Participation, Presence: An Existential-phenomenological Exercise in Fundamental Theology, in Three Rounds[6]

I

Me: 'Is there ammonia on Jupiter?' A bright student in my theology class: 'I don't know, but I know how to find out.' Me: 'How?' She: 'By spectroscopy—you know, the dark bands in the spectrum.' Me: 'Great! Think of a different answer to the same question.' Pause. Quasi-apathetic voice from the back: 'Who cares?' Me: 'Superb!' Silence. Me: 'You are both right.' I explain that there is such a thing as objective, scientific knowledge, but not apart from antecedent human interest—i.e. *participation.* We know something's got to be out there and it's worth knowing. But you poor stars and stones and trees and clever animals—lovely as you are, you'll never know what you mean, to yourselves, to us, to God.

---

[5] DS 3016 (emphasis added).

[6] Readers acquainted with patristic and medieval thought will notice that this section is indebted to the *trichotomy*: body-soul-spirit, or cosmology-anthropology-theology. Cf. my *God Encountered* (Collegeville, Minn.: The Liturgical Press, 1993-6; henceforth: *GE*), §102, 10, a-b.

I notice a handsome elm. Now I find myself looking at it, focusing on it by design. Slowly it comes alive. I 'decide' to let it happen. Now I am really *seeing* the tree: what *was* a living *object* (it still is, I suppose) has become a *presence*. To me, of all people. Not (or at least not to the same extent) to the passers-by in the park. It *appeals* to me; it calls; it *speaks*. An *encounter* without words has begun. A little later I realize: for a few moments there I lost possession of myself. Touched to the quick by *the tree's* presence to me, I extended *my* presence to *it*. I got 'interested'—*swept up into—this tree*. A case of *theōria*—contemplative self-abandon. My initial interest, conscious and intentional (*but non-mutual!*) as it began, has paid off: a tree has become, *unbeknownst to itself*, a treasured partner in *my* world (though in all likelihood not just in *my* world). Now a flight of fancy carries me into the whole sweep of cosmic evolution. I *participate* in it, *consciously*. *I interpret*. I recall Wordsworth's *Lucy Poems*:

> rolled round in earth's diurnal course,
> with rocks, and stones, and trees.

Now I sense/think: 'Why is there something rather than nothing?' or 'Bless the Lord, all things growing on the earth.'[7] In less than a minute, a tree has carried me from responsive contemplation to philosophic wonder to worshipful awe and intimacy. I believe. (Is that it?) My God. Goodness gracious. My goodness. My, my. YOU. *Fire*.

So here I am, after billions and billions of years of cosmic combination and decombination, in the mere nick of time, newly self-aware at the touch of a cosmic, *infrahuman* good, and lifting it up, along with my revived self, first to deeper awareness, then to thankfulness, then to the One Unseen. A living offering of praise and thanksgiving.

The two episodes suggest conclusions. (1) Whatever 'scientific objectivity' may be, it is invariably (if often unthematically) *embedded in something intentional*: interest, a sense of presence, encounter, participation, self-abandon, capacity for worship.[8]

---

[7] Dan. 3: 76 (LXX).

[8] Cf. the Greek fathers' conception of the spiritual soul as the *locus* of the human person's immediate and inalienable relatedness to God. It enabled them to regard faith as a quasi-natural endowment. Thus, Clement of Alexandria can write: 'Faith is some sort of immanent good; without seeking for God it acknowledges his existence and praises him as existent' (*Strom.* VII, X, 55; GCS 17, 40). Evagrius

(2) My moment with the tree was a true *encounter*; it yielded gratuitous (i.e. freely given) knowledge by participation, even though it was unsupported by any *antecedent* capacity for *mutual* intentionality. Note also that, though *gratuitous* in the end, the experience was optional from the start; moral duty played no part in it. After all, even the handsomest tree is only a tree. Still, lack of openness to at least *some* such experiences of aesthetic and spiritual intentionality would make me less human and so, *less moral*, for 'human acts and moral acts are the same thing,' as Aquinas, bold and clear as usual, writes.[9] Maybe less spiritual, too?

2

So here we are, closer to home; the issue of participation as a distinctively *human* phenomenon is on the agenda. Here, our first observation simply has to be: *among human beings, mutual intentionality is an antecedent given,* and a very compelling one to boot. Anybody who has travelled by train knows that the physical presence of even one human being is never a neutral, merely cosmic fact to us. Participation at the level of intentionality is simply part of being human. And like it or not, we invariably *project a presence* onto others, in a way things, plants, and even animals do not—not even our pets and domesticated mammals, or our fellow-primates. Our cats and dogs, of course, both beg for sentient attention and exhibit it; so do we, with some regularity; after all, we are sentient, too. But unlike animals, human beings also broadcast, simply in being around one another physically, tacit invitations (and indeed, insistent calls) for recognition, regard, and respect *of the consciously undertaken kind*. We are living, embodied invitations to *non-material communication*. On a train, if we do not wish to be bothered, we intuitively know that we do well to give fellow-passengers signals to that effect; only on this condition can we expect them to respect our desire, and in so doing respect us. No human beings, however alien their appearance and

Ponticus, who quotes Clement's oft-quoted statement (cf. e.g. *Philokalia*, II, (21)), elaborates it by adding: 'faith is an immanent good and it is naturally present in [people], even in those who have not come to believe in God yet' (πίστις δέ ἐστιν ἀδιάθετον ἀγαθόν, ἥτις ἐνυπάρχειν πέφυκε καὶ τοῖς μηδέπω πεπιστευκόσι Θεῷ); no wonder he can also characterize, in passing, the human intellect as 'naturally made for worship' (πεφυκότα προσεύχεσθαι). Cf. *Praktikos*, 81, 49; SC 171, pp. 670, 612.

    [9] 'idem sunt actus morales et actus humani' (*ST* I–II. 1. 3 in c.).

manners and however impenetrable their speech (or however numbing their mute stares), can avoid *'presenting'* (*'presencing?'*) *themselves to other human beings*; existing with others means: expecting to be acknowledged and responded to, if only by signs of amazement, helplessness, or lack of interest.

Obviously, at the sight of unfamiliar or seemingly hostile others, we may find ourselves *acting largely instinctively*, not unlike animals reacting to other members of their species: we may stand transfixed, dodge, act inquisitive, get interested in sex, lose interest and turn our backs, stare each other down and force a standoff, take to our heels, or spoil for a fight. But human communities all over the world have considered such 'pre-moral' reactions in-humane, uncivilized, embarrassing, immature, or at the very least incomplete. For the mere *availability* of any other human being is sufficient to create a situation of *intentionality*. We are captured by the human call for response because it encompasses us. *We cannot not-communicate with each other.*

All human beings intuit this, naturally. Inability to leave others alone is *a defining human trait. By nature*, we cannot not-participate. From this, it follows that we *should not* not-participate. For, first of all, trying to ignore others goes against the human grain: from the very *effort* it takes to *dis-regard* others, we *know* that it is unnatural and mulish to treat them as if they did not exist; attempts at ignor-ing are futile at best. But, second, in this way we also intuit that *wilful* efforts to ignore others are at least to some degree *immoral*; all efforts at reducing others to an infrahuman level are. And thus, indirectly, we know that, in making such efforts, odds are we would be stunting our own moral selves as well.

These modest opening gambits are already intimating vital con-clusions. (1) Being human *essentially* involves existing-with-others, *consciously*. We experience human 'co-existence' as a *natural* given, yet we know *it is never neutral*. We intuit that being-with-others is more-than-sentient; it is natively ('immanently') *intentional*, so it *must* be distinctively human.[10] This has consequences. If awareness of *mutual intentionality* is a strictly *anthropological* phenomenon, then 'running into others' already involves, *in and of itself*,

---

[10] Maurice Blondel was the first Catholic thinker to interpret this transcendental feature of humanity (he termed it 'immanence') as the inner predisposition to *action*, urging us on towards growth and development. In this essay, 'immanence' is inter-preted as the native human predisposition to encounter.

'encountering them'. If *Mitsein* is inherent in humanity's existential predicament, it encompasses us;[11] we cannot step outside it.
Mutual *regard* (i.e. mutual consideration, mutually participative
theōria) defines *us* before we ever define *it*, by embodying it in particular encounters. You can, of course, if somewhat perversely,
take this, with Jean-Paul Sartre, as proof that human encounters
are prisons with no exits to begin with; that all they do is drive
home to you your ontologically isolated self. You can also construe
it rather more positively, with Emmanuel Lévinas, as a call for
justice: without any ado, all those I encounter demand of me,
implicitly but unconditionally, that I do justice to them—a tall
order any day. No wonder bumping into others and not knowing
what to do—what to make either of ourselves or of them—makes
us self-conscious. But is it so surprising, really, that a sheer *given*
as mutual regard should involve some embarrassment? Is it any
more surprising than what experience tells us, viz. that it is distinctively human to acknowledge strangers by *greeting* them, even
if only tentatively?[12] (2) Among human beings, therefore, *deliberate*
interest and participation are never wholly optional; the only thing
subject to choice is what we make of our *given* mutual presence
and participativeness in *particular* situations ('how we handle
them'). Such choices, while often substantially deliberate, are
usually co-determined by a blend of cosmic accident and human
agency—our own or others'; none of us are as free as we like to
think we are. Consequently, the *particular kind of presence* which
we and those we 'run into' *actually succeed in establishing with
each other* occurs on a *range*. Martin Heidegger is right in noting
that cultures of inauthenticity imperil human co-existence by
making encounters virtually impersonal; but he also explains how
encounters can occur in various degrees of *objectivity*, while
remaining authentically personal. Martin Buber offers the same
observation by saying that in the long run we can keep engaging
in 'I–You' relationality only by interactions that involve elements
of distance and even separation: 'I–It'.

So elements of *distance* are part of every *particular* encounter.

---

[11] Cf. Martin Heidegger, *Sein und Zeit*, §§26–7.

[12] Recall that in the Hebrew Bible, especially in 1 and 2 Kings, greetings can take
the form of invitation-and-response (or question-and-answer): '"Peace?" "Peace!"'
('*Hašalôm?*' '*Šalôm!*': 1 Kings 2: 13); cf. 2 Kings 4: 26; 5: 21; 9: 11, 17, 18; 9:
22, 31; cf. also Gen. 29: 6; 43: 27; more ominously, 2 Sam. 20: 9.

They enable us to handle, weigh, wash, carry, help, describe, know, judge, and otherwise 'treat' others at various levels of *appropriate* care and regard, yet in substantially non-participative ways—i.e. 'clinically.'[13] Only on the condition that we *'place'* (i.e. interpret) the *objectifiable* 'things' that play a role in 'treatment encounters' in the light of the *non-objectifiable presence* that meets us in the other *person will we be doing justice to the other precisely as other.* In all *particular* encounters, therefore, the sense of *who* we truly are (and our willingness to discover *who we are able and willing to become* in the encounter) will define the depth of participation we are *able and willing* to engage in, and *vice versa. Are we going to try? And how far are we able and willing to commit ourselves?* Those whom we encounter have similar choices to face, of course. How do *they* understand themselves in our presence? And how far are they able and willing to commit themselves? And finally, how able and willing will *both we and they* turn out to put *ourselves* on the line in meeting *each other, in the moral universe that encompasses both of us,* even apart from this particular encounter? These (somewhat rhetorical) questions push us forward.

The answers to the first four questions just posed are of great human (i.e. moral) significance. Yet for purposes of present analysis and argument it is even more important to explore the final one: does our experience in *particular* encounters really suggest a *moral universe?* Do particular moral decisions point to something beyond morality? Could morality as we know and try to practice it have a wider horizon, and thus, *could morality be no more self-sustaining or self-authenticating than humanity itself, even at its moral best?*

3

For answers, let us begin by going back a step or two. Trees (or, for that matter, landscapes and stars and paintings and Mozart symphonies) only *invite* me to do justice to them; they leave the decision to me; at least initially, before they 'grab' me, I can make

---

[13] The word 'clinical' here is vital. It recalls habits of scientific objectification—one of *the* discoveries of the late sixteenth and early seventeenth centuries, as a reading of William Harvey's 1627 treatise *On the Motion of the Heart and the Blood in Animals* will confirm. 'Clinical' (from Gk. *klinē*: 'bed') suggests the posture of passivity (i.e. 'playing dead': non-responsiveness *intentionally* created), which the sick must adopt in order to let physicians 'work on them'.

of them what I wish; in any case, *I* pretty much decide how responsive (and responsible) I am going to let myself become. By contrast, human beings do not let me off so easy. They *demand*. Every single human encounter poses a moral challenge: justice. Still, not even our finest *particular* moral responses can never exhaust—i.e. do *full* justice to—the presence that faces us in any encounter with others. In the presence of others, the demand for justice is never definitively met. Thus, as Alasdair MacIntyre has so subtly shown, the satisfactions of the deliberate life taken by themselves go only so far; moral contentment with a life well lived fails to fulfil us in the long run.[14]

Besides, in today's global-communications world, *just what could the truly common good ever be?* And even if everything just had been well said and truly tried, would global justice not continue to elude our grasp? Full justice (i.e. the genuinely *common* good) is elusive, it turns out.

In this way, moral responsibility turns out to be limitless, not self-defining, let alone free-standing.[15] In the end, so we discover, the *anthropological* world of intentionality that encompasses us *is itself encompassed*. So are we participating in an endless presence, a limitless encounter? Having already been touched to the quick by Nature, and even more deeply by Humanity, are we getting yet another level of *theōria* to face—one fully *theological* this time? Let us try.

Human beings, Emmanuel Lévinas has taught us once again, cannot escape finding themselves put to a theological test whenever they meet others; the human demand for justice is unconditional. Over 150 years before, John Henry Newman elaborated a similar intuition, in his analysis of the phenomenon of conscience. After appealing to common human experience ('we have by nature a conscience'), he compares the experience of conscience with the sense of beauty:

[It] is *always* what the sense of the beautiful is *only in certain cases*; it is . . . *always* emotional. . . . it *always* implies what sense *only sometimes*

---

[14] *After Virtue: A Study in Moral Theory* (Notre Dame, Ind.: University of Notre Dame Press, 1981).

[15] This implies, of course, that Jesus' reply to the scribe's question (Luke 10: 29–37) is developing an unanticipated relevance in today's world. *Even in the empirical world*, doing justice to neighbours is no longer a task subject to moral definition but a limitless, *global* enterprise of freely undertaken compassion.

implies; . . . it *always* involves the recognition of a living object, towards which it is directed. Inanimate things cannot [of themselves] stir our affections; these are correlative with persons.

He then recognizes conscience's first, more *manifest* element: the *moral sense*. This is 'the rule of right conduct'—that part of conscience where our understanding of humanity and the world plays an essential role, and hence, the part where *change*, for the better or for the worse, can occur. But this very *mutability* suggests there must be more to conscience than the moral sense. So he writes:

conscience does not repose on itself, but vaguely reaches forward to something beyond itself, and dimly discerns a sanction higher than self for its decisions, as is evidenced in that keen sense of obligation and responsibility which informs them. And hence it is that we are accustomed to speak of conscience as a voice, a term which we should never think of applying to the sense of the beautiful; and moreover a voice, or the echo of a voice, imperative and constraining, like no other dictate in the world of our experience.

Now Newman is ready to explain what he has in mind, and he does so with the greatest care: '[In this way,] the phenomena of Conscience . . . impress the imagination with the picture of a Supreme Governor, a Judge, holy, just, powerful, all-seeing, retributive; and [thus it] is *the creative principle of religion*, as the Moral Sense is the principle of ethics.'[16]

Newman's sinuous prose conveys that he understands how *mysterious* conscience is. He knows that the moral conscience is part of (to use a modern idiom) humanity's 'transcendental' attunement to everything that exists, and ultimately, to God. But he knows something else equally well: like the attunement itself, conscience emerges in and through *particular moral experiences*. Accordingly, conscience *can* become the 'object' of *understanding*, but only by *reflection on moral experiences*. Besides, since the mature experience of conscience is a function of a *developing* moral life, conscience offers itself for reflection only to those *learning to live conscientiously*.[17] But, this, too, can occur only through and in con-

[16] Cf. *An Essay in Aid of a Grammar of Assent*, ed. Nicholas Lash (Notre Dame, Ind. and London: University of Notre Dame Press, 1979), 101 (italics and parentheses added for emphasis and to suit the present context).

[17] This has, of course, a negative counterpart: conscience, if worn down and stifled by habits of moral lethargy and sin, will move towards effective non-existence; it will then elude reflection as well. The hardened who reflect are few and far between.

crete *situations*—situations involving specific, objective, 'material' values 'out-there'. Thus, conscience's highest function (i.e. the sense of duty) will not emerge in us except in combination with a reliable, realistic, fairly articulate, ever-growing *moral sense*.[18] In other words: the genuinely mature conscience is the conscience that has come alive, thanks to the sense of duty resident in itself (i.e. in the last analysis, thanks to the sense of the transcendent God), to *the objective conditions of its own ongoing emergence.*

III 'MYSTERY'

So the tell-tale word has emerged: 'mysterious'. *Mystērion*: a Greek noun derived from the verb μύω (*myō*)

A Greek dictionary will inform us that *myō* means 'to close one's eyes' or 'to close one's mouth' But what does that *mean*? Let us try. *Myō* means: 'observing the kind of silence that becomes so eloquent that it elicits the kind of speech that reveals the Truth (while at the same time veiling it), and thus creates room for a sacred silence once again, inclusive, pregnant with truth, and intolerant of falsehood.'[19]

Our analyses have taken us to the threshold of (for lack of a better word) a 'Transcendent Presence'. It is analogous to the presences that greet us in the world of things and in the faces of others. But the former we can bring to consciousness by unilateral interpretation, and to the latter we can do justice by unconditional regard. Of both presences, we know that we know them, at least as far as our comprehension allows us. This amounts to saying we never encompass them fully, not only in the sense that there always remain more features to be discovered and known, but also

[18] It also follows that the mature conscience is *not* the individual conscience claiming to have successfully emancipated itself from the matrix of its emergence, and thus, autonomous and responsible to nothing and nobody but itself. Max Scheler has admirably shown this in *Der Formalismus in der Ethik und die materiale Wertethik: Neuer Versuch der Grundlegung eines ethischen Personalismus*, Gesammelte Werke, 2 (Bern and München: Francke Verlag, 1954); ET *Formalism in Ethics and Non-Formal Ethics of Values: A New Attempt Toward the Foundation of an Ethical Personalism* (Evanston, Ill.: Northwestern University Press, 1973)). Scheler's admirer, Pope John Paul II, has recalled the same truth in his encyclical *Veritatis Splendor*.

[19] This 'real meaning' of μύω is, of course, a periphrasis, not a translation. Quite probably, it sins by prolixity, if only slightly.

because our knowledge remains dependent on interest and mutual regard—that is, on participation. But about *this* Presence, we cannot know anything, since there are no 'its' to be known. Even less can we encompass It.

Still, It does invite us to agree to participate in It, 'for in Him we are alive and move and have being, as some of your own poets have put it: "For we, too, are of his kind".'[20] And: 'you have come to know God, or rather, *to be known by God*'.[21] And: 'For as for now, I know but in part, but then I will also get to know *the way I am known*.'[22] And: 'But those who love, they are *the ones who are known*.'[23]

That is to say, knowledge of It means: being content to be known by It, and to feel Its touch within us, which will transform us in all we do, not against our will, but not by dint of moral endeavour either:

For as much as you will it and desire it, so much you have of it—no more and no less; and yet it is neither will nor desire, but something you-know-not-what, that stirs you to will and desire you-know-not-what. Never mind, I beg you, if you know no more; just proceed ever more and more, so as to be ever active. . . . Let it be the agent, and you but the recipient; just behold it, and leave it alone. Do not interfere with it as if to help it along, for fear you might dissipate it all. You be but the wood, and let it be the carpenter; you be but the house, and let it be the landlord that lives in it. Be blind while it lasts, and cancel craving for knowledge, for it will hinder you more than help you. It is enough for you to feel enjoyably stirred by something you-know-not-what, as long as in your being stirred you think of nothing specific under God, and as long as your intent is nakedly directed to God.[24]

But It also greets us from everywhere and nowhere *outside us*: Glory displayed across the immeasurable heavens, wordless Word heard to the furthest reaches of the universe, Light as of a radiant,

---

[20] Acts 17: 28.

[21] Gal. 4: 9. (At the conference Gordon D. Fee kindly drew my attention to this passage.)

[22] 1 Cor. 13: 12b.

[23] I am adopting the lectio difficilior found in P⁴⁶: εἰ δέ τις ἀγαπᾷ, οὗτος ἔγνωσται; cf. Gordon D. Fee, *The First Epistle to the Corinthians* (Grand Rapids, Mich.: Eerdmans, 1987).

[24] *The Cloud of Unknowing*, 34, ed. Hodgson, EETS 218 (London–New York–Toronto: Oxford University Press, 1944 (for 1943); rev. 1958, repr. 1981), pp. 69–71.

irresistible Sun-beyond-sun, itself invisible, yet revealing and test-ing all,[25] 'uncircumscript, and al mayst circumscrive.'[26]

This Presence-beyond-all-presences will suffuse our world—the universe not only of our maturer knowledge, but also of our mature and tempered psycho-physical experience. That is to say, if we know It at all, we will know It only by participation, *yet never apart from everything and everybody else we know.* That is to say, It offers us no data that would enable us to encounter and under-stand It apart from all other things in the universe. For It has no separable 'its' to offer, to satisfy our desire for objectification.[27] This implies that It also resists our every *autonomous* attempt to know It apart from the *interior* witness which we cannot control; we know It only insofar as It discloses Itself to our interested, involved selves. Yet even as It invites us *from within*, radically, there is something irrevocably *Other* about It. But then again, if and when and as It dawns on us and we become unspeakably aware of It, both by the witness within us and by the charm and the moral appeal that comes to us from the world outside us, It will re-situate and re-create not only ourselves but also our entire world—everything cosmic that invites our perception or tickles our fancy, and (even more deeply) every human being meeting us, *without exception.* That is, It '*super-encompasses*' us, all other human beings, as well as anything in the cosmos that (unbeknownst to itself) could possibly attract our notice. All It 'does', therefore, is to invite us to agree to 'super-interpret', consciously and freely, the universe in

[25] Cf. Ps. 19: 1-6.

[26] Geoffrey Chaucer, *Troilus and Criseyde*, V. 1865. In lines 1863-5, Chaucer is imitating Dante (but turning reference into apostrophe): *Quell'uno e due e tre che sempre vive | e regna sempre in tre e' n due e 'n uno, | non circunscritto, e tutto circun-scrive* (*Paradiso*, XIV. 28-30). God's being 'uncircumscript' (cf. *Purgatorio*, XI. 2-3) means (1) all things are encompassed by the illimitable goodness which is God (cf. Dante, *Convivio*, IV. ix. 3); (2) it is better to say 'all things are in God' than to say 'God is somewhere.' On this point, cf. Aquinas' cautious explanation in *ST* I. 8. 1 ad 1: 'we can say that material beings are in something, meaning that the latter contains them. By contrast, spiritual beings contain the things in which they exist; for example: the soul contains the body. Hence, God, too, is in things as that which contains them. Still, we are using analogies taken from material beings when we say that all things are in God, inasmuch as they are contained by him.' Aquinas is taking his cue from Augustine, from whom he borrows the notion that the state-ment 'all things are in God' is preferable to the statement 'God is somewhere' (*in illo sunt potius omnia, quam ipse alicubi*). Cf. *De diversis quæstionibus*, LXXXIII. xx (CCL, 44a, 25; PL 40, col. 15)).

[27] This the central point of Jean-Luc Marion's elegant phrase *Dieu sans L'Être*, which must be understood to mean 'God Without Being It.'

which we participate, as well as ourselves and each other, in the light of Its presence, and in doing so, to enter into Itself, *entirely participatively*. Then, what we are apt to discover is nothing less than our true selves. For we have been *in* It forever in the first place; in entering It, we are only coming home, *as if for the first time*.[28] No words will ever do justice to It, but we can attempt to speak of It, though only to the extent that we are somehow *responsive to* It, as well as morally *responsible before* It, in all the things we do and undergo. And when we speak of It, we do so (1) schooled in the language of *responsive and responsible regard and affection*, which has over time made us capable of doing justice to other human beings, and (2) pre-schooled in the language of *informed and articulate wonder*, which has helped us articulate our conscious participation in the otherwise speechless (but ever so appealing) world of things. But when we try to speak of It as such, we find ourselves speaking *the language of mystery*, which is inseparable from silence—the sort of silence that has a way of being *eloquent*, so much so that it elicits words that reveal the Truth (while at the same time veiling it), and so makes room for sacred silence once again, all-encompassing, pregnant with Truth and unsympathetic towards untruth. This is where *theōria* turns out to be rooted in *theologia*: fully participative, contemplative *prayer*. So much for 'mystery'.

IV A MODEST PROPOSAL

What is the point of these past two sections? Answer: they are an effort to recapture, in the setting of the late twentieth century and by means of some of its idioms, *the integrated account of the cosmos, humanity, and God*, which, in a variety of related ways, has animated the Great Tradition of the undivided Church.[29] Obviously, the next question is how cogent the effort has been, and how persuasive. No doubt it is badly incomplete—the brush too broad, the

---

[28] Aelred Squire has well phrased this paradox, by calling it a 'creative recognition of what is already somehow obscurely known' and 'a long lost memory of their true selves'. Cf. *Asking the Fathers: The Art of Meditation and Prayer*, 2nd edn. (Wilton, Conn./New York and Ramsey, NJ: Morehouse-Barlow/Paulist Press, 1976), p. 15.

[29] I have argued that the same integrated vision undergirds Aquinas' five 'proofs' for God's existence. Cf. *GE* II/2, §102.

wall vast, and the paint a bit thin. Thus, in all probability, it is disputable.

Yet it may help us read the Great Tradition anew, both Israel's understanding of God as One and True and Faithful and the Christian understanding of God as Father and Son and Holy Spirit, *which is inconceivable apart from Israel's God.*[30] By way of a first round, we review some classical and some early, high, and late medieval instances in the Tradition, to get an idea of how it has understood God and humanity's relatedness to God and found ways to convey both.

V MYSTERY IN THE THEOLOGICAL TRADITION

By now, those familiar with patristic and medieval theology will find themselves on familiar territory. Before Aquinas ever discovered Aristotle's wealth of insight and knowledge, his theological world had been permanently shaped by an anonymous Syrian monk nowadays called Pseudo-Dionysius the Areopagite. From his work *On Naming God* he had learned that it is right to praise ('name') God affirmatively ('*cataphatically*') by using words taken from the world of things and human beings: 'we rightly say all these things about God, and [God] is [rightly] praised by means of names derived from all things that exist, inasmuch as all things whose cause he is are proportionate to him.'[31]

But, that said, Pseudo-Dionysius had plunged, breathtakingly, into the dark waters of 'un-saying' (*apophasis*):

But then again, the *most divine knowledge of God* is that which comes about by ignorance, by way of a union that surpasses the mind, when the mind, *taking its distance from all beings, and then also letting go of itself,* is united [with God] by splendors more than dazzling, out of which and

---

[30] Here lies one of the greatest (if not the greatest) weaknesses of the Cappadocian understanding of God, which has become normative Christian doctrine. The end of all living *theological* understanding and dialogue between Jews and Christians (which became final between ± AD 150–200) is decisive here. Even after Marcionism was abandoned, 'crypto-Marcionism' remained a bedeviling presence. For example, it led Gregory of Nyssa to set up his explanation of the nature of God—the opening gambit of the *Great Catechetical Oration*—as the *via media* between Jewish monotheism and pagan polytheism, as if the Church owed as little to the Synagogue as it did to polytheism, and as if the two were simply comparable.

[31] *De divinis nominibus*, 7, §3 (PG 3, cols. 871–2 AB; emphasis added).

in which it draws enlightenment, by the inscrutable depth of [divine] wisdom.[32]

Aquinas is clearer and especially more *systematic* than Dionysius when he writes:

> when we proceed towards God *on the road of removal*, we *first* deny everything corporeal of God. *Then* we deny everything spiritual as it is found in creatures, such as goodness and wisdom. *At that point*, all that is left in our minds is that *God is*, and nothing else; thus God *is* in a kind of perplexing fashion, so to speak. *Last of all*, however, we remove from God even this very *being* according as it occurs in creatures. At that point, God is left to dwell in a kind of darkness of ignorance; yet *after the manner of this ignorance*—at least as long as we are on our present way—*we are best united with God*, as Dionysius says. It is a dark cloud of sorts, in which God is said to dwell.[33]

Here Aquinas has taken us back to the roots of the tradition as it took shape in the century of Nicaea (AD 325) and Constantinople I (AD 381).[34] Here is how one of the period's seminal thinkers, Gregory of Nyssa, phrases what Aquinas was to write eight centuries later:

> This . . . [is] . . .what the soul experiences when it passes beyond its foothold in measurable thoughts, in its quest for *that which exists from all eternity and is immeasurable*: . . . it gets dizzy and does not know what to do, so once again it turns to *what is like itself in kind*, happy now to know this much about the Transcendent: . . . *it is different in kind from the things that it knows*. Thus, when reason touches on the things that are beyond reason, *that* is the 'time to keep silence.' . . . Thus, in the understanding of God, when the inquiry is about God's essence, then it is 'time to keep silence.'[35]

An acquaintance of Gregory's, Evagrius Ponticus, the courtier-philosopher-turned-churchman-turned-Egyptian-ascetic, writing

---

[32] Ibid.

[33] *In I Sent.* 8. 1. 1 ad 4. The last phrase alludes to Solomon's words at the temple dedication according to the Vulgate (2 Chr. 6: 1): '*Dominus pollicitus est, ut habitaret in caligine.*'

[34] On this complex subject, cf. Richard P. C. Hanson, *The Search for the Christian Doctrine of God: The Arian Controversy 318–381* (Edinburgh: T. & T. Clark, 1988).

[35] *In Eccles. Hom.* VII; PG 44, cols. 729–32; ed. Jaeger, vol. 5, pp. 412–15. Cf. ET [Gregory of Nyssa], *From Glory to Glory: Texts from Gregory of Nyssa's Mystical Writings*, trans. H. Musurillo (New York: Charles Scribner's Sons, 1961), 127–9. Cf. also *De vita Moysis*, II. 110–11 (PG 44, col. 359; ed. Jaeger, vol. 7/1, pp. 66–7; ET, pp. 79–80).

even as the harvest of the century's arduous growth in doctrinal understanding was being brought in, states the same, but with the bluntness characteristic of the desert monk and spiritual director. One of the many one-sentence statements in his *Chapters on Prayer* reads: 'If you are a theologian, you will truly pray, and if you will truly pray, you are a theologian.'[36]

So what you will acquire *if you will truly pray* (εἰ προσεύξῃ ἀληθῶς) is the knowledge of God (θεολογία). But what could Evagrius possibly mean when he writes 'truly pray'? To find an answer to this question, two of the many definitions in *De oratione* are useful.

Prayer, Evagrius explains, is 'the mind's *ascent* to God' (ἀνάβασις νοῦ πρὸς Θεόν) and 'the *removal* of thoughts' (ἀπόθεσις νοημάτων).[37] Let us examine both definitions closely.

One question must be: is the meaning of 'ascent' in the former definition *passive or active?* Put differently, does *anabasis* (ἀνάβασις) signify *release* from burdens or obstacles, or *self-emancipation* from them? One thing is clear: 'removal' (*apothesis* [ἀπόθεσις]: 'laying down') in the second definition implies conscious effort. So our question becomes: Is 'ascent' in the first definition the *opposite* of *apothesis* or is it a parallel (or, perhaps, a complement) to it? In other words, is *ascent/anabasis* to be understood as passive or as active? Does it convey receptivity ('allowing oneself to be attracted') or endeavour?

There are good reasons to think that Evagrius understands it in a *passive* sense, for elsewhere in the *Chapters on Prayer* he writes: 'If you *desire to see* the face of the Father who is in heaven, *do not seek to conceive* any form or representation at all while you are at prayer.'[38]

That is: 'If you desire to behold the face of God, try not to inject *patterns* or *conceptions* into your prayer.' Let us articulate what this implies. We have seen that Evagrius regards the soul as naturally made for prayer;[39] thus, he considers the desire to seek God's face

---

[36] Εἰ θεολόγος εἶ προσεύξῃ ἀληθῶς, καὶ εἰ προσεύξῃ ἀληθῶς, θεολόγος εἶ: *De oratione*, 60 (PG 79, col. 1180; attribution to St Nilus obsolete); ET *The Praktikos and Chapters on Prayer*, ed. John Eudes Bamberger (Spencer, Mass.: Cistercian Publications, 1970).

[37] *De oratione*, 35, 70 (PG 79, cols. 1173, 1181).

[38] Ἐπιποθῶν ἰδεῖν τὸ πρόσωπον τοῦ Πατρὸς τοῦ ἐν οὐρανοῖς, μὴ ζήτει παντελῶς μορφὴν ἢ σχῆμα δέχεσθαι ἐν τῷ τῆς προσευχῆς καιρῷ: *De oratione*, 114.

[39] Above, n. 8.

humanity's *native* aspiration. Yet he also regards 'true prayer' as *granted, not accomplished*; as *participative, not a matter of mastery in any sense, let alone of objectification.* That is, Evagrius thinks that while prayer is the most natural thing for us to be engaged in, he maintains that in order to pray genuinely we must suspend all intentional activity, such as interpretation and meditation.[40] This implies that he understands ascent/*anabasis* in a *passive* sense: in authentic prayer, he is saying, we find ourselves drawn by God; we do not work ourselves up towards God.

Let us make a first claim. Here it is. The Great Tradition's conviction about *the knowledge of God* is (1) that it is a matter of *theōria* (i.e. contemplative self-abandon), and (2) that it is, para-doxically, *both entirely natural and entirely God-given.* A millennium after the Cappadocians and Evagrius, the author of *The Cloud of Unknowing* was to make this very claim. In the plain, serviceable Midlands dialect, in which fourteenth-century English Christianity found and fostered so much of its experiential wisdom, identity, and manner, he writes:

If you were truly humble you would feel about this activity as I told you, namely, that God gives it freely, apart from any merit. The nature of this activity is such that *its presence makes a soul able to possess it and to experience it.* And that *ability is not available to any soul apart from it* [= its presence]. The ability to perform this activity is united with the activity itself, inseparably; hence, *whoever experiences this activity is able to perform it, and no one else*—so much so that *apart from this activity a soul is, as it were, dead, and unable to crave it or desire it.*[41]

The master of *The Cloud* has a contemporary in the Southern Low Countries: Jan van Ruusbroec. He, too, is turning a plain, serviceable dialect into a medium of exploration and understand-ing. He has the same experiential truth to share as his English

---

[40] This position is certainly part of the Great Tradition. In the late sixteenth century, when it was already getting lost, Teresa of Avila could still insist on it in *The Castle of the Soul*, in the passage about the two fountain-basins (IV. 2). She emphasizes that the interior flood that makes us irresistibly aware of God's presence comes from a source that lies deeper in us than the heart; it is inaccessible to any conscious attempts at finding either ourselves or God: *otra parte aún más interior, como una cosa profunda.* Two centuries earlier, Jan van Ruusbroec had written a brief treatise, *Het Boecsken der Verclaringhe* ((*Little Book of Enlightenment*; Ioannis Rvsbrochii *Samvel sive Apologia*); CChr, Cont. Mediaev., 101; Tielt: Lannoo; Turnhout: Brepols, 1989), to explain, in unmistakable terms, that union with God is not the fruit of deliberate self-consciousness or self-actualization.

[41] Cf. above, n. 24.

counterpart. But being a considerable theologian as well, he is closer to Gregory of Nyssa and Evagrius. This enables him to describe not only the fully apophatic account of contemplative, fully participative union with God described and commended in *The Cloud*, but also a fully trinitarian (and thus, wholly dynamic) interpretation of contemplative prayer. He does so by explaining that contemplative union is *the God-given actualization of what the human spirit simply is, by virtue of its very nature*: viz., the recipient, 'without intermission', of 'the impress of its eternal Image'. That is to say, the human spirit naturally participates in the eternal birth and mission of the Archetype, the Word, the Son:

through the resplendence of its eternal Image, which shines in it essentially and personally, the spirit abandons itself in the highest part of its living soul, to steep itself in the Divine Essence, and there enduringly possesses its eternal bliss. And it flows out again, along with all creatures, through the eternal birth of the Son, and is established in its created being by the free will of the Holy Trinity. And here it resembles the Image of the supreme Threeness and Oneness in which it is made. And in its created being, it accepts without intermission the impress of its eternal Image, just like the untarnished mirror, in which the Image constantly remains, and which renews, without intermission, the knowledge of [the Image] with new clarity, every time it is looked at anew. This essential unity of our spirit with God does not exist in and of itself, but it abides in God, and it flows forth from God, and it depends on God, and it reverts into God as into its eternal cause, and, accordingly, it neither parts from God nor will it ever do so.[42]

Jan van Ruusbroec has at last taken us forward to the *fully theological* understanding at the core of the Great Tradition: we know the One God by worshipful participation ('in the Spirit'), *and this participation occurs through and in the Eternal Word, Jesus Christ. The One God in whom we are alive and move and have being is the God who is in God-in-Three.* Not a trace of the trinitarian timidity that biases modern theology!

There is an unsuspected witness to the fact that this understanding of God is alive and well as late as the late fourteenth century: the great English poet Geoffrey Chaucer. When he brings

---

[42] *Die geestelike brulocht* [*The Spiritual Espousals*; *Ioannis Rvsbrochii De ornatv spiritualivm nvptiarvm*] (CChr, Cont. Mediaev., 103; Tielt: Lannoo; Turnhout: Brepols, 1988), 468–75. Cf. *The Spiritual Espousals and Other Works*, introd. and trans. James A. Wiseman (New York, Mahwah, and Toronto: Paulist Press, 1985), 116–18.

his *Troilus and Criseyde*—a lengthy tale of love, collusion, pander-
ing, deception, and death—to its conclusion, he follows the taste
of the period: he *moralizes*. But once he has finished lamenting the
hard moral lesson Troilus got to learn for his pains in courting
Criseyde's favours, Chaucer becomes *theological*: he turns to *prayer*.
Borrowing from Dante, who had echoed Aquinas, who in turn had
quoted Augustine, he writes:

> Thou oon, and two, and thre, eterne on lyve,
> That regnest ay in thre, and two, and oon,
> Uncircumscript, and al maist circumscrive,

And he continues:

> Us from visible and invisible foon
> Defende, and to thy mercy, everychon,
> So make us, Jesus, for thi mercy digne,
> For love of mayde and moder thyn benigne.[43]

In the first three lines, Chaucer shows he is aware, at least
unthematically, of two related truths. (1) Knowing God and
addressing God is knowing and addressing *the Triune God*. (2) Doing
so is and remains a matter of *participation*, for while defining everything that exists, God remains beyond all definition.[44] This is not
surprising; Dante and Chaucer simply share the traditional
Christian understanding of God. At the heart of this understanding
lies a profound (if often unstated) axiom. It can be put as follows.
Even if it should be possible (or even necessary) to make distinctions when speaking of God, such distinctions remain part of *the
language of mystery*—i.e. of participative knowledge and *theōria*. In
no way, therefore, do doctrinal statements state 'hard' (i.e. thing-
like) 'facts out-there' *about* God—facts stated (as it were) from a
point of view *outside* God; while *stating* (or rather, *formulating*)
truths, they do not *denote* them. Doctrines arise in worship and
witness, and must never be allowed to belie their pedigree; their
key function is and remains to ensure worship and to enable
witness. Accordingly, no doctrinal truth handed down to us by the
Tradition in human language is to be taken at face value, as if it
were denoting an 'it'—i.e. naming one or the other definite (i.e.

---

[43] Geoffrey Chaucer, *Troilus and Criseyde*, V. 1863-9.

[44] Note that both Chaucer and Dante use *numerals*—words with a purely *formal*
denotation—to represent the *names* 'Father', 'Son' (or 'Word'), and 'Spirit'. Plainly,
they regard the Triune God as *incomprehensible and undefinable*.

separable) reality, let alone two or more of them. This invites linguistic reflection on doctrine, of course, but this is not the time to go into this;[45] instead, let us conclude this section by pointing out two more theologically relevant features of Chaucer's lines.

First, the language moves *from doxology to soteriology*. The glorification theme is played first, in the three lines Chaucer borrows from Dante; in these lines, God is worshipped in a *universalist* perspective: *Thou . . . al mayst circumscrive*. The soteriological theme is played in the lines supplied by Chaucer himself; interestingly, they are a petitionary prayer obviously rooted in popular devotion. Yet, strikingly, the prayer starts *not with humanity* but *with the universe*. Chaucer prays for the triune God's protection against *the hostile powers-that-be in the cosmos*, liable to thwart humanity. Not until then does the poet address Jesus as humanity's Saviour, by means of an idiomatic syntactic device ('*so*') that conveys that the phrase ('*to thy mercy . . . so make us . . . digne*') is a *formal religious wish*.[46] But even here, very remarkably, Chaucer prays not (as we moderns might expect) for salvation or mercy, either for himself or for others, but *that all of us may be made worthy of the mercy revealed, promised, and indeed embodied, in Jesus*. In order to do so, Chaucer naturally uses the idioms of the Latin West: *he appeals to Jesus' mercy* in order to pray for the inner transformation of all—i.e. for what the Oriental Christian Churches call 'deification' or 'divinization' (*theōsis*). And like the Oriental traditions, he ends his prayer not by asking for the *intercession of the Mother of God*, but by appealing to *Jesus' love of her*; in other words, the Virgin Mary represents the fullness of what Chaucer has prayed for in behalf of all people: worthiness of God's mercy. At the heart of Chaucer's faith lies not humanity's sin and its needed salvation,

---

[45] This reflection, it must be added, should be informed not only by a (philosophical) understanding of analogy, but also by sound linguistic theory, to clarify exactly which features of language enable believers to refer reliably to realities that are by nature inaccessible to denotation. A fuller account of the manner in which metaphor and paradox refer to God, and indeed actualize the Presence of God in the world and humanity, would require treatments of, respectively, the manner of signification of 'myth', and the moral and theological significance of 'narrative' (cf. *GE* I, §41–3; *GE* II/3, §123, 7; §124, 10, a–b). It would also require a treatment of the rhetoric of metaphor and paradox (cf. my 'A Very Explicit *Te Deum*', forthcoming in *Horizons*).

[46] The use of '*so*' in this petitionary prayer is comparable to Chaucer's use of '*ther*' in religious curses and blessings. Cf. my 'A Note on *Ther* in Curses and Blessings in Chaucer', *Neophilologus*, 69 (1985), 276–83, and the literature cited there.

but God's immeasurable glory and boundless mercy, in which all of creation, and human beings in particular, are called to share, to the glory of God.

Second, one last feature of the last stanza of *Troilus and Criseyde* deserves comment. From a poetic point of view, doxology and soteriology run into each other in this text, *seamlessly*. Chaucer's lines do not show the slightest nervousness about the distinction (never mind separation) between 'immanent Trinity' and 'economic Trinity'—i.e. between *theologia* and *oikonomia*. Even towards the end of the troubled fourteenth century, Chaucer is still enjoying the undivided Church's integrated vision of God, humanity, and the universe.

The time has come for the last section. It is a rhapsody of intuitions and suggestions rather than an argument, but it may help suggest hermeneutical rules for future sallies into trinitarian theology.

VI Some Further Modest Proposals

What has been proposed so far is obviously predicated on a number of hermeneutical decisions. It is time to come clean on this. Let us start with the issue of *approaches*.

I

Theology and 'theologology'. Not very long ago, Harry Mulisch, a noted Dutch novelist and commentator since the 1950s, was interviewed on national television. At one point, Mulisch, never accused of modesty, offered his viewers one of his famous throw-away lines: he was the only living philosopher in the country. Visibly taken aback, the interviewer hinted that philosophy was being taught in all universities, presumably by philosophers. Mulisch explained, with the mock patience of the experienced teacher who has seen every folly, that all those professors were teaching not philosophy but 'philosophology.' Talking or writing about philosophers and philosophy does not make you a philosopher, he added. Point made.

One big problem with trinitarian theology is that it has elicited so much 'theologology'. One cause of this is simply *linguistic*. Like so many disciplines, Christian doctrine and theology employ *technical terms*. Now terminological language is not 'natural'; it is *entirely artificial*. Unlike 'regular' words, which have meanings that are both self-evident and flexible, *technical terms have only one meaning*, and that meaning is *stable*. This is due to the fact that unlike 'ordinary' words, terms are products of *definition*. That is, *only experts* understand terms and use them reliably (i.e. in the service of *understanding*). Hence, not only is it unwise for us ordinary mortals to use ponderous words whose meaning we do not know *exactly*; it is downright pointless to try to figure out what a technical term means by looking at it.[47] Thus, both to understand the *meaning* and to see the *point* of affirmations expressed in terminological language you must be an *expert*. Now experts are (or should be) 'objective'; expert knowledge must be *dispassionate*. This accounts for an important characteristic of technical terms: *they carry no connotations*, at least theoretically.[48]

Yet terms do intrigue us. This is because *in actual use* they very often do carry connotations. Terms look and sound 'learned'; people who use them are *knowledgeable*, especially if they use them nonchalantly. There is another problem: non-experts forget that terms create not knowledge, but the *presumption* of knowledge. So, to detect if expert So-and-so has *not just the training but also the knowledge*, you must ask his or her fellow-experts (who are apt to give you evasive answers, even if they have ideas about it). So, in the end, who is to tell, really? Who is checking on the experts? The moral: *beware of terms!*

This leads us to a liability inherent in the use of terms: they can function as *armour*. We frequently resort to terms for self-protection against unwelcome challenges, and even against *our understanding of our own reality*. It is a good idea to understand this well. In our day, the language of realism is often abandoned in favour of the language of self-conscious, quasi-professional expertise. The person who says, 'I am feeling horribly confused and impotent these days and I am getting emotional at the drop of a hat, please, what do you think, could a psychologist trained in this kind of thing help

---

[47] Example: *taken as a natural word*, 'poly-unsaturated fatty acids'—clearly a *technical term*—is nonsensical. How can something unsaturated be poly-anything? Isn't *x* times zero still zero?

[48] For present purposes, let us overlook cases where technical terms have become ordinary words again (e.g. 'inferiority complex'); such terms not only lose their scholarly accuracy; they also acquire connotations, by the back door, so to speak.

me?' is a lot more realistic than the one who says, 'You are right, I have some psychological issues to face.' Besides, the former phrase is far more *effective*: it calls for needed help; the latter merely cloaks the need for help by a show of apparent knowledge. Another example. The serene, unbiased expression: 'I have some serious theological problems' is an often-heard, wholly ineffective surrogate for: 'For God's sake, Jackie, stop it, faith in God doesn't mean a damned thing to me.' In both instances, the first speakers are inappropriately using the *relatively sterile* language of professional expertise to defend themselves against a fuller awareness of their own reality, and thus, from their ability to *commit themselves*.

In the park of Christian doctrine, this often happens, and trinitarian theology is no exception. Theologians and pastors, Karl Rahner included, have concluded that the doctrine of the Blessed Trinity ('One God in Three Persons') makes no vital difference in the lived life of most Christians today. And indeed, the sincerity of many professions of trinitarian faith is often in inverse proportion to their actual significance.[49] In this context, it is a mistake, of course, to remind people that the Blessed Trinity is a mystery; used in this way, 'mystery' merely means something like a thousand-piece puzzle that looks splendid until actually started.

Christian theologians must not resign themselves to this situation. Nor should they let themselves get fascinated by it; for too much focus on definitions might just make us the prisoners of the very formulas that now widely fail to support living faith in God. The doctrinal developments of the fourth century were defined in terms considered clarifying at the time, but *not with the aim of replacing mystery by formula*. Meant to *protect* a living and life-giving understanding of God, the formulas, while painstakingly arrived at, were never expected to *produce* that understanding. Today, they are unlikely to produce it either.

Thus, trying to force new understanding out of the classical definitions is like squeezing juice out of fruits dried sixteen centuries ago. For terms and definitions looking for a meaning are like monumental houses looking for inhabitants: some of us may try them; few will feel at home. Many recent treatments of trinitarian

---

[49] Cf. John Henry Newman's remark about the rationalist: 'He professes to *believe* what he *opines*.' *Essays Critical and Historical*, i (London: Basil Montagu Pickering, 1877), 35.

theology, orthodox, courageous, and often illuminating as they are, sound apologetic: we *have* the doctrines, so let us make as much sense of them as we can and handle the lacunae with appeals to 'mystery'. *Limiting trinitarian theology to insistence on, and discussions about, existing definitions and theologies will produce only theologology.* In the long run this is the death of living theological thought about the mystery of God professed in the Christian Churches.

2

How, then, to approach trinitarian theology today? Let me propose a two-pronged hermeneutic.

The first prong. Let me sing an old song. I have long felt that Christians who leave the church nowadays do so to a significant extent out of boredom. In church, you can count on finding some pretty good people and *ditto* fellowship, and some fine initiatives on behalf of the growing multitude of the disadvantaged, but no amplitude of purview, no ecstasy, no *theōria*—in sum, no sense of *participation in God, no mysticism.* The inner affinity with the Mystery *in whom we are alive and move and have being*—Father, Son, Holy Spirit—can grow on us only in the experience of God as 'the All': the God of each of us at the expense of none of us, the God who never comes alone but always with the entire cosmos and all of humanity. This experience is the heart of *common worship*, with its cosmic and universalist dimensions, its significant silence and significant speech, its significant gesture and significant motion-lessness, its interplay of the seen and the unseen—in sum, its *doxology made tangible.*[50] Prayerlessness and presencelessness are the bane of Christian churches today, it seems to me; 'praying-for-this-that-and-the-other', professions of the human need for 'salvation', and homilizing disguised as prayer have largely eclipsed praise and thanksgiving. Among theologians, overconcern with soteriological and ethical themes has bred, by default, a lack of taste for the mystagogical, liturgical, and mystical traditions (found in Christianity and in the religions) as major *loci theologici.* It is crypto-Pelagian to be too ethical in church. End of song.

[50] In a recent article, Robin Darling Young has shown that the Greek fathers assumed that the school of this type of contemplation was the Christian *liturgy.* Cf. 'Theologia in the Early Church', *Communio*, 24 (1997), 681-90.

The second prong. We need *a careful hermeneutic of the doctrinal tradition,* of the kind that respects the dynamics of the hermeneutical circle. That is to say, our interpretation of the Great Tradition must be inseparable from a deeper discovery of the *faith community and the culture in which we participate* (and hence, which we represent). For the Great Tradition is only as dead as today's churches will allow it to be. And on the other hand, only if the present churches engage today's culture with discriminating affection (and is ready to enhance that engagement) will they be communities of living faith. If today's church is to be revived by the living Tradition (as *Dei Verbum* of Vatican II insists), this can happen only if its understanding of the Great Tradition is the concrete shape of its respect for the Tradition's decisions and definitions. For these decisions and definitions invite not reiteration but *interpretation*; to understand our Christian selves in relation to the modern world, we must engage the *struggle for meaning* that made past decisions and definitions meaningful and, in the end, canonical. Our task today, therefore, is not to squeeze fresh juice out of them but to discover how and why they were dried, and how their meaning is to be reconstituted.

Is it possible to determine an agenda for theological hermeneutics that will fit the near future? Possibly. For the past two hundred years, the chief issue for both (Western) Christianity and the culture in which it has largely been living has been: the person of the *historical* Jesus who is the risen Christ now. Now the person of Jesus Christ was also the focus of the great debates of the fifth century, though for very different reasons. Could it be that in order to get the Great Tradition pushed further forward we must let ourselves be led further backward, to relive the great controversies of the fourth century, which dealt with *the Christian understanding of God?* Could the sophisticated and generous renditions of that struggle already offered by Richard Hanson, Manlio Simonetti,[51] and Rowan Williams[52] (to mention only three of the best) be pointing us in that direction?

I submit the answer is Yes. So let us suggest a few guidelines that may be able to help us interpret the Great Tradition, in hopes of recovering the Christian sense of God—Father, Son, Holy Spirit.

[51] *Studi sull'arianesimo* (Roma: Editrice Studium, 1965); *La crisi ariana del IV secolo* (Roma: Institutum patristicum Augustinianum, 1975).

[52] Cf. *Arius: Heresy and Tradition* (London: Darton, Longman & Todd, 1987).

3

Classical theism. This essay has proposed that trinitarian worship and doctrine have both supported, and been supported by, *an integrated account of the cosmos, humanity, and God.* This account has animated, in many related ways, the Great Tradition of the undivided Church. For this reason, one hermeneutical principle we will do well to adopt and apply is the following. It is wise to be sceptical when recent theologians and philosophers discuss the *classical* (i.e., at least implicitly, the 'Jewish–Christian') *conception of God.* For what many of us consider 'classical theism' is in fact a typical product of *modernity.*

Two fairly representative examples of this misunderstanding are the late Bishop John A. T. Robinson's *Honest to God*[53] and (at least in part) Elizabeth A. Johnson's book *She Who Is.*[54] The former was a bit of a *succès de scandale* in 1963; it proposed that the traditional 'theistic' image of a remote 'God out-there' had to be rejected as both unreal and un-Christian.[55] The latter, a solid, constructive monograph, saw the light in 1992, and combines a pointed, scholarly feminist critique of the patriarchal biases that have affected the modern Jewish–Christian understanding of God with a broad theological critique of the 'classical' conception of God. In this critique, the author proposes that 'classical theism' has understood God as remote and impassive.[56] But surely this is not true. For from the outset, the Most High God of Jews and Christians has been known as lovingly and mercifully present to the cosmos, and especially to humanity, and if anything, as a 'passionate God', as, in this century, Abraham Heschel was one of the first to point out once again.

Let us start with a hermeneutical principle of the first order. The remote, impassive, faceless 'God-out-there', which the West (including significant portions of the catholic West) has gotten used to, surfaced only at the confluence of a number of late medieval, early modern, and modern trains of thought and mentalities. The following bill of particulars is offered as a hermeneutical instru-

---

[53] (London: SCM Press, 1963).

[54] *She Who Is: The Mystery of God in Feminist Theological Discourse* (New York: Crossroad, 1992).

[55] *Honest to God*, esp. 29–44.

[56] Cf. *She Who Is*, esp. 19–21, 147–9, 224–5, 230–3, 246–8.

ment; it lists elements of the intellectual revolution called modernity that have had considerable theological consequences:

(1) the *nominalist* habit of locking *realities* up in *conceptual definitions,* combined with the *humanist* interest in *things for their own sake* (Louis Dupré);

(2) the fifteenth- to seventeenth-century habit of viewing the first of Aquinas' five ways to demonstrate God's existence (the *argument from motion*) as the most cogent, while ignoring the other demonstrations, and specifically the fourth (based on *humanity's* ability to interpret the great chain of being in terms of *graded participation* in God's truth, goodness, and worthiness of notice) and the fifth (based on humanity's intuition of the *natural finality* naturally resident in all things—a mirror of its own native desire for God);[57]

(3) the Reformation's decision to replace doxology with soteriology—the doctrine of humanity's sin and its salvation by divine grace—as the focus of the Christian faith, at the expense of (a) humanity's consciousness of its radical participation in the infrahuman universe and its silent doxology, and (b) the Great Tradition's stress on the *imago Dei* as the heart of humanity's abiding vocation to mediate between God and the cosmos;[58]

(4) the mid-sixteenth century Catholic decision to interpret nature and grace as two superimposed layers of reality, and hence, to interpret natural knowledge and faith (both of them frequently and very one-sidedly conceived as two bodies of true 'true information') as if they were two superimposed layers of reality;[59]

(5) the late sixteenth- and early seventeenth-century decision of Catholic theologians like Leonard Lessius and Marin Mersenne to view the issue of the existence and attributes of God as a matter of *natural knowledge*—i.e., respectively, of metaphysics and of early scientific cosmology (Michael J. Buckley)—a development that soon began to create the separate treatments of what the Great Tradition had known as (distinguishable but) inseparable: *theologia* and *oikonomia* (or 'immanent' Trinity and 'economic' Trinity);

(6) the concomitant development of the notion, prepared by nominalism, that apophatic theology and mysticism are free-

---

[57] Cf. *GE* II/2, §102. [58] Cf. *GE* I, §20. [59] Cf. *GE* II/2, §86, 10.

standing, self-authenticating acts of the human mind in relation
to God, and not forms of worship, let alone Christian worship
(Johannes Eckhart; Nicholas of Cusa);

(7) the early seventeenth-century decision to define humanity's
relatedness to God not in terms of participation in God but
mainly as a function of human *self*-consciousness and *self*-
assurance—a view that was to have momentous consequences
in the drift of nineteenth-century idealism in the direction of
modern atheism (Eberhard Jüngel);

(8) the resulting tendency to increasingly separate the world of
matter from the world of mind, culminating in C. P. Snow's *Two
Cultures*;[60]

(9) the tendency, among the inheritors of Isaac Newton's cosmological theology, especially among the physico-theologians in
the eighteenth century, to rewrite Aquinas' fourth and fifth ways
in wholly mechanistic terms, resulting in the 'argument from
design', which is coherent only if it is presupposed that the
'Artificer of the universe' (like any efficient cause) produces its
effects *wholly outside itself*;[61]

(10) the concomitant definition of unstable humanity's relationship to God in largely *fiducial* terms, and (by contrast) the
definition of the world of matter and motion as intrinsically
determinate and stable, and thus, as *related to God only indirectly*
(viz. by way of the eternal 'laws of nature', which were properly
created by God); this implicitly reduced God to the god of mere
motion;[62]

(11) the placement of God, from Descartes on, as the omnipotent
outside power that had given the material universe its initial
'nudge';[63]

---

[60] C. P. Snow, *The Two Cultures and the Scientific Revolution* (New York: Cambridge
University Press, 1959). Expanded edition: *The Two Cultures: And a Second Look*
(Cambridge: Cambridge University Press, 1963).

[61] A classic instance of this is the first chapter of William Paley's famous *Natural
Theology: or, Evidences of the Existence and Attributes of the Deity, Collected from the
Appearances of Nature* (repr.; Houston: St Thomas Press, 1972).

[62] Cf. the following lines in the well-known eighteenth-century hymn *Praise
the Lord! Ye heavens adore him*: 'Praise the Lord, for he hath spoken; | Worlds his
mighty voice obeyed; | *Laws which never shall be broken* | *for their guidance hath he
made.*'

[63] On this, Pascal wrote: 'I cannot forgive Descartes; in his entire philosophy he
would have liked to do without God; but he felt forced to have him flick his finger
(*il n'a pu s'empêcher de lui faire donner une chiquenaude*) in order to set the world in
motion; after that he had no use for God any more' (*Pensées*, ed. Brunschvicg, 77).

(12) the resulting dilemma between the understanding of God *either* as totally separate from the universe (Leibniz's *Monad*), or as identical with it, and thus, as the patron of its determinisms (Spinoza's *Deus sive Natura*);

(13) the resulting loss of the deeply traditional Jewish and Christian understanding of creation as eternally and ideally pre-existent with God (specifically in the Torah, in God's Wisdom or in the divine *Logos*) and thus, as inalienably loved by God;[64]

(14) the consequent loss, in Christian theology, of the understanding of the *Logos* as the eternal pre-condition, 'in' the Triune God, for the possibility of any creation, in relation to which God must be said to be both sovereignly loving and sovereignly free, i.e. that God is in reality as well as essence distinct from the universe, as well as ineffably transcendent over it, while at the same time not outside it, but rather at its core.[65]

4

Trinity and Judaism. Without any elaboration, let me make another vital claim: the early modern decision to relegate the issue of God's existence and attributes to philosophic Reason implied a dismissal of the Jewish Scriptures as irrelevant to Christian theology. So, to recapture the Great Tradition's full trinitarianism, Christian theologians will simply have to go back, not just behind Augustine and the Cappadocians, but also behind the first two Councils, all the way back to the Scriptures and the Christian writings of the second century, when the affinity between Christians and Jews, though far from flourishing, was still alive. The words of Paul in the Acts of the Apostles that God 'has never left himself without

In the long run, this move was to lead to the 'non-interventionist' *deus otiosus*—God on a perpetual vacation, which in turn is a throwback to ancient conceptions of gods as leading entirely carefree, and indeed, irresponsible lives.

[64] Aquinas (*ST* I. 115. 2 in c. and ad 4; cf. *In II Sent.* 18. 1. 2; QD de Ver. 5. 9. ad 8) appeals to Augustine's *De Genesi ad litteram* to point out that the 'seminal ideas' (*rationes seminales*) of everything that lives and changes in the universe (pre-)exist *principaliter et originaliter* in the Eternal Word of God, as 'ideal ideas' (*rationes ideales*), but adds that it is preferable to call them *rationes causales* than *rationes seminales*. The notion of *rationes praeexistentes in Verbo* is part and parcel of Jan van Ruusbroec's universe of meaning, as the quotation above (n. 42) makes clear.

[65] Cf. Vatican I: [*Deus*] *praedicandus est re et essentia a mundo distinctus, . . . et super omnia, quae praeter ipsum sunt et concipi possunt, ineffabiliter excelsus* (DS 3001).

witness',[66] and the recognition of Jesus as 'the faithful and true witness' and 'the beginning of God's creation'[67] must fill the void left by patristic trinitarianism. The New Testament interprets Jesus as 'the Lord's servant'; it is embarrassing that this has left virtually no trace in classical trinitarian thought.[68]

5

Theologia and oikonomia; *doxology and soteriology; 'immanent' and 'economic' Trinity.* Over the past four or five centuries, the intellectual developments just listed have 'trickled down': they have become, mostly unthematically, part and parcel of the *modern* 'Western' mentality and consciousness; they are supported, in no small measure, by humanity's self-emancipation from slavery and subjection to the cosmic powers—of both the strictly cosmological and the human kind. The successes of science and technology are an integral part of this self-emancipation. So are the successes of the rise of historical consciousness, and of human self-understanding, which is inseparable of the awareness of history. Small wonder it often looks as if what Newman feared has come about: the replacement of Christian doxology and soteriology by human self-cultivation and by rational Christianity's efforts at defining salvation on its own terms. Small wonder, too, it is hard to believe in Father, Son, and Holy Spirit today. We are the reluctant heirs of a silent revolution which has imperceptibly blurred *the synthetic vision of cosmos, humanity, and God* that had slowly trickled down from the Christian Church and become the *pre-modern* West's tacit, yet normative framework of cultural assumptions. At the centre of this vision, *though quite often implicitly,*[69] stands Jesus Christ.

---

[66] ἀμάρτυρος: Acts 14: 17.

[67] Rev. 3: 14; cf. 1 Tim. 6: 13.

[68] P. Smulders's interpretation of the fifth similitude in the *Shepherd of Hermas* contains interesting suggestions on this point. Cf. 'Dogmengeschichtliche und lehramtliche Entfaltung der Christologie' (*Mysterium Salutis: Grundriß heilsgeschichtlicher Dogmatik*, vol. 3/1 (Einsiedeln–Zürich–Köln: Benziger Verlag, 1970), 389–476), 395–7.

[69] The writings of the master of *The Cloud of Unknowing* are a good example of this. Christ does not *seem* to play a part in the unitive prayer he commends, but this is due to the author's tacit assumption that such prayer takes place 'in' Christ. And since he believes Christ is present in the Church, he can also urge his readers to defer to its sacraments and its traditions. This raises an important issue in trini-

Pope St Pius X inaugurated our century under the motto: *Instaurare omnia in Christo*: 'to bring all things to a head in Christ'. At the end of the same century, Jesus Christ does turn out to have been the object of the keenest theological questioning—much of it needlessly doctrinaire, much of it undesirably modernist. Yet it is and remains part of the Christian Churches' theological task to respond to the central question of Mark's Gospel: 'Who do *you* say I am?' In attempting to do so, they will either succeed in capturing and recapturing the profession of faith of the Great Tradition, or (God forbid) fail to do so. The distinctive feature of this profession of faith is Jesus the Christ, known and professed as the eternal Son of the living and loving God, for us and for our salvation born of woman, unjustly put to death, raised from death in the Spirit of God's Holiness, and awaited in watchfulness and prayer, against the Day when he will come in Glory to do final justice to the living and the dead.

The modern era is finding such a unified trinitarian vision of humanity and the universe hard to sustain. For one thing, it regards its monotheism, not as a mystery of worship and wisdom, but as a victory of Reason; many of our contemporaries have tacitly traded the living God for a remote 'deity' that somehow 'created' the universe. For another, many of us are inclined to accept ethics as a satisfactory substitute of faith. Finally, we tend to value godly experience more than God; thus many of us are apt to trade worship for religious self-consciousness, and propose Jesus as the (an?) admirable example of that self-consciousness. I could go on and on. But let me keep that story for another day.

tarian theology. In the past three-quarter century, physicists have learned that the outcome of their experiments substantially depends on the set-up of the experiments themselves, and that statements of physical facts do not, in fact, do justice to the 'facts', which are significantly indeterminate. Theologians can learn from this that the *actual experience* (the spiritual 'fact') of being in the Father's presence in the Son, Jesus Christ, can be indeterminate, too; it does not (and need not) involve any intellectual or affective awareness of the trinitarian doctrines. Gregory of Nyssa, Evagrius, Bonaventure, the master of *The Cloud of Unknowing*, and Jan van Ruusbroec (to mention only five theologians I have studied) all claim that the experience of the mind being lifted up into God is *agnostic*; Ruusbroec even calls it 'dying into God'.

The Trinity Depicted and Proclaimed

13

The Trinity in Art

DAVID BROWN

Because Christianity is founded upon a written revelation, the danger has always been that the power of the word will be exaggerated. So, despite the continuing protests of mystics over the ages about the limitations of language, precisely the same kinds of test for doctrinal orthodoxy or linguistic propriety have come to be applied in areas where they are either less suitable or indeed quite inappropriate. This is in my view one of the major stumbling-blocks which has plagued the Christian appropriation of art. A verbal checklist is applied, rather than care being taken to ascertain what it is that the artist is trying to achieve. The element of imaginative engagement is thus missed, as too is the fact that, because artists have not the same freedom to qualify as have writers, their metaphors have to be at once more forceful as well as—inevitably—more easily subject to misinterpretation. Such contrasts, though, far from being a weakness, can have much to teach us about the explication of doctrine. The extent to which different sorts of issue are raised by the visual as distinct from the verbal is well indicated, I believe, by the various types of presentation to which artists have resorted in developing imagery to highlight the significance and relevance of the doctrine of the Trinity.

Over the course of the centuries, quite a number of different forms of allusion have been attempted. At the risk of over-simplifying, I propose in what follows to identify three main types of approach. Inevitably, to some degree any type of classification prejudges issues, detecting common lines where others may prefer to see none, but whatever faults the method may have, it at least enables us to avoid a purely chronological investigation. So I propose we look at artistic representations under three heads, what I shall call triadic, incarnational and societal images. Very roughly what I mean by each is as follows. By 'triadic' I shall understand those images which focus on symbols of threeness, whether abstract such as a triangle or semi-representational such as three identical heads. By 'societal' I mean those where the primary focus is on relationality,[1] with its personal character stressed, and so one is immediately conscious of some form of inter-action taking place. Finally, by 'incarnational' I intend reference to those images where the primary idea involves some form of allusion to specific events in Christ's life. As we shall observe, over-lap is inevitable if characterisations of this degree of vagueness are used as our starting point, but the differences of emphasis are, I believe, significant and so worth highlighting. All three types have in fact been subject to severe criticism, but I shall contend that more often than not such criticism misses its mark because it judges by the wrong criteria. Precise theological statements have never been the aim, but rather visual metaphors that invite further exploration and involvement. The possibility of such involvement is, however, dependent on specific background assumptions, and it is absence of any awareness of those background assumptions that has more often than not plagued proper appreciation of what artists have been trying to achieve through such images.

I Triadic Versions

I begin here because, though historically the least common, such images are also at once the most ancient and the most modern. Though not in general unsympathetic to modern art, I do want in this particular case to suggest that, initial appearances notwith-standing, it is the modern versions which are in general the less thought-provoking or profound. To see why, let us begin with modernity. Perhaps the problem has to do with motivation. For the almost universal preference in modern times for symbolic allusion seems to have been inspired less by enthusiasm for the general trend in modern art towards abstraction and much more by revul-sion from traditional forms of representation. Derisive comments

---

[1] 'Societal' is used rather than 'social' in order to avoid any automatic associa-tion with a social understanding of the Trinity. As will become apparent later, though the two (art and model) are often connected, this is by no means requisite or inevitable.

about the Father as an old man and the Spirit as a bird are commonplace. That the worries inherent in such a critique are misconceived, I shall argue in due course. What, though, also needs to be acknowledged is that modern abstract representation also carries with it its own set of problems.

The principal of these is that, while functioning as useful reminders of trinitarian doctrine, such images are seldom effective in inspiring any fresh reflection on the nature of the doctrine, far less any suggestion of its relevance to ourselves. Louise Nevelson's work in New York might be used by way of illustration. Columnar forms and wall configurations are made triadic, and as such defended as a way of evoking the Trinity without it 'accosting' us.[2] Such muted reference certainly reminds us that we are in a church, but scarcely carries us beyond that point. John Piper's tapestry in Chichester cathedral is more direct, but still quite subdued. It is the symbols of the three persons that one notices first and only then the triangle that unites them. A level of subtlety is introduced by the way in which the intended reference of the three symbols as trinitarian only becomes retrospectively apparent as the triangle behind them finally forces such a reading.[3] So we are certainly offered aesthetic and intellectual pleasure as we explore the tapestry, but it would be harder to argue that there accrues any deepening of one's religious understanding.[4] A better contender might be the piece of sculpture recently commissioned from Stephen Cox for Newcastle Cathedral. Egyptian alabaster marked into three segments is the idiom employed, but this is combined with the piece as a whole being used to evoke the sense of broken bread and poured chalice, and so both the source of trinitarian doctrine in the life of Christ and of its continued significance in the worship of the Church.[5]

One modern image much discussed is Anselm Kiefer's 1973

[2] In St Peter's Lutheran church. For illustration and commentary, J. Dillenberger, *A Theology of Artistic Sensibilities* (London: SCM, 1987), 170–1.

[3] It was commissioned in 1966 by that major patron of the arts, Walter Hussey, while Dean. Against a wider frame of the four elements above and the symbols of the four evangelists beneath, a green equilateral triangle has superimposed on it a sun disc to represent the Father, a tau cross the Son, and flames the Holy Spirit.

[4] Much the same might be said of his design for the stained glass in the lantern of the Metropolitan cathedral in Liverpool, where three primary colours interacting is used to evoke the doctrine.

[5] Installed with the help of an Arts Council Lottery grant of £33,000 in August 1997. An ellipse made of porphyry is used to represent the tilted chalice.

diptych *Vater, Sohn und hl. Geist*.[6] The lower painting is of a dense forest with three trunks so named from which there emerges the log cabin that constitutes the frame of the upper painting. Within this cabin are three identical seats with flames of fire upon each, while through the cabin's three windows there is to be seen nothing except thick snow. It seems clear that Kiefer intended to say something about the tension between Germany's pagan and Christian inheritance; clear too that he is pessimistic about the ability of Christianity to communicate to the wider world.[7] But most relevant here is the way in which the painting takes up the theme of the Trinity also building upon pagan interest in triads,[8] for, if we are to understand why triadic images were once so popular in Christian art, we will need to come to terms with their pagan antecedents.

In the pagan Celtic world in particular the representation of divinity as three appears to have been extremely common.[9] Sometimes it took the form of three identical figures, sometimes one figure with three identical heads, sometimes small variations between them. There are also variations in what type is most popular in which location. For instance, in Germany two identical matronly goddesses are found flanking a younger third, while elsewhere one finds three identical figures distinguished only by what they hold. Again, the area round Rheims has yielded particularly fine examples of identical triple-faced deities, while elsewhere we find differentiation not only of age but also sometimes even of sex.[10] Scholars are uncertain how far differentiation must go before we should speak of three deities rather than one, and indeed it has been suggested that there may even have been a comparable uncertainty in the worshipper's own mind.[11] What, however, does

[6] For illustration and discussion, R. López-Pedraza, *Anselm Kiefer* (London: Thames & Hudson, 1996), 50–2; for a theological discussion, M. C. Taylor, *Disfiguring* (Chicago: University of Chicago Press, 1992), 290–305, esp. 296, though, inexplicably, the plate (34) only reproduces half the painting.

[7] The tension is suggested by the way in which trees need to be destroyed for a log cabin to be made; the lack of influence by the fire having no effect on the snow outside.

[8] The three trees are given Christian labels and grow into the three chairs.

[9] For a discussion with some illustrations, M. Green, *Symbol and Image in Celtic Religious Art* (London and New York: Routledge, 1989), 169–205. For the occurrence of related imagery among other pagan European peoples, R. Pettazzoni, 'The Pagan Origins of the Three-Headed Representation of the Christian Trinity', *Journal of Warburg & Courtauld Institutes*, 9 (1946), 149–57.　　　　[10] Ibid. 174.

[11] Ibid. 203–4.

seem clear is that such repetition was intended to indicate intensifying power, the presence in the deity of the relevant attributes to an unparalleled degree. One can see a related way of thinking operating where animals are given an additional horn or three phalli. The triad was the Celtic way of indicating the presence of something rather more than natural power.

Why three should have been chosen rather than, say, two or four is hard to say. Suggestions have included a reflection of social structure, the notion of the divine as all-seeing, or even an allusion to phases of the moon.[12] In the absence of any suitable literary evidence, only speculation is possible. What can, however, be asserted is that this use of repetition as indicating divinity continued well into the Christian era. Abstract triads are found, as in the seventh-century Fyvie stone where three circles inside a larger circle is used, or again with the three eggs found inside a bird's nest sculpted on the magnificent ninth-century Kildalton cross.[13] Triple-faced heads were once also very common, but, sadly, almost all were destroyed at the Reformation, though occasionally an inconspicuous location has preserved them, as is the case with an early fifteenth century misericord at Cartmel priory.[14] Nor was the phenomenon by any means confined to what had once been the domain of Celtic paganism. An early example from Rome itself is now in the Vatican museum. A sarcophagus telling the story of the fall and redemption opens with God as three bonded, bearded men creating Eve from Adam on the ground, while in the next scene God now as a young man addresses Adam and Eve, with his trinitarian character this time identified by three identical stars

[12] George Dumézil in *Jupiter, Mars, Qurinius* (Paris: Gallimard, 1941) and in a number of later books argued that a general Indo-European pattern is to be found, and this reflects the way in which society was divided between priests, warriors, and farmers. Wilhelm Kirfel in *Die dreiköpfige Gottheit* (Bonn: Dümmlers Verlag, 1948) suggested a pattern of influence spreading from India through Iran and Thrace to Greece and Rome and then still further west. But this fails to explain the huge variations in the popularity of the image, with it prominent in Hinduism and among the Celts but really very muted in the classical world.

[13] For discussion and illustration of the former, M. Lines, *Sacred Stones, Sacred Places* (Edinburgh: Saint Andrew Press, 1992), 11–13 (though unconnected, the parallel with Dante's final image in the *Divine Comedy* is worth noting). The latter remains in situ on the island of Islay. Its more famous face contrasts Cain's killing of Abel with Isaac's voluntary sacrifice; its Trinity occurs on its western side.

[14] This variant is of a crowned king with three noses and three mouths. For illustration, J. C. Dickinson, *The Priory of Cartmel* (Milnthorpe, Cumbria: Cicerone Press, 1991), 59.

above.[15] Though Roman religion did have triadic elements, they were scarcely dominant,[16] and so it seems implausible to suggest this as the source; nor need we postulate a Celtic sculptor. More likely is the Christian dogma interacting in the sculptor's mind with the thought that the repeated unnatural figure would suggest something greater than human personality. If so, there is an important element of engagement with that part of the narrative for which such a representation is chosen. Adam, we all know, was made in the divine image, but the three heads underline for the observer at once both the similarity and difference thus established between creator and created: God is in our image, but then also so much more.

Somewhat surprisingly, the Renaissance brought both renewed interest in such images and their eventual condemnation. As the latter issue is the less complicated, we may note the attack first. This was initiated by the celebrated St Antoninus of Florence (d. 1459), well-known for his writings on economic theory, and it is in the context of his discussion of the payment of artists that he makes his comments. Along with pictures of Jesus entering Mary's womb at the annunciation fully-formed and the Child reading before appropriate years, the Trinity as a single person with three heads is condemned 'because it is a monster in the nature of things'.[17] Ironically, here we find Antoninus fully in accord with the naturalising tendencies of Renaissance art as it was to develop, and indeed giving it a further push in that direction. Yet, as we have seen, what had once most appealed about the image was precisely its unnaturalness as indicative of divinity. Definitive condemnation finally came in 1628 from Pope Urban VIII.[18] Even so the image did not entirely disappear. Not only did abstract triadic structures become an image of Catholic dissent in sixteenth-century England,[19] even as late as the nineteenth century we still

---

[15] For illustration and discussion, R. Milburn, *Early Christian Art and Architecture* (Aldershot: Scolar Press, 1988), 67, 68, 82 n.15.

[16] As Kirfel notes, archaeological survivals are limited to Hecate and Cerberus; op. cit., 181 ff. Cerberus has three heads, Hecate sometimes three bodies.

[17] *ST* IV. 8. iv. 11: 'Reprehensibiles . . . sunt . . . cum faciunt Trinitatis imaginem unam personam cum tribus capitibus, quod monstrum est in rerum natura.' For a discussion of his motivation, C. Gilbert, 'The Archbishop on the Painters of Florence, 1450', *Art Bulletin*, 41 (1959), 75–87, esp. 81.

[18] Constitution of the 11th of August 1628.

[19] As in Rushton Triangular Lodge in Northamptonshire, built in the late six-

find this particular variant of a triple-faced deity receiving venera-
tion, though admittedly in the remoteness of the Tirolese Alps.[20]

How popular that image had once been is well indicated by the
numbers that have survived despite papal condemnation not only
from Antoninus' own time but even from his own archdiocese of
Florence. Though by major artists, none could be classed as a
major work in its own right, and this no doubt in part explains
their survival. Even so, their range is worth noting. Probably the
earliest Renaissance example to survive is Donatello's three-
faced Trinity in the tympanum of the Guelph party niche in
Orsanmichele, dating from the second decade of the fifteenth
century.[21] From 1438 comes Filippo Lippi's representation of St
Augustine's vision of the Trinity as a three-headed figure piercing
his heart.[22] Pollaiuolo (d.1498), who also employs a triangular
arrangement of angels to link heaven and earth in his famous
series for the church of St Augustine at San Gimignano, uses a
three-faced Trinity in his allegory of theology on the tomb of Sixtus
IV (d.1484).[23] Finally, from 1511 comes Andrea del Sarto's medal-
lion of a three-faced head of the Trinity surrounded by four other
medallions of saints. In this last instance encasement in a glowing
sun is used to further underline the divine unity.[24]

None of these examples can, it seems to me, be assessed fairly
without due account being taken of the thought of the time. The

teenth century by Sir Thomas Tresham, the father of one of the conspirators in the
Gunpowder Plot of 1605.

[20] For an illustration, Pettazzoni, op. cit., 16b. Late examples also survive from
Russian Orthodoxy, varying in date from the sixteenth to the eighteenth century:
Kirfel, illus. 174–7.

[21] Kirfel finds the oldest three-headed Christian Trinity in a manuscript of the
Chronicles of Isidore of Seville: op. cit., 148. The oldest painting I have been able to
discover is a wooden altarpiece, now in the National Gallery of Umbria at Perugia,
by Ottavigno Nelli, and dating from 1403.

[22] For illustration and discussion, M. P. Mannini and M. Fagioli, *Filippo Lippi:
Catalogo completo* (Florence: Octavo, 1997), 29, 97–9. Done as one of the scenes on
the predella of the altar in an Augustinian church, it balances an unusual annunciation to the Virgin of her death, where the choice of imagery may also be due to
Augustine.

[23] In the former case the unusual triangle of angels is held together by a chalice
placed beneath the foot of Christ who is crowning his mother: N. Pons, *Pollaiolo*
(Florence: Octavo, 1994), 86.

[24] For illustration and brief discussion, A. Natali and A. Cecchi, *Andrea del Sarto:
Catalogue complet* (Paris: Bordas, 1992), 38–9. Donatello had also used the imagery
of sun and rays, but his figure was crowned and considerably older. Kirfel speaks
of an 'uralte Motiv' deriving from Egypt or still further east: op. cit., 149.

neoplatonism of the Renaissance very strongly endorsed the notion of a common theology, that paganism should be seen as an anticipation of Christianity, and indeed this attitude was shared by St Antoninus himself.[25] The leading intellectuals of the movement, however, in particular Pico della Mirandola (d.1494) and Ficino (d.1499), carried the argument a stage further, in finding triadism in the world everywhere about them, and in seeing in this a reflection at one and the same time both of the triadic structure of God and of his ultimate unity.[26] A surprising but perhaps inevitable conclusion of such a line of thought was that even negative triads could be taken to point in the same direction. So, for example, appeal was even made to the existence of three-headed Cerberus in classical mythology, and this may explain in part why the same triple-headed image could be used of the Devil or of humanity in conflict with itself, no less than of God himself.[27] Perhaps Dante's use of both negative and positive trinitarian imagery should be seen as an anticipation of such attitudes.[28] Certainly, the simultaneous use of the image in opposed senses very effectively enabled the idea to be conveyed that the negative image need not have the last word; instead of ultimate division, there was the possibility of complete integration. This would seem to be the idea behind Titian's intriguing *Allegory of Prudence*, represented by a three-headed man with three animals beneath. The present time of the middle-aged face in the centre is given a lion below to indicate someone who has successfully integrated within his life both the ferocious determination of the wolf of the past (the youthful zeal of the face on one side) and the faithfulness of the dog of the future (the old man on the other). In other words, the idea is of a present reality in

[25] e.g. *ST* IV. 10. vii. 4: 'De verbo eterno seu filio dei multa dixit Plato . . . et satis clare.'

[26] The influence of their ideas on the art of the time is pursued in detail in E. Wind, *Pagan Mysteries in the Renaissance* (Faber & Faber, 1958), esp. 1–127 and 241–62.

[27] For an illustration of a three-headed Antichrist, B. McGinn, *Antichrist* (San Francisco: Harper, 1994), 148; for a three-way facing figure as humanity in conflict, note the example in Hexham Abbey, and also that by Grünewald in Berlin.

[28] The work culminates in a vision of the Trinity as three intersecting circles and colours, but on the way the three women who guide him seem to be treated as an image of the Trinity, while in Hell the Devil and his minion, Cerberus, are alike portrayed as three-headed and as all God is not. For the role of Mary, Beatrice, and Lucy, D. L. Sayers (trans. and ed.), Dante: *The Divine Comedy I* (Baltimore: Penguin, 1949), 328; for Cerberus, 104 ff. (Canto VI. 13 ff.); for Satan, 286 (Canto XXXIV. 28 ff.)

which past memory and future hope are suitably balanced and modified through present integration.[29] But undoubtedly of most significance for this line of thinking are the various figures of the three Graces, which were regularly taken to imply reciprocal relationships of love that bring an ultimate unity, and indeed this may well be an important factor behind so famous a painting as Botticelli's *Primavera*.[30]

In rehearsing this history my objective has been to challenge the supposition that modern triadic representations of the Trinity are subtle in their allusions to the doctrine, whereas three-faced heads are crude and naïve. Of course, from our perspective that is the way that they must appear, but that is not, I contend, how they would have been received at the time. Augustine's writings were used to justify not only the perception of an analogy of the Trinity within the human soul, but the detection of such analogies every-where, with suitable reinforcement for the argument then provided by a revived neoplatonism. It was such considerations that led so many Renaissance patrons and painters to believe themselves justified in re-appropriating this particular image from the classical and pagan world. In doing so, however, the objective was no mere academic exercise. Rather, the thought appears to have been that the Trinity thus understood could bring unity to a world—and human beings—which, because it and they were in the divine image, already had the makings of such a unity. The irony is that the Church put an end to such representations not because of theological or philosophical objections to the underlying theology, but on apparently quite secular grounds: lack of naturalism. Yet if a unity that is not of this world is to be suggested, as God's surely must be, is lack of naturalism not precisely what is required of our imagery, and so the pagan intuition in this case correct after all?[31]

[29] For a discussion, with the Egyptian roots of this particular image stressed, E. Panofsky, *Meaning in the Visual Arts* (New York: Doubleday, 1955), 181–205.

[30] Pico's claim that 'the unity of Venus is unfolded in the trinity of the Graces' is explored in Wind, op. cit., 113–27. Cf. also E. H. Gombrich, *Symbolic Images*, 3rd edn. (London: Phaedon, 1985), 31–81.

[31] In a recent article the Christian doctrine of the Trinity has been described as 'an implicit disruption and subversion of the Indo-European ideology': J. Milbank, 'Sacred triads: Augustine and the Indo-European Soul', *Modern Theology* (1997), 451–74, esp. 462–3. While some of the author's points hit their mark, it seems to me unlikely that Christianity's mission would have been quite so successful, had there not been already within the classical world an existent neoplatonic triad on

II Societal Versions

Without doubt the most popular image for the Trinity today is the famous icon of Andrei Rublev, based on the appearance of the angels to Abraham at Mamre.[32] Because the faces of the angels are alike, there are obviously some connections with the previous section,[33] but I place it here because societal interaction has now become the principal theme. A continuous dialogue of love is taking place between the gaze of their eyes, a dialogue bonded by the circle that implicitly encases them. Their interrelation is further underlined by the complementary character of the various balance of colours that make up their robes. Yet, though the image is a powerful one, it only indirectly engages our involvement, through the link in their gaze being mediated by means of the chalice in the centre of the painting.[34] I talk of indirect mediation, because though the Eucharistic involvement of the Trinity is thereby indicated (and reinforced by the blessings offered by Father and Son), there is nothing explicitly to draw us into the picture. Indeed, none of the three angels offer even a partial gaze towards the viewer.

That fact makes it all the more surprising that this is the image to which appeal has so often been made by those who think the doctrine of the Trinity central to a proper understanding of society, among them Moltmann.[35] Such a notion seems to have been no part of the intention of the artist. Moreover, account must surely be taken of the huge contrast that exists between any such divine society, however understood, and its supposed human equivalent. It is one thing to say that human society can on occasion provide an analogy for what the nature of God might be like; quite

which to build and within wider paganism the image of triads as a sign of intensifying power. The former already offered intelligibility as the second 'person', and the latter the possibility of the absence of 'hierarchy and heterogeneity'.

[32] Painted about 1411, it is in the Tretyakov Gallery in Moscow. The extent to which it is an advance on early representations can be observed through comparison with a Greek icon of the same scene from the late fourteenth century: K. Weitzmann, *The Icon* (London: Chatto & Windus, 1978), 131.

[33] It would be interesting to reflect why this image has gained in popularity, as that of the Graces has declined. Could gender issues be involved?

[34] Established Orthodox convention insists upon identifying the central figure with Christ, and sometimes argues in support the balance of his robes (indicating humanity and divinity). Against, though, is the fact that only the figure on the right gazes at the chalice and only his staff forms a cross with the fold of his robe.

another to argue the other way round, and suppose that human beings ought, so far as possible, to conform to this pattern. What the latter argument ignores is that human beings are still developing, and one of the main ways they do so is through contrast, in childhood through learning to differentiate themselves from their parents and in adulthood through alternative possibilities being opened up to them beyond any particular social group.

In western Christendom we find an early adoption of the same image in the church of Santa Maria Maggiore in Rome, but it never became very popular, in part because in the middle ages in the west Mamre became primarily an image of the virtue of hospitality.[36] Added to that was the Renaissance and Reformation retreat from reading the passage in question (Genesis 18) as in any sense the description of a trinitarian experience. Here one might contrast the treatment of the scene in Rembrandt and in Murillo. The latter by portraying three identical angels continues at least to allow the old reading, whereas Rembrandt leaves us in no doubt that he has discarded it,[37] as does Chagall in the twentieth century.[38] But here it is to Murillo's alternative societal image that I particularly want to draw attention.

Murillo was not the only artist to adopt the iconography known as the Two Trinities, but his representation is certainly the best known.[39] In this iconography what we have is the holy family

[35] He acknowledges this 'wonderful' icon as the inspiration for his social understanding of the Trinity and its implications for humanity in the preface to one of his books: J. Moltmann, *The Trinity and the Kingdom of God* (London: SCM, 1981), xvi.

[36] The mosaic in Santa Maria Maggiore was commissioned by Sixtus III (d. 430), and pictures three incidents connected with the story: for illustration, J. Hall, *History of Ideas and Images in Italian Art* (London: John Murray, 1983), 88. Just a century later at San Vitale the figures are more sharply differentiated, and hospitality rather than trinitarian revelation may already have become the main point: G. Bovini, *Ravenna* (Ravenna: Longo, 1991), illus. 19, 20.

[37] In Rembrandt's etching (now in Melbourne) the number of angels has for no obvious reason been reduced to two with no similarities between them. By contrast, in Murillo's painting (National Gallery, Ottawa), though the wings are abandoned, the three figures are so alike and interacting with one another as to invite a trinitarian interpretation. In Tiepolo's version, both traditions are rejected in favour of a mystic vision: for illustration, M. Levey, *Giambattista Tiepolo* (New Haven: Yale University Press, 1986), 34.

[38] Chagall's version (in Rheims Cathedral) is closest to Rembrandt's, with Abraham primarily engaged with one angel.

[39] Zurbarán painted the theme twice, as did Murillo. The earlier and less successful dates from 1640 and is in the National Museum, Stockholm: for illustration, *Murillo* (London: Royal Academy of Arts, 1983), 75. The latter, dating at most seven years before his death in 1682, is in the National Gallery, London.

linked to the divine Trinity through the infant Christ, who does duty as a figure both human and divine. An early attempt at such a pattern is provided by an illustration in the early eleventh-century Anglo-Saxon Aelfwine Prayerbook. On the right of the manuscript painting an almost identical Father and Son are gazing lovingly into one another's eyes, while on the left the Holy Spirit hovers over Mary who holds the infant Christ portrayed as a smaller version of himself as adult.[40] Though heaven and earth are thereby interwoven, an obvious difficulty lies in the repetition of the figure of the Son. Moreover, there is no suggestion of an analogy of relation between heavenly society and earthly, whereas undoubtedly this is one of the main aims in Murillo's version. As with most of Murillo's art, nowadays there is a tendency to dismiss his achievement as mere sentimentality,[41] but this is to ignore his own family history and the wider background of Spanish society at the time. His native Seville was in a period of decline, to which the population were reacting with intense penitential fervour.[42] One finds this reflected in Murillo's series of paintings of the parable of the prodigal son, and indeed it has been suggested that in them the human father is deliberately made to look like contemporary representations of God the Father.[43]

But penitence was not the only issue, there was also acute suffering and the issue of God's response to it. The city had been subject to plague, famine, and earthquake,[44] and the artist's own history was far from a happy one. He lost both his own parents early, while his wife and most of his own children were to precede him to the grave.[45] So, in considering his two representations of the topic, particularly the second completed towards the end of his life, it is important that we do not see a false idyll where there had

[40] For illustration and discussion, B. C. Raw, *Trinity and Incarnation in Anglo-Saxon Art and Thought* (Cambridge and New York: Cambridge University Press, 1997), 152–60, cf. 148, ill. XVb.

[41] In the eighteenth century, it was common to reckon him second only to Raphael.

[42] All secular plays were banned in 1679, in part as a result of the penitential mission of the Jesuit Tirso González de Santalla.

[43] M. N. Taggard, *Murillo's Allegories of Salvation and Triumph* (Columbia: University of Missouri Press, 1992), 9–66, esp. 23.

[44] Half the population died in the plague of 1649, and there was a terrible famine in 1651. Plague returned in 1676, followed by torrential rains in 1677 and an earthquake in 1680.

[45] Both his parents died when he was 9. In 1664 he lost his wife, and only three out of his nine children were to survive him.

been none. Rather, the suggestion appears to be that, as the holy family was threatened with anguish and sorrow but not destroyed, so our earthly families can be carried through death and tragedy to a new and deeper unity beyond the grave. If to this interpretation it is objected that it places too heavy a reliance on the artist's own special circumstances, let me once more underline that his experience was commonplace in the Seville of the time, and indeed it was, though admittedly to a less intense degree, the pattern in contemporary Europe as a whole. We need to transport ourselves back into a world where loss of wife and children were the norm rather than the exception; only that way will we remove the glaze from our eyes that sees only sentimentality, when something much more profound was in fact at stake.

Admittedly, there was a negative side. In the later middle ages, the extended family had been given a semi-trinitarian image with Mary, while holding the infant Christ, also made to sit upon the knee of her own mother, Anna. Commonly known by its German name of *Selbdritt*,[46] the image was sometimes given reinforcement through the notion of one family endorsing another by including the Trinity in the frame. A case in point would be Fra Bartolommeo's version in San Marco in Florence which has a three-faced Trinity hovering above.[47] While scarcely raising the same level of problem as the cases where statues of Mary opened up to reveal a Trinity, there certainly was a danger of too easy an equation between heavenly and earthly realities. That issue was to repeat itself in the case of the Two Trinities. As I have already tried to indicate, to use the human family to draw one into relation with something analogous is a quite different pattern of argument from suggesting that the Trinity itself provides the endorsement for some particular earthly institution or way of behaving. Yet there can be no doubt that the Counter-Reformation did sometimes resort to the latter type of appeal. This is perhaps most obvious in the way in which its use of Joseph as an argument for a greater sense of responsibility on the part of men in the moral and religious life of their families was allowed to expand into seeing Joseph as the

---

[46] *Heilige Anna selbdritt*—Saint Anne as herself the third.

[47] Bartolommeo (d.1517), who became a Dominican in 1500 under the influence of Savonarola, originally intended the painting for his large altarpiece in the Sala del Gran Consiglio. Savonarola, though, also endorsed the notion of trinitarian vestiges: *Triumphus Crucis*, 3. 3.

analogue of a heavenly Father.[48] Even today, devotional books on the holy family sometimes attempt the comparison, and suggest that Joseph be seen as our point of access to the divine Father, and so the nearest present equivalent of someone rightly to be obeyed.[49] Such attitudes left the way open for Murillo's painting to be understood rather differently from the exposition I have given above, as simply providing the divine endorsement of family life.

Although Murillo's commissions certainly reflect the Counter-Reformation's interest in Joseph,[50] I do contest the fairness of imposing such a reading on his *Two Trinities*. The youthful painting could perhaps yield such an interpretation, especially once account is taken of the high prominence given to Mary and Joseph and of the way in which God the Father might be seen as an older version of Joseph. But with the later, definitive version, matters are quite otherwise. God the Father has been deliberately increased in scale and alertness, while both Mary and Joseph are positioned at a lower level than Jesus, with the result that Jesus' gaze heavenward and his parents' dependence on that gaze become the central perspective. I conclude therefore that, though both variants of what I have called the societal image of the Trinity have been used to endorse social trinitarianism and with it particular understandings of society, this is by no means an inevitable consequence of such art, and it should thus be judged by independent criteria.

III Incarnational Versions

Here I have in mind the typical representations of the involvement of the Father and Spirit in the incarnational act of redemption, through portraying the former as an elderly father or Ancient of Days looking down from the sky and the Spirit as a dove hovering over the Son. The use of the latter symbol clearly derives from Christ's baptism, but the best known images of this type are in fact

[48] E. Mâle, *L'Art religieux après le concile de Trente* (Paris: Librairie Armand Colin, 1932), 313–25. 'C'est ainsi que fut glorifié saint Joseph qui, dans la Sainte Famille, apparaissait comme l'image de Dieu le Père' (325).

[49] e.g. A. Druze, *Discovering Saint Joseph* (Slough: St Paul, 1991), esp. 135, 187. Obedience to Joseph is a recurring theme, and, following Olier, used to endorse the authority of priests (69).

[50] As in his various paintings which depict Joseph holding the Child or leading him by the hand. For examples, L. Kagané, *Murillo* (St Petersburg: Aurora, 1995), 96–9, 124–5, 128–31.

of the crucifixion, and indeed were to acquire a distinctive name from nineteenth-century German art historians: *Gnadenstuhl* or 'Seat of Mercy'. One of the earliest examples dates from 1132.[51] Though now applied more widely, the term was originally intended specifically to refer to those instances in which the Father is himself seated, and holding the dying or dead Christ.[52] In such cases, the allusion is clearly to the mercy-seat of the Old Testament, and the way in which this image is taken up in the New.[53] However, I do not wish to confine myself quite so narrowly here. Instead, what I want to reflect upon is the reasons why this and related imagery have been so frequently attacked. What I shall contend is that the grounds are misplaced, because more often than not they represent a misconception of what the artist was trying to achieve.

The attack in the English Reformation on this particular image is well known. What is less well known is that it seems to have been not just part of the general assault on images, but also strongly motivated by revulsion against the particular form of imagery employed in this case. As early as Wycliffe it is specifically singled out as leading to a debased understanding of God; Queen Elizabeth attempted to stem the tide of destruction, but again in an influential tract by Anthony Gilby it was this image which was to be highlighted; finally, by act of Parliament in 1643 all remaining examples were consigned to oblivion.[54] But in response to the repeated contention that the image is unworthy and demeaning of God, the question must be raised whether the fault did not also lie sometimes in the viewer, in the failure to allow other than a very literal reading, and, if so, whether the attack should not be seen as part of a much wider cultural change, the retreat to a more literalist interpretation of Scripture that foreclosed the more multivalent possibilities of the past.[55]

[51] A German portable altar, now in the Victoria and Albert Museum in London.

[52] There are two excellent examples of the genre, both with the seat fully visible, in Edinburgh and London. The former has Hugo van der Goes' Trinity altarpiece of 1479, originally intended for a collegiate church of that dedication in Edinburgh; the latter, a splendid one of about 1410 from Austria.

[53] e.g. Exod. 25: 17-22. In the New Testament the imagery is taken up at various points, e.g. Rom. 3: 25, Heb. 9: 5.

[54] M. Aston, *England's Iconclasts* (Oxford: Clarendon Press, 1988), I. 76, 78, 99; R. Marks, *Stained Glass in England* (Toronto and Buffalo: University of Toronto Press, 1993), 232. For a rare example of a survival, ibid. 35.

[55] Though hard to prove, another factor may have been resistance to portrayals of a passible Father, showing obvious signs of grief.

However that may be, this has been by no means the only form of critique in modern times. Also requiring note is a resurgent Orthodoxy which claims that, while the incarnation legitimated representation of the Son, this remains precluded in respect of the Father.[56] As a matter of fact Orthodoxy is replete with such images,[57] but the modern Orthodox tendency is to regard them as degenerate, and as created under Western influence. Art historians would in any case contest whether Orthodoxy has ever been as free from external influence as it would like to see itself when at its best,[58] but here let us note a rather different form of objection, and that is whether to use this type of argument against artistic representation of the Father does not undermine the fundamental equality of the persons. In the original iconoclastic controversy the argument for legitimating imagery from John of Damascus and Theodore the Studite was that God in becoming incarnate had in effect drawn or painted himself and so repealed the Old Testament prohibition against portrayal of divinity.[59] But if one person, why not all? It is not as though the Son thereby revealed specific characteristics which the Father lacks, or that we are thereby portraying what the Son actually looked like. Orthodoxy of course sometimes does make that latter claim,[60] but even were this true, it still would not seem to me to establish the necessity for some absolute difference. Though one hesitates to make such a funda-mental and divisive criticism, it is hard to resist the conclusion that such objections really stem from residual notions of the Father as in some sense superior to the other two persons in virtue of being their

[56] L. Ouspensky, *Theology of the Icon* (Crestwood, NY: St Vladimir's Seminary Press, 1992), 287–409. Condemnations by Muscovite Councils in the sixteenth and seventeenth centuries are noted, one of 1667 describing the image in question as 'altogether absurd and improper' (371).

[57] Including some that modify the image in interesting ways, as in an eighteenth-century example from the Greek monastery of Toplou, which places the dove in the middle perched on a globe of the world.

[58] In its origins there are heavy borrowings from the pagan world, while in the case of El Greco it is now argued that he was already subject to Western influence long before he moved west from Crete. Cf. R. Cormack, *Painting the Soul* (London: Reaktion, 1997), 167–217.

[59] For examples of the argument, John of Damascus, *Orations on the Holy Icons*, esp. I. 15; II. 5; III. 8 and 26. The *aperigraptos* had become *perigraptos* (circum-scribed).

[60] As in the story of the *acheiropoietos* icon, allegedly made by Christ himself in response to a request from King Agbar of Edessa.

arche or source.[61] Perhaps however, rather than expressing it thus, the objection could be put more neutrally by saying that space must be left for God to be other than incarnate, and such a prohibition would at least preserve such an insight.

The question then becomes whether this is the only way of underlining that claim, or whether some of the criticized images, when correctly understood, do not make the point equally well. Take Masaccio's great painting on the subject, probably from shortly before his death in 1428 at the age of 27.[62] Art historians often wax lyrical over his naturalism and in his innovating use of light and perspective, and it is indeed true that he gives us a sense of the Trinity being presented to our vision in a chapel whose arch vault recedes before our very eyes. What, however, is not always noted is that, while the naturalism of the donor with his ear pushed back by his cap is in one plane and the crucified Christ in another, the Father exists quite outside space altogether. Masaccio thus succeeds in conveying the idea that, while the Son entered our space-time horizons, the Father did not. In short, the Father is imagined rather than seen, and the structure as a whole thus takes us from the corpse at the bottom through crucifixion into a world totally beyond space and time. Admittedly, the same claim cannot always be made for those who use the *Gnadenstuhl* image. Dürer in giving a papal tiara to the Father draws him forcibly back into our world, while Ribera's intention seems to have been to capture a single eternal moment renewed at each Eucharistic sacrifice.[63] But Masaccio is by no means alone in conveying the sense that the meaning of God is not exhausted by the depiction. El Greco's *Trinity* would be an outstanding example.[64] Not only is Dürer's papal tiara replaced by the headgear taken at the time to be indicative of the

---

[61] Ouspensky talks of 'the unrepresentable divine essence' (308). Some modern Russian theologians, though, have defended such representations: ibid. 385 ff.

[62] In Santa Maria Novella in Florence and only restored to view in 1861. For illustration and example of a treatment against which I am reacting, J. Takács, *Masaccio* (Budapest: Corvina, 1980), Tafel 25–7. Against my interpretation is the shelf on which the Father appears to stand; in favour is Masaccio's failure, uniquely in this case, to use foreshortening.

[63] In the Prado, Madrid. Shared conventions rather than direct dependence on El Greco is the favoured view: A. E. Pérez Sánchez, *L'opera completa del Ribera* (Milan: Rizzoli, 1978), tav. XX, n. 98.

[64] For a comparison of the work of El Greco and Dürer, R. G. Mann, *El Greco and his Patrons* (Cambridge and New York: Cambridge University Press, 1986), 32–6, ill. 6–7.

office of the Jewish High Priest and discrete cherubs used to indicate the throne, more importantly there is also a profound sense of movement from this world into that of the divine. Moreover, because it is the human body of the Son that is being drawn into this new world, the painting suggests the possibility of a similar transformation for ourselves.

This is not to say that the *Gnadenstuhl* image was without its problems. On the contrary, patrons and artists were alike aware of the difficulties, and that is no doubt why we find various alternative solutions being explored. Let me briefly note seven such alternative formats, taking them in historical order. As we shall observe, they achieve varying degrees of success. Roughly contemporary with Masaccio's *Trinity* is Van Eyck's famous polyptych *The Adoration of the Lamb*. In the lower painting Christ is portrayed as a lamb shedding its blood on the altar, while in the upper the Father is given a human form he never had, and the dove beneath at the top of the lower painting used to link them both. With symbolic forms of representation so prominent, one might detect a return to the more abstract formats that characterized earlier allusions to the Trinity, such as that in San Clemente in Rome, where originally, it is sometimes argued, each of the persons had only a symbolic representation.[65] Certainly, some art historians have seen this painting of Van Eyck's as essentially conservative in its approach compared with his later treatment of religious themes.[66] What, however, I find most interesting in the painting is the artist's treatment of the Spirit. The vertical axis of the three persons finds its strongest focus in the rays of light emanating from the dove which has been encased in a sun, the symbol, as we have seen, once used to indicate the presence of God in its totality. Thereby any demotion of the Spirit is avoided, while the fact that its arc is incomplete forces us to complete it through incorporating the Father above. At the same time the sheer scale of the Father prevents us from reading any of the images too literally.[67]

Towards the end of the same century Fillipo Lippi gave the

[65] Created before 1128, it shows a hand stretching down to a cross on which twelve doves are represented. The less impressive figure of Christ himself may be later. For illustration, C. R. Dodwell, *The Pictorial Arts of the West 800–1200* (New Haven: Yale University Press, 1993), 158.

[66] So C. Harbison, *Jan Van Eyck: The Play of Realism* (London: Reaktion, 1991), 193–7.

[67] Note also St Christopher, leading the pilgrims, out of proportion on the right.

imagery a quite new context by applying it to Christ's nativity,[68] or rather an apparently quite new context, since there are significant overlaps once one probes more deeply. On its surface the painting can easily come across as a sentimental picture with none of Van Eyck's mystic depths, but closer inspection discloses a programmatic painting about prayer, sacrifice, and denial. Initially we are attracted by the benign gaze upon the child of the Virgin and heavenly Father, and think no more of the finger in the Infant's mouth until we look more closely at the landscape. Then we discover its invitation on the right to sacrifice with the pelican and stacked logs, and on the left to rocky steps which carry us beyond the young Baptist to a praying St Bernard. Thus, though a direct vertical links the three persons of the Trinity, the steps on either side imply the possibility for ourselves of sharing in that divine life, arduous though that might be.

Bellini's *Baptism of Christ* dates from the beginning of the sixteenth century.[69] Unlike Piero della Francesca's more famous painting of the same scene, the Father is given a face, but like that other painting there are once more three angels in attendance, whose presence is almost certainly, in part at least, necessitated by the desire to hint at the trinitarian unity. But this is by no means the sole device used. Christ's loin cloth is tinged with the same pink as the Father's robe, while a more accurate reflection is indicated by the presence of the same complementary colours as those worn by the Father in Christ's upper garments which two of the angels hold in safe-keeping nearby. A quite brilliant device is adopted as a means of acknowledging the participation of the Holy Spirit in that same divine unity: a second bird is introduced at the forefront of the picture—a parakeet with exactly the same colouring. An additional purpose served by the angels is to indicate the possibility of our own involvement in the scene. The second is already kneeling, while the one nearest to the viewer is just beginning to embark upon the process. The intersection of heaven and earth is thus seen as having an impact on our world, with the angels functioning for these purposes at one and the same time as members of both sides of the divide.

Not much later Dürer completed his very different *Adoration of the Trinity*. Here we are closer to the *Gnadenstuhl* format, but with

[68] For illustration and comment, Mannini and Fagioli, op. cit., 52 and 127.

[69] R. Goffen, *Giovanni Bellini* (New Haven: Yale University Press, 1989), 163-7.

David Brown

two major differences: first, the dove of the Spirit is made the summit of the painting, hovering as it is over Father and Son alike; second, a great host of humanity joins in the adoration. What is interesting, though, about the various groups, in contrast to those in Van Eyck's *Adoration*, is that, although heaven and earth are distinguished, the painter places himself alone on earth, with the Church, whether dead or alive, moved to heaven. The fact that this includes the donor and his son-in-law might seem like self-serving cringing on the part of the painter, but, significantly, both are shown needing the help of others to see the vision, in the one case from a cardinal, in the other from an angel. The question of which time-space realm the Church inhabits is thus set acutely before us.[70]

Titian's mid-century *Trinity in Glory* abandons the vertical, and places the Spirit at the centre, to preside over Father and Son on either side, each of whom is dressed in blue and holds a globe.[71] The change might be thought to make for a static composition, but far from it. There is much more a sense of movement than was the case with Dürer, and in fact the painting gives the impression of all humanity being drawn heavenwards. Also in contrast to Dürer, monarchs no longer wear their crowns. The emperor Charles V is plainly dressed in white, with his crown at his feet. Ecclesia is also much more prominent. In Dürer she appeared on the sidelines, holding a chalice; here in the centre of the painting she presents the ark that is the Church to the Trinity above. Of particular interest is the dove with an olive leaf in his beak perched on top. Such double representations of the dove are to be found in other painters,[72] and may have served the function of warning that imagery is being used here, and not any simple reality. In this case it would seem particularly apposite since the most common modern theory for the source of the imagery at Christ's baptism is that it derives from the story of the Flood and so alludes to the notion of baptism as a new creation.

Next, an example from the eighteenth century, Tiepolo's *St*

---

[70] The influence of Augustine has been suggested: E. Panofsky, *The Life and Art of Albrecht Dürer*, 4th edn. (Princeton: Princeton University Press, 1955), 125–31.

[71] In the Prado in Madrid. For an illustration, F. Pedrocco, *Titian* (Florence: Scala, 1993), 52.

[72] e.g. Crivelli's *Annunciation* in the National Gallery, London, where the dove of the annunciation is repeated in the dove in the background that brings news of the new status for the town of Ascoli Piceno.

Clement Adoring the Trinity.[73] This time, Father and Son are aligned, with the Spirit portrayed as flying from them towards the pope. Initially, though, the painting is a disappointment since it seems so full of suggestions of wealth and only the Father seems to engage the pope's eye with Christ strangely distant. But closer attention suggests a rather different focus, with the axis of the Son with his cross raised aloft paralleling the cherub sitting beneath the pope and ready to hand him his papal cross. In other words, we have an argument to the effect that the Father sends the Spirit upon the pope to enable him to become Christ-like by taking up his cross, and so the initial distance in Christ's gaze is deliberate, in order to suggest that chain of events. Finally, as a rare example from the twentieth century, we might note the work of the German-born artist, Hans Feibusch, in the church of St Alban's, Holborn, in London, dating from the 1960s. This magnificent mural behind the high altar of *The Trinity in Glory* shows some interesting differences from the original sketch. Whereas originally the Father had dominated the picture,[74] now he recedes into the background with, most significantly of all, Son and Spirit roughly aligned and breaking the spatial bound of Alban's vision to enter our own space.

There are four main conclusions which I want to draw from this survey of incarnational imagery. The first is that the accusations that God has thereby been wholly naturalized are quite unfair, and caused by misreadings of the pictorial frame. Normally, there is some way of indicating that not all of the content belongs to this world, whether through the medium of where the horizon is placed (the usual convention), through the Father stepping out of the frame altogether as in Masaccio, or through the subtle play of symbolism as in Bellini's angels or Titian's repetition of the dove. Unadulterated naturalism is thus more in the eye of the careless observer than any part of the artist's intention. Second, what is of interest to the latter is less the doctrine as such or the raison d'être of its unity and much more its relevance to us. So it is the point of access to the divine which is stressed, and with that its ability to carry us beyond the events of this world into the transcendent realm. That is why it is never enough simply to note the three

[73] W. Barcham, *Tiepolo* (London: Thames & Hudson, 1992), 70–1. Unfairly, in my view, contrasted with another Trinity of his by Levey, op. cit., 75–7.

[74] For the original sketch, D. Coke (ed.), *Hans Feibusch* (London: Lund Humphries, 1995), 72.

figures in line but also how often the line interests with a horizon
to suggest contact, or else ascent invited by other means such as
Filippo Lippi's two rock-hewn staircases. Third, of the three images
it is the Father's which is consistently the least successful, though
here it seems to me that the artist is less to blame and more the
restraints of Scripture. For the requirement of fatherhood, particularly when reinforced by the image of Ancient of Days, seems to
have inhibited further development, whereas the vagueness of the
allusion to the dove at Jesus' baptism allowed more room for
creative possibilities. The result is no ordinary dove in several of the
paintings which we have discussed, with it in effect becoming a
figure of the sun. Nor was this by any means the only option that
was explored. In the early fifteenth-century *Rohan Book of Hours*
the artist experiments with the Spirit as a curtain of wings and as
a playmate of the Christ-Child on the Father's lap, while in the
sixteenth century we find the dove skimming the waters of the
Jordan, or drinking from the chalice into which Christ's blood
flows, thereby symbolizing the source of our own sustenance.[75]
Finally, one might note that the question of trinitarian relations is
largely ignored and indeed to some degree subverted, not, I think,
because of the conceptual difficulty of the issue but because of the
way in which such considerations would have run foul of the
visual impact of the imagery. Instead, every imaginable relation
between the three seems to have been explored in artistic attempts
to achieve dramatic and visual power. To judge matters on formal,
doctrinal grounds would, it seems to me, be tantamount almost to
a category mistake, for we have no reason to believe that the
demands of the visual will always pull in precisely the same
direction as doctrine or purely verbal imagery.

IV   CONCLUSION

In Olivier Messiaen's great organ work, *Méditations sur le mystère
de la sainte Trinité*, the three persons of the Trinity are each given
clearly defined musical themes, which are heard both separately
and interwoven.[76] The ear is thus allowed to hear both distinctness

---

[75] For illustrations of the latter two images, J. Clifton, *The Body of Christ* (Munich:
Prestel, 1998), 64–5, 116–17.

[76] Messiaen provides a detailed commentary with the score on the 'language' he

and underlying principles of unity. It is not true that there is no possibility of similar temporal developments and movement in art. Clearly there can be, as the artist invites from the viewer deeper exploration of his theme, and things come to be noticed that did not engage the eye at first glance. Movement can also be suggested by the position of the figures or by the direction of the gaze of figures within the frame. Even so, there is still this difference, that these kinds of dynamic are much less under the control of visual artists. There is therefore a greater need to make assumptions about anterior knowledge, as well as ensure that the first impression is decisive in eliciting further reflection. These are features which we have observed in respect of each of the three types of imagery which I have distinguished. Renaissance triadic heads and Murillo's *Two Trinities*, for instance, convey a rather different and more powerful meaning once they are placed in the historical context of their background assumptions. But that does not mean that all is therefore dependent on those background assumptions. On the contrary, artists have sometimes felt the need significantly to modify those assumptions in order to achieve the decisive initial impact. That proved particularly so in respect of the way in which the *Gnadenstuhl* image came to be modified.

Perhaps the greatest literary image for the Trinity is that which concludes Dante's *Divine Comedy*, but visually it is quite unappealing,[77] and much the same might be said of the images of the book with which the New Testament canon ends, which even a great artist like Dürer could only succeed in making at most, in my view, faintly comic. Our eye does not make quite the same demands as our ear or our intellect. In reading we can quickly decode metaphors into simpler language or else complement with alternative images. When a painting is set before us, this is something which we cannot do, and indeed part of the power of such images must lie in their refusal to be decoded and so fade from the memory. The tragedy of much of the history of Christian attitudes towards art is that simple verbal tests have been mindlessly applied to works of the visual imagination, with the result that instead of

has employed and its relation to Scripture and Aquinas. This includes the marking of specific sections as *Père*, *Fils and Saint Esprit*: op. cit., Paris: Alphonse Leduc, 1973.

[77] For a visual example of the problem C. H. Taylor and P. Finley, *Images of the Journey in Dante's Divine Comedy* (New Haven: Yale University Press, 1997), 264.

such images being allowed to feed the imagination and so deepen faith, they have been treated as faulty intellectual exercises. What is properly required of us is that such visual images first be allowed to stand in their own right, and then perhaps, so far from merely complementing verbal approaches, they will be able to offer their own critique of them.

Plate 1: *The Holy Trinity* by Titian, Prado, Madrid. Photograph: The Bridgeman Art Library, London. Cf. 348.

Plate 2: *The Holy Trinity with the Virgin and St John* (fresco) by Tommaso Masaccio, Santa Maria Novella, Florence, Italy. Photograph: The Bridgeman Art Library, London. Note how the image of the Father is not contained by the vault: cf. 345.

Plate 3: *Baptism of Christ* by Giovanni Bellini, Santa Corona, Vicenza.
Photograph: The Bridgeman Art Library, London. Cf. 347.

Plate 4: *St Augustine in His Study* by Filippo Lippi, Galleria Degli Uffizi, Florence. Photograph: The Bridgeman Art Library, London. Cf. 335.

14

Preaching the Trinity: A Preliminary Investigation

MARGUERITE SHUSTER

I Introduction

A moment's reflection reminds us that the Trinity is, at least implicitly, everywhere in Christian worship. We normally begin our Christian pilgrimage with baptism in the triune Name. If we are married in the church, the Name of Father, Son, and Spirit is invoked. The 'Gloria Patri' honours Father, Son, and Holy Ghost; the 'Doxology' praises them. We may not sing 'Holy, Holy, Holy', often called the finest of the trinitarian hymns, every Sunday; but much traditional hymnody refers in successive verses to the Persons of the Trinity. And the most common benedictions are trinitarian in form: even that from Numbers 6: 24-6 adumbrates the Trinity by the threefold repetition of '*lord*'. References to God in prayers and preaching, too, shift readily (if sometimes imprecisely, to the finicky ear) among the Persons. Rarely indeed, however, will one hear *explicit* reference to the Trinity. In fact, when Steve Davis and I consulted about my writing on the topic of sermons on the Trinity, we both suspected that the only sermon either of us had ever heard on the Trinity was preached by him- or herself. We thought this might have potential for being a very short paper!

In one sense, of course, this alleged deficit is scarcely surprising; since, as critics of every form of abstraction never cease reminding us, the term 'Trinity' is not found in the Bible, so a 'biblical' preacher cannot be condemned for failing to use it. Some would go further and argue vociferously that we ought to emulate Scripture's concreteness and modesty and not clutter our minds and speech—and certainly not our sermons—with ancient Greek philosophical speculation. Surely (and with this point I agree), people's deep sense of the Trinity will be shaped primarily by devotional and liturgical practices in which the presence of the Trinity is, indeed, more often assumed than named. It would be a loss, not a gain, if the awe of encountering God in worship were bartered for self-conscious manipulation of studied verbal formulas.

But that taking this tack will not finally suffice for even remotely reflective people is obviously the reason doctrine was developed in the first place. The question is just *why* we (and Scripture) speak as we do, and why it could be dangerous even, or especially, to our life of devotion and worship if we were to come to speak quite differently.[1] When theological faculty and clergy fail to be a bit diligent in the precision department, not only does language begin to slip, but the slippage tends to be cumulative. Over not so very great a period of time, the language of worship comes no longer to convey accurately what Christians have traditionally believed (most especially in churches that do not rely on a traditional, set liturgy, of course), and so worshippers are no longer imbued virtually unconsciously with sound doctrine.[2] I suspect this question of doctrinal precision is more critical today than it has been for a long time, for two reasons: first, persons in the average congregation are stunningly ignorant of Christian fundamentals, lacking anything faintly resembling the routine catechetical instruction of an earlier era;[3] and second, interfaith dialogue brought on by day-to-day encounters with increasing numbers of persons from other lands and non-Christian traditions puts pressure

---

[1] I will say at the outset what I will press further later on: I do not agree that we are so shut up to our own experience that we cannot appeal to anything beyond our subjectivity, and that to suppose we refer to anything 'out there' is illusion. I acknowledge, of course, the inevitable distorting character of position and perspective.

[2] I have granted above the serious danger of succumbing to a wooden formalism. Still, those shaped by the content of orthodox tradition may safely exercise a certain freedom of reformulation that quickly becomes hazardous when indulged by those who have not been shaped by that tradition. (A brief probe of books promoted as Protestant 'worship resources' will yield a harvest of crass heresy that should suffice to sober even the most optimistic.)

[3] One preacher notes how astounded Dwight L. Moody was when, speaking to a group of Scottish schoolchildren, he asked who God is: instead of seeing the downcast eyes and hearing the embarrassed mumbles to be expected of American children, he got the unison response, 'God is a Spirit, infinite, eternal, and unchangeable in his being, wisdom, power, holiness, justice, goodness, and truth' [from the Westminster Shorter Catechism, in which these children were well instructed] (20, pp. 60–1: for the sake of economy, references to sermons on the Trinity will be by number: see Appendix 2).

on us to be clear about what we consider essential to our own understanding of 'God'. To fail in our preaching to give our people any intellectual tools to help them understand why Christians speak as they do, leaves them with good grounds to consider Christianity incoherent or at best sloppy in its fundamental structure and the Christian God as something no more recognizable than what someone described as an 'oblong blur'. Not least important, they are also left without means to give any sort of coherent response to those from other traditions who might ask them for an accounting of the hope that is in them (1 Pet. 3: 15).[4]

II METHOD

As a means of testing the seemingly obvious hypothesis that very few sermons deal explicitly with the Trinity, I reviewed the subject and Scripture indexes of the thirteen-volume *20 Centuries of Great Preaching*[5] and volumes 34 through 76 of *Pulpit Digest*.[6] I checked all references to the Trinity or to Trinity Sunday, to all of the New Testament texts assigned for Trinity Sunday by the Revised Common Lectionary, and to fifteen other texts commonly cited in discussion of the Trinity.[7] This procedure generated some twenty

---

[4] This point was already made by Read in 1956 (2, p. 32).

[5] Clyde E. Fant, Jr., and William M. Pinson, Jr., *20 Centuries of Great Preaching*, 13 vols. (Waco, Tex.: Word, 1971).

[6] Earlier volumes were incomplete in the resources immediately available to me; and I also judged that forty-three volumes would provide an adequate sample for my immediate purposes. (Of the forty-three volumes, a very few issues were missing, one of which contained a sermon, apparently on Exod. 3: 1–14 and Rom. 11: 33–6, indexed as referring to the Trinity.) Editors of the volumes are as follows: 34–48, Ralph C. Raughey, Jr. (with Samuel McCrea Covert serving as 'Senior Editorial Advisor' from the middle of the 38th through the 48th); 49–52, Charles Wheeler Scott; 53–62, Charles L. Wallis (with the help of Charles L. Allen and E. Paul Hovey up to November of 1973, and W. F. Edwards taking over in May of 1982, until the end of the year); 63–5, James W. Cox; 66–76, David A. Farmer.

[7] While use of the Revised Common Lectionary is obviously anachronistic, my point was to focus first on texts currently considered both relevant and basic. The additional texts do not exhaust the possibilities but were chosen because they at least allude to (or may be taken to allude to) all three Persons of the Trinity. I did not pursue texts important to the development of the doctrine that refer to only two of the three Persons because I assumed that if the subject index did not suggest that sermons on such texts treated the Trinity, the texts in themselves would be unlikely to provoke such a sermon. That such a conclusion is unlikely to be broadly wrong may be seen in the chart (Appendix 1): only one of the non-lectionary trinitarian texts generated a sermon explicitly on the Trinity. When the text contains a range

sermons on the Trinity, with three preachers represented by two sermons each; and a few more in which the Trinity was at least mentioned in passing, or in which the whole structure of the sermon was strongly trinitarian (however, a trinitarian structure is not the same thing as an explicit reference, and I did not treat it as such). None was dated earlier than 1930. The results may be tabulated as presented in Appendix 1.

No Roman Catholic authors turned up in this sample. Desiring to represent them as well, I looked explicitly for sermons on the Trinity by Roman Catholic theologians. Surprisingly enough, a contemporary collection of 120 of Karl Rahner's sermons arranged according to the church year yielded nothing: there was no sermon for Trinity Sunday.[8] Turning to stalwarts John Henry Newman and Ronald Knox, I did find three substantial sermons. However, since my procedure here was entirely different from that which I used to obtain my other examples, and since two of the pieces are nineteenth instead of twentieth century, I touch rarely on these sermons in my general analysis but instead remark upon them separately.

The sceptical might rightly wonder, with respect to the *20 Centuries* and *Pulpit Digest* collections, if something besides ministerial resistance to doctrinal preaching could be at work here—like, for instance, *editorial* resistance to doctrinal preaching. That question cannot be entirely laid to rest with regard to the *20 Centuries* volumes, which are prepared by the same two people throughout.[9]

---

of verses, I looked at sermons on texts with overlapping verses or even on a single verse within the range, if the verses involved held any promise (e.g. regarding Matt. 28: 16–20, I certainly looked at sermons on Matt. 28: 19, but not at sermons only on Matt. 28: 16; regarding sermons on John 3: 1–17, I looked at sermons on John 3: 16, since that text alone could conceivably generate a sermon on the Trinity, though as a matter of fact it did not in my sources). When several texts were listed as texts for the sermon, I used for this analysis only those that figured somehow in the sermon itself (and there was seldom more than one that did).

[8] *The Great Church Year*, ed. Albert Raffelt (New York: Crossroad, 1994). Nor is there a sermon on the Trinity to be found among those included in the summary of Rahner's sermons on additional texts at the back of the book.

[9] However, one may at least note that Clyde Fant is not theoretically averse to doctrinal preaching. Indeed, he wrote elsewhere, 'The divorce between theology and practical homiletics is a primary reason for the parish minister's ongoing frustrations with preaching. Divorce may not be quite the proper term, however, since for many people theology and homiletics have never been wed. For some, they have never even been introduced' (*Preaching for Today*, rev. edn. (San Francisco: Harper & Row, 1987), xi–xii).

However, with respect to *Pulpit Digest,* the influence of editorial taste is clear and overwhelming: in volumes 53–65, there are *no* sermons designated for Trinity Sunday (one sermon on the Trinity from 2 Cor. 13: 14 appears in the issue for May–June in vol. 53, but it is not labelled as being for Trinity Sunday; and several editors were assisting in the transition taking place at this time), one implicit but not specific reference to the Trinity in a sermon on Matthew 28: 19, and one meagre, passing reference to the Trinity in a sermon on, and structured by, 2 Corinthians 13: 14 (the texts being two that will pull a reference if anything will!). These volume numbers correspond exactly to the editorial tenures of two people (Charles Wallis and James Cox; see note 6 above).

Another factor might be assumed to be the sheer difficulty of preaching on the Trinity, a factor that works against a preacher's efforts to meet those standards of excellence that at least in theory are applied to published work. Insofar as it is harder to preach on the Trinity than, say, on the love of God, one would suppose that sermons of the former type would be under-represented in print even if (contrary to my actual assumption) an equal number of such sermons were preached and submitted for publication. (This aspect of the question draws attention to the possible significance of the lectionary, or at least close attention to the Christian year, as providing discipline for preachers and editors alike.)

In any case, in the remainder of this paper, I shall first offer some general observations on the way the Trinity was treated in the general sample of sermons I examined. Then I shall briefly compare and contrast three groups of sermons: those on 2 Corinthians 13: 14, those explicitly on the Trinity which were not an exposition of any text (these two categories being the only ones with enough individual exemplars to provide any basis for internal comparison), and the three sermons by the two Roman Catholic theologians. Finally, I shall offer some reflections on issues facing the contemporary preacher who wishes to preach on the Trinity. And, lest there be any doubt, I should make explicit that my critique is made in the light of Nicene and Chalcedonian orthodoxy—a position I myself hold, though I recognize that it has come under attack from many quarters.

III General Observations

This is a survey of relatively recent historical materials, with all but one of those Protestant sermons analysed in any detail dating from the second half of the twentieth century. The time span is too short to show discernible changes in complexity, depth, or level of abstraction of the sermons: none of these sermons makes heavy intellectual demands on the hearer. (By contrast, if one looks to much earlier sermons in the *20 Centuries* collection and to the Roman Catholic sermons, one certainly can see a striking difference in the intellectual focus necessary to listen to them.) Of the twenty Protestant sermons on the Trinity, it appears that all were preached by clergy ordained in 'mainline' denominations; but there are too few individuals involved to suggest any denominational trends.[10]

On the structural side, it is remarkable how many of the sermons had only a single verse or no verse at all as their stated text (14 of the 20, as well as all three of the Roman Catholic sermons), and how many of the remaining half dozen really made no use of the full text as it develops. That is, whether allegedly text-based or not, the sermons tended to be topical, and hence rather generic, sermons on the Trinity, which gave them a somewhat surprising underlying sense of sameness, despite differences in style and theological precision among the various preachers.[11] As might be expected, a particularly strong tendency was to design the sermon around God's successive self-revelation in history (e.g. in creation, in Jesus, and at Pentecost; or, more subjectively, in an alleged instinctive sense of God's fatherhood, God's revelation of his character in Christ, and God's gift of his presence and power in our hearts and consciences in the Holy Spirit (sometimes these two schemas were mixed in a not very consistent way); see sermons 1, 5, 6, 9, 10, 11, 15, 17, 19). That the sermons should have an almost exclusive focus on the economic Trinity could easily be

---

[10] Of these sermons, six were preached by Episcopalians, four each by Presbyterians and Lutherans, two each by Baptists and Methodists, one by a minister of the United Church of Christ, and one by a minister whose affiliation I could not identify.

[11] Contrast no. 4, a sermon for Trinity Sunday on John 10: 30 that the preacher acknowledged did not deal with the whole Trinity (nothing on the Holy Spirit), but that skilfully and homiletically effectively expounded the text.

predicted simply on the grounds that homileticians of our day fear being condemned as 'abstract'; which tends, unfortunately but sometimes with reason, to be translated 'obscure, irrelevant, and dull'.[12] (And it is true that a few of the sermons whose authors were insufficiently concerned about such complaints took on something of the aura of a thin 'lecture for the laity'. These contained, perhaps, somewhat fewer infelicitous phrases than did sermons by some of the other preachers who were plainly striving for relevance, but they left the 'so what' question nowhere in sight.) Still, that preachers should feed resistance to abstract thought by subtly or explicitly scorning theological formulations and, especially, bashing the Athanasian Creed without mercy (sermons 1, 7, 8, 17, 20; contrast 11 and, especially, RC1 and RC2), I take to be unfortunate.[13] Such resistance to thinking theologically makes it easy for a preacher to assert confidently, for instance, that rephrasing the Trinitarian baptismal formula in terms of Creator, Redeemer, and Sustainer changes 'the language but not the meaning' (18, p. 43); leaving those having an informed feminist consciousness but only modest theological sophistication with no other hypothesis but sexism or sheer ignorance of modern trends to apply to preachers or theologians who resist this change.[14]

On the positive side, the preachers frequently made perfectly sound and clear observations. They often insisted not only that

[12] Contrast one sentence in no. 17, p. 27: the biblical story 'all has to do with what is either the most important question to which we can seek an answer, or one that is totally meaningless—the reality, the name and nature of the one true God and the possibility of both knowing him and loving him'. This sentence is the only strong assertion in these twenty sermons of the possibility that seeking to understand something about God's nature (God's *essential* nature?) may be a worthy human enterprise; the other sermons say much about mystery but seem not to be concerned about whether human experience reflects anything more fundamental.

[13] The scorning of credal formulations tends to be accompanied by the hazardous practice of canonizing one's own experience. For instance, 'I will be interested in and informed by the experiences of Paul, Augustine, Luther, and Wesley. But I will never, as long as I try to be a morally responsible person, subordinate my experiences to theirs. . . . I simply cannot turn over to anyone else the responsibility of stating the ultimate theological implications of the experiences I have in my own life' (9, p. 36). Few of us would take such assured responsibility for so much as repairing our cars. Or, for what must come close to being a maximally ambivalent (not to mention syntactically hopeless) statement, take this: 'Contrary to our thinking, the doctrine has been given a place of seeming importance, whether or not we are aware of it' (12, p. 37).

[14] My objection is not, of course, to the effort to make clear that God is not characterized by gender, but rather to the substitution of the economic for the immanent Trinity.

Christians do not worship three Gods, but also on the point that the oneness of God is a hallmark of the Judaism in which Christianity is rooted, so that anything resembling tritheism would have had enormous barriers to overcome (1, 2, 6, 12, 17, 18). Many of them emphasized that the doctrine of the Trinity was not thought up by theologians with nothing better to do, but was founded in irreducible Christian experience (1, 2, 5, 6, 7, 8, 9, 10, 12, 17; for example, the perfectly straightforward, 'The whole idea of the Trinity came as a result of the incarnation, the impact of Christ's life, and the ensuing experience with the Holy Spirit at Pentecost' (12, p. 38)). Several were able to speak positively of the doctrine as preserving an important mystery that points to the greatness of God (2, 12, 14, 17; also, especially profoundly, RC1).

On the not-so-positive side, the frequency of doctrinal gaffes, sometimes even in pieces wherein much was right, was simply dismaying—everything from modalistic and tritheistic statements and those speaking too weakly (even if not, in this sample, explicitly adoptionistically) of the divinity of the Son, to matters of confounding the Persons and denying the unity of the operations *ad extra*. (See Appendix 3 for samples—not an exhaustive collection!)[15] Several of the titles themselves beg for a fair measure of correction—sometimes forthcoming, sometimes not, in the sermons: 'God Speaks Through Many Voices' (9; well, yes; but for a sermon on the Trinity?); 'The Three Faces of God' (15; modalism?); 'One God, Our Mother' (16; again, for a sermon on the Trinity?); 'The Triangular God' (18; one may consider the symbol appropriate without embracing such a title); 'You Need Three Gods in One' (19; from a homiletics professor who surely should know better, and who did, for the most part, do better in the sermon itself).

Illustrative material and application understandably proved to be weak spots overall. They seemed to be managed best by those who did not seek analogies for the Trinity as such but who worked with one Person at a time; but this tactic meant that achieving unity (sermonic, but also with respect to the Godhead) and strong movement in the sermon was a challenge. (See Appendix 3 for problematic analogies to the Trinity—some with a sort of *vestigia*

---

[15] My dismay is related to these being published work; one can only assume that the efforts of less recognized preachers are unlikely to represent an overall improvement.

trinitatis flavour, but in any case none that would reverse the conventional judgement that analogies can be counted on to fail. One of the problems with analogies in such a crucial and difficult doctrinal arena is that the preacher needs to say something about their limits if they are not to mislead; yet illustrations that must be explained lose much of their force as illustrations.)

It should also be noted that many of the sermons that were not as a whole on the Trinity or did not refer to the Trinity by name nonetheless made perfectly good and orthodox remarks about the three Persons, such that trinitarian thinking was clearly pre-supposed and would likely work itself into the consciousness of hearers. As a particularly striking instance, consider these strong opening paragraphs in a sermon for Trinity Sunday that thereafter abandons the trinitarian theme entirely in favour of a missions/discipleship sermon on Isaiah 6: 8–9a:

On every Sunday in the year in some way the Church gives voice to its faith in the Holy Trinity—Father, Son, and Holy Ghost; for that is the great center of its faith. But on this one Sunday in the year, Trinity Sunday, we make the reaffirmation of that faith the emphasis of the day.

Together with the faith that God the Father, Creator of heaven and earth, is one and yet in His nature three-fold so that the Incarnation of Jesus Christ only showed us in time what was true in all eternity, and the manifestation of the Holy Spirit at Pentecost only expressed in history something which is of the everlasting nature of God, we also think today of the greatness and majesty of God. The inner richness of God, marked by our faith in the Trinity—the belief that, while in one sense God is indivisibly one, there is yet something like a society within Him—is also paralleled today by our faith in His wonder and greatness and glory.[16]

[16] Samuel M. Shoemaker, 'The Church's Commission in Our Day', *PD* 35, no. 205 (May 1955), 41. Similarly Billy Graham, in a sermon on the fruit of the Holy Spirit, remarks: 'The Bible teaches us that God is in Three Persons. God is One, but He is manifested in Three Persons. God the Father, God the Son, and God the Holy Spirit. Don't ask me to explain it—I can't. It's impossible for me to explain to you the Holy Trinity. I accept it by faith. God the Father, God the Son, who is equal with the Father in every respect. God the Holy Spirit, who is equal with the Son and with the Father in every respect' ('The Fruit of the Spirit', *20 Centuries*, vol. 12, p. 320). Again, Robert Murray McCheyne affirms: 'Each person of the Godhead has made Himself over to us to be ours. The Father says, "I am thy God"; the Son, "Fear not, for I have redeemed thee"; the Holy Ghost makes us a temple: "I will dwell in them, and walk in them". Is it much that we should do all we can for Him—that we should give ourselves up to Him who gave Himself for us?' ('Do What You Can', *20 Centuries*, vol. 4, p. 281). Yet again, in a high Calvinist sermon on our dependence on each Person in the Trinity for all our good, Jonathan Edwards says: 'Each person of the Trinity is equally glorified in this work: there is an

In my judgement, little better appears in any of the sermons that actually end up being on the Trinity; and one can only wish that this preacher had continued with the exposition of his stated theme (though one also wishes that the preacher had said simply '*God* . . . is one and yet in His nature three-fold' rather than '*God the Father* . . .': slips are easy to make!). We also find in a sermon for Pentecost Sunday the slightly awkward but nonetheless Trinitarian phrase, 'the Holy Spirit—the other self of God the Father and God the Son';[17] or again, in an evangelistic sermon, 'God's love of us makes him the great evangelist. He seeks us out and calls us home. He is the author of the good news. His Son brings the news through a ministry centering in his life, cross, and resurrection. The Holy Spirit applies it to our hearts.'[18] But, alas, one also finds the simply odd, like this remark in a sermon emphasizing Jesus' presence in our midst: 'Jesus is always in the midst of the revealed Godhead—Father, Son and Holy Spirit. He is always the Second Person in the Trinity. Where, on a number of occasions, we have reference to the Trinity, such as at Jesus' baptism or in a benediction or a baptismal formula, Jesus is always the Second Person— in the midst';[19] a mixture of the true and the misappropriated that is hard to disentangle.

On the other hand, a number of preachers preached sermons on baptism or discipleship or the Great Commission based explicitly on Matthew 28: 19 that manage not even to mention the 'baptismal formula', much less the Trinity;[20] similarly sermons on salvation[21] or on baptism[22] that make no reference to the Holy Spirit. It is hard to avoid the conclusion that preachers who achieve such feats have determined ahead of time that they will not allow their text greatly

absolute dependence of the creature on every one for all: all is of the Father, all through the Son, and all in the Holy Ghost. Thus God appears in the work of redemption as all in all' ('God Glorified in Man's Dependence', *20 Centuries*, vol. 3, p. 80).

[17] Johnstone G. Patrick, 'The Power, the Presence', *PD* 42, no. 288 (May 1962), 29.

[18] Elmer G. Homrighausen, 'Unfinished Business', *PD* 61, no. 497 (Jan.–Feb. 1981), 14.

[19] Wilbert D. Gough, 'Jesus in the Midst', *PD* 53, no. 400 (Mar.–Apr. 1973), 8.

[20] See sermons in *PD* June 1963, 39; Nov. 1968, 45; Mar. 1970, 41; Jan.–Feb. 1985, 51; and in *20 Centuries*, vol. 8, pp. 162–4 (a sermon by Walter Rauschenbusch on 'The Kingship of Christ' in which baptism but neither the Trinity nor the baptismal formula is mentioned).

[21] *PD* July–Aug. 1927, on John 3: 1–16.

[22] *PD* Nov. 1971, 45, on Eph. 4: 1–16.

to impinge on what they intend to say. (Incidentally, it is also interesting to note the texts that yield not a single sermon, or only one or two, in a forty-year span: analysis just of the Scripture indexes of various preaching journals, to note the texts used and those ignored, might make a provocative study.)

IV COMPARISONS AND CONTRASTS

Sermons on 2 Corinthians 13: 14 (nos. 5, 7, 11, 12, 13). In these five sermons, the prevailing neglect of interesting features of the text is very striking. Only two of the sermons (5, 12) mention that the verse comes at the end of 2 Corinthians; only two specify that it is a benediction or blessing (5, 11): not a very impressive showing for those concerned about context and genre in the interpretation of Scripture. Just one of the sermons (5) starts, as does the text, with 'the grace of our Lord Jesus Christ', reflects on why the benediction begins as it does, and allows that insight to give direction to the sermon (nos. 7 and 12 refer to the order in the middle of the sermon, but in a way that essentially buries the point).[23] The two remaining sermons (11, 13) use a threefold structure but begin with the Father.[24] One's sense that the preachers by and large intend topical sermons is confirmed by the fact that in speaking descriptively of the Persons, they do not tend to focus strongly on the specifics of the text (grace, love, fellowship: only no. 13 largely restricts itself to these). Rather, they treat more generally of their economic roles, most often with heavy and even disproportionate emphasis on the First Person as Creator, thus obscuring the apostle's striking choice of 'love' as the defining characteristic of the Father. Indeed, one sermon (7) speaks briefly of the three specifics of the text but then uses an analogy in which

[23] These two sermons I see as structurally weak in any case, with way too many preliminaries and generally too much going on, further compromised by a sort of defensiveness. (Contrast sermons 4 and 7 for strikingly different levels of effectiveness by the same preacher: the earlier sermon, in my judgement, is greatly superior, and partly because it seeks to do less.)

[24] In my judgement, sermon no. 5 is, of this group, both most faithful to the text and most effective sermonically; though no. 11, which relies in a positive way on the creeds, to the neglect of the text, also works rather well; as does no. 13, which does not intend to be a sermon explicitly on the Trinity (it is a sermon on essentials entitled, 'If This Were Your Last Sermon' (I personally disagree rather strongly with some of the preacher's assertions; but the sermon is nonetheless effective)).

the Father is characterized by law, the Son by love, and the Spirit
by life: surely not a helpful way to illumine a text, nor a helpful
way to maintain the unity of the Godhead. Another (11) focuses
on the Apostle's Creed as a starting point for its treatment of the
Father and Son, then refers to the text and to the Nicene Creed for
its discussion of the Holy Spirit.

Sermons not specifying a text (nos. 6, 9, 14, 15, 16). All of these
sermons were designed for Trinity Sunday, and all but one (16,
which is only very obliquely on the Trinity, while more intentionally expounding the feminine in God) are structured—apart from
sometimes lengthy and counterproductive preliminaries—in a
'Father, Son, Spirit' order. Two put heavy emphasis on the Father
as Creator (9, 15); three emphasize that Jesus reveals the heart of
God (6, 9, 15; no. 14 rather emphasizes the atonement); all but
one (16)[25] at least allude to God as present in the Holy Spirit. They
are by definition topical sermons; but it is nonetheless striking that
three of the sermons (6, 15, 16) not only do not expound a particular text, but do not refer to any texts at all, though one may
grant that their authors had scriptural witness in mind in a
general way. Several in this group of sermons appeared to be
particularly characterized by efforts of their authors to be, in some
sense, *au courant*[26]—a tendency that may reinforce perceptions of
the usefulness of taking a text, at least for those who suspect
that trendiness is no assured predictor of truth and substance in
preaching. Denominational distinctives were prominent in one
Presbyterian sermon (14): an approach to Communion from a
covenantal perspective, with a simple and orderly treatment of the

[25] No. 16 does say, 'The Holy Spirit broods over you as surely as the Holy Spirit
brooded over the chaos at the first creation, enabling you to come out of yourself
and say, "*I Am!*" To be able to say, "I am," is to be God-like' (p. 20): this is, indeed,
a kind of presence, but the whole tone is very far from what Christians usually
ascribe to the Spirit's role. Indeed, to say 'I am' in a 'God-like' manner may more
than just verge on blasphemy.

[26] References to death as an adventure and allusion to 'the death of God' and
the 'ground of all being' (6); resistance to 'dogmatism' and lengthy applause of
scientists' belief in design (9); problems of distinguishing 'male' or 'female' from
'masculine' or 'feminine', the issue of shame, God as manifested in Christ as 'fully
integrated', and assorted allusions from Jungian psychology (16): that these
matters relate remotely indeed to the Trinity is the point at the moment, not their
intrinsic value or lack thereof as preaching material. These three sermons are also
relentlessly experiential, in the sense of giving individual experience a kind of
absolute authority.

economic roles of the Persons in the upholding of the covenant. Both the shortest (no. 6, 2½ pages) and the longest (no. 9, 8 pages) of the twenty Protestant sermons on the Trinity happened to be in this group—a point not particularly significant in itself but still indicative of the considerable variety that would be expected and did in fact appear in this group.

Roman Catholic sermons. The two sermons by John Henry Newman and the one by Ronald Knox differ very greatly from the Protestant sermons in their manifest theological sophistication and precision of thought and statement.[27] They are blessedly free of careless blunders. They are also far longer on direct and unapologetic doctrinal teaching, far shorter on illustration (apart from reference to large numbers of supporting biblical texts—at least a dozen in each sermon), and significantly more cautious in the use of analogy. Newman, in particular, dealt primarily with the immanent Trinity, with a refreshing assumption of its relevance unexampled in the Protestant sermons. One cannot with assurance, though, attribute these striking differences simply to the Roman Catholicism of the authors, since Newman is from an earlier century; and both Newman and Knox were persons of far greater and more lasting stature, not to mention more thorough education, than that of most contributors to a monthly preaching journal.

However, for all their theological precision, these sermons tended not to be especially structurally 'tight' or to have strong movement—factors that I suspect would contribute, almost as much as their intrinsic intellectual difficulty, to problems hearers might have in grasping them and being motivated to stick with them.[28] In my view, they all attempted somewhat too much and went in too many directions. Only one (RC1) showed much focus

---

[27] As a matter of accuracy of detail, one should note that both sermons of Newman are dated about 1839, when he had begun to question his adherence to Anglicanism, but before his official conversion to Roman Catholicism in 1845. Thus, Anglicans might with reason claim these sermons. The preface to the first volume of his *Sermons and Discourses* notes that Newman himself had wished to suppress everything he had written before 1845 but was dissuaded by a friend, to whom he later expressed thanks. Knox, of course, was also a convert from Anglicanism.

[28] While the reader can certainly discern underlying design and unity in the sermons, I suspect the sheer quantity of material and complexity of development would be likely to overwhelm this unity for *hearers*, who do not have the luxury of looking back and sorting out the argument.

on any particular text (in this case, the idea of the divine Name in Matthew 28: 19—an idea soon abandoned, however, in the course of a 14-page sermon in which Newman sought to cover a great deal of ground). Another (RC3) gave three of its seven pages to the Trinity, as a background to its purportedly primary concern with the divinity of Christ (with attention to both incarnation and redemption—again, a big assignment for treatment in a few pages).[29] Application, beyond instruction in thinking rightly about God, tended to be in short supply, though one sermon (RC2) succeeded movingly in grounding our human hope for final peace in the happiness, completeness, and rest of the eternal God.

While these sermons are edifying to read for someone who cares about theology (especially in contrast to some of the sloppier and, if I may put it that way, more self-indulgent Protestant sermons), one gets indication that not only modern congregations could be expected to struggle in listening to them: Newman half-apologetically, half-chidingly remarked to his hearers, 'You may well bear once in the year to be reminded that Christianity gives exercise to the whole mind of man, to our highest and most subtle reason, as well as to our feelings, affections, imagination, and conscience' (RC1, p. 299)—a superfluous remark were resistance not foreseen. It is evident, then, that even the most talented and experienced scholar-preachers have long found sermonic exposition of the doctrine of the Trinity to be a somewhat daunting task.

---

[29] This sermon was allegedly on Col. 1: 15, with the verse cited in Knox's own translation: 'He is the true likeness of the God we cannot see; his is that first birth which precedes every act of creation'. This is a translation of the text that avoids by paraphrase the perplexities the RSV and NRSV might create for the modern reader ('He is . . . the firstborn of all creation'), and which the phrase πρωτότοκος πάσης κτίσεως has indeed generated in the history of doctrine. However, since the sermon was not centred in any one text, this 'amplified version' immediately affects only a paragraph or two of the whole. (For historical materials supporting not only Knox's interpretation but also Lightfoot's yet broader conclusion, ' "He stands in the relation of πρωτότοκος to all creation", i.e. "He is the Firstborn, and, as the Firstborn, the absolute Heir and sovereign Lord, of all creation"', see J. B. Lightfoot, *Saint Paul's Epistles to the Colossians and to Philemon* (repr., Grand Rapids: Zondervan, 1959 (1879)), 144–50. See also Gerald O'Collins, *Christology* (Oxford and New York: Oxford University Press, 1995), 33–5).

V Reflections

That preaching on a subject as abstract as the Trinity is difficult is not exactly news: indeed, while I teach a course in preaching Christian doctrine, I must admit that I myself do not assign a sermon on the Trinity for precisely that reason. Not only is the Trinity unique, but it is essentially without analogy, and hence makes it problematic to find compelling illustrative material. I suspect it is not without reason that the venerable practice of finding intimations of the Trinity in the created order has fallen on hard times. Not only can it, like allegorizing, lead to a certain excess of creativity; but also, it is vulnerable to the latest scientific discoveries. For instance, even if the figure of protons, neutrons, and electrons constituting one atom were not problematic for other reasons, it now leads an educated hearer to contemplate neutrinos, gluons, and quarks as objections (at which point she is no longer listening to the sermon!).

Furthermore, helping people understand why they should care, at any level beyond discussing what the various Persons of the Godhead provide for us (and which could be done by a tritheist or a modalist), requires thought. And it is very easy to fall off the trolley almost anywhere: the level of precision of statement required to avoid what the Church has considered to be doctrinal error is sufficiently great that many very good and well-informed preachers nonetheless can be found saying things that they surely would not wish to defend (a remark no doubt applicable to many of the statements quoted in Appendix 3). After pondering the possibility that discretion may indeed be the better part of valour in such matters, one may decide to avoid such rocky shoals altogether.

Add to the counsels of discretion, contemporary homiletical wisdom regarding the challenge of relating to an entertainment-oriented, fast-paced, personal-needs-obsessed culture: this wisdom would not give much immediate encouragement to the preacher who senses a need for deeper theological roots both for his or her own preaching and for the congregation to which he or she ministers. Narrative preaching that draws hearers into the story and lets them draw their own conclusions without laying on anything 'dogmatic' in tone or substance; pop-psychological approaches oriented towards feeding self-esteem and fostering coping skills; 'mini-sermons' that will not tax the attention spans of those accustomed to fast-moving images rather than to 'talking heads'; endless personal anecdotes and rather indiscriminate or self-serving self-revelation that seek to keep everyone feeling secure and cozy in the same [sinking?] boat; even verse-by-verse studies that comfort fundamentalist hearers who want to be assured that what they are hearing is biblical—none of these exactly lends itself to the disciplined proclamation of Christian doctrine.[30]

Even on seminary faculties, where one would hope for better, one finds 'theology bashing' to be great sport in certain quarters; so that students not drawn to systematic thought can find plenty of support for their already powerful avoidance mechanisms, not only from people in the practical department, but also from biblical studies people who resist what they fear to be homogenization of disparate texts and traditions, and yet again from those philosophical and constructive theologians who are deeply persuaded that anything resembling a dogmatic formulation constitutes by definition a breach of epistemic modesty. As a result many ministerial students graduate without being able to say anything coherent about their faith, and cover their ignorance and possible embarrassment by heaping scorn on everything but the experiential. Schleiermacher—who, not so incidentally, made his treatment of the Trinity a sort of postscript to his thought—casts a very long shadow. And, of course, it might be added that relativistic trends in society contribute their own share, as do theological commitments to doing all of one's theology 'from below' (which makes any sort of discussion of the immanent Trinity next to impossible).

I am well aware, then, that I am swimming against a powerful tide when I plead for a rebirth of doctrinal preaching in general, and even more so when I include in that plea difficult doctrines like that of the Trinity.[31] For that rebirth to take place, it seems to me

---

[30] I should clarify that I am not in principle opposed to narrative preaching or to the use of *lectio continua* as part of a full-orbed preaching ministry, though I would resist their exclusive use. I am, however, in principle opposed to the other techniques or ways of proceeding that I have lumped together into the same sentence.

[31] I am somewhat cheered to note two new 1997 volumes on doctrinal preaching: Millard Erickson and James Heflin's *Old Wine in New Wineskins* (Baker) and Robert Hughes and Robert Kysar's *Preaching Doctrine for the Twenty-First Century* (Fortress). Apparently people at different places on the theological spectrum share at least something of my concern. Neither of these volumes, however, gives substantive help with preaching on the Trinity.

that at least two things must happen. (1) Seminaries, ordaining bodies, and, one hopes, local congregations, must insist that prospective pastors be better educated theologically and refuse to pass, ordain, or call them until they can get the basics straight. Inability to say something clear and sensible about a fundamental doctrine, without resorting to jargon and *too-quick* retreats behind the shelter of mystery, is very good evidence that one does not understand it. (2) Ministers and laity alike must rediscover that there are real joys of the intellect, and that there are adventures to be had in exploring even that which is finally beyond one's grasp.[32] These two requirements interact: people (and especially ministers) who assume that doctrine is boring and irrelevant will not bother to learn it; people who do not know what they are talking about make a muddle that seems to establish that theology is only for those who have nothing better to think about or do. My own experience as a pastor leads me to believe that lay people are eager to understand their faith, provided doctrine is presented cogently and with its relevance elaborated. Many, however, have simply given up asking theological questions because they have become so accustomed to getting nothing enlightening by way of answers.

At the risk of being pulled under by a rip tide, I would like further to plead that in preaching, one not focus so exclusively on aspects of Christian faith as experienced that one altogether lose track of the traditional assumption that there is a truth, however imperfectly grasped and expressed, that lies behind the experiences. With respect to the Trinity, that means not completely losing track of the immanent Trinity in favour of the economic Trinity (while granting that most of one's exposition will probably deal with the latter). What is at stake here, in my view, is the question of whether God 'really is' who God reveals himself to be. If so, one can test one's experiences of God against that revelation, anticipate that God's ongoing activity will be consistent with his revelation, and stake one's life upon the character and faithfulness of God

---

[32] Note the helpful remark of David H. C. Read, in his sermon engagingly entitled 'The Thrill of the Trinity': 'We mustn't downplay the theology and think of it as an attempt to reduce a vivid religious experience to a series of propositions. There is a thrill of the mind as well as of the heart' (17, p. 30). Similarly in an earlier sermon: 'Isn't our first duty to re-educate ourselves in Christian doctrine, to lay hold of Christian truth for ourselves until it so lays hold of us that we are impelled to pass it on?' (2, p. 32). I consider it exceedingly unfortunate that this point of view was so seldom represented in this sample of sermons.

(granting, of course, that our appropriation of the revelation will be imperfect; but giving a certain weight to the tradition of saints who, looking in the same direction, have reported seeing something resembling the same thing). If not, one may ask if there is really anything that deserves the name of revelation at all. Are we absolutely shut up in experiences that are not only individual, but also so subject to cultural settings and trends that our efforts to see God are in the end only exercises in looking into a mirror?[33]

Indeed, if one gives maximum weight to experience, one may with reason suggest placing, say, Mohammed on a level with Jesus: apart from an essential Trinity, there is no reason why God might not manifest himself through any number of worthy prophets in different lands and at different times. Some have supposed that were life to be found on other planets, we might need to re-evaluate the place of Jesus:[34] possibly true, if one abandons the immanent Trinity; surely false if one holds to it. (I recognize that many would find the former outcome to be not only reasonable but highly desirable. By contrast, I am assuming—indeed, reasserting—here that biblical language regarding the Father, Son, and Spirit is such that it does provide grounds for speaking of an immanent Trinity.) It follows, of course, that I am not happy about replacing immanent with economic language in the baptismal formula or the liturgy of the church in general. (While I actively affirm the use of feminine imagery and language for God, I am not yet satisfied with any of the attempted solutions to the language problem overall, especially since I am concerned about the long-term effects of using impersonal language, even in the form of such locutions as 'Godself': the issue is not just aesthetics but a distancing abstractness.)

I do not see it as critical, doctrinally or for preaching, whether one prefers an individual or a social model of the Trinity, however; I take both to be approximations. The individual model has the homiletical advantage of keeping clear that the character and will of the Persons, and hence God's demand on our lives, is not divided and does not have components that can be played off

---

[33] I do not wish to be utterly unsophisticated about the power of one's life-situation in determining what one sees; all I intend to assert is that if that is the final word, to speak of God revealing himself is meaningless.

[34] e.g. Nancey Murphy, 'Jesus and Life on Mars', *Christian Century*, 113, no. 31 (30 Oct. 1996), 1028-9.

against one another. It may also help guard against some of the crasser ways of speaking about the Atonement, such as those that make a mere victim of Jesus. On the other hand, the social model better facilitates an understanding of God's nature as love and may reduce tendencies to picture God as, say, creating the world because he was lonely or as relating to human beings out of need.

When it comes to the specifics of sermon design, I would encourage preachers not to assume that the doctrinal sermon can take the place of a well-designed adult Sunday school class, in which a lecture format is appropriate and in which one can explore a doctrine in some depth and in an orderly way, without the fifteen- to twenty-minute time constraint placed on the typical sermon in a mainline church. My affirmation of the joys of the intellect and of the willingness of the laity to think does not translate into a proposal that sermons should be mini-lectures, 'to be continued next week'. In fact, I take a rather hard line in demanding that sermons be sermons, with decent structure and movement, a measure of emotive power, and a sermonic purpose that goes beyond the simply intellectual. For this reason (and some will perhaps consider this counsel surprising), I caution *against* strictly topical doctrinal preaching for all but the most experienced and skilful: my experience is that it tempts the preacher almost beyond bearing to take on too much and to become abstract and academic in the counter-productive sense. People tend, in my judgement, to have better success with taking a particular text (usually longer than a single verse) and expounding sermonically how a given doctrine, or aspects of a doctrine, come to life *in that text*, with its own colour and particularity.[35] This approach does not entail a refusal to refer to any other passages (though a tendency to scatter must be curbed); nor does it imply that one supposes the doctrine to be fully formed in a single passage, such that there is no need to have the broader context of the doctrine in mind. On the contrary, the person with any kind of systematic understanding of the doctrine at issue will preach in a way that is consistent with that broader understanding and not involve him- or herself in undoing next week what was said this week. All it entails is finding a way to help oneself not take on too much; and also, by attention

---

[35] As I implied above, I was surprised at how few sermons in my sample really probed any verse in any depth, much less took a more substantial passage and treated it seriously.

to the particularity of the text, to give one's sermon both scriptural integrity and the texture and detail that effective sermons require. This approach also helps hearers see for themselves where aspects of key doctrines come from, and it enables preachers to take up the doctrine from several angles without just being repetitious. If preachers were, say, to take for several years running a different one of the lectionary texts for Trinity Sunday, and from it preach a sermon on the Trinity, preacher and congregation alike would be better informed about this foundational doctrine of the Christian faith.

APPENDIX 1: TEXTS USED BY PROTESTANT PREACHERS

	Sermons on the Trinity		Sermons referring to the Trinity		Sermons having no reference to the Trinity	
	20 Centuries	*PD*	*20 Centuries*	*PD*	*20 Centuries*	*PD*
Lectionary texts						
Matt. 28: 16–20		2 same preacher		1	1	10
John 3: 1–17		2			4	18 (mostly on John 3: 16)
John 16: 12–15 (or 6–26)		1 (more on H.S.)			3	4
Rom. 5: 1–5						9
Rom. 8: 12–17					1	3
2 Cor. 13: 5–14		5 (or 4)		0 (or 1)		
Other typical texts						
Matt. 3: 16–17						3
Luke 1: 35						5
Luke 3: 22						1
John 14: 11–26				2	3	5
Acts 2: 33						2
1 Cor. 12: 4–6	1			1		5
Eph. 2: 18–22					1	4
Eph. 4: 4–6			1			7
1 Thess. 1: 2–5						
2 Thess. 2: 13–14					1	
Titus 3: 4–5					1	1

Heb. 2: 3-4			
1 Pet. 1: 2		1 (same sermon as 2 Thess. ref.)	
Jude 20-1			
Rev. 1: 4-5		1	1
Other texts used			
Exod. 3: 1-14	1(+1 secondary)		
Isa. 6: 8-9a		1	
Mark 14: 8		1 (weak)	
John 1: 38-9	1		
John 10: 30	1		
Acts 1: 8			1 (weak)
1 Cor. 12: 9-31		1 (strong)	
Gal. 5: 22-6		1	
1 John 4: 1-2	1		
Rev. 22: 13		1	
no text (used)	5		

APPENDIX 2: PROTESTANT SERMONS ON THE TRINITY

(arranged by date, earliest first)

1. Coffin, Henry Sloan, 'The Home of the Soul'. John 1: 38-9. Presbyterian. *20 Centuries*, vol. 8, pp. 302-8 (1930).

2. Read, David H. C., 'In the Name of the Father, and of the Son, and of the Holy Ghost'. Matt. 28: 19. Presbyterian. *PD* 36, no. 217 (May 1956), 31-6.

3. Hulme, William E., 'The Coming of the Holy Spirit'. John 16: 5-11, 14-16, 20-2. Lutheran. *PD* 40, no. 266 (June 1960), 23-7.

4. Ferris, Theodore P., 'The Meaning of the Trinity'. John 10: 30. Episcopalian. *PD* 42, no. 289 (June 1962), 23-8.

5. Horne, Chevis F., 'Experiencing the Trinity'. 2 Cor. 13: 14. Baptist. *PD* 47, no. 343 (May 1967), 35-40.

6. Riddle, Sturgis L., 'What Do We Mean by Trinity?' No text. Episcopalian. *PD* 47, no. 343 (May 1967), 33-4+.

7. Ferris, Theodore P., 'God in Three Persons'. 2 Cor. 13: 14. Episcopalian. *PD* 49, no. 365 (May 1969), 33-6.

8. Griffin, Dennis V., 'Blowing with the Wind'. John 3: 1-15. Lutheran. *PD* 48, no. 355 (June 1968), 35-8.

9. Bosley, Harold A., 'God Speaks Through Many Voices'. No use of text, though Acts 14: 8-18 is listed. Methodist. *PD* 50, no. 375 (May 1970), 29-36.

10. Krumm, John M., 'Will the Real God Identify Himself?' 1 John 4: 1-2; also lists Exod. 3: 1-15. Episcopalian. *PD* 51, no. 385 (May 1971), 33-7.

11. Gibson, Raymond W., 'Will the Real God Please Stand Up?' 2 Cor. 13: 14. Methodist. *PD* 52, no. 395 (May 1972), 23-8.

12. Bailey, Robert W., 'The Mystery of God's Revelation'. 2 Cor. 13: 14. Baptist. *PD* 53, no. 401 (May-June 1973), 36-41.

13. Brokhoff, John R., 'If This Were Your Last Sermon'. 2 Cor. 13: 14. Lutheran. *PD* 58, no. 433 (Sept.-Oct. 1978), 65-9.

14. Leyden, Stuart G., 'A Trinitarian Communion'. No use of text, though John 14: 25-31 is listed. Presbyterian. *PD* 66, no. 479 (May-June 1986), 31-4.

15. Cheadle, Jeffrey B., 'The Three Faces of God'. No text, though the lectionary readings are listed—Prov. 8: 22-31; Rom. 5: 1-5; John 16:12-15. Denomination unknown. *PD* 67, no. 485 (May-June 1987), 15-19.

16. Jones, Alan, 'One God, Our Mother'. No text. Episcopalian. *PD* 69, no. 479 (May-June 1989), 19-22.

17. Read, David H. C., 'The Thrill of the Trinity'. Matt. 28: 19, with all lectionary texts listed—Isa. 6: 1-8; 1 John 4: 13-15; Matt. 28: 16-20. Presbyterian. *PD* 71, no. 503 (May-June 1990), 27-30.

18. Barnett, Roger A., 'The Triangular God'. 1 Cor. 12: 4-6, with 1 Cor. 12: 1-11 and Rom. 8: 9-17 listed. United Church of Christ. *PD* 73, no. 515 (May-June 1992), 42-4.

19. Brokhoff, John R., 'You Need Three Gods in One'. John 3: 5. Lutheran. *PD* 74, no. 522 (July-Aug. 1993), 74-7.

20. Vaughn, J. Barry, 'Our God: Unity and Community'. Exod. 3: 1-14. Episcopalian. *PD* 75, no. 527 (May-June 1994), 60-2.

Roman Catholic Sermons on the Trinity

RC1. Newman, John Henry Cardinal, 'The Mystery of the Holy Trinity', in *Sermons and Discourses* (*1825-39*), ed. C. F. Harrold (New York: Longmans, Green and Co., 1949), 292-305.

RC2. Newman, John Henry Cardinal, 'Peace in Believing', in

Sermons and Discourses (1839–57), ed. C. F. Harrold (New York: Longmans, Green and Co., 1949), 12–19.

RC3. Knox, Ronald A., 'St Paul and Christ's Divinity', in *The Pastoral Sermons of Ronald A. Knox*, ed. Philip Caraman, SJ (London: Burns & Oates, 1960), 498–504.

Appendix 3: Examples of Problematic Moments

Modalism

In context of discussion of fourth- and fifth-century meaning of *persona* and its sense of 'mask': 'the same actor might well play many different roles' (7, p. 34; leans heavily towards modalism, as indeed the *persona* language can promote). Not an isolated problem in this preacher: 'there are three things that (the child) sees in his father—law, love, life—each one quite different from the others, but the father is the same. . . . He is the same person, but the child experiences him in three different ways at three different periods in his life' (p. 36).

Christians 'always intended a portrayal of God as one being experienced in three aspects' (18, p. 43).

Denial of Unity of Operations *ad extra*

'The Spirit works only in the area of redemption—the area of the Son' (3, p. 24; statement is in the context of a discussion affirming the *filioque* (without the technical label)).

'God, the Father, has decision making power—to create the heavens and the earth, . . .' (14, p. 30).

Confounding of Persons

'The Spirit of God, who had revealed himself as fully as he ever could in human terms, did not die with his human incarnation in Jesus' (6, p. 34).

'Jesus so perfectly revealed the Father-image of God in his own life . . .' (11, p. 25); also, 'God the Father Almighty, the God who was revealed in Christ Jesus, and God the Holy Spirit are all one and the same' (p. 28; one wishes the preacher had simply omitted 'the same'; similarly, see 4, pp. 27, 28).

Tritheism

'Christianity is different from all other religions by having three Gods in one' (19, p. 74; the author does later deny this seeming tritheism, and also denies that each Person is one-third of God).

Miscellaneous

'Christ was God's word to man—his final and ultimate word, based upon but superseding all other words' (9, p. 30; one wonders how Christ is 'based upon' other words; later, the sermon suggests a Schleiermachian view of Jesus' 'God-consciousness' but no strong sense of his divinity: 'he was the most completely God-conscious and God-trustful person of whom we have record', p. 33). Similarly, ' "Holy Spirit" indicates certain things that Christians had discovered in their life and fellowship together' (p. 34; though later development suggests the preacher really means more than this).

'Jesus embodies all of the attributes of God' (11, p. 16; obscures economic limitations of, say, omnipresence: a Calvinist, at least, may speak of the omnipresence of the Son but not of Jesus as incarnate. Granted that the preacher intended to speak only of Jesus' revelation of God's moral character.)

'God . . . now become divine Spirit in us . . .' (12, p. 41; implies lack of eternity of the Spirit).

'The doctrine of the Trinity is an explosive understanding of "God" as the sign of a loving, nonjudgmental community that is not only unshockable but also able to bring the power of laughter to heal our *shame* and to celebrate our fundamental goodness and acceptability' (16, p. 21, italics in original; really??).

Inadequate Analogies

Helium as detected on the sun, then found in the laboratory to be nonflammable, then employed as a fuel within airplanes (1; purely local).

Atom which is one but can be divided (2; but the atom has a large number of very different and unequal constituent parts).

Government made up of three branches (2; divides the substance, implicitly denies the unity of works *ad extra*).

Person as consisting of 'Me-in-myself', 'Me-revealed', and 'My spirit' by which I am present even in my absence—which was elaborated as, 'by God the Father we really mean "God-in-Himself" . . . God's private life of His own, His innermost being'; 'God has a life that existed before all worlds were. God the Father is this God-in-Himself' (2, p. 35; I should rather have thought that this description applies to the immanent Trinity, not to the Father alone); and again, 'The Holy Spirit is God the Father present everywhere; God the Son revealing Himself everywhere' (2, p. 36; surely a confounding of the Persons).

Space mission promised by Kennedy, accomplished by Neil Armstrong and his colleagues, made present to us by invisible radio waves (14, p. 34; divides the substance, implicitly denies the unity of works *ad extra*).

Index